Birds

THROUGH IRISH EYES

Birds

THROUGH IRISH EYES

Anthony McGeehan with Julian Wyllie

The Collins Press

For W. G. 'Billy' Hilditch (1938–2001),
a teacher of nature study who brought me
scenes I treasure.

FIRST PUBLISHED IN 2012 BY
The Collins Press
West Link Park
Doughcloyne
Wilton
Cork

British Library Cataloguing in Publication Data
McGeehan, Anthony.
  Birds : through Irish eyes.
  1. Birds—Ireland. 2. Birds—Ireland—Identification.
  3. Bird watching—Guidebooks.
  I. Title II. Wyllie, Julian.
  598'.09415-dc23

ISBN-13: 9781848891623

Design and typesetting by Burns Design
Typeset in Goudy and Trade Gothic
Printed in Poland by Białostockie Zakłady Graficzne SA

Photographs in prelims: p. i: (top) Skylark; (bottom) Turnstone; p. ii: Red Grouse.

CONTENTS

SPECIES ACCOUNTS IN ALPHABETICAL ORDER

ACKNOWLEDGEMENTS

This book is the product of a collective, collaborative process. While I wrestled with blank A4, checkers steered the emerging words into something that was accurate and better. Words and pictures change nothing unless their influence spreads from between these covers. I know that everyone's wish is that the birds themselves will be the beneficiaries of all our efforts. Contributions great and small mean that I am a little lost in adequately expressing gratitude. Some of you unselfishly heaved great rocks of personal observations on to the cairn of knowledge; others gave me a reference, a phrase or a photograph – vital cement that added solidity. I hope I have used your gifts wisely. Without the faith and optimism that the writer received from his wife, Mairead, the content might have gathered terminal dust and cobwebs (in places unreachable by a Hoover). Thank you all!

Editors

Edward 'Ned' Brinkley
Joe S. Furphy
Alexander Lees
Neville D. McKee
Frank Murphy
Craig Nash

Additional Assistance

Jim Beattie; Daniel Bergmann; Dominic Berridge; Dermot Breen; Kieran Buckley; Brian Cachalane; Oscar Campbell; Edward Carty; Ann Clarke; John Doherty; Ken Douglas; Frode Falkenberg; Drew Ferris; Owen Foley; Julian Friers; Steve Gantlett; Tim G. Gordon; Ricard Gutierrez; Paul Hillis; Flora Irwin; Eleanor Keane; Paddy-Joe and Regina King; Yvon LeCorre; John Lusby; Patrick P. Mackie; Bruce Mactavish; Kevin Mawhinney; John McCullough; Graham McElwaine; Richard Millington; Steve Newton; Julia Nunn; Michael O'Clery ; Ken W. Perry; Ian Poxton; Elizabeth Rice; Edward B. Rickson; Magnus Robb; Julie Roe; Angela Ross; Heiko Schmaljohann; Don Scott; John Scovell; Stephanie Sim; Mark Smyth; Jola Tabor; David Tierney; Antero Topp; Peter Walkden; D. I. M. Wallace; Jim Wells; Pim Wolf; Jean Wood; Magdalena Zerebeic.

Photographers

Arie Ouwerkerk: *Great Crested Grebe* (p. 93); *Slavonian Grebe* (p. 94); *Hen Harrier,* (p. 107, male); *Shore Lark* (p. 314).

Artur Tabor: *Goshawk* (p. 5).

Brandon Holden: *Canada Goose* (p. 29); *Red-breasted Merganser* (p. 56–57); *Osprey* (p. 100); *Arctic Skua* (p. 165, lower); *Iceland Gull* (p. 180).

Bruce Mactavish: *Garganey* (p. 40); *Scaup* (p. 47, bottom); *Common Scoter* (p. 53); *Leach's Petrels* (p. 78); *Goshawk* (p. 111); *Grey Plover* (p. 136); *Waxwing* (p. 252).

Christian Assaguel: *Red Kites* (p. 101, 102).

Craig Nash: *Ruddy Duck* (p. 59); *Little Gull, left-hand adult* (p. 183).

Graham Catley: *Red Kite* (p. 103).

Graham Clarke: *Ring Ouzel, female* (p. 259).

Jared Clarke: *Little Auk* (p. 199).

John Doherty: *Terns in flight* (p. 189, topmost group); *juvenile Swallows* (p. 238, bottom).

Julian Hough: *female Scaup* (p. 45).

Kathryn McGeehan: *several street names* (p. 1).

Kjetil Schjolberg: *White-tailed Eagle* (p. 96–97); *Golden Eagle* (p. 98).

Paul Hillion: *Ring Ouzel, male* (p. 260).

Rene Pop: *Pintails* (p. 39).

Rudi DeBruyne: *Grey Partridge* (p. 62); *Quail* (p. 64).

Raphael LeBrun: *Balearic Shearwater* (p. 74).

Remo Savisaar: *Capercaillie* (p. 4 & p. 61).

Richard Millington: *Woodcock* (p. 151).

Richard Steel: *Corn Bunting* (p. 307).

Robbie Brookes: *Grey Phalarope* (p. 164); *Woodlark* (p. 234).

Sindri Skulason: *Gadwall* (p. 36); *Common Scoter* (p. 52); *Goosander* (p. 58, main image); *Shag* (p. 87); *Knot* (p141, upper); *Black Guillemot* (p. 198, bottom); *Snow Bunting* (p. 302).

Steve Gantlett: *Smew* (p. 55, inset), *Black-throated Diver* (p. 67); *Bittern* (p. 88); *Barn Owl* (p. 208).

Steve Arlow: *Jack Snipe* (p. 148).

Steve Young: *Little Gulls* (p. 183, except left-hand adult); *Great Spotted Woodpecker* (p. 215, lower).

Tom McGeehan: *several street names* (p. 1).

Tom Shevlin: *Nightjar* (p. 211).

[All other photographs taken by author. Photoshop compositions by author.]

Smew, female.

LOST VOICES

THIS BOOK attempts to provide an overview of the state of our birds in the twenty-first century. Alas, most of the class is in rotten shape. It is tempting to speak of defeat and paint a picture of the last few centuries as an era of unremitting destruction of countryside and wildlife. Is Garrison Keillor writing about us when he says in *Leaving Home* (1987), 'We'll look back on all the good things we surrendered in favour of deadly trash and wish we could return and reclaim them. We may sit in a cool corner of hell and wish we had kept the ballpark, built the shops elsewhere, and not killed off all those cornfields'? I hate to deliver such gloomy tidings; I prefer to light a candle that illuminates where it all went wrong and hope that knowledge might beget change.

William Thompson's *The Natural History of Ireland* (1849–52) was an exhaustive union of documentation and original observation. Robert Lloyd Patterson wrote as a patriarch about his beloved hunting grounds in *The Birds, Fishes and Cetacea of Belfast Lough* (1880). James Burkitt placed metal numbered bands on the legs of Robins so that he could follow the fortunes of individual birds, which enabled him to tell a remarkable story – 'A Study of the Robin by Means of Marked Birds' (1924). Edward Armstrong's poetic writing in *Birds of the Grey Wind* (1940) still dazzles, as does Kay Milton's perception of landscape-scale conservation in *Our Countryside, Our Concern: Policy and Practice of Conservation in Northern Ireland* (1990).

Despite the wisdom that our forebears bequeathed, much has changed. Belfast Lough, for example, was once a wetland paradise providing Wigeon for local tables and oysters for the smart set in London. Today, market forces continue to divest the countryside of hay meadows, wet grassland and winter stubbles replete with seeding weeds and sufficient unharvested grain to help farmland birds through the winter. Several appear to be vanishing for good, among them the Corncrake, the recollection of whose voice still turns country folk into storytellers of gentler times. Old perfection has become modern ruin. Kestrels, Barn Owls, Lapwings and Yellowhammers are 'family silver' species whose names are starting to toll like a list of departed souls. Although it is a pipe dream to expect farmers to turn back the clock and embrace Amish principles, much could be done by offering alms – an uncultivated strip here, a hedgerow allowed to thicken there, or a few rows of crop left to feed mouths through the winter.

True, there exists a new understanding of the inter-relationship connecting all forms of life, including us. Indeed, 'biodiversity' is touted like a new religion. Unfortunately, in a 2010 poll, 80 per cent of the British population thought this was a washing powder.

But there is good news too. Eiders grace the coast like never before and Buzzards have returned to float regally overhead. The popularity of natural history television programmes is sky high and gardens have become the 'in' place for recreational birdwatching. Many of you want to do more. Conscience money flows to conservation organisations in the often naive hope that eco-warriors will protect more than just the birds outside our kitchen windows.

While we wait for someone to come along who might echo the words of Theodore Roosevelt – 'Spring would not be spring without birdsong' – this book is designed to take you to the next level. Who do you call if you want to know the identity of a ball of feathers that looks about as familiar as a probe from outer space when it lands on the lawn? Or makes you exclaim 'Wow!' when it hits the sea and detonates blue water into white. Birds' humble lives ignite a huge sense of wonder in ours. Maybe, by recognising them, you will cultivate an interest in their survival.

Is hindsight our only view?

THE RAZING OF THE GREENWOOD

OURIST BOARD PROMOTION of our landscape's archetypal green beauty is an ill-informed representation of the historical record. Collective amnesia means that we have come to accept the degraded state of both the countryside and the seas around us. We have lost a connection to ancient times and the natural order of millennia. Nobody alive today has seen the primordial beauty that was once Ireland. Changes creep up on us, unnoticed by younger generations who tolerate pollution, urban sprawl and long, stressful commutes to work. Specifically, an affinity with woodland has been airbrushed from our minds. The forest has gone and so have its birdsong, colours, cooling nuances and magnificent large animals. We live in an age of remnants. Ghosts of former woodland survive only through the accident of clinging to ground too steep, poor or wet to be exploited. Even there, ubiquitous grazing by sheep extinguishes saplings. Contemporary stands of timber exist as crops, established to meet needs demanded by a consumer society, such as daily newsprint and cheap building material. Plantations are not forests. In some places, benevolence has spared sentinel tall trees or groves whose humanised grandeur harks back to the extinct wildwood. Declan Kiberd (2000) writes that, well into the 1700s, field labourers sang a Gaelic lament for the fallen forests: 'What will we do for timber, now that the last woods are laid low?' (O'Tuama & Kinsella 1981).

After the last Ice Age (roughly 10,000 years ago), during which it is unlikely that trees survived in what became Ireland, the pulverised rock and gravel from the retreating ice cap bequeathed a blank canvas to colonising plants. Terra firma gradually attracted a mantle of greenery. Birch and willow were probably among the first trees to be established. At first the impact of humankind was negligible. Mesolithic people (hunter-gatherers) used wood for everything: weapons, accommodation and fuel. Around 5,000 years ago Neolithic farmers arrived and began to clear ground for tillage and grazing. To feed a growing population, more food – and therefore more land for production – was needed. Coinciding with the arrival of these farmers, tree pollen began to decline, while grass and cereal pollen increased – signs of agricultural expansion. In early Christian times, Irish peoples lived by a body of custom that enshrined woodland veneration. Trees were ranked in value and listed in common law. Penalties were imposed for cutting them down. A poem in the eighth-century *Hisperica Famina* records how monks 'hew the sacred oaks with axes in order to fashion chapels'. In a society

In modern Ireland, you have to search far and wide to discover a fragment of broadleaved woodland that stirs the imagination and provides a glimpse of the country our ancestors knew. Contemporary land use has relegated wild forest to the status of a relic afforded heirloom status as 'nature reserve'. However, acorns are not time capsules – they still make mighty oakwoods.

Like the headman of a lost tribe, the male Capercaillie exudes nobility. When forest clothed Ireland, giant males roamed dark woods, flanked by harems of smaller females. Bone evidence from several locations confirms that the Capercaillie survived until at least the thirteenth century. Remains of Woodpigeon, Woodcock and Wild Boar accompanied remains of Capercaillie from a Mesolithic site at Mount Sandel, not far from the River Bann. Such happy hunting grounds – a paradise lost.

lacking a cash economy, property such as timber produce and cattle were the main riches.

In spite of the vastness of the woodlands, their survival over millennia, and the multiple benefits of wood, people did not conceive ideas of possession until the cleared land was put to use during Tudor times (1485–1603), when the question of ownership became crucial. This lies at the heart of understanding the conflict between long-established Irish society and the impact of colonisation (Neeson 1997). The over-exploitation and ultimate eradication of woodland resulted from military action and the policy of plantation of Scottish and English settlers in Ulster that accompanied it. An alternative view is expressed by Atkinson (in Faulkner & Thompson 2011): 'Historical evidence shows that [at the time of the Plantation] Ireland was already reduced to one-third as wooded as England, with only 2–3 per cent woodland cover, owing to clearance for farming.' Nonetheless, leafy refuges became a gathering place for opposition, much like Sherwood Forest was for the legendary

Fierce, powerful, secretive: the reputation of Ireland's Goshawks turned the bird into hard currency. In the sixteenth century, tenants were required to record and safeguard nests from which young were taken for earls, some of whom were contracted to supply the birds to British monarchs for falconry. Henry VIII and Elizabeth I were both customers. Elizabeth also sanctioned deforestation. After her reign, the bird became extinct.

Robin Hood. Elizabeth I (Queen of England and Ireland 1558–1603) expressly ordered the felling of all tree cover to deprive the Irish of shelter: 'The war waged on Irish soil became as much a war against the trees, against the Irish environment, as it was against anything else. The inhabitants of the island and the environment became as one' (Horgan 2010).

Wolves and 'wood-kerne' (dispossessed Irish) were bracketed together. Fairley (1975), in recounting the demise of the Wolf in Ireland, touches upon the rationale behind the destruction:

> The clearing of trees was necessary too for the expansion of agriculture, and it was done as part of a deliberate policy of eliminating the retreats of wolves, of both the two-legged and four-legged varieties. These rebels, known also as tories, were hunted down with much the same measure of mercy afforded the Wolf.

In 1610, Lord Blennerhasset, acting to supervise and safeguard the expansion of settlements, recommended 'periodic manhunts to track down the human wolves to their lairs'. Oliver Cromwell, in power from 1653 to 1658, dealt the animal a fatal blow. Having exterminated Wolves in Britain, he turned Ireland into a free-for-all for trappers by offering staggering rewards: £6 for a female and £5 for a male. Hunters from Britain seized the opportunity and, by 1786, the noble canine, whose presence in Ireland can be dated by the study of bones to at least 34,000 BC, was extinct.

Paradoxically, although the face of Ireland was in the process of being permanently disfigured, Queen Elizabeth I exacted payment from some planted landowners in the form of Goshawks for falconry. Nests in the remaining squire-owned forests were protected for this very purpose. A Tudor poem, 'The Image of Ireland', written by J. Derricke in 1581, lionises birds of prey obtainable from Ireland:

The Goshawk [female] first of the crew,
Deserves to have the name:
The [female Peregrine] falcon next for high attempts,
In glory and in fame.
The tiercel [male Peregrine] then ensueth on,
Good reason 'tis that he:
For flying hawks in Ireland next,
The [male Goshawk] place should be.

Archives dating from 1686 (D'Arcy 1999) mention 'among the feathered kind, there breed in Ireland hawks which, from their preying on wild geese, are called Gos-hawks, of which those that breed in the north of Ireland are the best in the world.' In those days virgin forest stretched from the western shore of Lough Neagh and embraced the Sperrin Mountains. The region was the largest surviving woodland in Ireland and was referred to as Glenconkeyne.

In the century following the defeat of combined Irish and Spanish forces at Kinsale in 1601, a systematic devastation took place. By 1711, the country was almost treeless and had become a net importer of timber (Foster 1998). Chevalier De Latocnaye (1798) penned a scene redolent of nuclear winter: 'They had not left wood enough to make a toothpick in many places.' Great numbers of 'undertakers' – English or Scots planters on forfeited lands who 'undertook' settlement work – spread across Ireland throughout the sixteenth century, felling wood at a rapacious rate. Timber was so profitable that often the amount for which an estate was bought was recovered from the sale of the felled trees. This holocaust was fuelled, therefore, by the twin goals of profit and prevention of shelter for native insurgents.

From the mid-sixteenth century to the dawn of iron-hulled shipping, the economic fortunes of Britain were underpinned by the need for a steady supply of timber. In the absence of any silviculture policy in Ireland, legions of axemen ruthlessly obliged. From the mid-seventeenth century onwards, industrial development made further inroads. Furnaces of the iron industry gobbled up raw timber day and night. An acre of oakwood provided one ton of charcoal and it took two and a quarter tons of charcoal to make one ton of iron (Neeson 1997). Rackham (1976) claims that in areas given over to long-term ironworking, such as west Waterford, there is evidence that some woodland was preserved or even replanted. Elsewhere, ad hoc clearance was almost universal. Increased demand for barrel staves, furniture, utensils, iron tools and wood for export as wine casks (the last forests of Cork and Kerry were sacrificed to cask French and Spanish wine) meant that Irish timber continued to go up in smoke or out of the country as fast as it could be transported overseas.

By the end of the eighteenth century, most of the country was reputed to be largely devoid of trees and even saplings (Kee 1972). Later, the pillage became more complete. According to Mitchell (1976), by about 1850 Ireland was:

> ... a ruined landscape, almost destitute of any wooded growth. The countryside must have presented an extraordinary appearance; fuel was in such short supply that, apart from within the oases of the walled and guarded demesnes and around farmers' houses, there was nothing, not a tree, not a bush, to break the view of the bare landscape. Even the landowners' wooded gardens later succumbed. Woods that survived earlier cutting enjoyed only a brief respite before they vanished in the First World War, and when that was over, 200,000 acres (81,000 hectares) of woodland had disappeared, and less than 1 per cent of Ireland was covered by forest.

Ireland had in effect become Easter Island. Paltry redress commenced during the late eighteenth century, and descendants of the planters and entrepreneurs who had deforested the land set about limited reafforestation. Some lamented the loss of the magnificent wildwood, among them Frederick Lord Dufferin (1826–1902) when he beheld the treeless state of much of his demesne at Clandeboye, Down; a situation that he rectified. The Dublin Society (later the Royal Dublin Society) encouraged tree planting and between 1766 and 1806 some 25 million trees were established in new woods. Alas, such pea-sized restoration was too late for Ireland's Wolves, Wild Boars, Wild Cats, Brown Bears, Great Spotted Woodpeckers and Capercaillies – the Cock-of-the-Woods. In 2011, Lichen Ireland, a project that probed tree cover nationwide, concluded that it was impossible to find woodland with continuity spanning more than four centuries. Put another way, in the blink of time between the end of the reign of Elizabeth I and the coronation of Elizabeth II in 1952, a mere 349 years, a whole ecological framework was lost.

Farmers: Birds Need Help!

THERE IS NO getting away from it: modern farming has become more of a business than a way of life. Like the rest of us, farmers have to make ends meet. Capital has been invested, loans have to be paid off and a return has to be made. Yet, if bad weather throws a spanner in the works, the chances of a good harvest can be ruined. Then there is the volatile world of market prices for milk, cereals, poultry and livestock to consider. Financial worries are never far away. Around 75 per cent of our land is farmed, a far greater proportion than in most of the world. Into this mix come all the birds that need to make a home on farmland. Are their lives not important too?

To understand the dependence of birds on their farmland habitats, it is worth answering the question of how farming became an industry. Before social change divorced people from living on the land in small, self-sustaining communities, there was no need for commercial farming. Gone were the days when relentless subdivision of land left families subsisting on holdings of a fraction of an acre, reliant on a milking cow, laying hens and potatoes. Throughout the eighteenth and in the early nineteenth century, farmland developed its patchwork of small fields through the widespread planting of hedges as stock fences and delineations of ownership. Costs were low, labour was plentiful and machinery was limited. Draught animals were the main source of power. Fertilisers were mainly organic, supplied by the farmer's animals. Since farmers lacked chemicals, weeds and soil fertility were controlled by judicious cultivation, such as sowing clover to fix nitrogen, and by crop rotation. By the nineteenth century, land in eastern Ulster had been harnessed to produce food for export to Britain and to grow flax, a cash crop to be processed into linen. Flax was grown on over 100,000 hectares of land. With the arrival of globalisation, cheap foreign produce was imported, depressing local agriculture, whose fortunes were only revived when governments introduced guaranteed prices.

Today, mixed farming practices have been abandoned to accommodate contemporary triffid-like machinery and the demands of the Common Agricultural Policy. In less favoured districts small, family-run farms make little or no profit. On individual holdings, the strategy has been to concentrate into larger units: prairies of potatoes, acres of barley and oceans of oilseed rape. Luckily, many farmers decline to live on windswept deserts, green or otherwise. But it is not just the dimension of space that has changed; so has that of planting time. Spring sowing that allowed birds to forage on tilled ground and then rear young among growing crops became impossible once new seed varieties for autumn sowing were perfected. Moreover, crops have become cleaner of weeds as a result of effective herbicides and exposed weeds are covered by autumn cultivations. Earlier harvesting also meant that nesting among standing crops became a death warrant. Equipped with the wherewithal to force-fertilise the countryside and make it deliver, agricultural scientists thought like control freaks, aiming to grow two blades of grass where nature grows one. A variety of methods achieve domination. Drainage and applications of lime, slurry and artificial fertilisers boost yields. Tractor-mounted sprayers kill weeds. Existing sward is obliterated with a broad-spectrum herbicide, and the ground is reseeded with alien grasses, typically perennial ryegrass, bred for fast growth.

Far fewer people now work in the countryside. Those who do are often cocooned in cabs. Modern agriculture is dependent on machinery, high-yielding crop varieties, chemical fertilisers and pesticides. In the past, those who worked the land had vital contact with the world beyond the human. Nowadays such awareness is lacking. Most farmers just want to finish up and park the tractor before bedtime.

Field structure often has to toe the line to allow efficient use of large combines and forage-harvesters. Watercourses and ditches are canalised or replaced by underground drainage conduits. Hedges are trimmed to resemble picket fences or reduced to wire curtains. Nesting cover disappears, as do the insect sanctuaries that feed birds. Whitethroats, summer visitors from Africa, find fewer places to breed on farmland than ever before.

Honey Bees, which pollinate one third of the food we eat, such as tomatoes, beans, apples and strawberries, have declined by an alarming 50 per cent in the last twenty-five years. Never mind the obvious explanation – the colossal scale of destruction of flower-rich habitats in which the insects feed – there is a much more insidious killer in the environment. New research (Whitehorn *et al.* 2012; Henry *et al.* 2012) has shown, for the first time, that common crop pesticides seriously harm bees by damaging their renowned ability to navigate home. Neurotoxins, the pesticides investigated in the studies, are applied to seeds and permeate through the plants' entire system of life. The chemicals end up in the nectar and pollen on which the bees feed. Not only did many foraging bees 'disappear' because they failed to relocate their colony, the colony lost almost all its ability to produce queens, needed to survive the winter and found new hives.

Farm ponds are another vanishing habitat. Originally used to water animals (but also of great wildlife value) they are increasingly rare, grown over through neglect or filled in, and substituted by piped water and troughs – often a discarded household bath.

The Northern Ireland Countryside Survey of 2000 indicated a 30 per cent increase in ryegrass-dominated grassland in under a decade (Faulkner & Thompson 2011). Lush, fertilised fields become purged of botanical variety. Intense management, such as tight grazing or repeated cutting for silage, prevents plants from setting seed. Who would have believed a few years ago that cattle rearing would involve keeping cows indoors and feeding them with unprocessed grass monoculture – a denial of the animals' innate behaviour? So-called marginal lands, often nature's last stand, become the final frontier, awaiting conversion to human use. Whenever conservation poses a threat to livelihood, comfort or convenience, the expedient choice is to liquidate the natural capital. Many wildflowers are locally extinct, as are the insects that relied upon them. Impoverished remnants of vanquished flora and fauna are sidelined to the edges of silage fields. In the past, hay meadows burst with life: cutting them late in the season allowed plants to set seed; and cutting and removing hay left an open sward in which fallen seed germinated and insects could lay eggs.

Despite the fact that hedgerows are commonly cut with a mechanical hedge-cutter operated from a tractor, the potential still exists for the trimmed hedge to be left with a mitred top and intact saplings. By leaving the ground layer undisturbed, grasses and 'weeds' can set seed and, in the course of summer, push

Hawthorn hedges provide nutritious berries in winter and aromatic, insect-attracting blooms in spring. Alas, the camera lies. An eye-level view suggests a cornucopia of luxuriant vegetation. The reality is thin veins across barren fields. If the base is allowed to thicken, and an adjoining strip is left to allow natural vegetation to proliferate, small mammals can thrive, becoming important prey for beneficial farmland birds, such as Kestrels and Barn Owls. In this way, hedges can become battlements, not embattled.

through the hedge. The hedge now offers both shelter and the provision of a food supply late in the breeding season. By doing less, the hedge has more. Thin and gappy hedges are red herrings; wide 'battlement' hedges with undergrowth and trees are red carpet. It may be much better to widen an existing hedge, even by creating a 'no go' strip alongside it, than planting a new one. Hedges also provide cover for flocks of finches and buntings. Wary of ambush by Sparrowhawks, small birds prefer to feed near hedges where they can dive for cover. Oases of hedge and scrub in a sea of uniform farmland inevitably concentrate bush-nesting farmland birds. Research undertaken through Queen's University (Adderton 2005) has shown that many hedgerows are not wide or dense enough to offer adequate protection against Magpies and Hooded Crows. By using data loggers and analysing gizzards to assess diet, it emerged that Magpies were the main nest predators and that predation was the main cause of breeding failure in broods of Song Thrush and Blackbird. Outside the breeding season, crow numbers were maintained at a high level by easy access to invertebrates in animal dung, especially when brought to the surface by slurry spraying. Crows are smart and have the wit to follow hedgerows sure in the knowledge that, given few breeding places, songbird clutches inevitably await discovery. In contrast, scrub is safer. When prioritising existing habitats, it is important to remember that wetland and old grassland – unploughed, unfertilised and never drained – are far

more beneficial to birds, plants and animals than hedges. Furthermore, preserving remnant trees in pasture creates a buttress against loss of diversity.

Adult birds sustain themselves by eating a variety of foods whose availability is determined by the seasons. In other words, the day's dinner is dependent on the natural cycles of food sources. When it comes to rearing nestlings, many birds are totally reliant on insects. Insect life ought to be at its most abundant in summer but, increasingly, its sanctuaries have come under attack. Regular ploughing exposes pupae and adult insects to marauding gulls and crows; herbicides destroy food plants, with rough grassland and wetland refuges sprayed, damaged or lost, often by being amalgamated into existing monocultures. Assailed on all sides, the land is groaning. After decades of cultivation, crop yields are falling across Europe. Increasingly, ploughing is being seen as a harmful activity that inverts the soil and decimates its web of life. 'Conservation tillage', using low-pressure tractor tyres, making fewer passes and seeding crop into surface detritus, has been shown, in side-by-side trials, to be every bit as efficient. Undisturbed soil develops a protective mulch, allowing earthworms to increase, benefiting soil aeration and rooting for crops. Into the bargain, a natural cycle is restored, from fungi to beetles – which consume slugs. Setting aside the conservation benefits, the saving in cultivation time and fuel costs is huge. 'On a global scale, the value of functioning, intact

As land was cleared on a massive scale for timber and agriculture during the seventeenth and eighteenth centuries, an opportunity was lost to retain former coppice systems that preserved woodland. When felled, broadleaved trees grow multi-stemmed trunks from the cut stump. The renewed 'underwood' is a valuable, endlessly renewable resource. Moreover, wildlife endures. Coppiced woodland and farmland go hand in hand across many north European countries – regions where birds, mammals and wildflowers flourish.

ecosystems is priceless: yet we invest so little in protecting them' (AL, pers. comm.)

Faced with spiralling costs and diminishing returns, many farmers have thrown in the towel and 'For Sale' signs are commonplace. Others have managed to make money by renting fields to agricultural contractors – for chemically boosted yields of silage, root crops or arable – or through house-building by 'replacing' an old dwelling with a new house. As part of this process, mature trees and parcels of habitat are destroyed and unwanted building materials dumped, often in small, fragile wetlands. Wet hollows are a favourite for desecration. Meanwhile, black plastic from big bale silage festoons stream banks and flutters from hedges. What a mess. Even before the implications for wildlife are taken into account, this despoliation of rural areas is appalling. Surely we cannot indefinitely escape the consequences of damaging the environment, even if few bother to defend the rights of plants and animals to exist outside human dominion?

In truth, many farmers *want* birds on the land but are not told how to achieve this. Agri-environment schemes exist and do make a difference. In the present economic climate, however, they face an uncertain future and have unfortunately created a 'benefits dependency' among some who regard looking after the natural world on their property as nothing more than an income stream. Little can be done about such single-minded profit motives. Others, however, are knowledgeable and will do what they can to help. Here is one helpful suggestion. A recent study by the Game and Wildlife Conservation Trust investigated three types of seed mix for the edge of fields: grass margins; wildflower-rich margins; and a legume-based mix. Of the three treatments, legumes (such as clover, trefoil, sainfoin and lucerne) attracted the highest number of pollinators and delivered the greatest weight of insects eaten by chicks. Dr J. Holland, head of farmland ecology at the trust, has said:

> Grass-only strips remain the most common type of field margin established using [UK-based agri-environment schemes] but there is a weight of evidence demonstrating the superiority of flower-rich field margins to provide food for insects and birds. We need to persuade farmers to replace or supplement the unproductive grass margins with those containing flowers. (www.gwct.org.uk).

Grant-aid schemes put money in farmers' pockets. Here 'wildbird cover' has been sown that supports Linnets and Yellowhammers through the winter. Plantations containing native trees further enhance the potential for wildlife.

THE GOLDEN RULE when learning to identify birds must be 'Look for Yourself'. Written articles and illustrations are no substitute for first-hand field observation. Indeed, it is often not until you have studied something in life that the full benefit of reference sources can be appreciated. The legion of advances in identification that are with us today have not arisen out of blasé 'I'll name that bird in one' techniques. Most species have absolute characters that will always identify them, for example a Robin's red breast, the stumpy tail of a Wren and the hovering habit of a Kestrel. But many other supporting characters can be learned or discovered. These come into play when views are brief or distant.

You come across a small brown bird with a streaky chest. It is marked like a thrush but is petite and, unlike true thrushes, its back is patterned. Do not neglect mannerisms. The tail bobs and its gait is hesitant and mincing – a walk, not a confident thrush hop. An agile, active sprite, it flits about after insects and flies off uttering a squeaky *sit ... sit*, repeated persistently. On the wing, the action is jerky, not silky and powerful. Behold a Meadow Pipit. However, not every pipit-like bird is a pipit. Skylarks are superficially similar. However, they shuffle low to the ground in a creeping walk. A Skylark bill is stout and, more often than not, its telltale crest is sleeked down and invisible. Airborne, the flight is strong, somewhat undulating, and accompanied by rippling *chirrup* calls. Hence, on just a few nuances, a species can be named confidently – and by sound alone.

From left: Meadow Pipit, Skylark and Song Thrush.

ACQUIRING KNOWLEDGE of plumage terminology is the next step. Daunted? Fear not. From a Starling to a Sparrowhawk you will find the same feather groups (tracts). Because the layout is similar, you can practise naming parts on common species – even on a pet Budgerigar – at any time. Not surprisingly, larger birds have more feathers, although the number of tracts remains the same. For example, gulls and shorebirds have more rows of small 'lesser' coverts than songbirds: compare the spread wing of Linnet (p. 15) with the flying Black-tailed Godwit (p. 13). On any feather, the pattern and colour on the underside may be different from that on the upper side. Into the bargain, the overlapping arrangement of feathers on the wing and tail will, automatically, show detail from above that is masked when viewed from below (and vice versa). However,

birds' bodies are not uniformly covered with feathers. The belly is unfeathered, although swathed by long feathers growing across it from the flanks. Because the belly is bare, warm skin is accessible to incubate eggs and keep chicks warm. This hidden area is the brood patch. While it is possible to produce a worthwhile description based on features shared by humans – forehead, crown, back, belly and so on – it is more satisfying to locate and name a field mark precisely. Birds are ordered beings and their wings pivot beneath a cloak of overlapping covering feathers, aptly named 'coverts'. This is why, as soon as the wing is stretched, some plumage closes and other tracts pop into view. For clarity, no better explanation exists than 'Birds' Feathers', a chapter in Jonsson (1992).

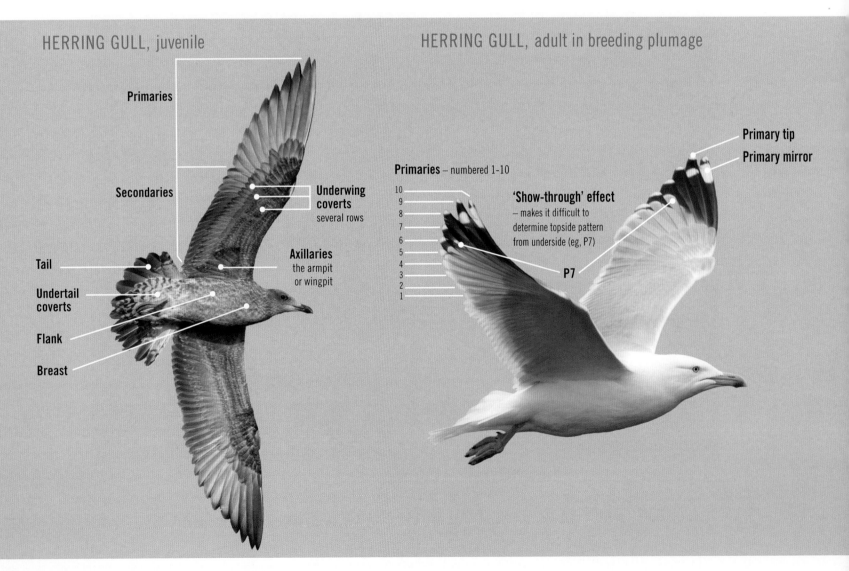

HERRING GULL, juvenile

Primaries

Secondaries

Underwing coverts
several rows

Tail

Axillaries
the armpit
or wingpit

Undertail coverts

Flank

Breast

HERRING GULL, adult in breeding plumage

Primary tip

Primary mirror

Primaries – numbered 1-10

'Show-through' effect
– makes it difficult to determine topside pattern from underside (eg, P7)

P7

Primaries

With the wings folded against the body, only the outer edges of the primaries are visible.

Tertials

Three innermost secondaries. On a folded wing, these broad feathers appear to ride on top; sometimes they break the outline and resemble a step. On adult gulls, tertial tips are bright white and form a bold crescent or fan (see Common Gull, p. 174). Importantly, once the wing opens, mechanical action slots the tertials below the rear scapulars. Note the change of position in the spread-wing image.

Greater coverts

On this image, the lower scapulars mask all but the tips of the greater coverts

Back

Scapulars

Three upper rows visible

Tertials

Greater coverts

Alula

Three feathers — corresponding to a thumb

Secondaries

Scapulars

Primary coverts

Back

HERRING GULL, immature

BLACK-TAILED GODWIT

Wing 'hand'

Wing 'arm'

Scapulars and back

The scapulars overlap the base of the wings. In effect, they are shoulders. It can be tricky to tell where 'scapulars' end and 'back' begins. Together, they are sometimes called 'mantle'.

Lesser coverts
several rows

Secondaries
Greater coverts
Median coverts

Inner primaries

Outer primaries
outer four dark and contrast with inner six

Rump

Tail

Leg

Foot

Wingbar (or wingstripe)

Note how white combines across two different feather groups to create a uniform white bar. White links the tips of the greater coverts with the bases of the primaries. Other species use different feather groups to create a wingbar. Redshank's wingbar (p. 160) combines white secondaries with white inner primaries.

ICELAND GULL

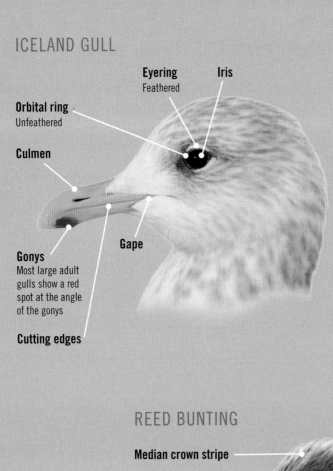

Eyering
Feathered

Iris

Orbital ring
Unfeathered

Culmen

Gonys
Most large adult gulls show a red spot at the angle of the gonys

Cutting edges

Gape

RINGED PLOVER

Supercilium
Side of head above eye – the eyebrow

Cheek

Forehead

Nape

Lores
Tiny feathers between eye and bill

Gape

Throat

REED BUNTING

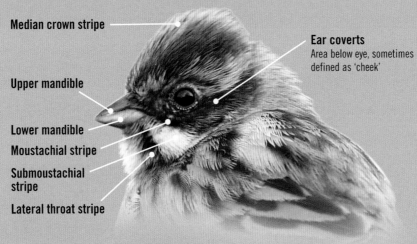

Median crown stripe

Ear coverts
Area below eye, sometimes defined as 'cheek'

Upper mandible

Lower mandible

Moustachial stripe

Submoustachial stripe

Lateral throat stripe

COMMON SNIPE

Tail

Tertials Hard to see actual wingtip due to overlapping tertials

Scapulars In this pose on Common Snipe, scapulars are being held high, thereby revealing coverts

Coverts

Crown stripe
Supercilium

TEAL, female

Scapulars

Flank
Part of body, not wing

Cap **Eyestripe**

Speculum

Tertials

BRAMBLING

Median coverts
White, almost entirely overlapped
by lower scapulars

**Back and upper
scapulars**

Greater coverts

Base of primaries

Tertials

Secondaries

Primaries

LINNET

Back The back and scapulars are often contiguous and lack a clear division

Lesser coverts
Median coverts
Greater coverts

Alula Slate-coloured

Primary coverts Slate-coloured, overlap base of primaries

Feather shaft

Feather inner web Note white margin to outer web of, especially, inner primaries

Emargination Narrowing of outer web

Eyering

Ear coverts

MISTLE THRUSH

Tertials
Rump

Uppertail coverts

Median coverts

Greater coverts

Secondaries

Primaries

LISTEN

BIRDS COMMUNICATE. They tell friends when they are anxious and broadcast to attract a spouse or repel an enemy. Song is one of the most effective means of setting out their stall. A male without a territory is of little account, and even a male with territory needs a mate to make it worth defending. Guile is also part of the language and – just like us – they have a curious ear. Male Swallows rally others by false alarming. The point of crying wolf is to discover the whereabouts of mates suspected of conducting affairs.

Croaking or buzzing could have met birds' communication needs. Thankfully they did not: instead, we are blessed by sophisticated messaging systems that are complex and beautiful. Each of 10,000 species has a unique voice. But not all sing. A few ground rules distinguish divas from dummies. Drake waterfowl flash finery at females and some do little more than grunt. Eagles, masters of the air, use the sky as a stage and perform spectacular flips and rolls. Others are closet romantics. Bullfinches are shy and one of the few birds that are truly monogamous. They sing quietly and only serenade the object of their desire when she is within earshot. Old hand male Great Tits build up a galaxy of notes because richness of song confers status. Youthful songbirds that mumble maiden songs (called plastic song) have a harder job finding a mate. What self-respecting female would take a singing apprentice for a husband – a choirboy rather than Frank Sinatra?

In undergrowth and woodland, voice matters more than looks: a triumph of radio over television. Tricks abound. A male Wren that inserts a novel note may steal a march on opponents. Mimicry is rife. Resident Starlings are listening posts. They imitate shorebirds when they overhear the composers practising for performances on tundra. Other mimics are mobile. Sedge Warblers are trans-Saharan migrants that bring imitations of

There is a rough relationship between song and plumage. Stunning looks seldom need an elaborate vocal accompaniment, whereas Plain Janes sing to draw attention. Science tends to portray nature as a feelingless universe – tantamount to snobbery – where function and form set the rules. Skylarks are oblivious to human attempts to comprehend their mental processes. Each bird improvises its own suite of perfectly articulated runs and trills in a sustained complex composition. The soloist uses scales, durations and intervals to impress its peers. From opera singers to rock stars, we do the same.

African birds with them when they return to breed. Singing burns calories and may interfere with feeding time. One tactic is to sing when the opposition is otherwise engaged. That way, only your voice gets heard. Mistle Thrushes frequently sing during rain, a time when other species pipe down. The habit earns them the nickname 'Stormcock'. Dusk on a still evening triggers serenading by Song Thrushes, especially in late winter when little else fills the airwaves. However, for most, spring is a time for 'pistols at dawn'. Even after a blustery night the air is often calm and cold before first light, facilitating the widest dispersion of sound.

How did birdsong evolve? It is probable that basic unmusical notes formed the vocabulary of prehistoric ancestors that were progressively honed and embellished as species competed. Birdsong, in other words, is evolution's soundtrack. By way of a corollary, where population density is low and contention for a partner is minimal, songsters sing less or truncate song length, as many Wrens do on Inishbofin, Galway (AMG). A solitary pair of Robins at Copeland Bird Observatory scarcely bothered to sing (NMK).

> Enough of science and of art;
> Close up those barren leaves;
> Come forth – and bring with you a heart
> That listens and receives.

When William Wordsworth wrote those words he was encouraging us to be attentive. Bird sound comes from a unique structure, called a syrinx, which lies deep within the chest. As the windpipe enters the lungs, it forks and enters a chamber strengthened by cartilage. This is the syrinx. From it, air transits to the lungs. By opening and closing valves and selectively inflating and deflating lungs and windpipe, the bird can blow air and modify resonance. Depending on species, windpipe length exerts influence. As with the pipe of an organ, the longer the cylinder, the deeper the sound. Unlike humans, birds take tiny breaths that top up air circulating within all parts of their anatomy. The combination of continuous air supply and internal 'bagpipes' bestows versatility. Grasshopper Warblers can sing continuously for twenty minutes and appear not to draw breath. Blackbirds sometimes yodel through a mouthful of worms.

A phone rings. A person speaks, one of hundreds known to you and millions whom you do not know. Every voice is different and the same is true for birds. If you listen, each is identifiable. In all skills, it is important to know the range of possibilities. Painters understand colours, musicians know notes, poets weave words – otherwise they cannot be creative or fully admire the works of others. Likewise, if we are able to distinguish sounds, our knowledge expands. Personal reminiscences have a deeper meaning when we detect that the sound denotes a migrant freshly arrived from overseas rather than a resident, or that an unassuming note may have a glorious creature as its source.

Describing songs in words is difficult. A phonetic handle that works for one listener may not work for another. Sonograms, a kind of graph of each note against time and pitch, are a forensic

Small and with a costume that could hardly be more modest, Wrens sing to broadcast ownership of a plot of undergrowth and to woo a mate. No two carollers sound exactly the same. Females pick the best singers as mates; multi-syllabled vocalists are preferred. Reed Warblers do likewise (see p. 251).

way of pictorially representing sound. In a sonic blueprint, patterns are revealed that would otherwise escape the listener, such as rises in pitch or a telltale regularity of gaps between phrases. Unintelligible lines of consonants and vowels masquerading as catechism in field guides seldom helps. A better plan is to describe what the vocalisation *sounds like*. You need a picture in your head. A Wren singing open-mouthed, its orange gape glaring on a tubby torso that swivels as it belts out a complex aria, is transformed into a miniature Pavarotti. Put simply, when you hear the composition, try to invent a means of remembering it. Be imaginative. A dentist's whining drill? The dying chug of an engine failing to start? Perhaps the notes suggest a spiral staircase for an ethereal ascending song. The piercing *teu, teu, teu* of a Greenshank might bring to mind the terse dots of Morse code. 'It works for me,' should be your mantra. Oddly enough, the wackier the comparison the more likely you are to succeed. You only have to 'get' the sound once. Then, like knowing a human voice, you ought to remember it forever.

Plink! Not so long ago, I found myself surrounded by hundreds of foreign tongues in North America. Cavernous woods were alive with challenges. *Plink!* The note came from a tiny, pot-bellied Swainson's Thrush lurking in undergrowth. I thought, 'It's a droplet plopping into a half-filled tin bucket.' In that instant I entered the eeriness of a dark castle with slimy walls glinting like the watchful eye of a lizard, the silence punctured by an ominous, echoing water drip. I never struggled to identify Swainson's Thrush after that (and I still sleep with the light on).

BEFORE YOU START

ARS JONSSON, for many the greatest living bird painter, wrote:

> One winter I decided to try to obtain some definitive knowledge of the colour, markings, shape and movements of the House Sparrow – to specify its general appearance. To my astonishment, I discovered new lines and shapes, new colours and patterns, new traits of behaviour, new postures, and the upshot is that I am unable to produce a satisfying picture of such a well-known species! (Jonsson 1976)

By the same token, photographs in this book have been chosen for realism, rather than unnatural close-up portraits. It is not feasible to capture any more than a moment in time, let alone portray a range of plumages.

Thanks to the Internet, additional support can be tapped by entering a species title under Google Images. The best European search engine is www.birdguides.com. Go to 'Iris (Photos)' and select from the drop-down menu.

To scrutinise birds in the hand, there is a fantastic resource on a Spanish database entitled 'Identification Atlas of Birds of Aragon', located at www.ibercajalav.net.

For recordings of songs and calls, www.xeno-canto.org is indispensable. Xeno-canto is a user-driven online collection from many parts of the world. Recordings are free and can be downloaded. The database is continually growing, and for each species, the number of recordings varies (by April 2012, Great Tit recordings had reached 232). Recordings are listed under various headings, such as song and call, and a sonogram of each can be displayed while listening (in 'Remarks', click '[sono]'). A sonogram is a graph of sound, plotted against time (horizontal axis) and pitch (vertical axis): the higher a sound's pitch, the higher the trace on the graph. By listening to the sound, especially calls, and simultaneously observing a graphed pattern, a much clearer understanding emerges and helps commit the sound to memory.

The choice of ultimate field guide is a shoo-in. It is Lars Jonsson's *Birds of Europe* (1992). For birdwatching locations in all parts of Ireland, *Finding Birds in Ireland* (Dempsey & O'Clery 2007) is an excellent guide.

Few birds are as confident in our presence as House Sparrows. Non-paying passengers make journeys on the London Underground and on cross-Channel ferries. They also dine free.

SPECIES ACCOUNTS

MUTE SWAN
Cygnus olor

Right: With few predators or, indeed, humans to bother them, Mute Swans feed sedately. Although some visit fields and graze grass, most feed by upending and craning their long neck to uproot aquatic vegetation.

Below: Mute Swans adopt a characteristic 'busking' posture. Its function is to demonstrate threat. The male (left), the larger sex with a more prominent bill-knob, is a formidable protagonist.

MUTE SWANS are far from mute. Adults hiss menacingly and group interactions are accompanied by sotto voce sneezes. Flight identification is possible by sound; an unoiled creaky *whump* is audible a kilometre away. The heavyweight has to work hard, a by-product of flight technology straining at weight-load limits. Take-off requires up to 50m of taxi room. For want of sufficient runway, individuals can become trapped in confined spaces.

Where did our Mute Swans come from? According to popular belief, they are feral. Trusting behaviour and year-round presence on lakes and ponds sustain the notion that they are tainted through human contact, a bird that has gone soft. In many European countries they were deemed royal property and introductions extended the natural range. Thompson (1849 52) even slights the species by referring to it as 'The Tame or Mute

Swan' and states that it is not known to have occurred in a wild state in Ireland, although he believed that it occasionally reached Britain from 'its native abode in north-eastern Europe'. Nonetheless, it was well known a century earlier, as evidenced by Smith (1749), who, writing about Cork, remarked 'The Tame Swan is frequently met with near gentlemen's seats on their ponds and reservoirs.' Such second-class credentials were swept aside by the authors of *The Handbook of British Birds*, who declared:

England: Evidence for former theory of early introduction fallacious. More likely to have been originally indigenous in Lincolnshire, Cambridgeshire, Hunts, Norfolk, Suffolk and probably Thames. Original wild stock gradually brought by capture and pinioning into semi-domestic condition,

As cygnets grow, they moult downy white coats and acquire fawn plumage. The bill lacks a conspicuous black knob and slowly turns orange-grey in the bird's second year of life.

beginning prior to AD 1186 and ceased to exist as a wild race. From thirteenth to eighteenth centuries all Mute Swans were property of crown and, under royal licence, communities, corporations or private persons. Under licence, marks were assigned to all qualified owners. (Witherby *et al.* 1938–41)

Writing about Ireland, Witherby *et al.* (1938–41) state: 'No evidence of swan-keeping and early history unknown. Now generally distributed. Wild migrants may occur.' Whatever their ancestry, Mute Swans are certainly mobile. One ringed in Northern Ireland shifted to Scotland's Outer Hebrides. A pair from Chester crossed the Irish Sea, making landfall in Down before returning to Chester.

In a remarkable match to the best of us, Mute Swans pair for life and stay together beyond their years of fecundity. Breeding birds are most productive between the ages of six and twelve. Some graze on fields during winter, the preferred habitat of Whooper Swans. While the two are easy to distinguish by head pattern, structural distinctions are useful, especially at a distance when they are facing away or upending. On land, Mute Swans waddle with swinging hips; Whoopers walk. On water, the neck is curved and the wings are often arched, especially in males asserting dominance. The tail is conspicuously longer than the wingtips and forms part of the trademark on boxes of Swan Vesta matches.

BEWICK'S SWAN
Cygnus columbianus

Bewick's Swans nest on Siberian tundra and cygnets are reared on wetland margins. All migrate to Europe and stage in the Baltic, especially Estonia. Aided by protection and milder continental winters, fewer and fewer now make the annual trek across the Irish Sea.

IN BYGONE TIMES, writers and wildfowlers drew a distinction between resident Mute Swans and 'Wild Swans' – Whoopers from Iceland, Bewick's from Siberia – that arrived to spend the winter. These evoked a sense of wonder and were incorporated into legends and fairy stories. Their charisma was enhanced by beautiful, desolate 'whooping' calls. There is some uncertainty about which was commoner. Quoting Thompson (1849–52), Patterson (1880) expatiated: 'There are two species of Wild Swan known to visit Ireland, and of these Mr Thompson considered Bewick's Swan to be of the most frequent occurrence.' Ussher and Warren (1900) were more unequivocal: 'We owe to Thompson the discovery that Bewick's is the wild swan that visits Ireland in the greatest numbers, a fact which all subsequent observations have confirmed.' Such historical facts become intriguing when the status of Whooper Swan, nowadays a regular winter visitor, is viewed in a nineteenth-century context. Ussher and Warren continued, 'The Whooper Swan ... occurs in about the proportion of one to 25 Bewick's Swans, and is therefore a much rarer bird. The only locality which it visits every winter is Lough Swilly, but it is occasionally found on Lough Foyle.'

Until the closing years of the 1990s, flocks of Bewick's could be encountered around Lough Neagh and on polders alongside Lough Foyle. All that has changed. Counts chart a steep drop in numbers. In the mid-1980s an estimated 2,300 wintered in Ireland, constituting around 14 per cent of the western European population. Results from a census in 2000 painted a sharp decrease to 382. By January 2010, the total had shrunk to handfuls. The decline contrasts markedly with an overall increase in the northwest European population, which grew from approximately 7,000 in 1970 to 30,000 by 2000. Our decrease appears to be caused by milder winters curtailing journeys to the far reaches of the historical wintering range. An alternative explanation is that the birds have simply shifted their winter quarters. Before there was talk of 'climate change', Bewick's Swans were common winter visitors in western Scotland but rare in England; however, since the 1930s the opposite has been the case. When they were common in Ireland, migrants did not arrive until December and departed in late February, demonstrating that harsh European weather was always the trigger. Fluctuations are borne out in Ussher and Warren:

> Sir Ralph Payne-Galwey [The Fowler in Ireland (1882)] states that 300 to 400 remained [at Lough Gill, Kerry] during the frost of 1878–79, while in January 1881 [another cold winter] there were about 800.

Compounding the attraction of modern short stopping, protection and tailored habitat management on a network of large reserves has lured many to remain there, rather than trek west.

The scale of size difference between Whooper and Bewick's Swans can be gauged from measurements. Whooper is 50 per cent heavier and both its wingspan and neck length exceed that of Bewick's by 20 per cent. Bewick's is also blacker-billed. Yellow is restricted to a 'butter pat' rather than its larger relative's 'wedge of cheese'. In concert, the features convey a svelte, demure form. For airborne flocks, compact physique translates into the dexterity and tight synchronisation of smaller wildfowl, on a par with Brent Geese. Voice can be a useful distinction from Whooper, although in practice is hard to come by. When not in large flocks and maintaining a hubbub of tremolo bugling, small bands 'toot' rather than trumpet. The notes often come singly or in pairs, rather than the longer series typical of Whooper.

WHOOPER SWAN
Cygnus cygnus

Whooper Swans are majestic. Bugling calls attend many activities, and are most evocative when they announce the arrival of an airborne troupe. Inset: Whooper Swans are long-billed and sport a Roman nose. In their first winter, cygnets are ashy with a pink and black bill. Yellow appears on the bill during spring and, by the following winter, just a few grey feathers remain on the head and neck.

POLAR WHITE PLUMAGE, a black and buttercup bill and triumphant bugling across wind-lashed loughs evoke an altogether different experience from the Mute Swan. In fact, Whoopers are predominantly terrestrial. On account of a short tail, an upending Whooper can be told from a longer-tailed Mute, whose protruding appendage extends past the wingtips. Furthermore, especially waddling, Mute Swans carry the head and bill in a forward tilt well below horizontal; Whoopers hold the head upright, periscope style. The angle is close to level and the countenance is square-jawed with a flat-topped crown. Mute Swans have sinuous necks that develop a 'waist' before reaching a sagging head. On Whooper, because the eyes are not engulfed by black skin, facial expression is benign. Head profile is smooth and planed, without knobbly contours. Often neck plumage is tinged copper, natural staining caused by iron compounds picked up from Icelandic lakes.

Distinctions from Bewick's Swan are more subtle. While the two wild swans differ in size, intermixed loafing or feeding flocks have a habit of presenting higgledy-piggledy arrangements consisting of the long and the short and the tall, yet all may be the same species. Only when alarmed and standing to attention does the dumpier stature of Bewick's emerge. The three most reliable distinguishing features are neck length, head shape and the amount of yellow on the bill. Whooper Swan has a relatively long neck, often showing a kink at the base. The head and bill align smoothly, creating a Roman nose. On adult Bewick's, the head looks slightly bulbous and less 'fused' to the bill: less Concorde, more jumbo jet. Given a clear view of bill colour, it becomes obvious that, on Whooper, yellow colouring extends beyond the nostril and ends in a point: on Bewick's, the yellow ends bluntly, above the nostril. Juveniles have uniformly grey bodies, becoming whiter through feather replacement as winter progresses. Their bills are black-tipped and pinkish-grey in those areas destined to turn yellow, the first hint of which appears in late February. Some flecks of fawn, typically around the head and neck, remain into the second year of life. Quite when the juvenile voice breaks is unclear, but it is certainly not during its first winter, when the best a juvenile can do is emit a raspy squeak.

Wintering Whoopers in Ireland are predominantly of Icelandic origin, although not all leave Iceland. Over 1,000 remain, mainly in waters fed by warm geothermal activity. Many are ringed or fitted with a variety of tags. Since 1986, co-ordinated counts of the flyway's population have been organised at five-year intervals. Tallies for Ireland between 1986 and 2000 ranged from 12,000 to 18,000, roughly 65 per cent of the flyway total. Following arrival in the northwest during October, especially on flat coastal fields on the shores of Lough Swilly and Lough Foyle, flocks follow a roving itinerary. Departures for Iceland commence in the second half of April. Flight altitudes are normally low, seldom higher than 500m, although one flock was famously discovered by radar at 5,400m over Belfast International Airport. In recent years a few pairs have attempted to nest.

Lead poisoning, from ingested pellets, is not uncommon among swans that feed in regularly shot areas. These clog in the gizzard and are slowly degraded by digestive juices, dissolving into fatal compounds. Three particles of shot are sufficient to poison a swan; just one will kill a duck. Lead remains in soil for many years, so the danger persists. Furthermore, despite protection over the bulk of migration routes, many swans have been shot at and carry remains of lead in their tissues. Alternatives to lead shot in shotgun cartridges cannot come quickly enough.

BEAN GOOSE
Anser fabalis

Brown, earthy tones pervade almost all plumage areas, leaving orange legs and bill to catch the eye.

DURING THE TWENTIETH CENTURY, Bean Geese rarely strayed across the Irish Sea. With little more than a few hundred in eastern Britain, no significant overspill materialised and the core wintering range remained on the continent. In recent years, all that has changed. The species is returning. Formerly it was common; the main recipient of the epithet 'The Wild Goose':

Sixteen were observed on 12th September [1845] flying over Belfast Bay; during the following six weeks great numbers appeared, many occasionally on one day. Throughout every month until January inclusive, and when there is no severe weather, wild [Bean] geese are occasionally seen passing in a

southerly direction. In the last week but one of December 1837 several groups, each of about twenty, appeared over Belfast Bay, the weather during the week being extremely wet. (Thompson 1849–52)

A decline took place during the latter half of the nineteenth century. Debates relating to changes in status in Ireland are often conducted in a narrow dimension that fails to take account of events just across the way in Scotland. There too, Bean Geese started to disappear during exactly the same era (Watson 1986). Particularly in Ayrshire and Kirkcudbrightshire, land reclamation and improved drainage reduced habitat. As ground dried out,

After an absence of more than a century, Europe's Bean Geese are showing signs of including Ireland as part of the species' winter range. Another welcome change is that they are not, so far, being greeted with a hail of shot.

marsh plants became extinct and re-seeding installed new grasses that, ironically, proved palatable to Greylag Geese. Local belief held that the increase and spread of Greylags in the old haunts of Bean Geese deterred them. The decline became noticeable about 1870 but Bean Geese were still the commonest grey geese on the Solway in 1886. In the uplands of Ayrshire flocks of fifty or more were fairly regular at least until 1927, but were replaced by Greylags during the decade 1938–48 (Hughes-Onslow 1949).

Bean Geese combine rich dark brown upperparts, flanks, underwings, neck and head with a 'glowing' pale brown chest. Bill colour is variable. Some are essentially dark-billed, apart from

a small dab of orange behind a dark nail; others are more extensively orange-billed. They are (apart from the Greenland White-fronted Goose) the only grey goose with orange legs. Bean Geese vary in size and proportions. Birds breeding in Siberian tundra are squat and not dissimilar in size from White-fronted Geese; those breeding in taiga wetlands are larger and also longer-necked. However, all are rather 'fat-faced' with a lumpy dark bill base. A useful, albeit rather subtle, field mark is the presence of light-edged tertials. Even at long range, distinct white edges to these feathers, which are almost plain on White-fronted Geese, are diagnostic.

PINK-FOOTED GOOSE
Anser brachyrhynchus

PINK LEGS AND FEET are a feature shared by both Pink-footed Geese and Greylag Geese. Other grey geese are orange-legged. In the field, trying to determine whether a wary goose has orange or pink legs can be difficult, if indeed the legs are even visible. An old name – Short-billed Goose – was much more descriptive. The bill is mainly dark with pink restricted to behind a dark tip. On many, the patch of pink resembles a sticking plaster. Pink-footed Geese are dumpy and dark, something of a titch. The head and upper neck are earth brown, contrasting with an almost sandy-brown lower neck and belly. At rest, some adults show a 'blue rinse' tinge across the back.

Pink-footed Geese breed in the Arctic with concentrations in Spitsbergen and Iceland. During winter, these populations remain separate. Those from Iceland winter mainly in Scotland, from where handfuls travel across the Irish Sea. The species used to be a great rarity: D.C. Campbell picked out the first Irish specimen from among shot wildfowl on sale in a poulterer's shop in Derry city in October 1891. The bird was killed either on Lough Foyle or nearby on Lough Swilly, Donegal. Because geese are sociable, lone out-of-range Pink-footed Geese mingle with other species. Occasionally they become permanently attached to a flock not of their own kind. Romance shone on one such individual when a stray of the opposite sex arrived. Although no nest was found, a family party containing two recently fledged juveniles was among a post-breeding flock of Greylag Geese at the Quoile Pondage, Down, in the summer of 2004 (AMG). When storms coincide with the final stage of migration from Iceland to Scotland, flocks divert to windward. Some finish up here, where they may remain for the winter. Perhaps befitting their smaller stature, Pink-feet have a slightly high-pitched voice. Their yappy *ink, ink* is distinctive, even when heard among a cacophony of other geese.

Dumpiness is a hallmark of this, the smallest 'grey goose'. Nimble grazing habits, a high-pitched voice and aerobatic manoeuvrability in flight chime with diminutive size.

WHITE-FRONTED GOOSE
Anser albifrons

WHITE-FRONTED GEESE breed across tundra in Europe, Siberia and Alaska, with an isolated population in Greenland that differs in several alluring respects, making it the grand dame of the tribe. Increasingly, it has been mooted as a full species in its own right – the Greenland White-fronted Goose. Flocks are quarrelsome but watchful. An appointed lookout, usually a sentinel adult, stands immovable, leaving family groups free to graze grass and roots. Bickering and yapping are commonplace. In flight, en masse flights are unparalleled. White-fronted Geese freely form chevrons and V-formations. Lofty legions embroider the sky like columns of marching ants.

Greenland birds spend the winter in western Scotland and in various parts of Ireland, the majority on the Wexford Slobs. Ussher and Warren (1900) provided a summary of status that was both accurate and evocative: 'A regular and often an abundant winter visitor to the great bogs in all the provinces.' A small population spends the winter in parts of Fermanagh, especially across the comparatively unspoiled wilderness of the Pettigo Plateau straddling the border with Donegal. The birds are hard to pin down. Flocks were formerly regular on the polder landscape adjoining Lough Foyle, where extensive fields of root crops harboured a winter wildfowl spectacular. The habitat has recently been vanquished, converted to a desert of lawn turf and biofuel willow coppice.

Those that winter on the Wexford Slobs utilise a habitat that did not exist until a little over a century ago. Faced with hunting pressure and the inexorable loss of remote oases of bogland, the extensive new pastureland on the shores of Wexford Harbour offered sanctuary in a time of crisis. The truth is, even on the slobs, farmers tolerate the birds only because they serve as quarry. The National Parks and Wildlife Service (NPWS) manage some fields. Viewing opportunities are limited and, once the bird's fortunes are seen in the context of almost total extirpation from most of the rest of the country, their status looks more like imprisonment on alien, fertiliser-fed grassland than anything that evolution might have brought about.

Parties pass along the Irish Sea coast, hugging the coast to Wexford, or head west to Wales or southwest Scotland. Although some 'within-winter' movements occur, the bird shows a high degree of winter site fidelity (Wilson *et al.* 1991). Around 85 per cent return to the same site in successive winters. They are similarly loyal to staging areas in Iceland and breeding grounds in Greenland. In spring, the majority depart during the second week of April. Routes plotted for twelve satellite-tracked birds from Wexford showed that in 1997, most departed on 7 April, including one that moved to Lough Foyle, where it stayed a week until departing for Iceland on 16 April. In 1998 and 1999, most departed from Wexford in mid-April. After a non-stop flight, all arrived in western Iceland between 17 and 22 April. Here they fed for about a fortnight before crossing the Greenland ice cap and arriving at Disko Bay on the west coast around 9–11 May, ultimately reaching ancestral breeding grounds, located around seventy degrees north, one week later.

Hunted for centuries in Greenland and Iceland (where it is now protected), the bird is understandably wary. Adult plumage is unmistakable. Juveniles lack the frontal 'sheepskin noseband' and also the black belly barring shown by adults. Peter Scott is credited with distinguishing the unique appearance of Greenland's breeders, recognised as *A. a. flavirostris* (yellow-billed) in 1948. Not only is the bill yellow-orange, it is also marginally longer and narrower than in other, pink-billed populations; and these birds are somewhat larger and swarthier in plumage. Over recent winters small groups of European White-fronts have straggled west to Ireland. One explanation is that they have actually travelled here annually but have been overlooked due to a more than superficial resemblance to Greenland stock. All White-fronts have a pleasant voice, not unlike the musical yammer of a pack of beagles.

Geese are social, and young and old can often be compared directly. With age, White-fronts become progressively darker-bellied, whereas yearlings lack belly barring in their first winter. Dried mud has attached to legs and bills, effectively masking bright orange bare parts.

GREYLAG GOOSE
Anser anser

Although extensively introduced into numerous areas of Western Europe, feral birds, originally released but now living independently, occasionally rejoin wild brethren. Indeed, some streetwise breeders flaunt a badge of boldness and raise families on ornamental lakes. More typically, uninhabited islands are favoured for nesting. Variation in bill colour is not unusual. On all grey geese, leg and bill colours can be tricky to determine at distance.

IT MAY COME as a surprise to learn that, during the nineteenth century, Greylag Geese were scarce. Thompson (1849–52) saw very few, encountering them only as fare in Dublin markets. Just one of his correspondents was familiar with the species, in Connacht, where small groups frequented upland pastures and cultivated fields. Harris (1744) recorded that the 'great harrow goose' was found in bogs in the Ards Peninsula at Kirkiston. An octogenarian friend of Thompson remembered that a relation often 'robbed nests in this very locality, *Kirkiston flow*, the period of his doing so was previous to the year of 1775. There is little doubt that the [Greylag Goose] was the bird alluded to, as it formerly bred plentifully in the fens of England, though for a considerable time they, as well as the bogs of Ireland, have been deserted by it.' A semi-domesticated population centred on Castle Coole, Fermanagh, is believed to date back to around 1700. When fresh recruits were added in 1960, the birds spread into the surrounding district. Similarly, releases at Strangford Lough in 1967 became the seed corn of a local population that stood at 527 by March 1986 (Merne 1986). An all-Ireland count in July 1984 turned up 977 'naturalised' adults at thirty sites (Cabot 2009).

In the eyes of the purist, today's populations lack unblemished wild credentials. Fearless bread-guzzlers in Belfast parks become wary once they fly on to farm fields or breed on uninhabited islands, such as those on Strangford Lough. Sages have learned to use the system and enter our domain on their terms. While some interchange takes place between bona fide migrants and settled groups, a banded individual at Belfast waterworks had not moved far in eight years; its recorded movements spanned a mere 2km. Others roam widely and are interchangeable members of populations that migrate to Scotland and Iceland. A marked bird at Anne's Point, Strangford Lough, on 29 December 2010 had

spent two winters out of fifteen in Ireland, passing the remainder in the northeast of Scotland and travelling to Iceland on at least one occasion (OC). Two clocked up a run of February and March appearances in the Lough Neagh basin between 2002 and 2011, with elaborate itineraries connecting summer homes in Iceland to winter quarters in various parts of Scotland, northern England and Ireland. One was faithful to fields at Deerpark, Antrim, in the month of February from 2002 to 2010; the other moved east from Donegal to stage at Portmore Lough in March 2011. Flocks from Lough Neagh's hinterland travel to Iceland. Once there, the species exhibits streetwise nous, tolerant around farms and villages but suspicious and unapproachable in habitats where humans are the exception (AMG). An unknown proportion of Iceland's breeding population winters in Donegal, Dublin and Louth. Most head to Scotland and then cross to Ireland in mid-winter.

Greylag Goose is the bigwig from which all domestic geese are derived, domestic geese, some of which closely resemble wild specimens. Domestication has had little effect on altering calls; the gruff voice sounds the same. Noble savages generally limit calling to taking flight or preparing to land, especially when coming in to roost. The typical call is a three-note *drrrunk, unk-unk* that seems to chime with a solid build. A pinkish-orange bill is heavy and conspicuously bright, even at long range. Identifying a species of 'grey goose' from its flight silhouette is something of a black art. Recognition is, at best, putative unless plumage or calls can be gauged. Greylag is thick-necked, the head is bulky and the bill is broad-based. The front-end profile resembles an Eider. If patterns are discernible, identification can be made by checking the underwing: whitish-grey at the front and contrastingly dark, blackish-brown behind.

CANADA GOOSE
Branta canadensis

Taxonomists waver over the number of recognisable 'forms' of Canada Geese. Certain populations have increased and expanded range, so a few distinct races are now less well separated in the wild. Among its ranks, the bird has evolved into sizes ranging from 'Giant Canada Goose' (the largest goose in the world) to the tundra-nesting 'Cackling Goose', little larger than a Brent Goose. The white chinstrap is used in social signalling.

'AND I AM DISPOSED to believe that some of the victims [Canada Geese shot on different parts of the Irish coast] may have been truly wild. The species seems to me as likely to visit this country occasionally as some other American birds do so.' Thompson (1849–52) wrote those revolutionary words in a bygone era when Swallows were still believed to hibernate in lakebeds. At the time, the Canada Goose had already been introduced into parks, gardens and ornamental ponds in several parts of Ireland. It is quite possible that these original founders, at least some of which came from Castle Kennedy in Dumfries and Galloway, provided the nucleus for flocks that still exist in parts of Fermanagh and on Strangford Lough. Merne (1969) published an inventory of Irish waterfowl collections containing free-flying Canada Geese. The population stood at just under 200. Merne also listed records of putative wild vagrants (first detected in 1954) that arrived with White-fronted Geese migrating from Greenland to Wexford. In most instances these were small types not kept in collections, thereby authenticating a wild provenance.

Irrefutable proof that waifs cross the North Atlantic was determined when a Canada Goose trapped among Greenland White-fronted Geese on the North Slob, Wexford, in November 1993 was shot in Maryland, USA, fifteen months later. It was assigned as (Todd's) Canada Goose *Branta canadensis interior*, the form whose breeding range has recently expanded eastwards from Hudson Bay to Greenland. This discovery has real significance. Before 1970, Canada Goose was a vagrant to western Greenland, although it occasionally bred. Since then a rapid colonisation has taken place, especially during the 1980s and 1990s (Lyngs 2003). Most occur along central and southern parts of the west coast and there are reports that burgeoning numbers are 'out-competing' Greenland White-fronted Geese (Tony Fox in *Birding World* 14:59). In 1999, the overall Greenland population was estimated at 2,600 pairs.

Some contemporary opinion considers that, in North America, differences in size and appearance – small and dark in higher latitudes in the west and north, large 'conventional' types in the east and continental interior – form a tenable basis for a two-way split. Hence, Canada Goose *B. canadensis* and Cackling

Goose *B. hutchinsii*. Establishing unequivocal identification criteria is complicated and far from being resolved. Honest minds should heed seminal work by Anderson (2010), which demonstrated a wide-ranging orderly spectrum, incapable of being divided or compartmentalised. Rather than species division, there is a need for unison that embraces a spectrum of forms.

Ringing recoveries have revealed the winter whereabouts of Greenland's colonists. Most head south across the Davis Strait in late September, passing Labrador, New Brunswick and Massachusetts en route to wintering grounds in northeastern USA. A few have demonstrated a propensity to accompany flocks of White-fronted Geese, Barnacle Geese and Brent Geese departing for Ireland and Britain. Consequently, determining the provenance of lone Canada Geese among flocks of other geese is becoming feasible, based on field identification breakthroughs (Batty and Lowe 2001). When stray individuals conform in appearance to populations from which vagrants are most likely to be drawn, a wild candidacy is better assured. Several with bona fide credentials, strongly suggesting a wild origin, have appeared; most have been seen in Mayo, Sligo and on Lough Foyle. Having grown accustomed to the gangly messy beast that is feral Canada Goose, a small dapper prototype comparable in size to a Greenland White-fronted Goose (or smaller) is a breath of fresh air and, in the right circumstances, wild and free to boot.

This brings the argument full circle, back to the continued existence in Ireland of feral populations. In Britain, the species is regarded as a menace. Feral flocks damage wetland habitats by eutrophication – defecation enriches shoreline vegetation, eliminating plant diversity and polluting water. Mobs of other domesticated wildfowl wreak similar damage. Populations in royal parks are kept in check only by annual culls and, at several airports, shooting is necessary to remove flocks that congregate on grassland in flight paths and constitute a bird-strike hazard. Surely there is a case for removing Ireland's feral population? To placate the anticipated howls of politically correct posturing from conservation charities at the very thought of control (that is, killing), the removal or pricking of eggs could, over time, eliminate this unwanted introduction.

BARNACLE GOOSE
Branta leucopsis

Barnacle Geese gather in closely knit flocks. Face patterns vary, although youngsters are invariably dullest. Reared in Greenland, chicks face a tough start in life. To avoid Arctic Foxes, adults breed on cliffs from which goslings leap to join their parents below.

ON THE CUSP of October, Barnacle Geese from Greenland arrive over the horizon and touch down on islands along Ireland's Atlantic coast. Thousands spend the winter on the Scottish island of Islay, from where small flocks cross to north Donegal and, less often, the Skerries and Sheep Island, Antrim. During the nineteenth century, most wintered along the shores of Dundalk Bay, Louth. Thompson (1849–52) was able to spy them when travelling by horse-drawn coach to Dublin.

Extensive sandy coast exposed by the receding tide, bordered by short pasture, is the favourite haunt of the bernacle [Barnacle Goose]. The greatest haunt is an immense shallow sandy bay, bordered by an extensive tract of pasture and marshy ground, called Lurgan Green. This locality is known to me from observing it on the way from Belfast to Dublin, which I have rarely done without seeing large flocks (numbering sometimes between 300 and 400) either on the sands or greensward little raised above it. I have seen them within shot of the coach, as regardless of its passing as a flock of tame geese, indeed more so, for the latter would have had the impudence to cackle, while the bernacle had the good sense to remain silent. No person having been permitted to fire a shot about Lurgan Green was the reason for their tameness. They were captured here in little pitfalls dug in the earth, without being in the least degree injured.

The scourge of habitat change wrought by agriculture rendered the birds homeless and, during the twentieth century, an increase on Wexford's North Slob may have comprised those displaced from Louth. Right up until the late 1950s, as many as 2,000 wintered there and on Lambay Island, off the Dublin coast. Then, for unknown reasons, all haunts along Ireland's eastern seaboard were abandoned. A handful – some of them wounded – were relocated from Mayo and established on the islands of Strangford Lough. The scheme's noble intent was to coax the birds to regard the area as their winter home. Regrettably the attempt failed. Instead, although wild-reared, the birds chose to take up permanent residence and nowadays 350 reside on the lough's islands (PPM).

Barnacle Geese graze grass, but specialise in eating clover stolons. The stolons, which creep along the soil just below surface vegetation, are the plant's starchy storage organs. Although heavily grazed in winter, the clover replenishes itself in summer. On the main Irish haunt, the Inishkea Islands off the coast of Mayo, pastures are short and amount to little more than a sward of plantain (Plantago spp). By pecking at an extremely fast rate – up to 250 pecks per minute – with a peculiarly short bill, the birds are able to nibble in ways that other geese cannot.

To avoid predators, chiefly Arctic Foxes, nests are constructed on ledges among vertical cliffs or on low islands. Chicks begin life by leaping into space and hoping that their coat of fluffy down will protect them from the pummelling that awaits them when they hit the ground – usually scree at the foot of nesting cliffs – up to 50m below. The luckiest jumpers manage to land upright, breaking their fall with splayed feet. It was not until 1891

that the first nests were found in east Greenland, and more nests were discovered in Spitsbergen in 1907. Later it was proved that Barnacle Geese breed in Arctic Russia, on the island of Novaya Zemlya. These three areas remain the core. Each population is discrete and adheres to migration routes and home ranges. Greenland breeders reach Iceland in early September and gather on mossy plains in Vestur-Skaftafellssysla and Austur-Skaftafellssysla. Here they bide their time and watch the weather. When a deep depression sweeps over us and triggers a cool northwesterly airflow, the birds seize the moment and fly south. Like a hen celebrating the laying of an egg, they only cackle after they have made it back. In 2008 Ireland's population amounted to 12,200.

Barnacle Geese look essentially monochrome, but chequerboard upperparts glint of blue. The black-and-white bust is reminiscent of a nun's habit. Facial colour is variable and unrelated to age or sex, ranging from snow-white through buff to pale lemon yellow. Adults have tricoloured wing coverts that lie in parallel rows, the biggest to the rear. Each feather is silver-grey with a white-edged black terminal band. Youngsters are similar to adults, but lack the white fringes and the overall shade of silver-grey is duller. This makes for less contrast. Because juvenile feathers are more rounded, there is a messy look to plumage arrangement. Adult upperparts have a tiled architecture. All ages have stony-white underparts with diffuse scalloping on the rear flanks. On youngsters, the background colour is less bright and the scallops can appear murky. Variation complicates matters. Some young betray their age by the presence of random white snags among black neck plumage, as though a kitten had pulled stuffing out of a cuddly toy.

Where do Barnacle Geese come from? Surely not barnacles? Crazy as it seems, this fanciful notion became enshrined in folklore. Greenoak (1979) takes up the story:

In his The Herball or General Historie of Plants, John Gerard (1597) mentions 'the Goose Tree or Barnacle Tree grows in the north parts of Scotland [Orkney]. Certain trees grow shells of a white colour tending to russet, wherein are contained little living creatures ... which falling into the water do become fowl, which we call Barnacles.'

The myth may have a basis in real life if you allow that the tiny feathery appendage (a kind of modified leg) with which the barnacle fans microscopic particles of food towards its mouth could conceivably be mistaken for the wing feathers of an emerging bird. Ireland's human inhabitants reached the same conclusion centuries earlier than Gerard. In 1185, Giraldus Cambrensis, a Welsh monk who travelled around Ireland, recorded in Topographia Hibernica that 'Bishops and religious men in some parts of Ireland do not scruple to dine off these birds at the time of fasting, because they are not born of flesh.' Irish logic decreed that, if they hatched from barnacles, they were really fish and could justifiably be eaten on Fridays and during Lent. Maybe, after all, the collective noun should be shoal?

BRENT GOOSE
Branta bernicla

BRENT GEESE are small, scarcely larger than Mallards, and are creatures of the coast. They are gregarious, but unlike grey geese do not fly in wedge formations. Over mudflats, they shift in lines at no great height, writhing and undulating in graceful ribbons. The voice – *krrowk* – is low and rolling, with a guttural quality. To breed, they trek to Canada's vast empty quarter and scatter across tundra, grazing on grasses and sedges and nibbling ground-hugging flowers. At high latitudes things can go horribly wrong if ice and snow smother ground at egg-laying time in early June. Preliminary research suggests that most pairs become acquainted at age two or three and settle down to breed roughly two years later. Most relationships are monogamous and last until one of the pair dies. Youngsters stay with parents until their first birthday. Clannishness is deeply ingrained and each generation tends to follow in the footsteps of its forebears, feeding and staging at familiar places all the way from Ireland to Canada. Iceland is a key refuelling stop.

On returning to Ireland, the bulk of the population congregates initially on Strangford Lough's green mudflats, swathed in eelgrass and leafy algae. As verdant mudflats become depleted, the bulk of the population travels clockwise to estuaries straddling the entire coastline of Ireland. Some criss-cross the landmass: from Strangford north to Lough Foyle or overland from the east coast to Sligo. Especially in Dublin, Brents have become habituated to people; passers-by and grazing geese ignore each other. When eelgrass became diseased in the 1930s, numbers crashed. A dieback has not happened for several decades and the species is thriving. Based on systematic counts at key staging areas in Ireland and Iceland, the population stood at around 35,000 at the end of a successful breeding season in 2011. Family units stay together throughout winter, even in the midst of

Family groups stick together and elders regularly keep things in order, admonishing pushy feeders and asserting dominance. Youngsters have parallel rows of pale edges across the wing coverts and develop a white neck brooch during their first winter. Inset: With winter quarters in Ireland and breeding grounds in Arctic Canada, Brent Geese expend massive amounts of energy during migration. Often, all effort is wasted and no young are produced. Setbacks apart, the population is flourishing.

massed feeding frenzies. Juveniles have pale fringes across the lower back and a poorly developed 'brooch' on the neck. As winter progresses and easy pickings diminish, juveniles are presented with a choice between thinly spread shoreline algae or abundant terrestrial grasses. In family units, they appear to be driving a switch to feeding on fields once eelgrass has been eaten out. However, the new diet seems to be borderline junk food. When they reach nesting grounds, marked grass-guzzlers weigh less than shoreline feeders. As a result, breeding performance is inferior.

Ireland's wintering birds, which hail from Canada, have light-coloured underparts and are referred to as Pale-bellied Brent Geese. Dark-bellied Brent Geese nest in Siberia and winter around the shores of the North Sea. Although dusky below, the upperparts are slightly paler than the belly. Moreover, the flanks have a delicate pattern of smoky pale scallops. A more striking form hails from Alaska. Entitled Black Brant, this bird has a blackish overall appearance, relieved by a white frontal collar and flanks slashed with white. Because all Brent Geese nest in the Arctic, the convergence of latitude shrinks distance between respective ranges and wanderers sometimes attach themselves to populations that are not kin. Rather than rejoin their own ranks, vagrants opt to associate with populous hordes. As a result, they synchronise migration routes and arrive with our Pale-bellied Brent Geese.

SHELDUCK
Tadorna tadorna

FEW WATERFOWL are as instantly recognisable as Shelduck. The sexes are closely similar, just one of several attributes – upright stance, terrestrial habits, persistent pair bonds and prolonged parental behaviour – that establish an affinity to geese. Males are larger and have a knob at the base of the bill, resembling a small red balloon or shield. The bulge, which is brittle in winter, enlarges in spring, becoming soft and fleshy and filled with oily matter. Shelduck may be a derivation of 'shield duck', on account of the bill's architecture. Indeed, in older books, the bird was named 'Shield-drake', later corrupted to Sheldrake. On the other hand, the term 'sheld' is a dialect word meaning variegated or particoloured, betokening piebald plumage. Shelduck feed by sieving wet mud for minute molluscs, scarcely larger than poppy seed. Ninety per cent of stomach contents consist of Laver Spire Shell (*Hydrobia ulvae*). The snails occur at up to 300,000 per square metre of mud. They feed on silt, fungi and phytoplankton, which they scrape from sediment.

Shelducks are quarrelsome and noisy. Disputes seem to be a way of life and are accompanied by female 'child-imitating-a-machine-gun' chatter and wheezy male whistles. Bickering ceases when young appear in early summer. Rabbit burrows and underground chambers are used for nesting, explaining why incubating females have no need of camouflage. Both parents guard ducklings and squabbling neighbours bury the hatchet and amalgamate broods into a crèche. Up to eighty have been seen together. A recipe for disaster? Apparently not, because the Everton mint colour scheme of youngsters may denote a bad taste. Thompson (1849–52) was aware of repugnant culinary qualities. 'It is generally considered to be bad as food ... strong

and having a heavy disagreeable smell.' Parents are indefatigable, but perhaps an off-putting taste packaged in a suit of warning colours is the real secret of duckling survival.

Except for the year's crop of juveniles, the population disappears in July. Ringing confirms that many embark upon a spectacular trans-Pennine flight to extensive sandbanks in the Waddenzee, the vast intertidal shoreline running north from Holland to Denmark, where a minimum of 100,000 – almost all the western European population – congregate to moult, during which time they are flightless. Uncertainty surrounds the origins of around 4,000 that moult at Bridgewater Bay in Somerset. Are they Irish? Eltringham and Boyd (1963) speculated that, because over one third of freshly moulted adults left Somerset on a westerly bearing and overflew Wales, they were most likely destined for Ireland. The species is a confident migrant and a commute to Somerset would require a flight lasting no more than a few hours. Conjecture also attaches to the source of Shelducks that arrive on the Cromarty Firth in northeast Scotland. Is this where Ulster Shelducks moult?

Youngsters do not travel to moulting grounds until they are one year old. There is no point; juvenile wing and tail plumage last approximately fifteen months. With few exceptions, juveniles are the only age-class present on estuaries during late summer. They lack a breast band. By late autumn, following a moult of head and body plumage, they more closely resemble adults. In flight, the wings show a light trailing edge. When at rest, coppery tertials are pale-fringed and some wing coverts are etched with frilly fretwork.

Shelducks feed at the tideline or in shallows, sifting mud through lamellae (tiny comb-like teeth) on either side of the bill, and sieving small invertebrates from the surface sediment.

WIGEON
Anas penelope

WIGEON HAVE IT ALL. They are good-looking and know how to whistle. Feeding packs on grassland effectively mow the sward and revisit it to enjoy a fresh bite. Both sexes are peppered with distinctive field marks. Drakes affect a Mohican hairstyle with a marzipan stripe crowning a terracotta head. The pink chest is juxtapositioned against a grey, canvas-textured body. Just before a pointy black tail, a white bum catches the eye. Muted female plumage is adorned with foxy shades. Both sexes have a neat 'cut'.

As early as March, flocks forsake Ireland and commence the journey back to northern latitudes. Ulster's population has crashed and the other three provinces are following suit, although not in quite such dramatic style. In the past, great legions spent the winter grazing eelgrass on Lough Foyle and Strangford Lough. At Belfast Lough, the city's expansion decimated the habitat. At Lough Foyle, where mudflats remain, numbers have dropped from 12,000 to 1,000. It may well be that most have shifted to winter quarters positioned at a lesser distance from the breeding grounds. In fact, as Strangford's population fell, numbers rose at Martin Mere in Lancashire (JSF).

In *Birds of Iceland* (1986) Hjalmar R. Bardarson writes, 'A few hundred Wigeon are resident and spend the winter along the coast of southwest Iceland. Ringing recoveries have revealed that large numbers winter in Britain and Ireland, and that a small number go to the east coast of North America. Iceland's population is probably a little less than 5,000 pairs.' So the bulk of Iceland's Wigeon still migrate south. It seems that many go to Scotland and southwest Ireland. Accordingly, it is safe to conclude that our missing multitudes were derived, not from Iceland, but from Scandinavia. Ringing data confirms the presence of breeding stock from Finland and Russia.

Riveting, beautifully written accounts in Thompson (1849–52) and Patterson (1880) evoke wildfowling on Belfast Lough. Initially small in scale, the activity grew into a commercial operation. Still, the demise of a great carpet of Wigeon and Brent Geese came about largely through other means. Thompson enumerated these:

Wigeon have latterly become very much scarcer in Belfast Bay, owing to different causes: the annually increasing shipping of the port; the steam vessels with their black smoke particularly alarming them; extensive portions of the sea-banks being reclaimed; the gas lights of the town; each and all of these together have had a tendency to make them change their quarters. But worse behind. The swivel-gun shooters, three of whom at least are at some portion of every day in pursuit of them. Their persecution, commencing soon after the arrival of the birds in autumn, has them pretty well driven away early in November, and few are killed between this time and Christmas. Wigeon are so much persecuted in Belfast Bay, that before the dawn of morning, multitudinous numbers rise from the banks on which they have been feeding all night and betake themselves to Strangford Lough, as a place of comparative safety, where they remain all day, but return [to Belfast] at twilight.

Had it been safe to do so, the flocks would have preferred to feed by day. Precise population figures will never be known. Counts from the late 1950s indicated that 5,000 endured, mainly to the west of the River Lagan (HD). In September 1966, a seemingly endless stream of hundreds was observed from Carrickfergus Harbour, Antrim, heading for Belfast, although they may not have halted there (AMG).

Drake Wigeon are not just a pretty picture – they also have a great voice. In French, the name is *Canard Siffleur* ('Whistling Duck'). Females emit a low chortle.

Left: Female plumage is foxy brown. Hues vary and some are loam-coloured. Identification is feasible on silhouette alone due to a short neck and bill. Wigeon bills are suited to grazing, with serrations along the edges that efficiently shear stems.

Below: During winter, dabbling ducks often stick together to feed communally and share security. Eighteen Wigeon, mostly drakes, are sprinkled among the Teal. For speed of recognition, key features are not resplendent plumage: in life views, the pointed, black-and-white rear and blaze of snow-white wing coverts (peeping out above the flanks) come into their own.

GADWALL
Anas strepera

UNTIL AROUND 1980, Gadwalls were uncommon. Small numbers, believed to be from Iceland, passed through during spring and autumn, a phenomenon that continues. While some of the current breeding population are derived from stock released by duck hunters, there is little doubt that the lion's share are colonists. In a corollary to Collared Dove, the species has marched west across Europe. Spreading from a core range located between the rivers Volga and Dneiper, prospectors settled in the eastern Baltic during the 1960s and the Nordic countries during the 1980s, followed by Denmark and the Netherlands, where the annual rate of increase hit almost 10 per cent during 2000–2008. In Britain, numbers have risen from 260 pairs in the early 1970s (Sharrock 1976) to over 2,000 (Holling *et al.* 2011). Nowadays many breed unobtrusively across a chain of wetlands all the way west to Galway and south to Cork. The origin of increasing numbers of winter birds is unclear. Are they immigrants from overseas or batches of new-found sedentary residents? Pairs and small flocks are undemonstrative and tuck themselves among shoreline vegetation. Some roost by day – a sign that feeding is probably nocturnal. Portmore Lough has become a summer moulting ground for 500 or more.

Drakes break the rules that apply to other male wildfowl; they are plain Janes, the antithesis of foppish. At first glance, a vat of grey engulfs all plumage areas. Close up, drakes are sublime, bedecked in a grey flannel palate, like hues of a lowering sky. The chest is dark and etched in chain mail; vermiculated sides appear pallid and uniform, and the head is ashen. Key features are a dark bill on an old face suggesting a mask of civility, relieved by a white speculum and black stern; the livery is funereal. In early spring a cloak of gold breaks the monotone when the drake's scapulars glint brassily. Freckled females are a close match to Mallards. Wait for a glimpse of the white speculum. Another sure identification option is to scrutinise the bill. Female Gadwall has a longitudinally striped bill, lacking the piebald pattern of black and yellow blotching shown by Mallard. Because her head is tinted grey, the bill's tramlines are emphasised. Especially on juveniles, the colour can be bright, close to tangerine. The bill transmits a fine tip and the head is vaguely angular; the forehead is steep and the nape slightly pointed. Gadwalls, when seen in flight from below, reveal a bright, whitish belly; on Mallards, the belly is fawn and diffusely speckled. Female quacking is similar to Mallard, although more pleasant. Drakes declaim a single dry, croaky quack (with a peculiar, hollow, wooden timbre). What if a putative Gadwall is standing on a shoreline, snoozing with speculum folded away and bill nestling among back plumage? Leg colour is a 'get out of jail card'. On Gadwall, the legs and feet are mustard-yellow, orange on Mallard. They are also obvious during upending feeding manoeuvres.

Gadwalls are steadily increasing in number and have become widespread both as a low-key breeding species and winter visitor. Undue competition with Mallard and Wigeon is avoided by feeding (often by upending) in open water and consuming floating vegetation. The largely white speculum is a diagnostic field mark.

TEAL
Anas crecca

DRAKES LOOK HAND-PAINTED. Among russet rushes and yellowing reeds the livery makes sense. They call incessantly with a musical piping; females are usually silent. During winter courtship, males toss the head skywards and flash a black and yellow 'hazard triangle' beneath the tail. As befits the smallest duck, they can be found in small, intimate locations, such as overgrown pools. Startled formations spring vertically into flight and intertwine like lines of dancers at a ceilidh. They eat seeds of marsh plants and feed mostly at night, often on land, when they can dine in peace. Females are the epitome of a brown speckled duck, except when an outstretched wing reveals iridescent green across a rectangular panel of the rear wing, hence the epithet 'Teal green'.

Intensive trapping on Mahee Island in Strangford Lough (PPM) reveals a wide spectrum of movements. Teal from Iceland and northern Europe pass through. Drake waterfowl, once paired with a female, abandon their own migration route and accompany her. Romantic attachments can explain dramatic 'detours' from one winter to the next. Formerly, Teal bred in suitable localities across Ireland and still did so during the 1960s on Rathlin Island, Antrim. Thompson (1849–52) lists haunts at Lough Mourne near Carrickfergus, pools at Wolf Hill above Belfast, Caledon in Tyrone, and Lough Beg, north of Lough Neagh. In an apocryphal remark, he quotes the proprietor of a Teal decoy near Navan, Meath, who complained, 'the country has been so drained and improved, that all kinds of wildfowl are now very scarce'. That was in 1845!

Such finery is impossible to improve. When Teal are animated and pirouetting in winter courtship manoeuvres, the raiment looks even better.

Teal forage, often nocturnally, along the shallow shorelines of lakes and marshes. They dabble and immerse the head to sift the tiny seed broadcast by grasses, sedges and rushes. Tussocks and tufts are thoroughly worked in audible, high-speed jabbing.

MALLARD
Anas platyrhynchos

THE MALLARD is the ancestor of the domesticated duck, which range from all-white Aylesbury to Khaki Campbell and the Indian Runner with its penguin-like stance. Echoes of domesticated stock can adulterate plumage among wild duck. Cayuga, the commonest type, is blackish or dark bottle green overall, save for a variable amount of white on the chest. Mallard has come to epitomise 'all things duck', including the female's loud quacking that has perpetuated the myth that all waterfowl quack. Pairs remain together only during courtship and there is fierce competition for females. So-called 'three-bird flights' consist of a duck pursued by two drakes. Peak activity occurs in early spring and the trio often fly erratically, their minds preoccupied. Thereafter, the female tends to all parental duties. She alone incubates and covers the clutch when feeding. Ducklings are born into a one-parent family and losses are severe. Later hatches, coinciding with maximum vegetation growth, fare better thanks to concealment.

Female dabbling ducks have brown, speckled plumage, serving as camouflage during the breeding season. Apart from size and structure, another means of telling species apart is to refer to that part of the inner upperwing known as the speculum (the Latin word for mirror). The analogy is apt because the plumage is iridescent and often contains a vivid colour, typically bordered in white. On Mallard it is blue, sometimes reflecting purple. Depending on posture, the folded wing may reveal just a glimpse of colour. On ponds and park lakes, the species is tame. The same birds are wary when away from benign habitats where they feel safe. Migrants arrive from Iceland and northern Europe in late autumn and some mingle with well-fed feral populations. In excess of half a million are believed to trek from Russia to Western Europe, including Ireland. Demonstrating their global reach, two ringed in the Canadian prairies were shot in England during winter.

Lengthening daylight in January signals all-out courtship. Aerial pursuit of one female by two suitors is commonplace. All three 'combatants' indulge in erratic flights – the female invariably in pole position – followed by boisterous displays on water.

PINTAIL
Anas acuta

Pintails are the epitome of elegance – and not just the drake. Ducks are readily distinguishable from other female waterfowl by their long neck and sleek lines.

PINTAILS have a svelte body form. In flight, the wings appear long and the neck and tail add to a 'stretched limousine' feel. Of all speckled female waterfowl, Pintails are the least brown, being closer to cool grey, with a virtually plain, fawn-coloured head and kind eye. Her bill is grey with a black ridgeline (culmen) and sides. In flight, watch for a stripy underwing. Other dabbling ducks show an eye-catching speculum on the upperwing. On female Pintail, bright colours are absent, leaving the speculum's bold white trailing edge as the most obvious feature.

Although occasionally encountered on freshwater wetlands, the main choice of wintering habitat is mudflats. One hotspot is the northeast corner of Strangford Lough, at The Maltings, until the 1980s the site of a distillery that spewed an outwash of waste barley, attracting a cornucopia of wildfowl. The distillery and boon of grain are gone but 200 or more return each autumn, sustained by eelgrass and mud snails.

Pintails winter as far south as Africa and migrate to Siberia to breed. Our wintering birds hail from two widely separated areas. Iceland is one, whose 500 pairs winter entirely in Ireland and Britain. Although scarce, small flocks can be seen arriving in autumn at Ramore Head, Antrim. A drake ringed on 21 July 1982 at Lake Myvatn in Iceland reached Wexford. Other ringed individuals hailed from Russia, Estonia, Latvia, Denmark and the Netherlands.

GARGANEY
Anas querquedula

GARGANEYS BREAK most waterfowl rules in that they are summer visitors, wintering in Africa. Tiny numbers breed in the marshy hinterland of a few large freshwater lakes, including Portmore Lough, Antrim, although luck is needed to see them because they feed unobtrusively among vegetation. Females arrive in late April but are immediately secretive; their reclusive nature is boosted by a brown, speckled costume. Basically, the female resembles a robustly built female Teal with a stripy head.

The bill is grey, lacking basal yellow, and the wing pattern is subtly different. In contrast, the male is dazzling. In flight his upperwings flash lavender-grey. August signals a departure south. Possibly for the first time, juveniles and adults that have finished post-breeding moult emerge from skulking among aquatic vegetation and can be seen. Coincident with their appearance, migrant Teals pass through – a lesson to look carefully at groups of pint-sized dabbling ducks in late August and September.

Despite their striking appearance, males are shy. Like most drake waterfowl, they do not quack: the call is an incongruous rattle, akin to strumming a steel comb.

SHOVELER
Anas clypeata

NEVER MIND the gargantuan bill, drake plumage is outstanding in its own right, with a white chest set against a bottle-green head and chestnut body. Courtesy of an XXL bill, identifying a female is a no-brainer. Her spatula is brown, tinged olive and fringed with orange. Shovelers are filter feeders. They dip the bill just below the waterline, sometimes for long periods. Groups often feed together, pumping and straining all the while. Some dabble mud in estuaries. The diet is variable, but contains more animal matter than that of other dabbling ducks, although some seed is consumed. Occasionally the outsize bill is used as an open-mouthed fly swatter to catch insects. In flight, drakes show sky-blue forewings, which are more subdued on females. Rapid wingbeats generate a low whistling, especially at take-off.

Shovelers are uncommon on marine coasts and seek out shallow freshwater wetlands and marshy meadows. The bird is wholly migratory and a winter visitor in unremarkable numbers. Once the wintering population departs for Scandinavia (and possibly Iceland, where small numbers breed) a few pairs arrive in spring. Irish breeding birds winter in the Mediterranean. On favoured Spanish wetlands, such as the Ebro delta, huge flocks wheel and perform aerial revolutions reminiscent of Starlings going to roost, a side of their character that we never see. Breeding pairs are more territorial than other waterfowl. Courtship behaviour is simple but mesmerising, and starts with both birds raising and lowering the head, keeping the bill more or less horizontal. This is followed by animated and synchronised head pumping, during which the male occasionally tosses the bill vertically. Eventually the happy couple swim around each other in tight circles, sometimes achieving a spinning momentum like an ice-skating duo. When broods hatch, the female becomes secretive and leads ducklings to concealed wet margins where they feed by pecking invertebrates until the bill develops its unique shape.

Below: male. Inset: female. Irrespective of sex, the spatulate bill is unmistakeable and is equally characteristic on a flying silhouette when, by comparison, the rear end looks short. Ducklings are borne with a miniature spatula. An azure forewing adorns drakes but is blue-grey on females.

POCHARD
Aythya ferina

During winter, female Pochards combine a grey canvas with soft brown. Overall, the texture suggests suede. The head's gentle contours are distinctive. A peaked crown slopes smoothly into the bill, whose tip is tapered. Despite being slightly blurred in the photograph above, the accompanying female Tufted Ducks have flat-topped heads and steep, short foreheads. Moreover, they show good contrast between back and sides, while the bill looks blunt.

Around Lough Neagh, wildfowlers use the epithet 'Redhead' for the species, although only drakes possess the coppery plumage. Females are nonetheless distinctive and have a bespectacled, 'intellectual' face.

POCHARD, like Scaup and Tufted Duck, are in the waterfowl division classified as 'diving ducks', so named because they dive for vegetable matter, molluscs and chironomid midge larvae. They are uncommon on salt water. The sexes share a streamlined silhouette. The head's profile slopes, smooth as a ski-jump, from a domed crown to an elongated bill. Acute angles are absent. Despite an aerodynamic shape, they are reluctant fliers and, if nervous, prefer to dive. On the wing they look remarkably plain since the upperwing is unpatterned. Plumage texture becomes obvious in close-up. From afar, what looks like a grey body sandwiched between a black stern and chest is revealed as a canvas of vermiculations. On fully adult males, a sequin-sized red eye sets off a russet head. In dull light the head can appear dark and coppery. Both sexes have a dark, blackish-looking bill (leaden on females) with a characteristic pale scuff, suggesting missing enamel, behind the tip.

Small numbers breed on lakes that combine rich bottom-feeding and dense shoreline vegetation. Nests are close to the water's edge. Until comparatively recently, thousands breeding in Latvia wintered on Lough Neagh. The average winter count during 1979–81 was 28,000. Most were drakes: the sex ratio was 8:2 between 1996 and 1999 (Evans and Day 2001). Since the turn of the millennium numbers have plummeted. One theory is that the birds may simply be cutting short the last leg of their migration because alternative feeding lakes in Poland and the Baltic States remain ice-free. If circumstances change, wildfowl prefer to remain closer to breeding areas. At Ireland's chief wintering site, Lough Corrib, Galway, a winter average of 12,000 during 1996–2002 decreased sharply to around 3,000 in 2008 and 2009.

Discussion of recent fluctuations in numbers of Pochard, Scaup and Goldeneye on Lough Neagh is included in the entry for Tufted Duck, where the threat posed by invasive Zebra Mussels (*Dreissena polymorpha*) is also explained.

TUFTED DUCK
Aythya fuligula

AT A CASUAL GLANCE it is easy to miss the colours on a seemingly monochrome drake Tufted Duck. In any case, identification is easy thanks to a tufted mane, black body and white sides. While the tuft may resemble a wild lock of hair, it can disappear completely when sleeked down during diving and surfacing. The eye is beady yellow and the azure blue bill has a black tip backed by a pale surround. In good light, the apparently black head is revealed to be purple, blue or green. Female plumage is a far cry from that of the male. Apart from a white belly and vivid wing stripe – both features shared by drakes – her livery is close to dark brown. Darkest are head, chest and back; the flanks are medium, rather than dark, brown. Her eye is amber and her tuft rudimentary. This is important because confusion is possible with other female waterfowl, none of which show any form of a tuft. Some exhibit a whitish noseband reminiscent of Scaup. Stippled dark pebble-dash makes it look dirty rather than pure.

Although tameness on some park lakes suggests domestication, it is uplifting to report that all are completely wild. The birds are wary in surroundings where they are likely to be quarry. In late winter most depart for Iceland or Scandinavia. A snapshot of recoveries of ringed birds, almost all shot, plots individual histories, for example from Iceland to Lough Neagh and from Kerry to Finland. Food is a mixture of vegetable matter, seeds, insect larvae and aquatic molluscs. High-pitched male voices are generally reserved for use during dawn and dusk courtship. Females call quite frequently in flight, a burry growl with a revving motorcycle quality.

Thompson recounts a tale in which he shot a brace in Belfast. As the story emerges, the location pales into insignificance, given the writer's resourcefulness in ensuring that his trophies were not lost:

When crossing the Long Bridge at Belfast on a frosty day at the end of January 1827, on my return from shooting along the shore of the bay, a flock of seven or eight Tufted Ducks appeared on the river within shot of May's embankment. [In 1827, the Long Bridge spanned almost 1 mile across an arm of estuarine mudflats as well as the course of the River Lagan. In 1849 a solid piece of Victorian engineering replaced the old bridge and was named 'Queen's Bridge' in Victoria's honour.] By hastening to the place I succeeded in killing a couple, which proved to be young birds, with white feathers bordering the bill, as in the Scaup, but of lesser extent. I had no dog with me and, annoyed at seeing the dead birds floating downriver, offered a reward to any boy of a party playing about, who would swim and bring the ducks to land. One fine manly little fellow at once engaged to do so, and swam out boldly – perhaps more so than his strength warranted – until near the middle of the wide river. Then, being almost within reach of the bird, he became faint. This was either from the cold of the water or over-exertion ... but his spirit was not to be beaten. He rallied and, at a few more bold strokes, laid hold of both ducks and returned safely with them to the shore. (Thompson 1849–52)

There is no such thing as a 'bad hair day' for a drake Tufted Duck, which always look dapper. During periods of active diving the crest is sleeked down and temporarily disappears.

While a white sheepskin noseband is a consistent field mark of female Scaup (right), some female Tufted Ducks (left) show rudiments. Other distinguishing features include, for Tufted, a light subterminal stripe behind the bill's black nail and, for Scaup, a 'defrosting' appearance prompted by concentric canvas bands on the back and sides. Note too the loftier head shape of Tufted and a few shards of a tuft. Scaup are typically wet-bum birds; Tufted Ducks prefer to keep the tail dry and hold it up, half-cocked. Brown tones differ subtly: honey-brown for Scaup, dark chocolate in Tufted.

Tufted Ducks have shown a sharp decline. On Lough Neagh, the wintering population dropped from 26,360 in January 2001 to 7,871 in January 2006 (Cabot 2009). Research has been undertaken, and there are detailed annual counts spanning at least forty years, back to the heyday of dizzy heights in *Aythya* (diving duck) numbers. Uncontrolled wildfowling and pollution are factors that have worried conservationists. Yet the driving force behind the lough's high winter concentration of Tufted Duck, Pochard, Scaup and Goldeneye has been the availability of chironomid midge larvae. Immense populations of non-biting midges, known locally as Lough Neagh Fly, inhabit almost the entire shoreline and provide a staple diet for diving duck and fish. Blessed with a shallow and gently shelving bottom, most of the lough bed is a happy hunting ground for waterfowl that snooze by day and feed at night. Midge populations are cyclical. Previous research demonstrated that the rise and fall in the midge population chimes with duck increases and decreases. However, feeding strategies and diet differ between species. Tufted Ducks take molluscs as well as midge larvae. Shrimps (*Gammarus*) and worms are also important items on the menu. Roach, which have been introduced, compete for some of the same prey as Tufted Ducks. Are Roach diminishing the birds' food supply? Pochard, on the other hand, feed almost exclusively on midge larvae that are not, apparently, eaten in large quantities by Roach. Of all diving waterfowl, Scaup show the least cause for concern. They too feed on midge larvae but choose to feed at greater depths, where larval size is bigger on average. A conundrum clearly exists. Thinking outside the box points to other factors that may be relevant. Although Tufted Ducks breed here, most originate from Iceland and the Baltic. Scaup come from Iceland; the bulk of Pochards are Latvian. No discernible change in migration pattern has been detected among Iceland's Tufted Ducks and Scaup. Breeding success at the main breeding location in Iceland – lakes in and around the aptly named Lake Myvatn, which means 'lake of the flies' – is dependent on the cycle of chironomid midges. When swarms occur, adult insects are consumed by ducklings, ensuring high breeding productivity. So, for the moment,

Iceland's migratory waterfowl are following traditional routes.

The same cannot be said for wildfowl that hail from northeastern Europe and Russia. Here, a slight increase in winter temperature has been a tipping point. Wetlands that, until the 1990s, froze over at the onset of winter are now ice-free. Increasingly, wildfowl seem to be voting more with their feet than their wings and are 'short-stopping', curtailing their migration. Human memories forget that, here too, winter could be so severe that the very wildfowl that we are losing in the twenty-first century were in the past forced to endure (or flee) big freezes. Armstrong (1944) provides a reminder: 'The Irish winters are milder than they used to be and the ducks are never frozen out of their feeding waters. There was a great frost in 1739–40 when the whole of Lough Neagh was frozen over, and again in 1815 when a bullock was roasted on the ice.'

Recent colonisation by an alien mollusc is more insidious than the vicissitudes of winter weather. Around 1993, along the River Shannon, Zebra Mussels (*Dreissena polymorpha*) were discovered on the hull of a boat imported from abroad. They arrived in Lower Lough Erne in 1996 and by 2008 had reached Oxford Island at Lough Neagh. Ireland is the latest part of the northern hemisphere to be affected by this invasive species that has spread west along Europe's canal networks from its nearest native range in the Black Sea. The mollusc coats everything from hulls, ropes and buoys to aquatic vegetation. Dense colonies smother bottom mud and could disrupt the great cycle of life sustained by the Lough Neagh Fly. Fly larvae (bloodworms) live in ooze and wriggle free to pupate and hatch as swarms of adults. At each life stage the insect is a vital food source – winged prey for Swifts in summer and nutritious larvae for diving ducks in winter. Zebra Mussels live for around three years and spread at an exponential rate by releasing millions of microscopic young that disperse in currents before settling to reproduce. They feed by pumping water and sieving algae. Somewhat ironically, water clarity increases as a result of infestations. For more information, visit www.doeni.gov.uk/niea or www.epa.ie.

SCAUP
Aythya marila

SCAUP come dangerously close to qualifying as boring. They feed mainly at night. Flotillas snooze the day away, head down and fast asleep in beaded lines. North Americans classify them as 'bay ducks'. Up to a point, this is true. They are unlikely to be seen on park lakes or small waters. Even larger lakes and reservoirs frequented by Tufted Duck, Pochard and Goldeneye seldom yield Scaup. Home tends to be large sea inlets and Lough Neagh. They are out there, loafing over deeper water where they dive for mussels, weed and (in fresh water) insect larvae and molluscs. The Irish population is believed to be derived from Iceland, where an estimated 10,000 pairs breed (Bardarson 1986). In early April, numbers increase on Lough Neagh as others, staging on their way back north, augment local concentrations.

In size and shape Scaup resembles a Tufted Duck that goes to the gym – muscular with a more voluminous body and head, including a slightly broader bill. The crown is lofty, like the end of a lollipop stick. Because the eye is slightly forward of centre, the head's apex falls at mid-crown. Other *Aythya* ducks show a peak towards the hind-crown. Males have a canvas-grey back. Field guide illustrations tend to overplay the extent of pale. In reality, just a little over half of the upperparts are pale, with the grey bleeding into black across the lower back and folded wings. Variation is considerable. Some look silver-backed with matching flanks. Others appear 'smoky' and have finely vermiculated upper flanks that extend ashen upperparts closer to the waterline. In sunlight, green head gloss is apparent, as is a bright china-blue bill with a tiny black shiny nail. In North America, wildfowlers refer to the species as Bluebill. The bill of Tufted Duck is tricoloured with the nail set in a band of black that encompasses the tip. On female Scaup, a white sheepskin noseband encircles the base of the bill. The texture suggests ermine and seems deep pile, deeper than adjoining head plumage. The forehead, bill base and chin are included in the white. In the breeding season a pale, off-white blob is acquired, low on the side of the head. During winter the head is plain dark brown. Some run close to blackish and a few glint green. Unlike female Tufted Duck, the upperparts

and flanks are obviously textured. Transverse whorls of frosty grey banding are arranged randomly across the back and flanks, suggesting 'defrosting'. Females and youngsters have greyer bills than adult males. Although the nail is, once again, shiny black, the bill mid-section often has inconspicuous light patches. Juveniles, because they lack pale eyes and bright nosebands, are fairly ugly. Smaller face patches are buff-coloured; juvenile females can have an off-white noseband as large as an adult. They possess a light blob on the side of the head (analogous to the adult female during summer) but have plain upperparts, lacking – until moult commences in early winter – any adult-type vermiculations. Their backs are dark brown but, on many, the flanks are lighter dun-brown. More unsightly are juvenile males, which, through moult, rapidly dispense with a rudimentary buff-coloured noseband and acquire sooty-black head plumage. The face is blackish and parts of the neck are brown. Some look capped. A badge of youth, the large pale blob on the side of the head, is sandwiched between a brown neck scarf and blackish plumage around a goaty eye.

Belfast Lough was formerly the chief wintering haunt. Mussel banks and acres of eelgrass sustained flocks numbering thousands. By 1980, they had virtually disappeared due to pollution, oil spills and habitat destruction. Since then, the dubious creation of a commercial shellfishery has led to a reappearance of large flocks. With 2,300 present during the winter of 2009–2010, views at Dargan Bay, Belfast, were reminiscent of Thompson's account:

> Scaup are, excepting Wigeon, the most numerous of all ducks in Belfast Bay. They sometimes appear in very large flocks and as many as 10,000 are considered to have been seen together. One of these great flocks is described as rising from the water with thundering noise. They do not all rise at once, but, commencing at one end of the flock, gradually take wing. The noise made by a multitude of these birds feeding in the little shallow pools exposed at low water on the sea-banks in the stillness of the night resembles the sound of a waterfall. (Thompson 1849–52)

Below: Where they gather in numbers, Scaups pack together and often snooze during daylight hours. This flock, disturbed by a Peregrine and about to roar into flight, portray standard plumage variation including, on some females, a diagnostic pale blob on the rear cheek.

Left: North America's duck hunters know drake Scaup as Bluebill. Colour and a broad, platypus shape makes the bill arresting. In close up, the head is green and grey vermiculations pervade the flanks, making them less pure than the unsullied, gleaming white of drake Tufted Duck.

Below: Monochrome drakes have a standard appearance, whereas females vary. Get-out-of-jail-card identification tips include white 'sheepskin' feathering at the bill base and a largely blue bill tipped with an isolated black nail. The head shape is subtle, yet diagnostic: domed, the apex above the eye, then a long sweep to the rear neck.

EIDER
Somateria mollissima

Blue Mussels, which grip underwater rocks, provide the mainstay of a diet that includes crabs. Mussels are prised free by the macho bill, then swallowed whole and crushed by muscular action in the gizzard. Eiders have a profile consisting of a straight line from crown to bill tip.

ALTHOUGH FLOTILLAS of Eiders are commonplace around most rocky coasts in Ulster, they remain a scarce sight elsewhere. Raft members dive for shellfish one after the other and then surface in rapid succession. Gulls invariably attend activities and try to snatch unswallowed food. Flocks serve as a courtship club. As with most waterfowl, winter is the season for wooing a mate. Swarms pack together and remain in close contact for days, even weeks, on end. A great throng of canoodlers can, offshore, resemble a floating mass of weed rather than birds. In still air, cooing is audible at a kilometre range. By April, alliances have been made and the rave disperses, scattering around the coast as females shift to islands to breed. Males follow but play no further part in domestic duties. Once ducklings are independent during summer, adults and older immatures come together to moult. For a time they are flightless. Drakes acquire a sooty-black eclipse plumage before changing back into their normal livery of white over black.

The species has undergone a subtle but nonetheless spectacular expansion from western Scotland into northeast Ireland and parts of Donegal. A century ago they were almost unknown. Indeed, during Thompson's lifetime (1805–1852) the only occurrence concerned, not a Common Eider, but a female King Eider, shot on 11 March 1850 'in Belfast Bay' (Belfast Lough). Yet, by 1939, Scottish colonists had established footholds. In 1941 four or five pairs were breeding on the Copeland Islands. Until the late 1970s, the species was still rather scarce and parochial pockets in Donegal and Sligo showed little sign of vigour. Then, for reasons that are not fully understood, breeding numbers underwent a step-change increase. By 1977, roughly 100 pairs were nesting on the Copeland Islands. Presumably, birds from here founded nuclei on remote (and largely predator-free) islands at Port Muck, Antrim, and in Strangford Lough. By 2009, 1,000 pairs were breeding in east Antrim and Down. Despite little interchange of population, those along the north Antrim coast matched the growth in numbers, with 170 pairs on Rathlin Island. Perhaps recently established commercial mussel beds in both Belfast Lough and Strangford Lough have been the tipping point that caused fortunes to soar?

Eiderdown comes exclusively from the female, who plucks it from her breast to line the nest. Bestowed with camouflaged plumage, she undertakes all incubation duties – piebald drakes would only draw attention. Off-duty females cover the eggs when they leave to feed.

LONG-TAILED DUCK
Clangula hyemalis

To dive, Long-tailed Ducks partially open the wing. Uniquely, they spread the wing's alula and use it as pivot that facilitates a steep, rapid dive.

IN MONOCHROME winter plumage, Long-tailed Ducks are sublime. Colour is restricted to a pink 'Band-Aid' across the bill, shown by males of all ages. Females have grey bills and are kind-faced with curiously stumpy rear ends. On drakes, the two central tail feathers are elongated – hence the name – but rapier thinness often renders them invisible. Nonetheless, the owner is fully aware of his raiment and, much as a puppeteer breathes life into an inanimate object, the adornment is whisked and flexed. The species is gregarious and usually encountered in small posses. The wings beat more deeply below the line of the body than above it. Fliers are tubby and swing from side to side, at the same time tilting the body to show underside, then upperside. Rather than glide and skid to a halt, they crash-land. If startled, all take wing. Remarkably, diving birds en route back to the surface spot commotion and emerge from the sea on a trajectory that launches them directly into flight (AMG). Feeding birds dive

Long-tailed Ducks are unique in several respects. Unlike other drake waterfowl, males moult in spring to acquire a mostly dark, chocolate-brown breeding plumage, mimicked by the female.

Although a 'perfect ten' in appearance, deep-water feeding habits seldom bring drakes close enough to admire.

vigorously. Between dives they prostrate themselves flat on the surface like penguins. Just prior to submerging, the wing's alula feathers are spread to act as a wrist and claw the surface for propulsion. Banks of mussels on the seabed are sought out, a preference that ties the bird to deep water some distance from shore. Frustratingly, most flocks lie beyond the reach of binoculars. Millions breed across northern Scandinavia and Russia and stream southwest in autumn. The Baltic hosts many, both during winter and on migration. During the latter half of the twentieth century enormous numbers died (as many as 10,000 each winter) due to oil pollution. Flocks often alighted on floating oil, mistaking it for less rough water. The source of Ireland's relatively small wintering population is unknown and could be drawn from either Europe or Iceland, some of whose population migrates southeast and overwinters around Scotland.

COMMON SCOTER
Melanitta nigra

A courting group in Iceland. Common Scoters are essentially marine waterfowl. Flocks remain offshore outside the breeding season and congregate over mussel banks, thwarting clear views – even with a powerful telescope.

FOR DUCKS that feed in the open, Common Scoters are difficult to see. Most views are of bobbing strings of black dots. Dundrum Bay, Down, is a key wintering area. Here, during the severe winter of 1962–63, an unprecedented 10,000 accumulated (JSF). Iceland's breeding population (approximately 300 pairs in 1986) is migratory. Could they winter with us? In late autumn at Ramore Head, Antrim, flocks arrive from the northwest, coincident with Whooper Swans and Great Northern Divers, hinting at an Icelandic, rather than Scandinavian, origin. However, the magnitude of Ireland's population is considerably larger, estimated at almost 10,000 in 2001 (Cabot 2009). Whichever way the numbers are crunched, the origin of most is the myriad lakes and wetlands stretching from Scandinavia to Siberia. From this vast breeding stronghold, not far short of 2 million empty into the Baltic in September. Those that reach Ireland are among those to have travelled furthest. Even today, detailed knowledge of the bird's movements is scant due to sporadic inter-site movements and a shortage of ringing recoveries. Overseas migrants travel to Britain to moult. The sea off Blackpool in Lancashire and Carmarthen Bay in Wales holds thousands. They are wary and rise in alarm at considerable distances – a worry, given potential offshore wind farm developments in the area (AL). During summer, dozens fly west off the Munster coast, their destination unknown.

On boot-polish black drakes, a tangerine sliver suggesting orange peel fronts a lumpen grey bill. Females and immatures are dark brown with light cheeks, making them appear dark-capped. On both sexes the wings are blackish but not entirely plain. In flight the primaries glint pale, especially on the undersides. Bivalve molluscs, mainly Blue Mussels up to 4cm long and cockles, form up to 90 per cent of the diet (Cabot 2009). Distance masks a playful character. Other wildfowl that mass on water, such as Scaup and Pochard, tend to roost by day, making them boring to watch. Not so Common Scoters. They wing-flap, as though the behaviour is a nervous habit. Clusters submerge and interact with each other by surfing, especially when a good swell is running, or launch into a short-lived flight and splash-land. The tail is pointed and moderately long; when frolicking it is whipped upright and, even at rest or when the bird is dozing, may be half-cocked. To dive, the bird springs forwards with closed wings (other species of scoter flick the wings open to dive). They regularly rear up off the water and shake the head forwards and down; the motion evokes a headbutt. Given the range of animated activity, it is possible to discern pale bellies on some. These are juveniles. Young males acquire black underparts during winter. As they do so, some are a patchwork of black and brown, especially in late spring when the belly is still whitish.

Actions speak louder than static shapes. Like other waterfowl, Common Scoters rear up to flap but – diagnostically – combine the action with delivering a headbutt against an invisible target.

The species is an aquaculturalist on a grand scale. Flocks graze mussel beds until the density of molluscs is diminished. Then they move on. The reduced pressure allows stocks to recover and, over time, equilibrium is reached so that optimum feeding conditions always exist in some part of a widely dispersed winter range. Thompson recorded the demise of 'some hundred individuals' in Drogheda Bay, a familiar story of human greed followed by failure to work out what the birds knew – do not kill the goose that lays the golden egg. Quoting his correspondent, R. John Montgomery, Thompson wrote:

Endeavouring to ascertain the reason of the diminution in numbers of the scoters in Drogheda Bay, the only one I can assign is this: there were immense beds of mussels in the mouth of the river, and in some places along the shores of the bay, which I suppose attracted them in such numbers. There has now sprung up a new trade in mussels to Liverpool, and from 200–300 people, chiefly women, are sometimes employed in collecting these shell-fish at low water, at the entrance to the river. They are washed there, put up in bags, and sent to Liverpool for consumption, where they meet a ready sale. The mussels are becoming scarce, as well as other shellfish, which I think accounts for the diminution of the scoters: certainly there is not one to be seen now. (Thompson 1849–52)

Ireland's population was carefully estimated in 1995 at 100 pairs (in Connacht, at Loughs Corrib, Ree, Conn and Cullin). A further 95 pairs breed in Scotland, amounting to an overall nesting total of under 200 pairs for Ireland and Britain (Underhill *et al.* 1995). Common Scoters formerly nested on islands across Lough Erne in Fermanagh. Breeding was first noted in 1905, increasing steadily to 152 pairs in 1967 (Underhill *et al.* 1995) but the population became extinct during the 1990s. Roach were introduced into Lough Erne and adversely affected the aquatic food chain, while a hydroelectric power station was constructed at Ballyshannon, Donegal, effectively preventing fledgling Common Scoters from accompanying their parents to the sea. Possibly the most serious change arose through an imbalance in the sexes of the breeding population. There were males, but very few females. A similar situation applies at other breeding lakes in Connacht and is due to predation by North American Mink. Female Common Scoters have become, literally, sitting ducks. Mink are a versatile predator and, like foxes, cache food. In Iceland, also blighted, about 700 Eider ducklings were killed and stored in one den. In Ireland, the occasional 'liberation' by misguided animal lovers of mink from fur farms condemns yet more native wildlife to death. With only six fur farms operating in the Republic of Ireland (2011), a licensing review is under way. Closure is devoutly wished. Alas, a change in the law will not prevent the animals' continued presence. Even remote seabird nesting islands are no longer safe; several intrepid swimmers have been trapped on islands west of Kerry.

GOLDENEYE
Bucephala clangula

GOLDENEYE used to be exclusively a winter visitor to Britain and Ireland. They hail from Scandinavia and northern Russia, a fact confirmed by individuals ringed in the breeding season in Sweden and Finland having been shot on Lough Neagh and Strangford Lough (respectively) in early winter. Tree cavities are used for nesting, old Black Woodpecker holes being a favourite. Imagine that – Irish wintering birds may have been hatched deep in the abandoned nest hole of Europe's largest woodpecker. Consequently, nest-boxes are readily accepted, and this benefaction has facilitated a range expansion. More than 200 pairs now breed in Scotland and one pair bred (in a nest-box) on Lough Neagh in 2000.

Waterfowl, and indeed all birds, can be recognised by silhouette alone. Goldeneye's anvil-shaped head and chisel bill are a giveaway. Adult females are brown-headed but grey-breasted, demarcated by a white, narrow-waisted boa. Goldeneyes fly fast and are noisy; their wings whistle. Groups congregate and commence courtship in midwinter. Drakes toss the head backwards and call rapidly in a voice suggesting a Mallard that has inhaled laughing gas.

Lough Neagh and Lough Beg are headquarters for the majority wintering in Britain or Ireland – or were. Numbers have fallen from around 13,000 for the three winters 1991–93, to 2,780 in January 2006. Food consists of caddis fly larvae, freshwater shrimps, spire shells and plant material, all of which appear to be available in sufficient quantity. The slump appears to be a result of curtailed migration; many are choosing to halt on European sites that have become ice-free over recent winters. In fact, uncertainty pervades a historical assessment of Ireland's wintering numbers. In late October 1956, fifty together on Lough Neagh

Above: Air chambers inside the lofted crown are linked to the sinuses and, it is believed, supplement the bird's air supply during dives.

Below: The high forehead and bright eye of both sexes readily distinguish the species.

was deemed a notable flock (*Irish Bird Report 1956*, p. 7), although 2,800 were counted across all parts of the lough in January 1960 (*Irish Bird Report 1960*, p. 7). Given the size of Lough Neagh and changing standards in census techniques, such as the use of telescopes, an accurate assessment of trends is not achievable.

Wildfowlers regarded Goldeneye as the most wary of ducks, famous for diving before shrapnel struck (probably, quarry spooked at the sight of an aimed gun barrel): 'An old male, fired at with a percussion gun from a distance of about twenty yards, dived before the shot could reach the spot; and its emerging and flying right off from the bosom of the deep were the act of the same instant'. (Thompson 1849–52)

SMEW
Mergellus albellus

A CHILDHOOD MEMORY of a photograph of a drake 'among the thawing ice-floes of Sweden en route north on spring migration' (Gooders 1970:323) fired my imagination. The bird was demure yet regal, a white nun with a black domino on its face and a fancy quiff. Caught in a swimming pose, reflections in its wake took on the air of a bridal train. In Ireland, grey-bodied females and immatures, rather than snow-white drakes, are the norm. Females and young males resemble each other but differ considerably from adult drakes, having white cheeks that contrast with a red-brown crown, leading to the sobriquet 'redhead'. The species is just about annual. Large freshwater lakes are favoured and salt water is generally shunned. As befits a member of the sawbill genus, the short bill is lined with tines and the bird dives to catch small fish and root out the larvae of aquatic insects. Shallow water is not an impediment as long as food is plentiful. Often one returns faithfully to the same haunt over successive winters. If it fails to do so, another seldom takes its place. Over the past decade, Portmore Lough in Antrim has emerged as a reliable location with as many as five, including at least one drake. Many breed in Russia and winter in the northern Black Sea, although some travel west towards Britain. Formerly, up to 8,500 occurred on Lake Ijsselmeer in the Netherlands. It appears that milder winters, meaning unfrozen lakes closer to the heart of the range, may have tempted them to cut short their migration.

Above: males, inset: female. During courtship the frontal crest is upraised. At other times it is sleeked down, making it invisible. Like Red-breasted Merganser and Goosander, the Smew is technically a 'sawbill'. Tooth-like tines inside its bill are designed to grasp prey. While some small fish are captured, most food consists of insect larvae and molluscs.

RED-BREASTED MERGANSER
Mergus serrator

Like two frisky thoroughbreds anxious for the off, a pair of mergansers steam this way and that before diving for fish. Rakish and animated, swimming is quickened with Moorhen-style body pumping while the face is frequently immersed to spot prey. Furious legwork propels underwater sorties. The species flies so fast that the wings whistle. The pilot of a light aircraft noticed that, when one travelled torpedo-like alongside, both plane and bird kept pace – at 120 km/h.

FRANKLY, the name is unfortunate. There is no red breast. An old wildfowling term was Scale-duck, coined from the drake's scaly flank bars on a white ground. Both sexes possess a punkish hairstyle. In cases where an English name is inept, it is worth examining the Latin title. Therein lies the word *serrator*, denoting the arrangement of tiny 'teeth' aligned along the inside of the bill. Mergansers occur in coastal waters and expansive freshwater lakes. Commonest in winter, small numbers remain to breed on uninhabited islets. Females are drab and one matriarch may tend young from several broods. One at Castle Caldwell, Fermanagh, had fifty-nine ducklings in tow (JSF).

Witherby (1938–41) makes reference to even larger crèches: 'In Ireland and elsewhere remarkable packs of young birds up to several hundred in number in charge of only one or two adults occur regularly between August and October.' No such fecund concentrations are known today. The bird's purple patch may be over. Indeed, it is a fairly recent colonist. Few bred in the mid-nineteenth century (Thompson 1849–52), a time when it was primarily a winter visitor. Nowadays, breeding and wintering numbers have both waned, each for different reasons. Predation, especially by released North American Mink, is undoubtedly a factor that curtails the efforts of many waterfowl that attempt to produce a new generation on Ireland's lakes. Winter visitors, on the other hand, may be choosing not to migrate here in the customary high numbers witnessed during, particularly, 1970–1990. Red-breasted Merganser is a circumpolar species and Ireland sits on the periphery of its global range. Ringing recoveries confirm southbound movements from Scandinavia, Iceland and Greenland, although most immigrants probably hail from Scotland. Perhaps we are victims of a double whammy: local breeders in trouble and a boycott by overseas travellers?

GOOSANDER
Mergus merganser

GOOSANDERS ARE GIANTS. Similar in size to Eider, they lack the latter's people-carrier stature. Their silhouette suggests a streamlined coupé. Being a sawbill, it uses tines aligned internally along both mandibles it uses to clasp fish. Breeding habitat is freshwater rivers where, because of a penchant for finny prey, the bird is disliked. To avoid ground predators, large holes in trees are used for nesting. If none can be found, a recess among boulders suffices. Despite persecution from anglers, rivers in Scotland, northern England and Wales have been colonised, as well as some Norfolk Broads. A few breed in parts of Donegal and Wicklow. More are seen in winter, when meagre immigration occurs. Being, in the main, a bird of fresh water, Goosanders are displaced when inland lakes freeze. Bouts of severe weather that commenced in November 2010 and continued in the early part of 2011 initiated an influx across the eastern half of Ireland. Reports culled from bird news media charted a rise from fifteen scattered over ten localities in November to in excess of a hundred at twenty-five locations after Christmas; most remained until March.

Drakes are unmistakable – marshmallow pink with a bottle-green mane. They moult into a female-like eclipse plumage during summer, which only disappears fully by December. A peachy glow among the folded wings and underparts are a clue to the bird's sex. Females are larger and more robust than Red-breasted Merganser, with a fox-coloured head appearing stuck asymmetrically on top of a whitish lower neck. Because many wildfowl become flightless during moult, they migrate to remote areas to grow new plumage in safety. Drake Goosanders desert females once incubation has started. Then, remarkably, the entire European population of drakes treks to four large fjords around Norway's North Cape. Job done, all shift to the nearby estuary of the River Tana where as many as 35,000 assemble and ready themselves for departure in late autumn.

Below: male, inset: female. The Goosander's saw-edged bill ends in a hooked nail, designed for raking small prey from stony riverbeds. Fast flight and a powerful swimming action are Goosander attributes. Unique among waterfowl, a mother will carry ducklings on her back and ferry them quickly out of danger. Her turn of speed is faster than theirs.

RUDDY DUCK
Oxyura jamaicensis

A displaying male Ruddy Duck indulges a bizarre technique to woo a mate. The bill is drummed against an inflated chest, producing an audible clicking and stirring the water into bubbles.

THIS PRETTY North American waterfowl became established when founders from a collection at Slimbridge in Gloucestershire escaped from captivity in 1953. Twenty years later, around seventy were breeding in the wild among reed-beds in freshwater lakes. By 1975, a post-breeding population of around 300 was centred on Somerset, Staffordshire and Shropshire. In 1991, 3,500 were counted in southern central England. As the outlanders prospered, some crossed to Ireland and Europe. Intriguingly, a few made it to Iceland. Might these have been vagrants from North America? Based on DNA samples, the answer is no – they originated from Britain. During the 1980s breeding became regular at several haunts in and around Lough Neagh. A decade later the nucleus dwindled. The reasons for the decline are unclear. One hypothesis is that, as with all exploratory range expansions, the initial phase of colonisation was experimental. If a species cannot build on a foothold forged by its infantry, long-term presence is unlikely.

When progeny reached Spain in 1991 and began to hybridise with White-headed Ducks (*Oxyura leucocephala*), an endangered European relative of the species, alarm bells started ringing. Could a native species be lost through inbreeding? Arguments have raged ever since. A controversial approach to the perceived problem has been the systematic eradication by shooting of all Ruddy Ducks in Britain. When the process began in September 2005, Britain's population was estimated at 4,400. By November 2009, 6,159 had been shot. The cull appears to be having a direct impact on the size of the population on this side of the Irish Sea. The peak winter count at Portmore Lough in Antrim shrank from forty-three in February 2009 to just one in February 2010. Since no cull was carried out here, the crash could be explained as a result of former annual immigration from Britain on a scale that was not suspected, or post-breeding dispersal (and possibly a moult migration) from here to Britain. Either way, the supply of pioneers has been snuffed out.

RED GROUSE
Lagopus lagopus

Male Red Grouse, Connemara. Where Red Grouse survive in redoubts untouched by introductions from Scotland, a distinctive ginger hue permeates the plumage, probably an adaptation designed to camouflage the bird in its local habitat.

A FEW RED GROUSE are still to be found on the last unspoilt tracts of moor and bog. A recent systematic field survey (2004) estimated that possibly no more than 400 individuals remain in Northern Ireland. For the rest of Ireland the most optimistic estimate is 4,000. Walking through occupied habitat means entering heart-attack country. Encounters take the form of a coronary-inducing explosion launching a peat-coloured rooster into skimming escape flight on fingered wings. If forewarned by croaky calls you might glimpse a head peeping among the heather.

Isolated by millennia, populations become attuned to their surroundings and evolve subtle differences in morphology. Irish and Hebridean Red Grouse *L. l. hibernicus* are less dark than British stock (Witherby *et al.* 1938–41). Their feathering is 'ginger nut biscuit'. Evolutionary mastery of disguise may well have been corrupted by introductions. Red Grouse surviving in northeastern Ireland could be descended from releases of British provenance. Commendable research, funded by the Department of the Environment for Northern Ireland (Environment and Heritage Service 2006), sought to assess the genetic uniqueness of *L. l. hibernicus*. S. Anderson and J. Freeland, geneticists based at the Open University, analysed plumage and faecal material from wild specimens and museum skins, garnered from Red Grouse across Ireland, Britain and parts of Europe, where the taxon is somewhat different and treated as a distinct subspecies, Willow Grouse. DNA sequences had 'a high overall level of similarity ... a reflection of the fact that they have all shared a recent common ancestor'. In essence, the genetic credentials of *L. l. hibernicus* did not rack up enough points to stand apart from *L. l. scoticus*, British Red Grouse. That said, genetic closeness does not necessarily rule out divergence in plumage, habitat choice, diet and certain aspects of behaviour: *L. l. hibernicus* are famously tight sitters and vocalise considerably less than *L. l. scoticus* (Witherby *et al.* 1938–41). Plumage differences in *L. l. hibernicus* may reflect locally adaptive camouflage to Irish and Scottish blanket bogs, or could be a manifestation of diet. However, there remains a conundrum: *L. l. scoticus* introduced to Ireland can apparently maintain their dark plumage (Hutchinson 1989). Taxonomic questions apart, evidence was found of a declining level of genetic diversity. Based on the timeline of samples, this deteriorated over the preceding 120 years, a consequence of range fragmentation and reduced population size: surely an alarm bell to spur protection?

Tall heather is used as nesting cover and the plant's shoots, flowers and seeds constitute an exclusive diet. Faecal analyses from blanket bog in western Ireland, where heather is thinly distributed, showed that the plant is still the most favoured food, forming 90 per cent of all fragments throughout the year. Insects gleaned around damp ground, especially craneflies, are important in the diet of chicks. The bird is under siege because most of its habitat has been ruined. Overgrazing by sheep, subsidised by government grants, has converted heather-dominated swards to wildlife deserts. Tough, unpalatable plants that sheep do not like – and therefore avoid – have come to dominate mountain pastures. Goodbye heather, hello barren vistas of matgrass and rushes. Once heather is grazed out, the plant (and therefore Red Grouse) has no way back. Whole Irish counties have been denuded. Pockets that survive usually do so only by the inadvertent protection afforded by boundary walls or fences. Conversion of moor to sheep walks, often by vandalistic heather burning organised clandestinely by graziers, and afforestation, have acted in concert to deliver devastation. As a by-product of afforestation and a lack of gamekeepers, many nest predators – specifically foxes and crows – have increased. Another insidious killer is Louping ill, a viral disease transmitted by *Ixodes ricinus*, a sheep tick. The disease first made its appearance in Britain around 800 years ago and it was probably introduced to Red Grouse habitats as late as the nineteenth century, the period when sheep farming expanded and brought the virus with it. Where present, the disease can wipe out 80 per cent of birds. On moors in Britain, successful control measures against Louping ill (and nematode worm infestations) include vaccinating sheep and dispensing medicated grit. Here, its impact is unknown. For detailed information, www.gwct.org.uk/ is indispensable.

Thompson wrote in halcyon times:

> On the range of the Belfast mountains, rising to nearly 1,600 feet in altitude, the grouse maintains its ground. In the evenings of summer and autumn, when taking a favourite walk to the mountain ridge to behold the grand prospect – above all to watch the going-down of the sun behind the distant mountains beyond Lough Neagh and see the expanse of waters steeped in lovely hues – the crowing of the grouse has almost invariably enlivened my walk home. (Thompson 1849–52)

CAPERCAILLIE
Tetrao urogallus

Female Capercaillie, Estonia. Wholesale destruction of Ireland's native forest consigned this giant woodland grouse to oblivion.

THOMPSON'S dispiriting account of the extermination of Ireland's Capercaillies is presented here in the hope (more than the expectation) that documenting the eradication of a wonderful bird from vanishing woods might stir action to bring back both bird and habitat.

That so noble a bird – the chief of the European grouse – and aboriginal inhabitant of our native forests should have become extinct, is much to be regretted; but by the felling of the woods its doom was sealed. In *Topographia Hiberniae*, Giraldus states that it was more common in Ireland than the Red Grouse, about the twelfth century. When the island was covered with native woods one can imagine this to have been the case, but even if less abundant, the nature of its haunts would cause it to be more frequently met with than the Red Grouse, and consequently lead to the belief that it was more common. Willughby (1676) observes, 'This bird is found on high mountains beyond seas, and as we are told in Ireland (where they call it Cock of the Wood) but nowhere in England.' He thus concludes his description: 'The flesh of this bird is of a delicate taste and wholesome nourishment, so that

being so stately a bird, and withal so rare, it seems to be born only for great men's tables'! O'Flaherty, in *West or H-Iar Connacht*, written in 1684, on page 13, remarked: 'I omit other ordinary fowl and birds such as wild geese, swans, *Cocks of the woods*, &c.' The Irish statutes 11 Anne, ch. 7, recite, 'The species of Cock of the Wood is in danger of being lost,' and prohibit the shooting of them 'for seven years.' Smith in *History of Cork* (1749) observes 'it is now found rarely in Ireland, since our woods have been destroyed.' Rutty, in *Natural History of Dublin* (1772), mentions, 'one was seen in the Leitrim about the year 1710, but they have entirely disappeared of late, by reason of the destruction of our woods.' (Thompson 1849–52)

Deane (1979) asserted that the Capercaillie was never a native bird, findings that were convincingly challenged two years later (Hall 1981). The debate was eventually resolved with the discovery of Capercaillie bones at the Mesolithic site at Mount Sandel, near Coleraine. D'Arcy (1999) contains a detailed and fascinating discussion that illuminates the bird's rightful place as a former resident.

GREY PARTRIDGE
Perdix perdix

AT SOME TIME in the 1980s the Grey Partridge became extinct in Northern Ireland. In the early part of that decade, coveys (groups of adults and young of several families) were still found in at least two areas: on arable fields near the west shore of Lough Beg, and in similar habitat around Clough, Down. The species was lost without a whimper: no conservation measures were put in place; nobody seemed to be aware of the crisis. Contrasting with conservation apathy in Northern Ireland, in the Republic of Ireland co-ordinated efforts by the Irish Grey Partridge Conservation Trust (www.greypartridge.ie) and the NPWS managed to save the species from oblivion. In 2002, a mere twenty-two indigenous individuals remained on cutaway bogland in Offaly. While not a traditional habitat, the skeleton bands had retreated here because, as railway tracks were cut across peatland to quicken its destruction through extraction, ridges of trackside spoil sprouted vegetation and became havens. In summer, insects (especially ants and their larvae) and seeds of grasses constitute food; winter mainstay comprises the leaves of weeds and coarse grasses.

With so few birds left, alarm bells rang. As insurance, a small contingent was imported from Estonia, whose population proved to be a close genetic match. Linear nesting strips of tussock-forming grasses (such as Cocksfoot) were established, as well as kale-based crops. Predators – Magpies, Hooded Crows, foxes and rats – were removed over a wide adjoining area. By the end of 2010 a miraculous turnaround had occurred. The population had increased to 980. Moreover, the actions allowed breeding Lapwings and Skylarks to flourish and sustained large winter flocks of Linnets, Reed Buntings and Stock Doves. In the autumn of 2011 a covey was reintroduced to sympathetically managed farmland near Dublin. Crucially, predators were again controlled, especially foxes, which kill incubating females.

Thompson referred to behavioural distinctions which still held true for both coveys observed in the 1980s (AMG):

> There is a singular difference in habit between the [Grey Partridge] of the north of Ireland and that of the opposite portion of Scotland. An Irish covey generally springs without uttering a call, but the Scotch covey shrieks with all its might when sprung. The Scotch birds too, even where very little molested, more knowingly take care of themselves than the Irish: their watchfulness is extraordinary. A sporting friend, who has had much experience in both countries, remarks that he has more than once seen every bird of a moderate-sized covey shot in Ireland, but never saw this done in Scotland. (Thompson 1849–52)

Nowadays, across Britain and most of Europe, the species is in steep decline. Agricultural methods and equipment pose a constant threat to nests and flightless, mobile chicks. Many losses

A valiant last-ditch effort managed to save Ireland's last coveys from extinction.

occur before the young are fledged. Even in Thompson's day, numbers fluctuated. Proving, as ever, to be ahead of his time, he gave plausible explanations:

From wet and cold summers the decrease may have originated, as about the same period Swallows became scarce. In 1846 and 1847 Swallows appeared again in their former numbers. To the fine warm weather in the early part of the summers of the last few years this increase is attributable: within which period a slow but gradual increase of the partridge has taken place. [On the other hand, decline has resulted from] the increasing population of the country and consequent diminution of farms; the law legalising the sale of game; and the constant opportunities afforded of sending it by steam-vessels to England and Scotland. Some persons imagine that the increased cultivation of clover – a crop that is cut early – has kept the numbers down considerably by the destruction of the nests. (Thompson 1849–52)

Research into population crashes across many parts of Britain and Europe has focused on aspects of ecology, particularly the food consumed by chicks. In a nutshell, newborns require insect protein to grow and become strong enough to digest seed. The Game and Wildlife Conservation Trust found that chick survival rates fell from an average of 45 per cent to under 30 per cent between 1952 and 1962. The introduction of herbicides in the early 1950s eliminated many crop weeds that were insect food plants, and by the 1980s the number of insects in cereals had fallen by at least 75 per cent. Since then, fungicides and insecticides have inflicted more damage, a state of affairs worsened by the removal of grassy nesting cover as fields were enlarged by removing hedgerows and field boundaries.

Numbers have dwindled sharply in upland regions where agricultural practices remained relatively unchanged and applications of herbicides were uncommon. During the period that Grey Partridge has declined in Great Britain, the number of Pheasants has increased dramatically, notably on private shooting estates that have, to the dismay of landowners, lost breeding populations of Grey Partridges. This state of affairs highlighted a possibility that adverse interactions with released Pheasants might be at the heart of the matter. One mechanism, by which the inadvertent favouring of one species over the other may have occurred, is in the loading of shared parasites. In a situation where two species host the same parasite, the more resistant carrier – in this case Pheasant – can be responsible for harbouring a parasite that, while posing little or no threat to it will, if transmitted to the less robust host, cause ill health. A corollary in humans is the common cold, which is a mere discomfort to most, but can be deadly to peoples who are outside normal contact with western civilisation. Similar interactions have passed on human diseases to Great Apes in Uganda. Pheasants and Grey Partridges share a range of gastro-intestinal nematode worms. One species, *Heterakis gallinarum*, is found abundantly in Pheasants. Where both Pheasant and Grey Partridge occupy the same habitat, the parasite spreads, and its infective egg stage can act as a carrier for pathogenic protozoans that can cause disease among Grey Partridges. Consequently, there appears to be firm evidence that the spread of parasites from increasing numbers of reared Pheasants has contributed to the decline in Grey Partridge numbers in the latter half of the twentieth century. (Tompkins *et al.*)

There are times when a sense of doom and demise makes me wonder if I would have found greater fascination in life if, in childhood, I had taken up an interest in astronomy: a universe, for the moment, safe from the ravages of *Homo sapiens*. Instead, I am left to feel the burden of birdlife being lost. But not all. Even in Ireland, where few 'get' the natural world, miracles occur. Forget Knock, visit Lough Booragh to see what is possible.

QUAIL
Coturnix coturnix

Highly secretive, Quail are usually heard but not seen. In flight they are long-winged, strong fliers. Despite their puny size, many are trans-equatorial migrants.

DURING THE NINETEENTH CENTURY Quail were found in summer wheat and barley fields throughout Ireland and remained on weedy stubbles throughout the winter. Across their European range, they are summer visitors. On the Indian subcontinent the species is resident, presumably linked to a year-round food supply. Although it is astonishing to recount it as fact, it would appear that Quail found a similar bounty of food here. They were commonly shot and brought to market. Thompson gives numerous insights into their status and distribution. The following passage is typical:

> Quails were very numerous during the winter of 1846–47, in the counties of Antrim and Down, fifty or sixty of them being occasionally brought from the country in one morning to the chief game dealer in Belfast. Although more Quails appear to have wintered in Ireland in the comparatively mild seasons of late years than formerly, I have the testimony of a veteran sportsman to the effect, that from his having met with them in the counties of Down and Antrim every winter during the last 65 years, he had always looked upon them as indigenous, and not as migratory birds. (Thompson 1849–52)

Other passages testify to the symbiotic link of Quail to wheat growing. 'In 1837 I learned that within the preceding eight or ten years the Quail had become much more common in Kerry, within which period cultivation [of wheat] had much extended.' Thompson also gave a clue to why the species was able to survive year round. 'The slovenly system of farming, unfortunately too common in Ireland, is, however, greatly in their favour, as the seed of weeds among the stubble supplies these birds during winter and at other seasons with an abundance of food.' Thank goodness for 'slovenly' Irish farmers leaving spilled grain and seeding weeds to sustain, not just Quail, but a host of other resident seed-eating birds. Ironically, the choice of wheat fields as the species' summer home may have had more to do with the weed seeds and soil invertebrates found among the shelter of the crop than with the ripening grain. Quail feed at ground level and, unlike sparrows, finches and buntings, are unable to reach grain until it falls. Nowadays the statistics for unharvested grains are frightening. Modern machinery gathers 99.7 per cent of arable crops, leaving just 0.3 per cent uncollected. In combination with weedkillers, fertiliser applications and heavy machinery that compacts soil and crushes life, the upshot is that farm fields have become biologically sterile growing media with no life except that which is force fed into them. Resident populations of Quail disappeared sometime during the late nineteenth century. Since then the species has become a rare summer visitor, usually detected by hearing its distinctive three-note 'wet-my-lips' call coming from monoculture fields of wheat or barley.

PHEASANT
Phasianus colchicus

When female ground-nesting birds shoulder responsibility for incubation, they often evolve plumage that is a camouflage masterpiece. For safety, chicks leave the nest soon after hatching.

PHEASANTS ARE NOT INDIGENOUS to Ireland; nor, given their limited powers of flight, could they ever have reached Irish soil under their own steam. They were introduced long ago. When, and by whom, cannot be ascertained. A journal written by Fynes Moryson, who was in Ireland from 1599 to 1603, contains the remark: 'Such plenty of Pheasants, as I have known sixty served up at one feast' (Moryson 1735). Clearly, the species has been around for over 400 years. The nearest natural range is along the eastern shore of the Black Sea, where it inhabits reed beds, thickets and forest. The ancient name for Georgia (Colchis) explains *colchicus* in the scientific name. Numbers are augmented by annual releases for shooting. Feeding stations filled with cereals sustain the sacrificial stock, which consume little else. Survivors that go bush adopt a more varied diet and feed on cereals, plant roots and stems (principally buttercup and clover), fruit, acorns, weed seeds, slugs, snails and earthworms (O'Huallachain & Dunne 2007). When immigrants established at Copeland Bird Observatory they decimated twenty-five pairs of Moorhens by voraciously out-competing them for food. Britain's Pheasant population – estimated at 90 million – accounts for more biomass than all other birds put together. Moreover, the amount of Pheasant carcasses available as roadkill sustains high levels of scavenging crows and foxes that, come the nesting season, turn their attention elsewhere.

Undoubtedly, the bird is beautiful. In particular, female plumage is superbly detailed. Since males take little interest in family matters, the female deserves the best camouflage available. In post-Plantation times 'nouveau riche' landowners nurtured further releases by planting coverts of ground-swaddling laurel and rhododendron, and assiduously protected quarry by employing gamekeepers who declared war on crows and birds of prey. Some raptor populations have since recovered, but infestations of alien shrubs remain and choke many planted woods. Such is the baggage of an introduced alien. More serious is the comparatively recently discovered link (Tompkins *et al.* 1999) between the parasite loading shared by Pheasant and other closely related species, notably Grey Partridge and, quite feasibly, Corncrake. Pheasant and Grey Partridge share a range of gastro-intestinal nematode worms, including *Heterakis gallinarum* (see discussion under Grey Partridge, above). Research has established that the spread of parasites from released Pheasants has contributed to an overall decline in Grey Partridge numbers in the latter half of the twentieth century. There is no reason to suspect that a similar deleterious impact did not occur on this side of the Irish Sea. A new worry is that 'novel' releases of Pheasants on some Irish islands may explain recent crashes in a dwindling Corncrake population. If, as seems likely, Corncrakes are susceptible to parasites carried by Pheasants, a silent killer may unwittingly be dooming an emblematic native species.

RED-THROATED DIVER
Gavia stellata

THESE DAYS, binoculars and telescopes deliver views of birds like never before. Has it become easier to identify divers? Not really. Distance and the interplay of light make assessment of plumage and structural distinctions difficult. When actively feeding, divers slink low and stay under for minutes, sometimes surfacing a long way from where they submerged.

The Red-throated Diver has a slim bill, and the lower mandible has a planed tip, as though put through a pencil sharpener. To boot, it is carried upswept, nose in the air, and the bird has a tendency to lean slightly forwards. Both Great Northern and Black-throated Divers carry their head and fuller bill in a level plane, with a sinuous neck and muscular chest. Red-throated has a kind eye – an isolated dark button in a sea of pale plumage, almost untouched by dark feathering. Beware confusion with Cormorants and Shags, immatures of which are whitish around the foreparts. However, even at long range, their diving action involves a spring or lurch well clear of the water. Divers slip smoothly under the waves in a movement executed with a deferential bow. Cormorant and Shag have beaver-like paddle tails; the appendage often flexes downwards – even in mid-air – as part of the diving action. Divers are almost tailless. In flight, large feet occupy the space where the tail ought to be and can do a convincing job of masquerading as one.

Red-throated Diver has a circumpolar distribution and occurs in an arc from Greenland and Iceland, through northern Scotland and thence to Scandinavia. Some breed in Donegal and flightless young were seen in Antrim in one recent summer. Although not commonly ringed, an analysis of British Trust for Ornithology (BTO) recoveries from Shetland and Orkney documents many movements to Ireland (Okill 1994). Worryingly, most records came from birds found drowned in fishing nets. Ringed birds from Greenland, Iceland and Scandinavia have reached the coast of Britain. Despite the lack of ringing data, Red-throated Divers from Iceland and Greenland probably constitute the bulk of those that winter here or pass north in spring, especially during April.

Moult is a fact of life for all birds. Some change appearance when they moult, acquiring a more exotic look, becoming Cinderella for the sake of courtship. Red-throated Diver, a grey wolf in winter fatigues, dons regal russet to attract a mate.

Leanest, palest and smallest of the tribe, Red-throated Diver's rakish build is further emphasised by a slightly uptilted bill, habitually carried aloft.

BLACK-THROATED DIVER
Gavia arctica

Around 200 pairs of Black-throated Divers breed on Scottish lochs, mainly in western districts. Small numbers winter around Ireland. At any distance, a sinuous shape echoes perfectly counterpoised monotone plumage.

THIS, the Scarlet Pimpernel of divers, is hard to get to know. Breeding haunts in remote parts of western Scotland could be the source of Ireland's wintering population, estimated at around 100 and clustered along the western seaboard. Except for a hotspot on the north coast of Clare, mobile feeding habits at 'recluse' range make Black-throated Diver a needle in a haystack. Most reports in Northern Ireland are no more believable than sightings of the Loch Ness monster. Questing for the rare produces false claims that are given credence through lamentably poor corroboration. A cavalier attitude clouds understanding, making it impossible to disentangle bona fide from fanciful. A few Black-throated Divers winter among the inaccessible islands – evocatively named 'pladdies' – of Strangford Lough, plying manifold channels and tongues of deep water.

The bird is as serpentine as a sea snake. When fishing, it ranges widely and follows tidal currents that carry finny prey. Followed by car along the shore of Donegal Bay at Mount Charles, one travelled a kilometre in under ten minutes,

appearing on the surface only six times and swimming under water faster than walking speed (AMG).

Winter plumage is, by and large, all we see. It might be tempting to conclude that, in comparison to others in the tribe, low-key distinctions amount to no more than subtle nuances for the middleman between Great Northern and Red-throated Divers. Actually, Black-throated Diver is sublime. Its attributes are a level, dagger bill; fifty-fifty separation of white and charcoal grey running horizontally across the face and vertically down the neck; blackish lores, suggesting sunglasses; and isolated white 'wheel arches' either side of a black stern. Hallmarks of Red-throated Diver are a ghostly face, tilted bill and slight forward lean. Great Northern Diver has a stout pale bill base (like sun-bleached bone), bespectacled eye and dark scarf that wraps partially around the side of the lower neck, breaking up the vertical symmetry of a dark hind neck paralleling a white fore neck. Jonsson (1992) is an indispensable reference.

GREAT NORTHERN DIVER
Gavia immer

Adults pair for life and nest on lakes scattered from Iceland to Alaska. Spectacular breeding plumage is shed prior to migration. Expert meteorologists, Great Northern Divers await the onset of northwesterly tailwinds before embarking on a transoceanic flight to our latitude.

FIRST THERE IS the regal name, redolent of Icelandic lakes, where many breed. Then there is the bird, hulking as a U-boat yet blessed with controlled grace and Buddha-like poise. Diving is executed with neither a spring of the body nor a flurry of tail movement. As with all members of the family, the tail is notable by its virtual absence. To submerge, the bird leans forwards and slides under the water. In swells, a more forceful lunge is deployed. On calm days a pair of whirlpools are left as a wake, stirred by the downward propulsion of huge webbed feet. Great Northerns specialise in peering underwater and they immerse the face to check for prey, in effect snorkelling. Shoaling fish are seldom taken. Instead, seabed-lurking flatfish and crabs are favoured. Back on the surface, a caught crab is twiddled and manipulated into position before being swallowed whole. As part of the process the crustacean is often 'washed' beforehand.

Gales disrupt fishing activities and harbours become a port in a storm, presenting an opportunity not to be missed. Close up, the eye is ruby-red and the bill, a bony edifice, has a cold blue look. Back pattern indicates age. Youngsters are decked with serried frosty scaling. Adults are more sombre, patterned with rectangular tiles. Two-year-olds manifest an almost plain soutane. Wintering birds do not arrive in strength until November and slip south through winter, rather than lingering. The leviathan is mercurial along the Irish Sea coast. Out west, it is more common, especially in April and early May when parties of black-billed adults sparkle like chequered flagships awaiting a fair wind. Aloft, the silhouette is goose-like, except for gangly feet resembling a jet fighter's landing chute. Winter-long Trappist vows are normally broken only on the breeding grounds. However, adults freshly arrived in autumn and still bestrewn in nuptial finery sometimes give a last hurrah. Stimulated by glassy calm – optimum broadcasting conditions – the haunting call feels like a requiem for the turn of the season.

As streamlined as a torpedo and powered by large feet, the heavyweight is lithe and fast underwater, easily covering 500m or more in the course of a single dive. This is a juvenile.

FULMAR
Fulmarus glacialis

Fulmars surf gusts of wind and treat them like escalators. They are inquisitive and come close enough to reveal a peculiar tubular bill with fused, external nostrils designed to extrude ingested salt and to locate food by smell. The bill's supernumerary structure classifies Fulmar as a 'tubenose'; shearwaters and petrels possess the same feature. True seabirds filter salt from the bloodstream in a conveniently placed gland in the head.

'THE FULMAR is extremely rare as a British bird, excepting at St Kilda, where it breeds annually in multitudes, and is their most valuable product; the eggs and birds themselves being used as food, and the oil for various purposes' (Thompson 1849–52). Sometime around the turn of the nineteenth century, Fulmars began a spectacular colonisation of the coasts of Scotland and Ireland. They first bred in Mayo in 1911, followed by Donegal (near Malin Head) in 1912. Today they are almost ubiquitous on coastal cliffs and occasionally occupy potential nest sites at inland quarries.

Most of the population is at sea between autumn and the New Year, when the birds disappear across a wide region of the North Atlantic. Recoveries from a long-term ringing project at Little Saltee, Wexford, chart a pattern of dispersal to three main areas: the Newfoundland Grand Banks and adjacent parts of the North Atlantic as far east as Iceland; European Arctic waters; and inshore coastal waters stretching from the North Sea to the Bay of Biscay, as well as Ireland's continental shelf. British studies map a broadly similar pattern (Macdonald 1977). Females are more widely travelled than males. Wheeling hordes over sea cliffs in the dead of winter contain males awaiting the arrival of females, for whom they defend ledges suitable for courtship and mating. Based on age, the peak of return movements to colonies occurs after the bird's fourth birthday. Established pairs mate for life.

Despite a superficial resemblance to gulls, these are seabirds. Think of them as mini-albatrosses, to which they are closely related. They share a lot of features, including a 'block of flats' bill that has a pair of external tubes through which the bird rids itself of excess salt. Technically speaking, bill structure defines the bird as a tubenose, a mark of a top-echelon seabird with a phenomenal sense of smell. Most shearwaters and petrels home in on feeding hotspots by whiffing the air, which is laced with dimethyl sulphide and pheromones released by algae. Both indicate areas of marine richness (Nevitt 2000).

Fulmars glide, using flaps to maintain momentum, and the wings beat stiffly, as if in splints. Over a smooth sea, the bird sweeps low and its wingtips score the surface tension. Silent in flight, they cackle and bray in colonies, and pairs duet when they meet. Just one egg is laid and the chick grows rapidly, reared on a diet of regurgitated seafood. Fulmars scavenge discards (offal) jettisoned during fishing activities and large numbers attend trawlers. Left to their own devices, they catch zooplankton and squid, mainly at night. Adults rearing chicks eat less offal and switch to nutritious clupeoid species of fish, such as Herring, to feed their young. Before they fledge, youngsters are abandoned for long periods. The baby has a secret weapon that keeps

If approached too closely, youngsters – and sitting adults – direct oily bile at all comers. For inadvertently trespassing birds, a heavy dowsing can clog plumage and cause death.

predators, and even inquisitive humans, at bay. If approached within several metres, the downy chick spits a stream of orange-coloured oily phlegm. Its aim is surprisingly accurate. The habit helped coin the species' name, which is derived from an Icelandic word meaning 'foul gull'.

Fulmars have become a marine mine-canary. Since 2000, they have declined by 37 per cent and stomach analyses reveal that 90 per cent of North Sea populations contain plastic: statistics that are, presumably, not unrelated. Floating rubbish is mistaken for food and inadvertently gobbled up. It is also regurgitated and fed to chicks. Some birds choke; others are slowly poisoned. An unknown number weaken and die through having less stomach space available for digestion. Worst affected are adult females fattening to breed. In some recent winters, notably 2004, hundreds succumbed through a domino effect: poor foraging conditions caused by mild sea temperatures that reduce concentrations of zooplankton; hunger; and a toxin-leaching bellyful of plastic. Legislation has curbed production of some industrial plastic, such as polypropylene beads; the bulk of ingested material comprises throwaway consumer rubbish, from water bottle caps to balloons and contraceptives.

GREAT SHEARWATER
Puffinus gravis

With each heave of the ocean, the ship lurched and was cleaved by wave tops whipped into frothy precipices. Yet the Great Shearwaters barely moved a wingtip, skimming rollers and sliding over hillocks of water, using minimal energy in – for them – perfect flying conditions.

LIKE A COMET cruising the cosmos, this sublime seabird slips through our part of the North Atlantic in autumn. Keeping well clear of land, it tacks ever southwards, tapping into a secret geometry steering a course to the Roaring Forties. How do we know it is there? Some are seen by vessel-borne birdwatchers or glimpsed from shore. The Irish Sea is a seldom-taken side road, whereas a marine eddy that brushes Ramore Head, Portrush, is more regularly used. Rugged west coast headlands, thrust like ramparts in the face of stormy seas, intercept most. During late summer, millions coil around continental shelves in the western North Atlantic. Food is plentiful and the birds gorge on small fish and squid on Newfoundland's Grand Banks and in areas southwest of Greenland. Fuelled up and fat, they are ready to migrate. The majority breed on Tristan da Cunha, midway between South America and South Africa. Using the prevailing wind, squadron after squadron head for the Equator. En route, tailwinds sometimes tempt skeleton bands to transit close to Ireland. Gales, huge swells and mountainous seas are no bother. The wings are used like sails; but, unlike canvas, cupped undersides and a flexible shape are more efficient in making micro-adjustments. By taking account of wind direction, freewheeling is possible – into the wind, across it, or with it. A wind blowing directly from behind is managed by obliquely shearing from side to side. Birds tagged with miniature transmitters clock up an average of 500km per day and continue until they reach the Argentine shelf. In light airs, they are forced to idle. For many, romantic globe-trotting ends in Irish territorial waters. Shocking evidence is emerging of a bycatch numbering thousands. Well offshore, Spanish and Portuguese longliners lay up to 70km of virtually invisible monofilament containing hundreds of hooks baited with fish, snaring and drowning hapless victims.

'Greater' than a Manx Shearwater, the bird is scarcely bigger than a Fulmar. But comparisons end there. Great Shearwaters skim low, so close to the contoured surface of the sea that they appear attached to it by an invisible magnet. They fly with a slouch. Outstretched boomerang-shaped wings hang slightly forwards and down. Progress is methodical and controlled, interjected with brief, almost nonchalant, deep wingbeats. Turns can be made on a sixpence and initiated by steering with just one wingtip. Steep soars add momentum by catching the wind. Watched in action over a stormy sea, the bird's technique is effortless, almost lazy. A dark cap is made distinctive by a white collar around its corners. The upperparts are brown but patterned with lighter fringes. The result is a zoned, frosty patchwork across mid-wing and back; the wing's hand is always dark and plain. While the underparts are white, fine black speckling dims the underwing. Dusky undertail coverts reach the belly and resemble a stain, best revealed when the bird banks. A thin white horseshoe butts up against a black tail, which, if discernible, means that your view was excellent indeed.

SOOTY SHEARWATER
Puffinus griseus

Sooty Shearwater is one of an elite group of seabirds that breed in the southern hemisphere but migrate into the northern hemisphere. They pass our way in autumn.

SOOTY SHEARWATERS nest on islands in the Roaring Forties. When the breeding season finishes, several million decant north over the Equator and feed during summer on the Newfoundland Grand Banks and off the coast of Greenland. Come late August, thoughts of home send them packing. En route they cruise past Ireland, especially during September. If you want to see one, set your alarm for autumn and keep checking the weather for onshore winds. Rough weather at sea is a boon to any long-winged seabird that speeds downwind, because their rate of progress is enhanced by a following wind. The downside of a free ride is encountering the coast, which must be detoured. Populations that track winds around the Pacific in an 'endless summer' migration clock up 65,000km on a round trip: a distance at least three times greater than a direct course from breeding stations in the South Pacific to winter quarters in the North Pacific (Shaffer *et al.* 2006).

Identification is not difficult, even at long range. An initial view suggests an all-black shearwater, larger and more athletic than a Manx Shearwater. Illuminated properly, the real shade is peat brown. When they are banking, silvered wing linings glint like chalk on a blackboard and resemble a film negative of the wing's overall shape in miniature. Against a dark sea, the underwings are a beacon. The wings are set in a crook and taper to a spear point. In gales, the bird travels fastest yet deploys fewest beats. High arcs are followed by long, knifing slaloms. Fliers pitch high, stoop, and race ahead by harnessing wind and gravity. Judicious flicks are used to steady and compensate, rather than propel.

MANX SHEARWATER
Puffinus puffinus

Above: Autumn migration from Ireland to wintering grounds off the east coast of South America is a rapid affair. Most avail of favourable northeast trade winds and do not halt until they reach Brazilian waters.

Below: Manx Shearwaters catch their prey by settling on the water and diving for it, using wings and feet to swim underwater. They feed mainly on small shoaling fish.

MANX SHEARWATERS have the long, graceful sweep and easy movements of an accomplished skier. A plain black-and-white livery conceals a globetrotting lifestyle. The world population was estimated in 1990 to be in the region of 280,000 pairs, most of which breed on two Welsh and one Scottish island (Skokholm, Skomer and Rhum). Approximately 30,000 pairs breed around the Irish coast, mainly on Kerry's islands. The Copeland Islands, with 5,000 pairs, hold around 2 per cent of the world population.

It seems that the Copeland Islands have been used as a breeding station only in the last century. Until the seventeenth century, monks from Bangor Abbey farmed the islands, rendering them unsuitable for burrow-nesting birds. Overgrown lazy beds are everywhere. Changes begun during late Victorian times, particularly the introduction of rabbits and the abandonment of farming, sparked colonisation. Where did the founders come from? Blood samples taken from 120 birds in 1977 were compared with Welsh data. The results showed a poor match. The Copeland birds were distinct. Perhaps Manx Shearwaters from Scotland established the colony? Ceaseless work by the observatory's volunteers (www.copelandbirdobservatory.org.uk) ensures that invasive scrub does not render the habitat unusable. Ringing recoveries testify to a long life expectancy: the oldest bird passed fifty years of age in 2003, although its age at ringing was not known. Less fortunate individuals have been picked up dead in Australia and at Lake Huron, Michigan, USA.

Youngsters complete a ten-week fledging period during September and follow an innate migration vector taking them southwest. Seen on active migration at sea, they avoid ships and seldom pause, clocking up an average flight of 450km per day. They pass the Azores and swing west into mid-Atlantic, crossing the Equator and heading for Brazilian waters. Once there, they track south until they reach journey's end: the rich 'delta' stretching east from the mouth of the River Plate over the Argentine shelf to the Falkland Islands. A few maiden flights go awry and collisions occur with telegraph poles and wires, exacerbated by the dazzle of unaccustomed light. Downed fliers are seldom injured but must be relaunched at night (to avoid being attacked) on the coast, preferably by holding them aloft and facing into a breeze.

The homeward route, commenced in March, is not the reverse of the journey south. Prevailing winds and feeding resources are factored into an itinerary that has evolved over millennia. A sinuous northbound stream arcs off the outer rim of islands in the West Indies. Presence here, mainly east of Guadeloupe in the Lesser Antilles, was only recently discovered through land-based sea-watching (Levesque & Yesou 2005) and data recorded from loggers. Ahead lies the Gulf Stream. Some continue to track north before pausing to feed on the edge of the Newfoundland Grand Banks. The majority, however, take a more direct line from east of the Caribbean and strike out towards the central North Atlantic, probably gathering over the mid-Atlantic ridge to refuel before completing the last leg to far-flung breeding stations. Quite how they find fertile zones over featureless ocean is a mystery, although provender may be signalled by the smell of dimethyl sulphide (Nevitt 2000), produced by marine phytoplankton and characterised as 'the smell of the sea'. In concentrated form dimethyl sulphide is used as a food preservative and flavouring agent. It has also been used as an attractant on marine bird-watching trips and is effective at drawing in small petrels, confirmation of the birds' highly developed olfactory sense.

Barely 20 per cent of young survive the first five years to reach breeding age. Older adults have a higher survival rate. Just one large egg is laid, weighing 15 per cent of the bird's weight and requiring fifty days' incubation. Although masters of the marine environment, Manx Shearwaters are wary of land-based predators, and come ashore at breeding colonies only during the dead of night. Eerie calling accompanies nesting activities and has prompted rookie lighthouse keepers to lock doors and re-examine personal views about ghosts. During summer, feeding flocks congregate in the Irish Sea and North Channel. Sometimes enormous numbers occur, suggesting that individuals from many colonies gather together on the same fishing grounds. This begs a question: how are 'fishing reports' communicated? Visits to feeding areas sometimes involve a commute of more than 330km each way to and from the colony (Guilford et al. 2008). Perhaps the body language of returning, well-fed birds, singles them out as Pied Pipers to others?

BALEARIC SHEARWATER
Puffinus mauretanicus

In global terms, the Balearic Shearwater is scarce. Handfuls reach Ireland's coastal waters, mainly during late summer.

ALL THE WORLD'S Balearic Shearwaters breed on small islets among the Mediterranean archipelago that gives the species its name. Rats and the growth of tourism close to breeding sites are having a devastating impact. 'The once uninhabited nesting islands of Formentera and Eivissa are now amongst the world's busiest tourist destinations, and the tourists and new residents have brought their cats with them' (Gutierrez 2003). The bird's fortunes appear grim and, unless measures are taken to control predators, the present rate of decline could result in extinction in less than fifty years. In the early 1990s the population was at least 10,000 individuals; by 2002 no more than 2,000 nesting pairs remained (Mayol 2003).

The birds nest early in the year and migrate west past Gibraltar and into the North Atlantic, concentrating in the inshore waters of the Bay of Biscay. In the new millennium a northwards shift in distribution has been witnessed off southwest Britain, where several hundreds now occur during summer. This change has been linked to a small but significant rise in sea temperature that has impacted on the distribution of the bird's prey. Put simply, as food supply moved north, Balearic Shearwaters followed suit. From July to October small numbers are present around Ireland, mingling with flocks of Manx Shearwaters, which the bird resembles in size. Identification rests on discovering a dusky 'airbrushed brown' shearwater. No two are the same, but even the cleanest have grubby wingpits and undertail coverts. Shape is distinctive: potbellied, with a smallish head on a projecting neck and feet that jut out beyond the tail. The darkest individuals, probably juveniles, can suggest a Sooty Shearwater. Although Sooty Shearwaters are a size larger and proportionately longer-winged – with underwings that gleam silver in a full tilt – a lone bird can be tricky. A useful steer is a pale throat on Balearic; Sooty Shearwater is uniformly dark on both head and chest. Moreover, flight style helps. Balearic employs long, at times almost fluttering, bursts. By October, Manx Shearwaters have departed for winter quarters yet a few Balearic Shearwaters linger, some even appearing during winter.

STORM PETREL
Hydrobates pelagicus

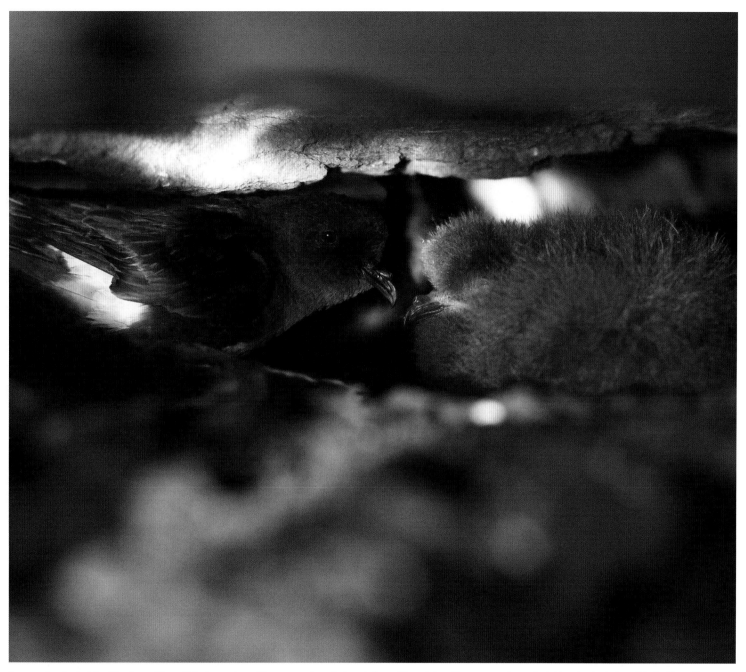

Supremely adapted for life at sea, Storm Petrels are forced to come ashore to breed. To avoid predators they come ashore at night and wriggle to safety inside wall cavities, scree slopes and boulder fields. A solitary chick is raised on partly digested marine organisms. Fully fattened by late summer, the baby is abandoned to grow plumage and make its own way out to sea.

SEABIRDS do not come any smaller. Despite weighing slightly less than a male House Sparrow, Storm Petrels live long lives, probably forty years and more. They forage by night and day with wings aloft and trampoline webbed feet off surface tension to pluck zooplankton and tiny fish from the cusp of the water column. At nightfall, bottom-dwelling marine organisms rise to the surface, especially during high tide closer to the coast. The birds follow suit. To breed, they are obliged to come ashore, a risky task undertaken in darkness. On terra firma they are feeble and rest on their tarsi, which is somewhat ironic, given their St Peter walking-on-water capability, from which 'petrel' is derived. Similarly, *Hydrobates* means 'water walker'. Non-breeders wander widely and tour existing colonies. For example, one ringed on 5 August 1977 at Skokholm in Wales was trapped the following evening on High Island off the west coast of Galway. At Copeland Bird Observatory, 'playback' (broadcasting sound to

Even in fast, fluttering flight, the wing's chalky underwing stripe is always visible and instantly diagnostic.

lure passers-by) produces memorable encounters. Extracted delicately from a mist net, the sight of a velveteen denizen of the deep sitting on the palm of a hand is enthralling. Sitters are placid and have to be elevated and faced into wind before they summon the urge to fly.

Making accurate censuses is an insoluble problem. Seabird 2000 estimates (Mitchell *et al.* 2004), based mainly on playback responses from occupied burrows, identified Kerry's offshore islands as a world stronghold. Between them, the Great Skellig, Puffin Island and the Great Blasket archipelago held upwards of 50,000 occupied burrows. Totals include vocalising non-breeders as well as incubating adults. Enormous numbers nest on the Faroe Islands and in Iceland. While the populations there are large, possibly exceeding 250,000 pairs, current estimates are 'based largely on guesswork' (Mitchell *et al.* 2004). Given that Ireland possibly holds as much as 40 per cent of the world population, the epithet 'British Storm Petrel' (Robb 2008) seems incongruous, if not jingoistic. Ussher and Warren (1900) stated that nesting occurred in Northern Ireland 'on two small islands off the north coast of Antrim'. Sheep Island was probably one of them. Current knowledge is vague, although active colonies may still exist at predator-free locations.

No nest is built and a single white egg is laid at the end of an underground passageway. Suitable labyrinths occur among rock scree and in lighthouse walls, revetments and under stone-pitched pathways. Mortar spells disaster and occasionally repair work has inadvertently entombed incubating adults and left others homeless. During daylight the troglodytes are silent. Come nightfall, males commence churring. The sound is an audible flag, and by cupping one's ears one can easily follow the gentle tom-tom to its source. Pressing an ear against the ground may help you get within a few centimetres of the crooner, possibly rendered visible by torchlight. Heavy musk pinpoints the lair just as accurately as sound. Before the technological age of head torches and playback, aroma was used as a survey technique. Hiccups punctuate purring. One listener likened the polite cough to 'a fairy being sick' (C. Oldham in Lockley 1983). Both sexes hiccup and can tell each other apart, an ability that escapes human ears. In tests, females respond more to prospecting males and spouses than they do to other females (James 1984). The bird's knack of locating a nest chamber in the dark was unravelled by de Leon *et al.* (2003). A chick's scent was impregnated among a range of tunnels containing the scent of others, and the youngster returned to the location smeared with its own signature, proving that sense of smell is how adults find the right burrow.

The discovery of a protracted fledging period was made by Mr Ryan, a lighthouse keeper writing from the Tearaght, Kerry, on 10 October 1885: 'The Stormy Petrels take a long time to get fledged. I am watching one that was hatched in July and it is not fledged yet' (Barrington 1900). The chick is fed exclusively on oil, a diet that created unforeseen problems for William Andrews in 1841: 'The young birds are singularly large and full in appearance, and contain an immensity of oily matter, which renders it difficult to preserve a specimen' (Thompson 1849–52).

Between late August and November, juveniles vacate nest burrows and disappear rapidly out to sea. Being close to land during daylight is dangerous. Peregrine Falcons patrol coastal waters, sensing the potential presence of seabird prey during inclement weather. Gales sometimes 'wreck' waifs inland as far as Lough Neagh. If the birds are fit, the displacement is temporary. Youngsters winter in the warm tropical seas off West Africa. Adults, however, travel much further. Crossing the equatorial doldrums they disperse over the cool Benguela Current that sweeps north from its Antarctic origin to enrich the windy corner of Africa from the Cape of Good Hope to Namibia. Others go even further and enter the Indian Ocean as far north as Mozambique to feed over upwellings rich in plankton.

Good views are possible from boats; pouring just a small quantity of cod-liver oil or 'rubby-dubby' overboard is often sufficient to attract one or more alongside. Overall blackness is relieved by a white rump and chalky underwing stripe, obvious in the wing's pit, along the inner half of the underwing. A thin upperwing bar is comparatively nondescript. By late summer many adults lack any sign of a bar and, through abrasion, show a rudimentary pale panel along the greater coverts. Fresh-plumaged juveniles show the upperwing bar to best effect. In autumn, small numbers come within viewing distance of the coast during gales. Despite buffeting winds, the species is an indomitable flier and holds to a direct line, powered by an energetic bustling flight. Bursts of flapping are frenetic. Beats are too rapid to count (unlike Leach's Petrel) and at times the wingtips appear to tremble. Caught among heavy seas, glides are of short duration and few dilly-dally, preferring to speed along. Nonetheless, time out is taken if a feeding opportunity presents itself. In an instant, the bird veers and backtracks. The action is as instantaneous as the effect of hitting a window.

LEACH'S PETREL
Oceanodroma leucorhoa

Leach's Petrels are noticeably larger than Storm Petrels (left-hand three birds). In light airs their manner of progress recalls a slow-motion tern. Everything changes in strong wind. Juveniles destined for winter quarters in the Gulf of Guinea are deflected inshore when caught out by autumn gales. Experiencing the blast for the first time, rookie fliers get into a flap. Some appear to lose the run of themselves and look encumbered by outsize wings – like one of us fitting on skis for the first time and being expected to know how to use them.

UNTIL A BETTER understanding of weather-related seabird movements emerged in the early 1980s, this species was something of an enigma. Huge numbers, estimated at several millions, breed in eastern Canada, while thousands nest in Iceland, the Faroes, St Kilda and the Outer Hebrides. All migrate south in autumn, many heading for the Bay of Biscay en route to tropical seas. In the past, gales were seen as the only agent that dumped storm-blown waifs across Ulster, but in fact Leach's Petrels are regular along most of Ireland's west coast during September. Onshore blasts are crucial, ideally from the northwest, a classic direction for tailwinds behind a vigorous depression. This recipe often reveals migrants tracking along windward coasts. Ramore Head in Antrim is a recognised hotspot.

Leach's Petrel is larger and longer-winged than Storm Petrel. Wingspan appears similar to Puffin and is almost twice that of Storm Petrel when viewed in blustery conditions, which affect shape. Battling into turbulence, Leach's flap, using short glides at erratic intervals. At times the bird appears not to be fully in control of wings that are a tad big for its body. In light airs, flight is strong and purposeful with deep strokes supplying plenty of lift but, pitted against high seas, many individuals seem to chicken out from attempts at strong flying. Ironically, midget Storm Petrels battle on. Instead, Leach's hug troughs, steadying themselves like a tightrope walker and making little real progress. The wings are cupped and the tail is spread, making its pointed corners catch the wind and flutter upwards. Although the tail is forked, the indent is seldom obvious. Occasionally the feet are partially lowered to kick off smooth patches of sea. Presumably this is an attempt to feed, though in the throes of a tempest, it looks more like a ploy to maintain momentum and prevent downwind displacement. When visible, grey upperwing panels and all-dark underwings are key distinctions from Storm Petrel. However, when seen against a grey sea in overcast conditions, Leach's and Storm Petrels are silhouetted. Because both are seldom present at the same time, plumage and size distinctions are nullified. Yet, even moving in silhouette, the two are identifiable. Leach's is long-winged and flies with sinewy, measured strokes that can be counted. Storm Petrel is much shorter-winged with bat-like 'trembling' wingbeats that are impossible to count.

The notched tail gave rise to the following incident, described by Patterson (1880). An acquaintance of Patterson's visited Tory Island off Donegal in 1845 to procure specimens of Storm Petrels. Small boys (with small hands) were paid a penny to grab the birds from burrows. Wondering if Leach's – known then by its older name of Fork-tailed Petrel – might also be available, the acquaintance offered tuppence. Remarkably, the wished-for quarry was produced, but the shortness of time required to procure it raised suspicion. Upon examination, it was discovered that the ingenious youth had, acting upon the principle of demand regulating supply, pulled out the central tail feathers of a Storm Petrel.

Nowadays Leach's Petrels are known to nest on a few uninhabited Irish islands. In southwest Donegal, small numbers occur at Rathlin O'Birne. The Stags of Broadhaven, Mayo, holds the majority, estimated at 300 pairs.

GANNET
Morus bassanus

Immature in flight over sea. Thanks to lithe wings that deliver effortless cruise control and a sharp-edged schnozzle designed to grip slippery prey, Gannet prototypes have roamed the world's oceans for at least the last 40 million years.

MORE THAN a quarter of a million pairs of Gannets breed on cliffs and offshore islands around Ireland and Britain. At some of the largest, such as Little Skellig, Kerry, clouds of brilliant white adults swirl in thousands like never-ending snowflakes. Juvenile plumage is ash-brown and covered with starry pinpricks. Offspring come to resemble their parents through a series of moults spanning the first five years of life. Until they do, they are marked out as immature and not old enough to breed. Laying is not synchronised, so by late July colonies contain newborn chicks and 'good to go' fledglings. Youngsters are leathery faced. Airborne, their gangly shape and chocolate-mousse colouring evoke a Pterodactyl. The underwing is two-tone and plumage contrast mimics the bone structure, creating a pattern resembling an X-ray. Fledged young weigh more than adults. Once they glide from nest ledges and land on the sea, some begin autumn migration by paddling until they have lost sufficient puppy fat to take off with ease. One-year-olds look much the same as juveniles but are distinguished by a white belly. In Scotland, dispersal of young was studied on the Bass Rock in the Firth of Forth (Landsborough Thompson 1975) and on Ailsa Craig, Firth of Clyde (Zonfrillo 1997). In October, sophomores demonstrated a primal urge to penetrate south as far as Iberia and Senegal. During November, some embarked on a lateral movement past Gibraltar into the Mediterranean; others continued south to tropical seas where they remained for a year.

The bird is a maniacal fisherman. Depending on the depth of prey, plunges can be vertical or oblique, from as high as 30m and striking at 100km per hour. Sometimes the diver corkscrews just before impact. In days when boats were made of wood and canvas, kamikazes ripped through sails unscathed but broke their necks and dislodged timbers in plummets at spilled, wriggling fish. Gurney translated a Latin account written in the fifteenth century by Robert Gordon that describes a booby-trap catching method employed by Scottish fishermen: 'The sailors prepare a smooth board, and make it white, and fasten Herrings on it; which they make fast to the stern of a fishing boat. [Gannets] seeing the Herrings, try to seize them with their bill, and drive it so deep into the board that they cannot pull it out again, and thus are taken' (Gurney 1921:195–6). In the heyday of the British herring fishery, around 1900, 750,000 barrels of fish were caught annually (800 herrings per barrel). Gannets, catching on average six fish per day, were estimated to have consumed at least 1,160,000 barrels.

At a time when many seabirds are declining, they are holding their own. Around the Irish coast, embryonic clusters on the Saltee Islands, Wexford, and at Ireland's Eye, Dublin, have become substantial colonies in the last twenty years. Success derives from an ability to fish up to 500km from home. At the end of an expedition, adults return fully loaded to feed a single mouth.

Above: Three adults. Binocular vision helps to spot fish and a lack of external nostrils streamlines the bill into a cleaving dagger. Just before piercing the sea, the wings swivel backwards and align with the body. This transforms the bird into a missile, capable of striking water headfirst with scarcely a splash.

Facing: Juvenile with out-of-focus adult. A diamond in the rough, almost every juvenile is an only child. Adults have no brood patch but manage to incubate a single egg by tucking the clutch beneath spreadeagled feet. To create maximum girdling area, webbing spans all four toes. Until babyhood down disappears, one or other parent remains in constant attendance to defend junior.

Pp 82–83: Little Skellig. To breed, Gannets patronise craggy, uninhabited islands. Although few and far between, colonies are sizeable affairs and most have been in existence for millennia. In Scotland, sea-fowling communities ate 'guga': fat, unfledged young. Similar exploitation pegged back the population at Little Skellig. By 1850, a mere 500 pairs survived. Today, thousands nest in peace. Better than historic, the spectacle is authentically prehistoric.

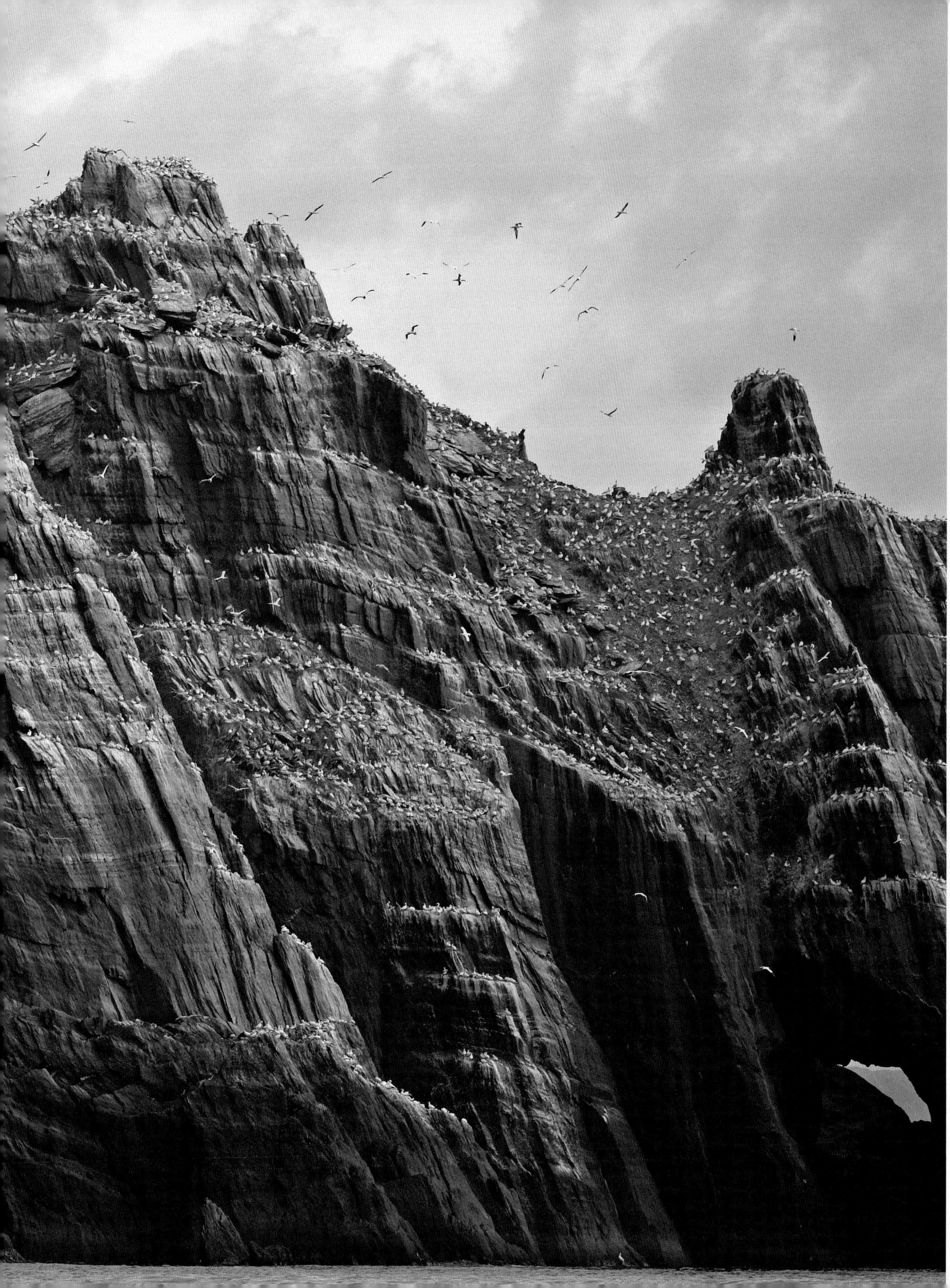

CORMORANT
Phalacrocorax carbo

Above: Structurally, Cormorant is goose-like, square-jawed and with a rather ferocious, vulturine hooked bill.

Opposite: The plumage of Cormorants and Shags is permeable. Modified barbs allow air to escape through feathers that admit water. The effect is to compress plumage – like donning a wetsuit – making underwater swimming fast and skilful. The downside is that the bird becomes waterlogged. The well-known heraldic pose is really clothesline time! Foreground: perched one-year-olds. In flight: (left) adult in breeding plumage; (right) first-winter.

FISH ARE NOT safe from Cormorants, relentless pursuers in both salt water and fresh. The species is colonial and socialises each evening at favoured roost spots, often in high trees near water. Daily commutes from Belfast to Lough Neagh are commonplace; breeders on Strangford Lough and along the north Antrim coast raise young with fish caught on Lough Neagh. Ringing returns indicate dispersal as far as France and Iberia. Adults are sedentary but young are imbued with wanderlust. The class of 1977 from Sheep Island, Antrim, reached Lough Neagh, Fermanagh, Cork, the Firth of Clyde and Cumberland. Two arrived in France and one in Spain. Most were shot. Immigrants come the other way. Chicks ringed in Wigtownshire have been recovered on Lough Neagh, while some from Wexford travelled north of the border.

As well as flapping heavily low over water, Cormorants cross the sky at height, causing confusion with geese. Because they fly in ribald skeins, the risk is increased. However, they intersperse glides between flaps – something geese never do – and have longer tails and a kinked neck, as though something is stuck inside. A swimming Cormorant sinks low when alarmed and leaps forward to dive, sometimes arcing in mid-air. On land, groups sit upright as black bottles, spreading the wings to dry before anointing them with water-repellent powder preened from a gland at the base of the tail. Unlike waterfowl, Cormorant plumage is not 'Gortex standard'. Spectacular breeding plumage starts to appear in late January. Silvery filamentous feathers (like tinsel) erupt and form a white balaclava. Older birds acquire most and males more than females. In counts at colonies in various parts of northern England and southwest Scotland, roughly 15 per cent of breeding adults were white-headed: 'It would seem that such birds are the elders of a colony and may be seven or more years old' (Stokoe 1958). The plumes are grown as a nuptial adornment and, on average, reach maximum extent in early March. Then, remarkably, they disappear. They are lost by moult, not wear. The moult starts about the time the eggs are laid – any time between late January and early April. The head then reverts to standard black. Another characteristic gained and lost in the same process is a large white blob on the rear flank, like a headlight on a dark road. Juveniles and immatures are dark brown with light throats. They have brown, proud chests and a whitish 'rectangular' belly. How to tell a Cormorant from a Shag, a major stumbling block for many bird-watchers, is discussed below.

SHAG
Phalacrocorax aristotelis

Swimming, Shags are 'snaky'. Close views create the opportunity to home in on subtle differences that distinguish them from Cormorant. In all plumages, the extent of feathering between the top of the eye and the culmen (the ridge of the bill) is a guide. On Shag, this 'fore face' is feathered; on Cormorant the equivalent area is bare. Shag has a thinner bill than a Cormorant, with a less malevolent hook. On some (facing page) there is no hook extension below the lower mandible. Bill shape is slimmest on young Shags; the lack of girth makes some look long-billed (left, lower). Juvenile and yearling Shags (left, upper) have an anaemic iris, emphasised by an orbital ring of light feathering. They look sleepless.

EXCLUSIVELY MARINE, Shags are an ancient life form that, once perfected, stayed the same; *aristotelis* is a nod to their venerable lineage. With Cormorants, they congregate on coastal rocks, promontories, buoys or piers to dry outstretched wings that are occasionally aired while swimming, especially when they are at sea and bereft of a perch. Canny breeders seek out inaccessible ledges near entrances to sea caves. Where they feel secure on uninhabited islands, pancakes of dead grass, seaweed and jetsam (frayed rope is a favourite) are sited on flat ground. Nuptial plumage, a forwards-facing tuft at the front of the head, is acquired as early as November. In sunlight, plumage is metallic. The scaly back is olive, whereas the head and neck are deep bottle green with a Peacock gleam. Shag's rakish build allows it

to spring clear of the surface to dive, flexing a paddle-shaped tail in mid-air as it does so. In both Shag and Cormorant the uppertail coverts are remarkably short – to facilitate access to the preen gland?

Shag's bill is narrow, with a waist behind an unimpressive hook. The mandible tips tend to merge and the hook scarcely protrudes lower than the underside of the bill. Especially at rest, it is easy to see where bill becomes face – head and bill are separate entities. Cormorant's bill has an overhanging, aquiline hook and the tong-like mandibles fuse into the face. Concentrate on the side of the lower mandible. On adult Shags, a lick of bright Dandelion yellow encircles the gape; in breeding condition, some adults have yellow across much of the lower mandible too. On youngsters, the entire lower mandible is insipid, mustard yellow. Cormorant has a 'bleached bone' lower mandible and a bright swatch of yellow-orange girdling the bare skin at the gape, suggesting a mandarin orange. Shag, in place of bare skin across the lower face, has feathering. The plumage is white and stands out as an isolated, pouted bulge, as if sucking a sweet. Young Shags are noticeably pale-eyed. Iris colour is glacial – something between icy green and blue. An arc of pale skin surrounds the eye, adding a quizzical touch. On Cormorants of equivalent age, the eye is darker and the pale orbit is narrower and much less striking. Shag is comparatively small-headed with, at rest, a high 'bearskin' forehead when relaxed and standing. Cormorant's contours peak across the rear crown, producing a pear-shaped profile. When fishing commences, head shape is unreliable because plumage is compressed. Shag, when swimming, is small-headed and wiry-necked with such a low centre of gravity that it could pass for a watersnake, especially when peeping below the surface. Ashore, underparts pattern is useful: plain fawn-brown on Shag but admixed with white across the breast and abdomen on Cormorant, whiter on older immatures. Cormorants invariably have black legs and feet. Young Shags have massive, flesh-coloured feet attached to dull legs overlain by a dark 'trouser leg'. Airborne, Shag looks potbellied, the neck cranes forwards and the puny head is held high. In terms of proportion, Shag's flappy wings look out of kilter with a lithe body, like a big suit on a small man. Only Cormorants fly overhead. Shags tend to hug the airspace immediately above the waves. Indeed, they may derive lift by doing so. Due to a phenomenon known as 'ground effect', flight is aided when wingbeats constrain – effectively trap – a pillow of air against a flat surface.

BITTERN
Botaurus stellaris

THE CHANCES of encountering a Bittern on this side of the Irish Sea are slim. Although the bird formerly bred among freshwater reed beds, Thompson (1849–52) felt that its survival was threatened by drainage and shooting. Ussher and Warren (1900) mention that, during the latter half of the nineteenth century, there were 'plenty enough' around Upper Lough Erne and they were also present in 'extensive swamps' north of Strabane and near Dungiven.

Dr T. R. Robinson recognised one killed on 12 November 1845 at 'Layde Bottoms', a mile from Armagh, as being an American Bittern *Botaurus lentiginosus*. Although the fresh skin was immediately forwarded to Thompson, the remains met a different end: 'It was very fat and made very good eating, for we roasted it!' Oliver Goldsmith (1730–1774), playwright, novelist and poet, provides first-hand testimony of growing up at a time when the bird was familiar. In his illustrated eight-volume *History of the Earth and Animated Nature* he included his personal recollections of Bitterns in rural Ireland:

It is from its hollow boom that the Bittern is held in such detestation by the vulgar. I remember, in the place where I was a boy [Kilkenny], with what terror the bird's note affected the whole village. They considered it as the presage of some sad event, and generally found one to succeed it. I do not speak ludicrously. If any person in the neighbourhood died, they supposed it could not be otherwise, for the 'Night-raven' [Bittern] had foretold it. If nobody happened to die, the death

of a cow or a sheep gave completion to the prophecy. Those who have walked in an evening by the sedgy sides of unfrequented rivers must remember a variety of notes from different waterfowl. None is so dismally hollow as the booming of the Bittern. It is impossible for words to give those who have not heard the evening call an adequate idea of its solemnity. It is like the interrupted bellowing of a bull, but hollower and louder, and is heard at a mile's distance, as if issuing from some formidable being that resided at the bottom of the waters. These bellowing explosions are chiefly heard from the beginning of spring to the end of autumn. However awful they may seem to us, they are calls to courtship or of connubial felicity. (Goldsmith 1796)

Nowadays, the species is a rare winter visitor. Silence and stealthy confinement within impenetrable wet habitat cloak the phantom and mask an understanding of its status. Migrants may be more regular than believed. In line with an increase in the British breeding population – eighteen sites held at least eighty-two booming males in 2009 – it is not too far-fetched to hope that the bird might someday return. Bitterns seldom fly, yet the Latin name *Botaurus stellaris* is a romantic commemoration of flight. The clue is not from *Botaurus* (applied on account of the 'booming' that resembles the bellow of a bull) but from a habit of spiralling high and circling out of sight, often towards nightfall. *Stellaris*, therefore, is a sobriquet hinting at the stellar realm into which it ascends. Oliver Goldsmith would have approved.

The Bittern is so exclusively adapted to wet reed beds – a vanishing habitat – that its existence is in jeopardy across many parts of Europe. Most of Ireland's wetland wilderness has long since been lost; so too have its once-thriving Bitterns.

LITTLE EGRET
Egretta garzetta

BIRDS HAVE A CAPACITY TO SURPRISE US. In little over a decade, the status of Little Egrets has undergone a dramatic transformation from vagrant to breeding species. Colonisation got off to a thunderous start when twelve pairs raised twenty-nine chicks at Rincrew Wood, Waterford, in 1997. Reasons for the expansion from Mediterranean wetlands are not clear. Perhaps, like westwards-moving Collared Doves in the 1960s, the birds found a vacant niche. Certainly, there is no competition in feeding strategy between this dashing new kid on the block and lugubrious Grey Herons. Typically, Little Egrets charge about in shallow water and tend to dash for dinner, rather than using 'old bachelor heron' tactics of remaining motionless in the hope that an unsuspecting victim makes a false move. Small fish are snatched, but shrimp (*Crangon crangon*) may be even more important prey. Preliminary results from research into the diet of nestlings in Waterford showed that almost 75 per cent consisted of shrimp; the remainder was small fish (Ronayne 2011). Small parties, hunched up and motionless, resemble tufts of Cotton Grass.

In breeding plumage, Little Egrets develop white head plumes and lace-like white diaphanous 'aigrette' feathers that hang like a bride's veil over the back. Facial skin turns bright custard yellow, so matching the feet, which resemble ankle-socks on black legs. There the flattery ends; the voice is a guttural *whaa*? said in a Belfast accent. Immatures have mustard-coloured legs and, outside the breeding season, insipidly coloured bare parts.

Many stay here for the winter. But not all. A 2009 nestling from Galway was discovered in October in the Azores, 2,133km from where it was born. Being the only small white heron, identification is straightforward. However, there might be an exception. History could be repeating itself, this time involving Cattle Egret *Bubulcus ibis*. Consequently, a small egret associating with livestock – a by no means unusual winter habit of Little Egret – may prove to be a Cattle Egret.

Above: Hope springs eternal. Who could have predicted that such a delightful bird might become a regular sight in Ireland? Ireland's colonists are the most northerly breeders in the world.

Below: Recently tested by two consecutive severe winters, hardy survivors have bred and made good their losses in the big freeze.

GREY HERON
Ardea cinerea

GREY HERONS have the look of a loner; the epitome of a patient fisherman – motionless, but primed with a hair trigger. The eyes focus along the line of the bill, facilitating a cobra-like strike. Included in a diet of fish, frogs and rodents are chicks and, given a chance, adult birds. Not surprisingly, the behemoth's lumbering flight silhouette generates commotion and unease among potential prey. Despite sedentary body language and a clunky flight, some travel far. Vagrants, quite possibly from Ireland, have reached eastern Canada. Ringing data has documented midwinter movements from Galway to Wicklow and Meath, while a juvenile from Norway was discovered wintering along the Irish east coast.

Heronries have been thoroughly surveyed in Northern Ireland. Eighty have been enumerated, of which approximately seventy are occupied annually. The largest contains 129 nests. Others, seventy-strong, are on islands in Lough Erne. Several nineteenth-century sites are still active, as at Ringdufferin, Down, where the species bred as long ago as 1830. In early spring the birds apply themselves to renovating twiggy nests that have taken a battering during gales.

Young herons are muted grey. Adults have a white forehead with inky-black locks sweeping back along the sides of the crown and culminating in a neck plume, like a balding bloke with an embarrassing ponytail. At rest, adults sport a flamboyant black-and-white epaulette, visible on the carpal bend of the folded wing. Pumped with hormones in preparation for breeding, a male's bill turns coral red for a short time. Calls are sporadic but loud – a strident, squawked and discordant *frank!* Silence mostly accompanies a stolid, ecclesiastical demeanour. Yet, come nesting time, a wide range of idle chatter is vented, from clicks to grunts.

Above: Based on the evidence of many years of ringing data, this juvenile probably faces a tough apprenticeship. Youngsters disperse widely. Two from France crossed the Atlantic and finished up in the Caribbean. Seventy per cent die in their first year. Those that survive can expect, on average, a further two or three years of life. Mature adults, with a well-established territory and detailed local knowledge, live much longer (up to thirty-five years of age).

Left: How much punch does that bill pack? Half of the bird's metre-long body is made up of muscular neck. Moreover, the bill is fused to the skull, effectively melding bill, head and neck into a single entity. An injured Purple Heron, a slightly built relation of Grey Heron, accidentally killed a man with a single stab to the head.

LITTLE GREBE
Tachybaptus ruficollis

Of all birds, Little Grebes seem most snug. Fluffy plumage traps air and provides an extra layer of warmth, as well as aiding buoyancy.

IN THE DAYS before bird books, local names tended to reflect essence more succinctly. Rather than the technically correct name of Little Grebe, the species was called Dabchick, by virtue of the rapid dip or 'dab' as the mite plops out of sight, along with a nod to character – its resemblance to a baby waterbird with a fluffed-up stern and dumpy shape. Do not be fooled into equating cuddly shape with an approachable nature. Most are shy and wary. If startled before submerging, the head and neck function as a periscope to check that the coast is clear when re-surfacing.

Little Grebes are sharp-faced shallow divers that forage within 1m of the surface. Home is fresh water, even small ponds and ditches. The titch is a master of living secretively along margins screened from the shore by reeds, rushes and willows. Labyrinthine underwater vegetation suits hunting requirements. Diet consists less of small fish and more of aquatic larvae, snails and tadpoles, meaning that food is most abundant where plant growth flourishes in clear sunlit water. An unobtrusive nature is compromised in the breeding season because courtship serenading indicates presence, although spotting the caller's whereabouts is another matter. The whinny lasts about three seconds, a trill that runs away with itself before losing momentum. Pairs often duet in a magical musical spiral. Courtship plumage comprises shiny black foreparts surrounding

a chestnut neck, coining *ruficollis* (rusty-collared). In sunshine the neck glints bronze. The effect of light accounts for a popular misconception affecting colour assessment of a fleshy flange at the gape. Field guides claim this to be yellow. Actually, it is mint green, although it can appear bluish or yellowish. The bill tip is whitish and pellucid. In non-breeding plumage, the sides of the bill are pinkish yellow.

Nesting activities peak in May, although the breeding season can run as late as September if flooding scuppers first attempts. The bird covers its eggs with vegetation before leaving the nest, frenetically so when panicked. Clutch size is variable. Typically just two or three two youngsters accompany successful parents, and are carried piggyback. Winter plumage is drab, relieved by a fluffed-up powder-puff rear. Refugees displaced from frozen lakes are regularly seen on estuaries, less so on exposed coasts.

The floating nest is anchored to vegetation. Eggs are hastily covered if danger threatens. When incubation duties resume, the bird festoons itself with strands of weed to improve camouflage.

GREAT CRESTED GREBE
Podiceps cristatus

FOR MILLENNIA Great Crested Grebes were commonplace until their dense, silky plumage became a must-have fashion accessory during the mid-nineteenth century. Muffs and coat trimmings, erroneously termed fur, along with feathers for hats and fishing flies gleaned from exotic breeding plumes, accounted for the deaths of most of the breeding population in Britain and Ireland. Across Europe, North America and Australia, more grebes and egrets suffered the same fate. In *The Economist*, dated 15 March 1879, 24,750 skins from Turkey, Russia and California were offered for sale. The slaughter was nearly unsustainable but it was a change in the attitude of consumers that saved the day. Thanks to outraged women who drew attention to the iniquity, laws were eventually passed to protect not just grebes, but birds in general. This change was truly tectonic and the tactics used were remarkable, given stuffy Victorian times. Radically minded women confronted their feather-bedecked peers and harangued them, even spying on their attire at church and mailing anonymous letters of complaint. Wallace (2004) captures the pace and direction of the mood swing:

> What was needed for national conscience to take active root was a cause célèbre and some impassioned advocates. The former was first publicly expressed by Alfred Newton who, in a letter to *The Times* on 28 January 1876, denounced the use of birds' plumage in female fashion. The latter corps was formed by lady propagandists who became formidable and formed vociferous bodies such as the Plumage League and the Fur, Fin and Feather Groups. To improve their propaganda, these precursors to the suffragettes recruited the pens and (after a brief feminist-like debate on whether men should be members) the full allegiance of luminary male apostles.

Like some latter-day fashion model, the beanpole that launched bird protection sits on the boundary between elegance and gaunt anorexia. In winter, when Cleopatran headdress is absent, its long neck looks pale and painfully thin, reminiscent of a coat hanger bobbing on water. In flight the resemblance is closer to Concorde. Along with a distinctive gangly shape, the wings are strikingly patterned 'fore and aft' with white. Famed for a walking-on-water courtship dance, Great Crested Grebes are to water what Swifts are to sky. From a floating nest moored or tethered among aquatic vegetation, chicks are carried piggyback-style and fed tiny fish and insects until, at about six weeks old, they learn to dive. Adults consume small feathers, plucking them from among their own plumage, and also feed them to chicks. The feathers line the wall of the digestive tract and form padding, trapping fish bones that are eventually regurgitated in a pellet, while also compressing prey and facilitating enzymes in the gut wall that liquidise dinner.

As a result of annual surveys between 1995 and 1999 (Perry *et al.* 1998), the breeding population of Great Crested Grebes at Lough Neagh, its marginal areas, islands and its associated lakes was established to a high degree of accuracy. During the summer of 1998 at least 2,017 pairs were found, establishing the area as a stronghold of international importance. Previous surveys had suggested about 750 pairs, while a 1975 estimate of around 300 pairs for the Republic of Ireland (Preston 1975) is in need of revision. Each August, a significant proportion of the population migrates to Belfast Lough due to a seasonal reduction in Lough Neagh's fish prey when Roach, the birds' mainstay, leave accessible surface waters and move deeper to breed.

Like Cinderella stripped of her finery, winter plumage is a far cry from courtship raiment.

During courtship and greeting ceremonies, riotous rufous tufts are fanned like a matador's cape. The spectacular 'fashionable' headdress and body plumage that provided a hand-warming pelt cost the lives of thousands, until outraged women put an end to the slaughter.

SLAVONIAN GREBE
Podiceps auritus

MYSTERY ATTENDS THIS NYMPH and makes it something of a *rara avis*, a situation that is compounded by the wraith choosing to winter beyond binocular range on large inlets. Lough Foyle and Strangford Lough are especially favoured; elsewhere in Ireland, numbers are tiny. During rare days of midwinter calm, it is possible to count fifty or more on Lough Foyle. When the sea becomes ruffled during windy weather, they are either AWOL or undetectable due to small size among choppy waves. A telescope is essential, as is local knowledge. Favourite areas are permanent water below the low-tide margin along the outer reaches of mudflats: underwater conveyors for fish prey that run with the tide. Grebes are present between October and March. Identification is not that difficult once a diminutive blob with white cheeks and a black 'woolly hat' pops into view; Little Grebe is not at home so far from the coast. Slavonians often mix with Great Crested Grebes. In spite of size difference and the latter's anorexic 'coat-hanger' shape, distance can deceive. In particular, a balled-up Great Crested Grebe can appear unnaturally small.

The origin of our wintering population is unknown. An estimated 500 pairs breed in Iceland. Bardarson (1986) states: 'The Slavonian Grebe is mostly migratory in Iceland. In April, as soon as the ice melts, it arrives on lakes. Departure commences in late September. A few remain off the southwest coast but many winter off the coasts of Europe.' Might a proportion migrate here? Closer, some breed in the Scottish Highlands. This is the only colony in Britain and numbers appear to rise and fall inexplicably, also a characteristic of the variable numbers, ranging from 20 to just over 100, wintering on Lough Foyle.

BLACK-NECKED GREBE *Podiceps nigricollis* and **RED-NECKED GREBE** *Podiceps griseigena* sometimes occur, almost always in winter plumage when their eponymous monikers do not hold true. Black-necked Grebe is the Michael Jackson of the tribe: lightly built, petite nose-in-the-air bill and heavily made-up face. Red-necked Grebe is a pig in the middle, falling between Great Crested and Slavonian Grebes but more dusky and stocky than either.

Like watching an old black-and-white television, we have no inkling of the remarkable colour transformation made by a Slavonian Grebe when it dons breeding plumage. Nonetheless, monochrome winter birds are dapper and gameful. Although not much larger than Little Grebe, small parties endure winter weather on wide sea loughs; small size makes detection difficult except on calm days.

WHITE-TAILED EAGLE
Haliaetus albicilla

THOMPSON'S DESCRIPTION of White-tailed Eagles gives us a poignant account of what it was like to live in a country with skies darkened by a winged colossus.

In Antrim, the Sea Eagle has an eyrie at Fair Head, the most lofty and sublime of the basaltic promontories of the northeast coast. When visiting this place on 16 July 1839, a pair appeared soaring about the headland. An intelligent man, long resident in the neighbourhood, stated that they build annually, very early in the season, on the same platform of rock, and the number of young was always two. Eagles are persecuted for carrying off lambs, turkeys and geese of tender age, as well as ducks and hens of all ages. In the island of Rathlin, the Sea Eagle is said to have an eyrie. This species, as well as the Golden Eagle, has been taken in Glenarm Park; and, on the 6 September 1837, two were seen on Galbally Mountain, near Garron Point. They are frequently met with [in the Mountains of Mourne in 1836] by Lord Roden's gamekeeper, but are seldom seen as low down as Tollymore Park. [By 1846] the same gamekeeper reported to me that he believed that there was only one eagle left in the mountains. The birds are accused of committing great devastation, 'killing a sheep every week,' and very often sweeping down and bearing off a goose from the farmyard. (Thompson 1849–52)

Despite feeding mainly on fish and carrion, an ill-deserved reputation for killing lambs doomed the giant to extinction; the same argument blighted Golden Eagles. In contrast to the latter's solitary nature and occupancy of a large territory over mountainland, most White-tailed Eagles' eyries were within sight of the sea. The birds were social and came together in loose aggregations, much as vultures or Bald Eagles do. The picturesque strands around Dunfanaghy, Donegal, were used as a loafing area for up to half a dozen at a time; rabbits on sandhills behind the beach made living easy and offered a change from hunting seabirds over the nearby cliffs of Horn Head, then a seething

Strands in north Donegal formerly held up to forty loafing White-tailed Eagles. Pairs nested along many parts of Ireland's coastline until the middle of the nineteenth century. Relentless, unwarranted persecution by shepherds, gamekeepers and the local populace – latterly for financial gain, given collectors' lurid interest in obtaining eggs and trophy specimens – led to extinction. Commencing in 1968, Norwegian offspring have been released in Scotland. The result has been the establishment of a surrogate 'wild' population. A similar initiative, modelled on the Scottish experience, is ongoing in Ireland, with the birds touted as a tourism asset.

A massive flesh-tearing bill dwarfs those of other eagles. The bird can glide for long periods on flat 'barn door' wings, although a short tail limits manoeuvrability. Youngsters are dark-tailed and take five years to develop a fully white appendage. As adults mature, the head also becomes progressively paler. Photograph taken in Norway.

seabird city described by Otway (1827): 'Nests were here and there on some boulder and broader prominence too high from below and too deep from above to be accessible from man. Young were as large as turkeys and the old birds, from thirty to forty at a time, floating in mid-air above, shrieking and challenging our audacity in molesting their sovereignty.'

On 25 June 1832 Thompson travelled to Horn Head, where he witnessed two eaglets, destined for captivity, being removed from the nest, and saw another nest with two eggs. Around the nest was littered 'many legs of rabbits and the remains of Puffins', confirmation of a diet devoid of domestic livestock. Over two days he saw five adults, believed to be all that remained, the local gamekeeper having killed thirteen over the previous four years. Ussher and Warren (1900) summarised status in 1894: 'Still one or two pairs in Mayo and Kerry. Has been destroyed or driven from former breeding haunts in Donegal, Antrim, Down,

White-tailed Eagles feed by catching fish, chasing seabirds and scouring habitat for carrion, requirements that tie them to the proximity of seabird colonies, coastlines and large wetlands. Photograph taken in Norway.

Wicklow, Cork, Clare, and Galway.' By 1900 the giant was gone, having been around for millennia and featuring in early Christian poetry and Celtic crosses, including seventh-century examples from Cardonagh, Donegal, not far from Horn Head.

Cataloguing the demise of an icon from our avifauna gives rise to feelings of disgust. Although decades of destruction here were matched in Scotland, the tables have recently been turned and the bird is back along the Scottish west coast, restored by reintroductions from Norway. Occasionally, youngsters wander out to sea, drawn to explore land on the far horizon – Ireland. Meanwhile, in Kerry, releases are taking place. Seen properly, identification of White-tailed Eagle is straightforward. In flight the silhouette resembles a barn door. The tail does not turn white until its owner is at least three. At all ages the appendage is short and shaped like a fan. Drifting high overhead, aesthetics take a back seat to the awe inspired by a majestic presence.

GOLDEN EAGLE
Aquila chrysaetos

Golden Eagles are active hunters. In addition to broad, powerful wings, a generous tail permits versatile twists and turns. This bird, photographed in Norway, has caught a young fox. Patrolling birds soar to great heights and spot prey at up to a kilometre below. Their eyeball is comparable in size to ours. Scotland's mountain wilderness remains in good heart and retains viable populations of eagles and prey, such as grouse and hare. The same cannot be said for Ireland's uplands. Here, recent reintroductions are maintained by supplementary feeding of a cosseted few transported from Scottish eyries and released into a beleaguered home range barely capable of providing sufficient food.

THIS LORD OF THE AIR is a free spirit of upland wilderness where time passes slowly. After a day sitting on a crag and digesting dinner, the gimlet-eyed searcher, equipped with eyeballs as large as walnuts, glides aloft to peer unseen over rugged hunting grounds. Oddly enough, colour vision is comparatively unimportant; prey is detected through contrast and, most of all, movement. Buzzards are somewhat uncharitably nicknamed 'Tourist Eagle' in the Scottish Highlands and the same confusion applies here. The unexpected appearance of a large bird of prey soaring on fingered wings quickly cements the notion that such a regal beast *has to be* an eagle. Look closely at the underparts. Golden Eagles are, at all ages, dark-bodied. From below, Buzzard plumage is variegated, with a pale cummerbund bounded by dark plumage. Alternatively, a large raptor drifting over a cliffed coastline may prove to be a White-tailed Eagle, some of which are spilling south following successful reintroductions along parts of the west coast of Scotland, or radiating north from similar schemes in Kerry.

Golden Eagles were purged from our heritage by persecution waged by gamekeepers and sheep farmers. Although wild prey consisted of Irish Hare, Red Grouse, rabbits and carrion, there is little doubt that poultry and lambs were sometimes snatched. This led to the bird's reputation being blackened, and it was made more culpable than warranted. Golden Eagles occurred at a low density over inland mountains; on the coast, piscatorial White-tailed Eagles were commoner. John Vandeleur Stewart (1832) described the status of each in Donegal: Golden Eagles were rare; White-tailed Eagles were common. Thompson (1849–52) commented that Golden Eagles were found sparingly 'in only the most lofty and retired mountain ranges'. Though one was killed in the Mountains of Mourne in 1837, a gamekeeper active in the district stated that over the nine preceding years he had 'never met with the Golden Eagle'. Other references include one captured and two others seen at Cleggan, Antrim, on 14 October 1835. From Glenariff, Antrim, around 1820, Thompson reported the ingenious use of a tethered eaglet placed in a field to encourage its parents to drop rabbits and hares as food, which were then appropriated by its human captor. If such a ploy had become widespread, farmers might have protected the species. Surely it is also the case that the bird was ousted to mountainous redoubts as a consequence of persecution on lowlands? In those parts of Europe, such as in the Baltic States and northern Sweden, where bogland and wilderness remain intact at close to sea level, Golden Eagles still occur.

With the refinement of game production over the course of the eighteenth century and the growth of zealous keepering aimed at eliminating birds of prey, all-out war was declared, which drew popular support from rural inhabitants. Only in uninhabited country did some birds escape the onslaught. In the second half of the nineteenth century the introduction of strychnine, laced as poison into bait, accelerated the annihilation. When the final pairs or lone individuals amounted to curios, they were shot to satisfy a selfish lust to own the last examples of a dying breed. As part of the destruction, nests were robbed for eggs, the payment for which was generous because of the danger of procuring the clutch from eyries in precipitous locations.

Golden Eagles breed in low numbers in remote parts of western Scotland. From 1953 to 1959 a pair derived from the Scottish population bred each year at Fair Head, Antrim. Arnold Benington observed them and, not surprisingly, was besotted. Watching adults and offspring on 22 July 1953, he wrote: 'Pure bliss. With difficulty I removed my gaze from the nest and let it roam slowly around the mountains, moors and glens. It was all familiar country to me, yet somehow today it was different. It had taken on a new significance – eagle country' (Benington 2009). Two things were remarkable about the event. First, the birds chose to nest on a sea cliff. Perhaps the absence of competition from extinct White-tailed Eagles enticed the birds to commandeer an eyrie of yesteryear. Second, it is claimed that some prey, such as Scottish 'blue' Hare, was captured on the Mull of Kintyre, 20km away across the sea (CDD). Scotland was the motherland and progeny may have dispersed there, rather than westward. Over subsequent years Scottish wanderers, mostly juveniles recognisable by white wing flashes and a white tail base, have reached Rathlin Island and adjacent parts of the north Antrim coast. One source from which potential breeding recruits might have come, the Kintyre peninsula, which harboured several pairs until the 1960s, has lost most of its breeding population due to afforestation, thereby removing hunting territory. Perhaps Islay, where several pairs nest, offers a better prospect?

Raptor enthusiasts have attempted to reintroduce Golden Eagles to part of their ancestral homeland among the hills of Donegal, at Glenveagh National Park. The long-term aspiration is to build a nucleus of pairs across a sweep of upland, within which human threats are minimised, including voluntary curbs on the use of poisoned baits to control foxes. Between 2001 and 2006, forty-six were released. The youngsters were taken from Scottish nests; in each case the smallest chick was removed. Often the second offspring does not survive and, if food is scarce, may even be killed and eaten by its older sibling in a heartless Cain and Abel ritual. All were reared in pens, without human contact, for several weeks before being released and fitted with transmitters. The first nest was constructed in 2005 and eggs were laid in that year and again in 2006. In 2007 two pairs attempted to breed and one chick fledged. It lived just three years and, in 2010, was found poisoned in Leitrim.

Although prohibited, the illegal use of poisoned bait to kill hill foxes and crows is a running sore. However, it should not be assumed that eagles are being selected as targets. Rather, they are unintended victims. Instead of tut-tutting at landowners killing foxes and crows, it is time to recognise the damage done by uncontrolled predators (camp-followers of human land use), especially to vulnerable ground-nesting upland birds such as embattled Red Grouse, Golden Plovers and Curlews. Misplaced ethical sympathies help no one. Mother Nature never intended Irish uplands to be smothered with conifer plantations that impinge on mountain and moor, or grazed to a green desert bereft of Golden Eagles and the chain of life upon which they depend. Wilderness is not an empty quarter; it is a mirror symbolising the wealth of the wild.

OSPREY
Pandion haliaetus

IN TERMS OF BREEDING range extensions, Ireland is usually in the slipstream of Britain. Successful colonisation there precedes establishment here, provided momentum is sustained. In reaching Irish soil, Little Egrets, Mediterranean Gulls and Collared Doves have founded outposts on the very edge of Europe. Ospreys, on the other hand, have, thanks to protection, not so much colonised Britain as rebounded. Nowadays there are at least 180 pairs across the water (Holling 2011). Because the species is migratory, wanderers drift west across the Irish Sea. Ringed individuals have been seen at Lough Beg, north of Lough Neagh, one of which had been ringed as a chick in Scotland. Sometimes singletons linger for weeks, and two have been seen together. The bird is becoming an annual passage migrant. Future breeding attempts would appear to be a possibility although, in 1973, a military commander encountered a nesting pair near the River Maine, Antrim (NMK). Ospreys are spectacular dive-bombing hunters of fish. They patrol the skies over large lakes and sheltered estuaries and hover to spot the ripple of prey. Dinner is usually quite sizeable so, like most large raptors, they spend considerable amounts of time sitting idle. They are almost unmistakable and tend to perch prominently on a tall tree or comparable structure. At Lough Beg, channel markers are used as resting places.

Hooked talons are handy for airlifting nest material, not just prey. To catch fish, Ospreys submerge fully. Occasionally the target is too large to carry and the bird is dragged under. At least one Osprey skeleton has been found attached to a fish.

RED KITE
Milvus milvus

RED KITES are big, lanky basketball players. Gangly at rest, with long limbs and a loping gait, launched into flight they exude elegance and agility. They are ballet on wings. The forked tail swivels freely and operates independently of wing hands that arch and thrust forwards. How can a raptor the size of a lumbering Buzzard be so graceful? Put simply, the shape is extremely aerodynamic, notably the broad wings designed to flex and cup the wind. By comparison, the body and spiky rudder are anorexic. The moving silhouette, never mind the bright ginger tail, is distinctive from afar. Closer views reveal a chequerboard of contrasts, from pale patches on the underwings to light upperwing diagonals and a frosty head on a russet body.

Acrobats pounce on rabbits, rodents and small birds. Carrion attracts them, but they also gambol over grassland in pursuit of earthworms. They are at home in lightly wooded, rolling countryside, particularly where hillsides provide updrafts enabling them to hang out aloft and scan open ground. The species was once widespread throughout England, Scotland and Wales, and scavengers were common in London streets during the Middle Ages. A Venetian ambassador of the time described exhibitionists swooping to steal bread smeared with butter out of the hands of children. Dextrous skills elicited a different response in rural areas when they snatched poultry – persecution followed. As numbers dwindled, just one fastness remained at the end of the twentieth century: the isolated valley woods and pastoral foothills of mid-Wales. Fears were expressed that a remnant population of around twenty-five pairs might not be self-sustaining – an assumption that was wrong – and grandiose reintroduction schemes have fostered the bird's return to parts of England and Scotland. Because Red Kites are regal and conspicuous, they have become a big hit with the public. Conservation organisations have found themselves in a 'win-win' situation by restoring the species to its former range in Great Britain.

Status in Ireland was summarised by Thompson in 1849:

The name of 'Kite' appears commonly in the catalogues of birds given in the Statistical Surveys of the Irish counties and elsewhere; but, as the larger species of the [birds-of-prey] are in some places called Kite and Glead [meaning 'glider'], as well as Goshawk or Goose-hawk, there can be no doubt that the Buzzard, or some common species, was generally meant. The mere fact of rewards having been offered for the destruction of the 'Kite' as one of the birds-of-prey, does not prove anything with respect to the veritable species. Smith, in his *History of Cork*, completed in 1749, could hardly be mistaken, as he does not content himself with stating that 'the Kite is distinguished from all other birds of prey by its forked tail,' but adds, 'that it remains with us all year.' He remarks, however, something that we should hardly have

Adult Red Kite, France. Easy movement of slender wings produces an elegant flight. Although somewhat bigger than a Buzzard, Red Kites are more graceful – a far cry from Buzzards' lugubrious 'flap-and-glide'.

expected: 'these birds are so common as to need no particular description.' But when the country was more richly wooded, and less populous than at present, it was much better circumstanced for the Kite. It is now unknown, not only in the County of Cork, but in the whole south of Ireland.' (Thompson 1849–52)

Elsewhere in his account, Thompson states: 'A native bird, either in a wild state, or preserved in a collection, has not come either under my own cognisance, or that of any of my ornithological correspondents.' His patrician style erred on the side of diplomacy and he refrained from casting aspersions on the veracity of earlier writers. Nevertheless, it seems that he raised an eyebrow at Smith's (1749) contention that, in Cork, Red Kites were 'so common as to need no particular description'. Ussher and Warren (1900) were more forthright. Their status summary reads: 'Rare and accidental visitor. No Irish specimen is known to exist.' They went on to say:

Thompson quotes Smith's 'Cork' reference from 1750, which states that the Kite with forked tail 'remains with us all the year,' and that 'these birds are so common as to need no particular description.' However, as Smith shortly afterwards tells us that the Hobby breeds on the sea-coast, we must use his statements with caution, especially as he was liable to be misled by the name 'Kite,' used in Ireland for both the resident harriers.

Smith's trustworthiness is undermined further when he reports in his *Ancient and Present State of the County and City of Waterford* (1746): '*Urogallus minor*, the Black Grouse of England, [is] also an inhabitant of the mountains.' He writes again about Black Grouse in his *History of Cork*, describing the species as frequent.

Adult Red Kite, France. Head colour pales with age. Red Kites perch freely and roost communally in sentinel trees. Silhouetted against bare branches, the long lean body resembles that of a gibbon.

Smith is, of course, wrong when he claims that Black Grouse occurred in Ireland. Even Thompson, who normally shied away from pointing out flaws, was moved to state: 'Were this description [Smith's claim that Black Grouse occurred in Ireland] taken from native birds, it would be decisive as to the species; but it is, instead, borrowed from the work of Willughby.' (Willughby's seminal work on England's birds was published posthumously, thanks to his mentor John Ray, in 1676. The first edition (in Latin) was followed by an English edition in 1678.) In other words, Smith was unreliable. At pains to establish facts, Ussher and Warren declare: 'The only record, however, of a Red Kite shot in this country is that of Sir Ralph Payne Gallwey, who describes his finding a young male, which he killed in Kerry, during the severe winter of 1880–81.'

Mindful to present all shreds of evidence, Thompson (1849–52) inserted: 'I heard from an old gamekeeper, who had lived for many years at Shane's Castle [Antrim] of a few Kites "with tails forked like Swallows' having been killed there." ' Might these

have been nesting birds or simply a toll of any that passed through? Throughout the eighteenth century gamekeepers on large estates were diligent in their work, and records for Antrim held in the Public Record Office of Northern Ireland testify to zealous and indiscriminate killing of birds of prey, crows, Cormorants and Otters at, among other areas, Portmore and 'Massereene' (which probably encompasses Shane's Castle). Statistics such as single claims in 1747 for Rook of 1,876 and 1,525 individuals indicate the scale of slaughter.

Is there a concrete basis for reintroducing the species into the north of Ireland, or do releases that commenced in Down in 2007 constitute deliberate dispersal of a bird that was never here? Either way, are such actions steered by public relations rather than any addressing of a conservation goal? There seems to be no 'trickle-down' collateral good news for other birds, wildlife or habitats benefiting from the introduction scheme. Perhaps conservation organisations ought to spend their time and money more wisely, rather than using it to garner publicity from plans to reintroduce an undeniably beautiful bird that is not unquestionably native to Ulster.

In other parts of Ireland, bone remains add credence to the bird's credentials as an extirpated species. D'Arcy (1999) states:

Bones of the Red Kite have been recovered from excavations at Wood Quay Viking site in Dublin. They date from sometime between the tenth and eleventh centuries. They were found in 'back-yard' situations along with the remains of other predatory and scavenging birds such as Ravens, crows, Buzzards, harriers and White-tailed Eagles. The list suggests that these Viking settlements were beset by a formidable collection of avian refuse collectors. Excavations at Lough Gur in Limerick have revealed bird bones from the thirteenth or fourteenth century. Here too, Red Kite bones were uncovered along with those of Buzzards, an unidentified eagle and numerous Ravens and crows. Red Kite bones found during archaeological work at Roscrea Castle, Tipperary, and date from the seventeenth century. The birds may have come to grief as quarry for falconers. There are many references from England and elsewhere to *kites* [italics added] being used for this purpose.

As Thompson (1849–52) was at pains to point out, no inference should be drawn that suggests 'kite' actually means Red Kite. In a study of the past status of the Buzzard in Britain and Ireland, Moore came up against the same problem, albeit for establishing a correct identification for records of Buzzard:

The main sources of information about the distribution of the Buzzard in the past are the writings of contemporary naturalists. Today the other large birds of prey are so rare that errors due to wrong identification must be slight. But when three species of harrier (*Circus* spp.), Red Kite and Honey Buzzard could all be seen more or less frequently in Britain, all records, except those of reliable ornithologists, are suspect. John Ray (1678) distinguished between the Buzzard or

Migrating juvenile Red Kite, Spanish Pyrenees. Youngsters have a shallow fork and the tail is ruddy brown. As it twists, the fork disappears. Due to persecution, Red Kites disappeared from England, Scotland and much of Wales. Thanks to protection, the remnant Welsh population eventually bounced back and began to expand. Potentially, a natural recolonisation of the bird's British range could have resulted. Rather than aiding recovery by native stock, resources were used to remove migratory youngsters from parts of the north European range and release them in Scotland. The birds' migratory urge brought several to Ireland, where they succumbed to poisoned bait. Nonetheless, successive introductions from Europe continued. Several regions of the British countryside have since become repopulated. Hailed as a conservation success, the same propaganda now attends similar unethical releases in Ireland.

Puttock, the Red Kite, the Honey Buzzard and the Bald Buzzard (Osprey) and the Moor Buzzard (Marsh Harrier) and 'Ringtail' or Hen Harrier, but probably few of his countrymen did. The situation was further confused because the words, Buzzard, Puttock, Kite, Gled, Glede, meant different species according to region – all could refer to Buzzard (*Buteo buteo*). Recognition of these sources of error must be taken into account before accepting any records of a Buzzard. (Moore 1957)

With large-scale release schemes across all parts of Great Britain, any chance of Red Kites naturally colonising Ireland from wild populations elsewhere has been nullified. In the natural way of things, wandering immatures generally provide a pioneering vanguard when a species attempts to expand its range. In the past, individuals of this age class periodically reached all parts of Ireland, for example from Germany, right up to the time when reintroductions commenced in Great Britain. Since 2008 the provenance of any Red Kite in Irish skies is forever tainted.

MARSH HARRIER
Circus aeruginosus

Skimming light as a paper dart, then interspersing floppy wingbeats to maintain momentum, a lone hunter stares fixedly for prey among an immensity of reeds.

ALTHOUGH IT IS UNWISE to use habitat choice as a golden rule in bird identification, a harrier seen wavering back and forth over reed bed will, most likely, be this species. Marsh Harriers do not so much hover as dangle in the air like a suspended puppet. They follow a low flight path and, powered by a few steady flaps, drift effortlessly with wings set in a V, looking ever downward in the hope of stumbling across an unsuspecting Moorhen, Common Snipe, duckling, frog or rodent. Reed beds are an ideal hunting ground and the bird's silhouette is the epitome of a quartering predator. In fact, since almost all the Marsh Harriers that reach us are immature, the birds' plumage is truly dark, irrespective of the light. Adult females show some relief, dint of a buff crown and throat. The same colour marks the leading edge of the inner wing, creating a passing resemblance to landing lights. Former haunts in Great Britain have been recolonised and a pair bred successfully in Northern Ireland in 2009. A sign of things to come?

Thompson (1849–52) wrote: 'Found in suitable localities over Ireland, and is resident.' He then went on to catalogue slaughter. 'Many years ago, a friend saw two of their nests on the ground in Island Mahee and Island Reagh, Strangford Lough, and shot the females rising from them.' The bird became extinct in the late nineteenth century. Gamekeepers were ruthless; and to boot, wetlands were drained. Like Bittern, Marsh Harrier's needs are habitat-specific. Reed beds and swamp intermixed with fen are its bailiwick. Such habitat was commonplace across lowland; raised bogs also provided succour. Decades of destruction began in the nineteenth century. The Bog Commission maps of 1810–14 charted many intact wetlands. The same documents, and the first maps produced by an Irish Ordnance Survey, now stand as a Doomsday Book of paradise lost.

D'Arcy (1995) narrates a grim tale:

The reclamation brought in train by the Commissioners of Public Works was such that over 100,000 hectares of wetland was drained or alleviated from prolonged flooding under the 1842 Act. The works continued for years and under the 1863 revision were continued for a further period. The effect on wetland-dependent birds must have been devastating. The disturbance caused by large gangs of men (hundreds together; tens of thousands in all throughout the duration of the works) would of itself have been significant. The fact that the drainage was carried out mainly during the summer (when the water table was at its lowest) must also have put intolerable pressure on birds like breeding harriers. The further episode of wetland drainage under the 1945 Arterial Drainage Act not only eliminated many tracts of reed swamp that survived the nineteenth century drainage, but reduced to insignificant fragments many wetlands that had remained (or regrown) to a size that would have been immediately attractive to harriers.

Thompson (1849–52) mentions a young Marsh Harrier kept in captivity that lost a leg and was fitted with a wooden replacement. The success of this prosthetic limb was remarkable: 'The dexterity it acquired with this stump, both in walking and killing rats, was astonishing. When a rat was turned out, the bird pounced at it, and never failed to pin the animal's head to the ground with the stump, while a few grasps of the sound limb soon terminated the struggle.'

HEN HARRIER
Circus cyaneus

MOST PEOPLE are familiar with the unique flight capabilities of harriers through their titular connection with a fighter plane. The real McCoy is an agile hunter of bogland, heather moor and newly afforested areas, gliding with wings raised above the line of the body, head crooked and eyes locked downwards, quartering the ground and holding to an invisible line from which it periodically re-casts over an adjoining strip. As well as breeding in small numbers in Ulster, Connacht and northern districts of Leinster and Munster, Hen Harriers are scarce winter visitors from as far away as Orkney. Females and youngsters are basically brown, save for a characteristic white rump, coining the epithet 'ring-tail'. Adult males are stunning, so pale and graceful on the wing that they can be taken for a passing gull.

In Ireland, Hen Harriers hunt mainly Meadow Pipits, Skylarks and Starlings (Scott 2010). Young Rabbits and Irish Hares, as well as Wood Mice and Pygmy Shrews, make up around one tenth of captured prey. Young of upland-breeding Curlew and Common Snipe are occasionally taken. Chicks of Red Grouse formed less than 1 per cent of quarry in a study of 600 pellets gathered from nest sites in the Antrim Plateau and Sperrin Mountains between 1991 and 2009 (Scott 2008b, 2010). In England, Scotland and Wales, Short-tailed Voles are an essential part of the diet during the breeding season. In the Isle of Man, where voles are absent, prey parallels that taken in Ireland, yet the species fares better, thanks to favourable habitat and a lack of Red Foxes.

Before being afforded protected status, Hen Harriers were shot for no other reason than they presented a target. Thompson (1849–52) was no different from these gunmen: 'The first that came under my notice appeared when a friend and I were in search of snipes, in a boggy spot among the Belfast mountains, when a female bird hovered above us in the manner of a Kestrel, and was not alarmed by our presence – her life fell sacrifice to my gun.' Persecution led to the breeding population going up in gun smoke and Deane (1954) reclassified the bird as a vagrant. Aside from direct slaughter and nest disturbance, a litany of changes – turf cutting, moorland drainage and ploughing, over-grazing, burning heather and so on – destroyed or degraded traditional haunts.

The bird was dealt an ace when widespread planting of conifers began in the late 1950s. Below a carpet of Sitka Spruce saplings, rank grass teemed with rodents and nesting Meadow Pipits. Prey in abundance and ideal nesting conditions too – the new forests were quiet and undisturbed. Although a temporary phase in the operation of a commercial forest – the tree canopy closes around fifteen years – the hope was that clear-felled areas might be reoccupied once the planting cycle resumed. That time has come. Regrettably, and for reasons that are not apparent, this has not happened.

A surprise was that some Hen Harriers constructed nests in trees. Don Scott made this startling discovery in July 1991 (Scott *et al.* 1991). The first structure was built on the deformed trunk of a Sitka Spruce and was nearly 5m off the ground. This was exciting. If the habit caught on, might tree nests protect eggs and chicks from predation by foxes? Data from the Isle of Skye put losses of clutches to foxes at 67 per cent. Being novel, the practice often led to failure when young fell into the impenetrable understorey. In a Herculean effort, more than twenty chicks were rescued, some being reared in captivity before being fostered to wild parents.

Since 2008, no Hen Harriers have nested in trees. Other threats have emerged to blight productivity and threaten survival, particularly in Antrim. Here, during the period 1980–2010, numbers have crashed from twenty pairs to seven, of which only three bred successfully in 2010. During this era, car rallies in forests and the inappropriate scheduling of operations led to nest desertions. In line with the implementation of EU Specially Protected Area designations, car rallies have since been banned during the nesting season (April to July). Wind farms are among a suite of new menaces. Companies have shown a cavalier attitude towards the hazard that turbine blades pose, and employees have been discovered removing mutilated corpses of Hooded Crows and Ravens from beneath them. An adult male Hen Harrier (with one wing severed) was found dead under a rotor in January 2007 (Scott 2008a). Breeding pairs around Slieveanorra, Antrim, have been displaced by the erection of wind farms. Despite alarm being communicated to the Royal Society for the Protection of Birds (RSPB) and the Northern Ireland Environment Agency, pleas were ignored and permission was granted for additional wind turbines. This approval was granted in the face of incontrovertible evidence demonstrating that local weather conditions regularly produce rain, drizzle and fog, obscuring rotating blades from flying birds. Devastated and rightly enraged, Scott's only outlet was to document the turn of events in *Irish Birds* (Scott 2008a) and to publish a letter in *Birdwatch* (October 2010): 'The Hen Harrier [killed by the wind turbine rotors] was reported to RSPB and other conservation bodies. Sadly, reports were not acted upon and consent was given a short time later for an enormous extension to the existing wind farm site. 'A recent spread by Buzzards and Goshawks into 'harrier country' is not without worry. Both are aggressive and have harassed and killed at least one Hen Harrier in Antrim (Scott 2010).

Over the course of more than a quarter of a century of almost weekly visits throughout the Antrim Plateau, Don Scott has amassed a store of knowledge and published his results regularly. Much of the content of his book *The Hen Harrier* (2010), a compendium that takes a strategic view, is a tale of woe. The raptor has become a golden goose for bird surveyors dragooned into the field by wind farm companies, the RSPB, the Northern Ireland Environment Agency, and a gaggle of environmental consultancy firms; and the unholy rush to gather data has produced reports whose recommendations masquerade as holy writ when dubious conclusions suit commissioning paymasters. The book contains a blow-by-blow exposé of the skulduggery, fleshed out in reportage reminiscent of Woodward and Bernstein's *All the President's Men*.

The sexes are strikingly different. The male's light plumage suggests an adult Herring or Common Gull. Gliding flight slows to a stall when prey is spotted. A successful hunter wobbles, tumbles and pounces to snatch quarry from the ground.

COMMON BUZZARD
Buteo buteo

Buzzards are similar in structure to a miniature eagle. Ample wings with fingered tips reduce drag, confer stability and create an impression of idle power. Typical prey is rabbits and rodents, although frogs and the chicks of ground-nesting birds are seized if spotted from the bird's aerial view or from a strategically occupied perch.

BUZZARDS ARE UNUSUAL among latter-day Irish birds of prey: they are increasing. Once they were found throughout the land. In Antrim, they nested along basalt cliffs. In Down, crowns of tall trees in wooded demesnes were preferred. The raptor was heavily persecuted by farmers and gamekeepers and became extinct at the end of the nineteenth century. In the 1950s Scots immigrants clawed back former range by establishing a bridgehead centred on Fair Head and Rathlin Island. Nowadays they are countrywide; only western parts of Munster and Connacht remain unoccupied.

The airborne silhouette is impressive, so much so that an aquiline build and slow gliding can, to the uninitiated, suggest the majesty of an eagle. However, proportions are dumpy and, irrespective of overall shade, all possess a telltale light cummerbund, never shown by Golden or White-tailed Eagle. Sleuths watch for rodents from a lofty perch such as a treetop or telegraph pole, and hover clumsily and ball up in flight before plummeting to the ground after rabbits. Voice is another giveaway, often mimicked by Starlings. Calling is frequent, especially in spring. On warm sunny days it is not unusual to hear mewing coming from the sky. The combination of warm sun on the back and rising pockets of air – thermals – means that several can effortlessly circle and climb so high that they are lost to sight.

SPARROWHAWK
Accipiter nisus

Pandemonium signals the appearance of a Sparrowhawk in a garden. Surprise is everything and gives an airborne hunter sufficient speed to overhaul prey that leaps from a standing start. Chases are hectic but short-lived. Plucking posts are used regularly; stray feathers identify victims.

Inset: Juvenile female carrying Blackbird. Fresh rufous fringes are a clue to age. Long bare shins, gangly toes and razor-sharp talons reach and snatch. As long as the target is hit, the hawk can bind and carry it off.

(Left): Most Sparrowhawks die from collisions sustained while hunting; (right): before delivering a *coup de grâce*, victims are sometimes mantled. Males are blue-grey above with barred underparts on an orange background.

BOOKS HAVE BEEN WRITTEN about this *enfant terrible* and nemesis of songbirds. Mad eyes etch ferocity into the face and the birds' boldness in pursuit of prey as large as themselves is legendary. Swallows and Hooded Crows have specific alarm calls that mean one thing: 'Sparrowhawk!' The executioner has long bare legs designed to snatch. Once gripped, hapless victims cannot escape talons that lock automatically. Kills are made at high speed. Short, rounded wings with deeply slotted primaries provide turbo-charged bursts; the long tail acts as a rudder. Swoops are made with the wings tucked in, the assassin hurtling past like a bobsleigh careering around a bend, red mist down and zeal unshakeable. Windowpanes may be struck, resulting in death. Almost two thirds of corpses examined at the Institute for Terrestrial Ecology in Cambridgeshire died from collisions with glass. In the thick of action fear of people is suspended and tales of psychos flying through open windows into rooms after cage birds are not uncommon. House Sparrows taking crumbs under al fresco café tables on Cape Clear Island, Cork, were singled out for attack – between the legs of both tables and diners (AMG). In these changing times, wind farms pose an insidious threat to displaying Sparrowhawks. At one site in Tipperary, two soaring birds were struck and killed by rotors within the space of three days in April 2010 (Cullen & Williams 2010). Weather conditions were excellent, prompting display. Worryingly, additional Sparrowhawks later used the same airspace, a wooded hillside topped by turbines. Their fate – or good fortune – remained unknown.

Males are colourful and sport blue-grey upperparts and bright brick-red underparts. Young birds resemble females but have bright coppery edges to the large feathers of the back and wings. At rest, all ages exhibit a small quantity of whitish blotches on the scapulars, suggesting that the bird has either lost feathers or been sprinkled with flour. Sparrowhawks never hover. Except when they cleave the air and metamorphose into streamlined phantoms, flight is unimpressive – drifting nonchalantly over trees or pursued by small fry and crows engaged in naming and shaming the killer. Do not be fooled. Once a target is selected Mr Hyde will be back in a flash. Females are almost twice the weight of males: sexes avoid direct competition since she can tackle larger prey, up to a half-kilo Woodpigeon. Newton (1986) judged that a pair could account for 55kg of meat a year, equivalent to about 2,200 House Sparrows or 600 Blackbirds. Eye colour varies between the sexes and darkens with age. Youngsters are yellow-eyed. Adult females are orange-eyed, mature males red-eyed. Iris colour may be a factor in mate selection, since older (darker-eyed) birds are more experienced hunters and therefore likely to be better partners (Newton & Marquiss 1982).

It is claimed that Sparrowhawk populations are regulated by the quantity of songbird prey available to them, which they do not diminish because they take a 'doomed surplus' that, somehow, would have died anyway. It is unquestionable that their numbers are in part regulated by prey abundance and it is also unquestionable that they will have an impact on prey populations. This can be maddening. One of possibly the only breeding pair of Wood Warblers in Northern Ireland was snatched when feeding young. This led to nest desertion. Sharrock (1976) cites songbird populations whose increase appeared to be due to a decrease in Sparrowhawk numbers: 'Since 1955, there have been reports of increasing numbers [of Bullfinches] and colonisation of more open habitats. This has been attributed to the decline of Sparrowhawks, which was brought about by toxic chemicals. Bullfinches are relatively bold birds, which feed away from thick cover, and it is presumed that their survival is improved by the decrease of their chief predator.' However, bring back the hunter and it will drive down the population of naive quarry until equilibrium is reached. Because Ireland has lost its native broadleaved forest and indigenous Goshawks, the 'mesopredator' (Sparrowhawk) has no enemy and has enjoyed a boom, albeit mitigated by human activities such as persecution. Goshawks, the top dog, formerly regulated Sparrowhawk numbers and much else too.

From the mid-1950s, the accumulation of pesticides had a calamitous effect on birds of prey. The value of a motivated observer becoming aware of the insidious nature of the crisis helped to bring damning evidence to light, thereby hastening legislation that tackled the problem. The observer was Arnold Benington and his role is documented in personal diaries, from which the following is an extract:

In the early 1920s near Moira, Armagh, I used to be able to go out early in the morning on my bicycle and visit two or three Sparrowhawk nests before breakfast. In half a day, in May or June, using the same transport, I could usually visit as many as six nests before dark. At that time inside a measured seven square miles of country around my home, there nested regularly eight pairs of Sparrowhawks, five pairs of Kestrels [and the same quantity of breeding Barn Owls and Long-eared Owls]. Since those days, however, a sad change has come over the numbers of birds of prey. Sparrowhawks have undoubtedly suffered most. From being a common species, quite suddenly they began to disappear. Territory after territory that I had known to be occupied consecutively for thirty years or more, now fell empty; and during my country walks, instead of seeing a hunting hawk every few days, I no longer saw one even every two or three months. I set out in 1959 to examine as many of the old-established territories as possible. I tackled the problem by taking a study area of some fourteen miles diameter, or approximately 160 square miles. My local district contained sparse woodland, some arable, good grazing, the town of Lisburn (population 18,000), several villages, and a fair amount of fenland along the adjacent shore of Lough Neagh. In this area twenty-two pairs of Sparrowhawks nested regularly. In the period 1956 to 1966, the population shrank by 73 per cent to six pairs. I examined all the nests regularly and noted a serious drop in fertility. That this state of affairs is largely due to organo-chlorides absorbed into the birds' tissues from horticultural and agricultural pesticides is borne out by analyses of infertile eggs that Ian Prestt kindly agreed to investigate at Monks Wood Experimental Station in Huntingdon. Most eggs contained four of the following persistent residues: dieldrin, DDT, TDE, heptachlore-poxide and DDE; with the last named always in greatest quantity. (Benington 2009)

Do Sparrowhawks migrate? Because adults jealously guard territory it is axiomatic that juveniles must find their feet elsewhere. Dispersal at the end of the breeding season is a fact of life and unsuccessful hunters quickly perish, either through a failure to catch prey or collisions borne of inexperience. Analysis of data from the Calf of Man Bird Observatory (McCanch 1997) provides evidence of dispersal by juvenile Scandinavian Sparrowhawks. From mid-October to November, movements chimed with large-scale Chaffinch emigration from southern Norway. Migrants reach the Calf of Man around ten days after leaving Scandinavia.

GOSHAWK
Accipiter gentilis

Juvenile plumage is spotted below and, overall, quite unlike that of an adult. This wild bird has killed a Herring Gull.

GOSHAWKS WERE DENIZENS of Irish forest for as long as the habitat existed. Fossil evidence is truly ancient and comes from far and wide. Remains from Mount Sandel, near Coleraine, date from 7000 BC. Some were kept as pets, but their chief use was for hunting. 'Hawking' was practised since prehistoric times and information concerning the whereabouts of eyries was prized. An export black market existed. 'As early as 1218 a Reginald Talbot was seized in Dalkey, Dublin, for illegally delivering a Goshawk to [an English buyer] and was heavily fined. In Richard II's reign a proclamation at Drogheda against exporting birds of prey was necessary to reduce the activity and searches were carried out at ports in Henry IV's reign (1400)' (D'Arcy 1999). One reason for attempting to stamp out illicit trade was to ensure exclusivity. Due to their value, especially to landowners among whose woods they bred, captives could be paid as rent to feudal overlords. By the sixteenth century, Goshawks were one of the most desirable presents to be sent from Ireland, and there is in existence a sixteenth-century inventory for eyries in Kerry and Limerick. (See further discussion in 'The Razing of the Greenwood', p. 2.)

During Tudor times the pendulum swung. Forest clearances exterminated the remaining 'big game' of Ireland – Wolves, Capercaillies and Goshawks. From the seventeenth century the species was no longer exacted as rent, so eyries were not protected. To boot, gamekeepers employed on newly created demesnes were instructed to protect game birds, especially introduced Pheasants, and eradicate raptors by shooting and trapping. Eradication of bird and habitat was complete by the end of the eighteenth century. Thompson (1849–52) stated: 'Cannot be included in [contemporary] Irish fauna with certainty. Bird preservers have told me of Goshawks, killed in Ireland, having been sent to them to be set up, but the species has neither been seen by myself, nor by any of my correspondents throughout the island.' Across the water, the sorry tale was repeated, but with one important difference: persecution affected the bird, less so its habitat.

Goshawks are widespread across Europe's forests and northern populations are partially migratory. Probably seeded by a combination of wandering immigrants and escaped – or deliberately released – falconers' birds, Goshawks have gradually re-established themselves in Britain. With a feeder population yielding progeny from Britain and possibly Norway, some have returned to Ireland. The newcomers' wild credentials are, unfortunately, tainted. Did they really reach here as part of natural recolonisation, or are most, if not all, a result of falconry birds gone bush? It is known that some were deliberately turned loose in Connemara (AOD). In Northern Ireland, at least three seen in the wild were reputed to have 'escaped' from captivity (JSF). Moreover, in a repugnant trade located near Dublin (www.falcoireland.com), captive Goshawks and other birds of prey are bred for export, mainly to Arab nations. Not only is this a likely source of escapees, but accursed interbreeding of Goshawk subspecies also occurs, contaminating Mother Nature's supreme handiwork.

Despite their size – females are roughly the size of Buzzard – Goshawks are secretive. Hunters watch for long periods from a hidden perch or take to the sky and circle aloft, scanning unseen for quarry. Observers who monitor active eyries in the Netherlands and in North America seldom see hunting activity. Woodpigeon dominates diet in Ireland, but fearsome hunters have been known to kill Sparrowhawks, Kestrels and Long-eared Owls.

Fleeting views have challenged identification skills for centuries. Matters are not helped by a widespread belief that recognition rests on the tenet that 'Goshawk superficially resembles a giant Sparrowhawk.' One way to debunk this fallacy is to go back to first principles and analyse Sparrowhawk shape. Airborne, Sparrowhawk is T-shaped. The wings are short, the tail is long and square-cornered and the head is short and neckless. Travelling flight is fussy and fairly unimpressive – 'anxious' wingbeats are followed by a diffident glide – and the bird seems to be stuck in a low gear. Goshawk flight is fluid and exudes idle power. Wingbeats are slow, steady and lofty on the upstroke; glides are direct; the hunter cruises in autopilot. The bird is a super-heavyweight. Females are up to six times heavier than female Sparrowhawk (Cramp et al. 1977–94) with bone-cruncher short legs three times as thick as gangly Sparrowhawk shins. If dragged along by large prey, such as a fox cub or hare, Goshawks use the free foot as a powerful brake by clutching the ground. Hefty hips look well padded and chest shape suggests a bulletproof vest. The tail looks less like a Sparrowhawk rudder and more like falcon undercarriage. The tip is blunt and somewhat rounded. Wing profile says Peregrine more than Sparrowhawk; the arm is broad and 'triangulates' to the hand. Especially, the trailing edge bulges. In tandem with the proportions of head and tail, the silhouette is cruciform rather than T-shaped. Juveniles, until they develop adult musculature, are more lightly built and look vaguely 'stretched'.

KESTREL
Falco tinnunculus

Most hunting is conducted from a stationary, aerial position during which the head is rock steady. Perhaps surprisingly, a headwind makes hovering easier. In calm weather, Kestrels frequently hunt from perches.

ALL IT TAKES is a split-second glance from a moving vehicle to identify a Kestrel. No other bird has such complete mastery of hovering, effectively parking in mid-air. The head is stationary, rebuffing even a stiff headwind. In light airs, gimlet-eyed gazers perch and peer fixedly at still vegetation, panning for a movement that means pay dirt. Males have a plain blue-grey tail with a broad inky tip. The head is grey and forms a strong contrast against russet upperparts. In Mediterranean countries perched birds can be almost invisible against terracotta rooftops. Females and youngsters are a chequerboard of blackish crossbars and speckles. Older females are grey-tailed (and even grey-headed). Adults of both sexes have black spotting on the flanks. Youngsters are more heavily streaked below, particularly on the chest; many have sandy-brown edges to the upperparts and wingtip outline. In flight, the bird can look 'floury'. Given a close view or a sharp photograph, check the primary coverts. On juveniles these feathers are unworn and show bright fringes.

Nest sites need to accommodate up to six offspring. A tree hollow, cliff cavity, inaccessible ledge or disused crow's nest provide sufficient floor space. On breeding territory much aerial play-acting takes place. Calls are frequent, a piercing repetition of *kee-kee-kee*. Sentinels hover at dawn and dusk, times when light levels ought to impair vision. This anomaly was noted long ago. 'I have remarked the Kestrel abroad at a very early hour in the winter morning ... observed one on the morning of 11 November examining a stubble field before seven o'clock, when there seemed little enough of light for an owl to plunder by' (Thompson 1849–52). We now know that Kestrel eyesight registers ultraviolet. Rodents leave faeces and urine trails that 'glow', and the Kestrel positions itself over hotspots, hoping that furred prey will come along any minute. This explains why aerial hunters do not comb ground systematically.

For reasons that are not fully understood, Kestrels seem to be quietly disappearing throughout Ireland. The decline has been catastrophic across lowland areas; marginal land across foothills and areas where young forestry plantations abut upland still

Dawn and dusk are good times to hunt rodents. Quarry is active and, amazingly, Kestrels track prey in ultraviolet vision.

retain nesting pairs. Interestingly, the ongoing northwards expansion across Munster and parts of Leinster of inadvertently introduced Bank Voles and Greater White-toothed Shrews may be providing bonus prey. In Britain, statistics compiled by the BTO show a gradual decrease from 1995 to 2008. One measure of change was the displacement of Kestrels by Buzzards as the commonest bird of prey hovering alongside roads. It has not been established whether this switch has arisen as a result of competition. In 2008 and 2009, BTO data charted a dramatic dip of 36 per cent. Although RSPB press releases were quick to blame intensive farming, this did not tally with the sudden drop. Factors peculiar to Britain, notably severe winter weather, may have been behind the fall. Kestrels are known to struggle to find food when the ground is snow-covered.

Here, a cocktail of factors may be at work. The growing and ubiquitous use of 'chuck-and-forget' sachets containing poison for rodents could be the main culprit. Research in England (Shore *et al.* 2001) showed that a worrying 70 per cent of dead Kestrels contained rodenticide residues. While many had residue levels that were sub-lethal, others had died by the anticoagulant effects of rodenticide poisons. It is probable that chicks featured among unseen casualties. The bird's plight has been exacerbated by the elimination of overgrown field margins and the butchering of hedgerows, reduced to stunted lifeless strips with no skirt of sheltering ground vegetation for mice, shrews and large insects such as grasshoppers. A chillingly familiar scenario has been observed during the course of ongoing Barn Owl surveys in Cork: 'It is obvious that parts of the Cork countryside are heading towards the same habitat problems as parts of Northern Ireland – lots of hedgerows gone, therefore giant fields. Neatly trimmed hedges and just posts and wire instead of a hedgerow subdividing huge wildlife-free tracts of grassland. And, sure enough, now very few Kestrels' (MOC).

Ironically, good habitat is sometimes created accidentally when industrial estates and retail parks spring up on suburban hinterlands, often near a nexus of roads and roundabouts. Rough grassland, harbouring small rodents, abounds. Then, as soon as the first employees arrive, pest control firms are hired to eradicate 'vermin'. Almost invariably, this results from scaremongering fuelled by the over-weaning Health and Safety Order, coupled with business clients who are brainwashed by clichés such as 'you are never more than two metres from a rat.' In no time a rash of ground-level baited traps appear and the local rodent population, which will repopulate itself regardless of periodic poisoning and become progressively immune to pesticides, becomes a silent killer of Kestrels and owls that consume dying animals. Such decimation occurred at Belfast Harbour Estate where, in the course of a wave of new office developments in 2002–2005, Kestrels, Barn Owls and Long-eared Owls vanished (AMG). The use of slug-killer compounds, broadcast on a wide scale by arable farmers, is another potentially insidious agent of death. Populations of grassland beetles and grasshoppers have plummeted, probably as a by-catch of slug-killer compounds (DB). Large insects are especially important in the diet of juveniles, but these may become a poisoned chalice through the effect of secondary poisoning accumulated in the bird's tissues by eating those that survive the chemical warfare conducted in the name of improved crop yields.

In the Netherlands, farmers welcome Kestrels as a natural means of rodent control. In 1998–99, a study of breeding success found that, of 917 monitored nests, 93 per cent were in nestboxes. This is a staggering statistic. Furthermore, 'chuck-and-forget' poisons are illegal. Although this does not guarantee that poisons will not be used illicitly, the sale of aggressive poisons is banned. Dutch farmers had got into the habit of putting a sachet of rodenticide under a roof tile along field edges. This has also been outlawed, and in 2010 the population stood at 7,000 pairs.

Fairley and McLean (1964) studied the summer food of Northern Ireland Kestrels by collecting 420 pellet remains from seven nests. Six were located in coniferous trees; the other was in a cavity in an ivy-covered Ash. By far the most important prey was Field Mouse. House Mouse, Pygmy Shrew, Brown Rat and Rabbit were included among quarry, as were juvenile Starlings – thirty-five wings beneath one nest site were itemised and twenty-five below another. The only other bird remains were one apiece of Blue Tit and Yellowhammer. Large insects were found in 71 per cent of pellets, although catching beetles would have been a thankless task when several mouths needed to be fed, and rodents were undoubtedly preferred, augmented by juvenile Starlings.

The absence of voles from our mammal fauna must contribute to the lower density of Kestrels compared to Great Britain and Europe, where voles often form a major component in the diet. Studies in England (Village 1982) have shown that more shrews are taken in years when vole numbers are low, but that lighter pellet weights result – which means that total food intake is reduced. While pellets facilitate a means of checking diet, some food items may be almost impossible to identify. Yalden and Warburton (1979) pieced together data on minutiae in pellet remains:

The most important surprising feature is the importance of invertebrate prey [which is unwittingly underestimated when pellets are analysed]. The chances of overlooking any vertebrate prey are negligible; both matrix and the various skeletal elements are, by comparison with invertebrate remains, extremely conspicuous. By contrast, the chances of overlooking a few caterpillar or grasshopper mandibles, or losing a few insect legs, are high. There is also the probability that some soft-bodied prey is missed completely [moth remains were verified through microscopic analysis of wing scales] and the likelihood of craneflies being taken is also high. Davis (1960) reported that 60 per cent of his March pellets contained sand, which was surely derived from earthworms, and mentioned one pellet entirely of fibre, which was probably derived from caterpillars. Therefore, invertebrates are numerically important and seem to represent 27 per cent of the weight of the diet. They represent an important alternative food source, particularly during the non-breeding season and especially at times when vertebrates are scarce or hard to find.

A study of hunting behaviour conducted over three years in an area of mixed farmland in Sussex (Shrubb 1982) revealed useful information. A seasonal pattern was noted in search methods, with most still-hunting (scanning for prey from a perch) in winter and hovering in summer. The timing of hunting sequences suggested that up to two hours were needed to catch the food requirement of about 40g, with a success rate of 50 per cent against mammal prey and 31 per cent for birds. Males took more insects and smaller birds than females, which preferred mammals. Youngsters killed beetles for themselves ten days after leaving the nest. At sixteen days, spells of continuous still-hunting lasting up to three hours were recorded, during which an insect was taken at an average of three-minute intervals. Hovering skills took a month to acquire; only then did the first youngster catch food by this method.

Kestrels are unable to catch prey under thick snow and are not adept bird-hunters, so they cannot switch prey during severe weather. It is likely that big freezes during recent winters inflicted heavy casualties. Across mainland Europe the northern limit of wintering distribution roughly follows the line of permanent snow cover. Indeed, northern birds are migratory, whereas those breeding further south are partial migrants and southern populations are sedentary (Coiffait et al. 2006). Kestrels from migratory populations winter in lowland Europe, with some reaching North Africa, including four BTO-ringed birds recovered in Morocco. Fifteen British-ringed birds have reached Belgium and four Norwegian Kestrels, all ringed in summer, have arrived in Britain, three of them in October. Singletons, assumed to be migrants, have been noted arriving along the Down coast in autumn (AMG).

MERLIN
Falco columbarius

Female Merlin. Small, compact and deadly, Merlins harry small birds in open spaces. Many are migratory and retreat to coastal lowlands or overseas to accompany prey. Nesting periods of hunter and hunted coincide, so that youngsters can learn to catch rookie passerines before they have mastered evasion techniques.

MERLINS ARE THE TITCH AMONG FALCONS. They are the most dogged and acrobatic of all birds of prey and specialise in low, fast pursuit. Prey is startled as if by a bolt out of the blue. Flight rhythm is snappy, 'changing gear' and undulating in shallow arcs, like a Mistle Thrush. It has been suggested that this superficial likeness could be a deliberate Trojan horse deception. In the Netherlands, migrants have been detected flying incognito among thrush flocks.

Merlins frequent moors and uplands during summer and shift to low ground – principally the coast – at the end of the breeding season. Meadow Pipits, Wheatears and Skylarks are top targets through the breeding season, with smaller shorebirds featuring during the winter months. Migrants travelling back and forth to destinations in the Arctic augment sightings. A 'Taiga Merlin' from Canada was discovered at Cape Clear Island, Cork, in autumn (Garner 2002); a youngster ringed near Reykjavik on 12 August 1992 was picked up dead at Annalong, Down, three months later; and a female ringed in Waterford on 3 March 1990 rested aboard a ship in the Denmark Strait on its way back to Greenland two years later.

Small numbers breed, invariably in upland wilderness areas.

Compared with the rest of Europe, Irish and British Merlins are unusual in nesting relatively frequently on the ground, mainly in deep heather or among bracken. Overgrazing by sheep has damaged or destroyed huge tracts of moorland, the bird's home. At the same time, crows and foxes have proliferated. All ground-nesting birds, Merlins included, suffer at the hands of these predators, which operate from sanctuaries among forestry plantations. On the other hand, could the small bird communities associated with conifers, such as Coal Tits, Siskins and Goldcrests, offer a new source of prey and supplement Merlins' diet? Such questions were answered in a study carried out in an extensive area in Galloway, southwest Scotland (Watson 1979). The aim of the research was to investigate the possibility that Merlins nesting in young plantations that replaced open moorland had undergone a change in quarry selection. Prey analysis showed that this was not the case, and suggests that most hunting is still undertaken in open country habitats, even though these were as far as 4km from the breeding site. It was concluded that, where afforestation is particularly extensive and increasing, populations of Merlins will inevitably decline, and in some cases disappear altogether.

PEREGRINE
Falco peregrinus

PEREGRINE FALCON is the fastest bird on Earth: a true dynast. Supreme speed comes through rising high above prey and stooping. The wings are tucked against the body and the bird reaches in excess of 200km/h before striking with its feet. Strong talons prevent escape by piercing flesh. Most powerful is the hefty rear talon that can exert a force capable of slicing deep into a human wrist; hence the need for falconers to wear thick gloves. Not only does it achieve breathtaking speeds, it is also able to withstand the G-force that comes with pulling out of a stoop. Fighter pilots would black out if faced with the sudden change in direction after a near vertical descent. After the initial impact, the assassin attempts to bind and bite through its victim's spinal cord to extinguish life before plucking. The *coup de grâce* is assisted by an indented edge along the side of the upper mandible – the tomial tooth. The energy demands of active hunting mean that much time is spent resting between sorties. Most hunts are unsuccessful: quarry can escape if it flies higher than its pursuer, thwarting the added acceleration of the hunter's stoop; and another tactic is to land on water, from where Peregrines are extremely reluctant to snatch prey.

Choice of hunting domain is wide. Canadian Peregrines head south for winter and some migrate at sea, coming aboard ships and using them as a base from which to hunt passing migrants. In England, urban sleuths assail prey at night, picking out targets silhouetted in flight against bright city lights (AL). Except on moonless, pitch-dark nights, nocturnal hunting is commonplace at Manx Shearwater colonies on islands west of Galway: one clifftop plucking perch contained the remains of fourteen shearwaters. In autumn, seabirds migrating several kilometres offshore are not safe. Gales are no deterrent. Leach's Petrel, a bird that appears inshore only during inclement weather, is proof that Peregrines are not fazed by heavy seas: thirty-two plucked corpses were amassed at Ramore Head and The Skerries, Antrim, during September 1987. In England's Peak District, breeding birds have killed Merlins and Ring Ouzels; a sign that too many Peregrines are a mixed blessing.

Rudimentary nests – little more than a scrape – are located on inaccessible ledges, sometimes in working quarries or on high buildings. The granite form of an off-duty male occupies a prominent perch while the female incubates a clutch or swaddles downy chicks. Approaching humans are spotted a long way off. If the male becomes edgy he slips away quietly and takes to the sky for a lofty look while the female sits tight. If a tipping point is reached, one or both birds start to alarm. Slow at first, the sound builds distress. An initial low sighing *gaaah* rises in pitch and becomes a wailing cadence – *gak, gak, gak*. The intensity of the racket matches the unease. If both call, the male's voice is the higher-pitched. The whine is deeply unsettling and designed to do one thing: make you back away, which indeed you must. Peregrines are nervous birds and prone to desert if tormented.

Established pairs reoccupy sites well before breeding and sometimes 'rotate' a choice of eyries, switching the site in some years. The larger-bodied female stops hunting early, even before laying, and stays near the breeding ledge. After fledging, young birds remain on natal territory for a few weeks, where parents feed them until their hunting skills develop. Adults are grey above with black crowns and dark, bandit moustaches set against white chests and barred grey bodies. Young birds are brown above with streaked underparts and a 'baby' moustache lacking gravitas. Outside the breeding season Peregrines range widely and some of the year's new generation cross the Irish Sea to Wales, southwest England, France and Iberia. A juvenile ringed in Antrim in July was recovered three months later in Portugal. Immigration also occurs. A 1988 youngster from Sweden was picked up injured in Tipperary in the autumn of 1989. Moreover, nestlings from southwest Scotland cross the Irish Sea.

One bird stands its ground when confronted by a Peregrine – Raven. Both vie for the ultimate nest ledge, each regarding itself as head honcho. Armstrong (1944) provides accounts of disputes on Rathlin Island:

> In May 1867 a collector robbed a Peregrine eyrie on a cliff. Not far distant was a Raven's nest. When the Peregrine returned to find her nest empty she acted as if the Ravens, with which she had hitherto been on good terms, had plundered it. Stooping furiously at the sitting bird she killed her and tore the nest to pieces. The cock Raven fought fiercely but eventually he, too, was overcome. The falcons forsook the place and never returned. More recently a desperate fight was observed between a Peregrine and a Raven. Stoop after stoop was foiled by clever manoeuvring on the part of the Raven, until, as the falcon sought to strike, the Raven swerved and managed at the same time to stab the falcon's wing. She fell to earth, sorely wounded.

Pesticides accumulated by Peregrines through eating contaminated victims that contain small, non-lethal doses have a disastrous effect on breeding success. The chemicals (organochlorine pesticides) affect the ability of adult females to produce eggs of normal thickness, and parents inadvertently crush their own clutches. Especially during the 1960s, breeding numbers crashed. Worried researchers succeeded in isolating the offending agricultural products – basically, seed-dressings – and the bird's fortunes recovered. Demonstrating that birds know the meaning of the phrase 'Never look a gift horse in the mouth', easy pickings presented by large numbers of urban-dwelling Feral Pigeons entice Peregrines to follow prey into built-up areas and even to nest there. Less welcome news for racing pigeon enthusiasts has been the fact that their prize possessions also taste good and can be zapped while en route. Some racing pigeons,

bred from renowned bloodlines, fetch several thousand pounds and as much as £14,000 has changed hands. Enthusiasts are convinced that the best birds, because they strike out from released flocks and into the lead, are the most vulnerable. Some fanciers confront the 'hawk problem' head on. Eyries have been attacked and eggs, young and adults destroyed. There is no doubt that Peregrines take pigeons and claims by individual fanciers of up to fifty birds being lost in a season are probably not exaggerated. Large female Sparrowhawks have also learned to hang around the vicinity of lofts and pick off returning birds. On the other hand, races are conducted to weed out the best, and inferior birds are deemed expendable. They become easy prey through taking time-outs over terrain that is unfamiliar to them. Undoubtedly, the keeping and racing of pigeons involves effort and money. Most fanciers accept a degree of risk in releasing birds into a wild environment.

Adult pair and juvenile. Youngsters are streaked brown and spend long periods exercising. The wings are flapped regularly before short practice flights commence. Peregrines are not born with gym bodies and need to develop powerful muscles to fly fast. Unsuccessful hunters die of starvation. Image is a Photoshop montage of a fictitious eyrie.

WATER RAIL
Rallus aquaticus

WARNING: if you can live with just hearing this species, rather than seeing it, you will avoid much frustration. Their vocal repertoire consists of a descant of chipping protest, strangulated squeals, grunts, and individual notes 'pumped up' until they peter out in a fading crescendo. As a rule of thumb, if you detect a piglet-like squeal coming from an impenetrable marsh, the caller is a Water Rail. Calm weather towards dusk is the best time to listen.

Although widespread in swampy habitats, public appearances are rare. That is a pity, because the phantom is adorned with spectacular plumage and spindly toes that clasp as surely as a monkey's tail. The foot operates like a snowshoe, spreading weight and enabling the bird to walk – even run – over soggy ground. Velveteen slate-grey underparts glow with a bluish light. As the wraith slinks through vegetation or stands motionless, facing away from danger, a streaked Dunnock-like back blends with the surroundings. Easing through tangles is accomplished by compressing its shape to slip, 'thin as a rail', between stems. Actions are jerky, coy and nervous. Having to spend time out in

the open is anathema, as though daylight might prove deadly. A long red bill is thrust forward in the manner of a fixed bayonet and the bird flees like a startled rat. Running is preferred to flight.

Diet is varied. Insects, molluscs, worms, seeds and berries are the mainstay, but small birds are ambushed: Wren, Little Stint and House Sparrow have been killed. How does a Water Rail, lacking a hooked bill or claws, subdue prey? It grabs the victim and then drowns it. Pairs are believed to separate at the end of the breeding season. When marshes freeze, denizens patrol margins, where sunlight keeps some habitat ice-free. Now the tables are turned: when venturing into the open, they can be spotted and seized by vigilant Grey Herons. In the days when lighthouses were staffed, the species was frequently recorded striking in autumn and early winter (Barrington 1900). Despite giving the impression of ungainly flight, migrants travel far. One came aboard ship over 800km west of Ireland and was fed small pieces of meat, which sustained it until it was released near Lisbon in Portugal.

Brief appearances are the norm. A Water Rail may emerge momentarily at the edge of marsh vegetation but an observer requires considerable patience. On the other hand, views are worth the wait.

CORNCRAKE
Crex crex

We hear it in the weeding time,
When knee-deep waves the corn.
We hear it in the summer's prime,
Through meadows night and morn.

BOTH THE WORDS of John Clare (1793–1864) and an onomatopoeic Latin title immortalise the Corncrake's rasping chant. Most people who grew up in rural areas before 1970 remember the sound, yet Corncrakes had become extinct in almost all of mainland Ireland by the late 1990s. A bird that, just thirty years earlier, was a summer soundtrack calling from fields and part of an unchanging order, was gone. What happened? As the sword fell, its demise was claimed to be a result of problems encountered in African wintering quarters. The combined effect of drought and overgrazing by goats in the Sahel region (allegedly an important staging area flanking the Sahara) was turning savannah grassland into desert. In truth, the death knell was due to events unfolding under our noses.

Males arrive in late April and extract a potpourri of animal and vegetable matter from herbaceous undergrowth. Based on stomach contents, Collinge (quoted in Witherby *et al.* 1938–41) found roughly 80 per cent animal matter and 20 per cent vegetable. Prey includes craneflies, beetles, earwigs, grasshoppers, slugs, snails and earthworms; vegetable food embraces seeds of Corn Spurrey and rushes, as well as grain. Foraging birds hide. One belied its presence by tapping snail shells on a rock (TG). Iris beds, clumps of Cow Parsley and nettles cloak the phantom until meadow grasses grow tall and lush. Males call to attract night-flying females passing overhead on migration. Calling is intermittent during the day and subsides completely between nine o'clock and midnight, a lull that appears to serve as a siesta before night-long, high-energy bellowing. Craking continues well into July, periodically abating during the period of incubation and the early rearing of young. Mystery shrouds breeding activities. On Inishbofin, Galway, some calling males move location during the breeding season (TJG). Presumably the birds are polygamous, as suggested by Cramp *et al.* (1977–94).

Accepted wisdom states that two broods are produced and that, job done, males migrate ahead of females and the summer's new generation. Witherby *et al.* (1938–41) depict the wing of a moulting adult showing all feathers growing synchronously, stating '[Renewal of remiges and rectrices] is acquired by complete moult, which is very rapid, all wing-feathers, wing-coverts and tail being shed simultaneously, August–September.' In this condition, flight would be well-nigh impossible and migration out of the question until some time in August at least. Occasionally Corncrakes are flushed from cover as late as October. These are either youngsters from second broods or overseas migrants, possibly from Europe.

Despite its ungainly fluttering flight, the bird is an

Males call with great regularity – from the same spot, in the same field and for weeks on end. No wonder the sound entered the human psyche and, for those who remember it, conjures up fond memories of long summer days in the company of nature.

accomplished flier, albeit to wintering quarters the limits of which are imperfectly known. The route taken is also uncertain. The principal range lies in a longitudinal band from Malawi through Zambia and Zimbabwe to eastern South Africa. Difficulties of detection hamper understanding, but a scarcity of records in western Africa suggest that, while some European migrants pass through Morocco, most may make diagonal flights across the Sahara to reach home ground in the eastern half of tropical Africa. Alternatively, some may winter undetected in tropical parts of western Africa, possibly Zaire, Congo-Brazzaville or northern Angola. In any event, many migrate through Egypt, bound for Sudan. Alas, Sudan seems increasingly prone to drought, which causes grassland to parch, and Egypt is a country rife with nets designed to catch Quail. Traps set along the Mediterranean coast of the Nile were estimated, in 1993 and 1994, to take a bycatch of a staggering 9,000 and 14,000 Corncrakes respectively (Baha el Din *et al.* 1996). It was estimated that about 9,000 people were involved in trapping and shooting in the coastal strip and that between 0.5 and 2.7 per cent of Europe's Corncrakes were taken per year, but such a low percentage beggars belief. An embryonic education programme was put in place and might have reduced the carnage, although the message was aimed at sparing Corncrakes, not preventing the deaths of an even greater number of Quail. Trapping blights others that pass south through Iran in autumn. Dozens, rather than thousands, are caught. Following rice harvest, youths and

Corncrake heaven. Alas, the shy summer visitor has lost its meadows and declined to near-extinction in Ireland. Old-style saving of hay provided a safe bailiwick within which nests survived and young fledged before fields were cut. Silage has spread like a flood across the land and changed everything. Offshore islands have become final holdouts. Even here, skeleton bands are threatened by cats, the overgrazing of habitat by sheep, and misguided introductions of Pheasants, which commandeer habitat and food and, even worse, probably pass on parasites shared by both species, debilitating the much smaller Corncrake, not the robust alien.

young men catch migrants among stalks in paddy fields using a combination of nets and dogs. State ornithologists have engaged with the trappers and suggest that an end to the practice is achievable (Ashoori and Zolfinejad 2008).

It is chilling to recount how numerous Corncrakes once were. A passage written by A. Ellison (1890) and published in *Zoologist* makes poignant reading:

Near Waterford these birds are so abundant this summer [1890] that during the cutting of a meadow of perhaps four acres, a hundred or more were driven out, the last perch or so that was left uncut in the centre of the field being literally alive with them. It is a curious sight watching the crakes rising in twos and threes from the ever-diminishing patch of grass or watch them scurrying mouse-like among the swathes of fresh-cut hay, while helpless young were destroyed in dozens by the machines.

Not surprisingly, most observers point to the advent during the twentieth century of mechanised mowing, first by horse, then by machine, as agents of death. Scything, even by teams of cutters, was less traumatic and allowed nests to be spared and broods to escape to safety in field margins. Mowing, conducted from the field's margins to the centre, was fatal. In smallholdings and on islands, late cutting of hay was done by hand; here, Corncrake numbers remained constant. Everywhere else, cutting machines became ubiquitous and were soon accompanied by a switch from a pastoral landscape consisting of hay meadows to one dominated by wall-to-wall silage. Growth is boosted to a tall, vigorous sward by spraying manure and dousing with granular fertiliser, while the natural world is kept further at bay by a firewall of pesticides and herbicides. Verdant fields might look inviting, but huge triffid-like forage harvesters chug over inert prairies taking two,

sometimes three, cuts to be baled and used as livestock feed. By the 1990s, farmland had been turned into a desert, albeit a green desert. Traditional hay meadows went the way of the dinosaur and the Corncrakes went with them.

Some still occur in parts of the west of Ireland and may yet recolonise Rathlin Island, where land-sympathetic management practices have been set in place in the hope that restored Scottish populations might spill new recruits south. Across the Republic of Ireland, final redoubts are on islands, notably where clumps of nettles have become established over abandoned areas of tilled ground. During the 1980s a healthy population in the flood meadows along the Shannon Callows numbered almost 200 calling males. Those days are gone. Nest-destroying unseasonable flooding and predation by 'gone bush' North American Mink have put paid to a vibrant nucleus. A depressing truism is that, once the bird is lost from a former stronghold, disappearance tends to be permanent.

The history of an increase (between 1993 and 1998) on Inishbofin, Donegal, offers a light in the darkness. Casey (1998) documented the events:

Inishbofin has an unusual social structure, in that it is inhabited in summer only, with islanders moving to the mainland when schools re-open in autumn. This means that most of the island is not actively farmed. Prior to 1993, the island was extensively grazed by sheep and cattle, and low numbers of Corncrakes were occasionally reported. The management of Inishbofin changed dramatically in the spring of 1993, when a local dispute led to the removal of all livestock from the island. Much of the area which had formerly been meadow and pasture was then ploughed, but not tilled. In late summer 1993, it was reported that two singing male Corncrakes were using the rough vegetation

Calm overnight weather produces a heavy dew and wet grass saturates plumage. Suddenly stepping from cover onto a wall, this Corncrake basked in sunlight to trap warmth and dry itself.

which had been allowed to grow up following the withdrawal of grazing. No active management was carried out in 1993, and the accumulation of that year's growth remained in spring 1994, when 12 singing males were recorded on the island. In summer 1994, the vegetation had already started to become rank, and much of this was mowed by BirdWatch Ireland in that autumn. Corncrake numbers reached a peak in 1995, when 27 singing males were recorded. However, it was not possible to mow the vegetation in autumn 1995, and no further management took place until the spring of 1996, when a small area was mowed. That year, 15 singing males were recorded. After the 1996 breeding season a small area was mowed. During 1997, only 12 singing males were recorded. An area of about four hectares was mown in September 1997. An improvement in numbers was noted in 1998, with 15–17 singing males on the island. Since 1995, a grant scheme has been in operation on the island, offering an incentive to landowners who agree to leave their land undisturbed until after 1 September and allow management to benefit Corncrakes. In terms of uptake, this scheme has been successful, but much of the land entered into the scheme is becoming less suitable, and is impossible to mow [for a variety of reasons]. It has been suggested that meadow areas should be ploughed, levelled and re-seeded.

Based on visits during 2008 and 2009 (AMG) no recent management beneficial to Corncrakes appears to have taken place. Several calling males were heard, albeit in reduced numbers. On other inhabited offshore islands, including Tory Island, Donegal and Inishbofin, Galway, numbers have gone into worryingly steep declines since 2007. On Tory Island, the unchecked grazing by a rogue flock of sheep, eating habitat and trampling nesting areas, emerged as a local problem that is far from insoluble. Domestic cats, the scourge of island birds the world over, stalk Tory's meadows and nettle beds, as they do on other key nesting islands. Some are silent killers and casualties die undetected. Occasionally a live victim is delivered to the moggie's owner. Even 'lightly injured' birds succumb through puncture wounds and trauma. By killing adults, cats inflict maximum damage on the bird's breeding prospects. Conservationists and some local opinion on Tory and Inishbofin have attempted to demystify the 'harmless' reputation of cats. As a result, several animals have been repatriated to mainland sanctuaries.

On Inishbofin, concerned islanders noticed a link between Pheasants and Corncrakes. Put simply, when Pheasants occupy Corncrake habitat, Corncrakes appear to move out. Since Pheasants were released in 2004, Inishbofin has lost almost all of a Corncrake population that received much TLC in the form of establishing early vegetation cover and ensuring late cutting of breeding habitat. Given the timid disposition of Corncrakes and the blundering presence of a big brother game bird, it is not difficult to imagine that Pheasants could outcompete their smaller brethren. A cock Pheasant, revved up to breed, is intolerant of other birds that stray into his bailiwick. A more

insidious link may also exist. Research has demonstrated a connection between the parasites shared by Pheasants and Grey Partridges, which have a harmful impact on *only* the partridges (see Grey Partridge account, above). Could it be that a similarly excessive parasite loading derived from Pheasants is having an impact on Corncrakes? Although conjectural, the possible relationship between recent introductions of Pheasants onto several offshore islands and the contemporaneous decline of Corncrakes, is a subject warranting post-haste examination. Although it makes depressing reading, Norris (1960) is worth repeating:

> When the British enquiry took place in 1938 and 1939, Corncrakes were still abundant in many parts of Northern Europe and in those parts of Ireland and northwest Scotland where mowing machines were absent or few and far between. Twenty years of increased mechanisation in agriculture – and in particular the development of the small and easily adaptable tractor – have produced a further dramatic change for the worse. In 1958, Dr Haartman produced a report on the present position in Finland and found very much the same set of circumstances that had been found in Britain, with the luckless Corncrake decreasing to vanishing point. For a bird that chooses to nest in meadows and lays up to a dozen eggs, the power to recover its former numbers would be very considerable if only the nests were left in peace. This has been discovered on several occasions when pairs have been successful in restricted areas where, for one reason or another, mowing is very late or non-existent. In such areas a reservoir of birds has soon been built up and in a short time the neighbouring meadows have again become populated. The Severn and Avon valleys above Tewkesbury are good examples; but once the sanctuary area is lost, the annual massacre of nests goes on and the voice of the Corncrake is seldom heard for more than a year or two. The future of the whole species must be in some danger, although just how serious this is, is hard to assess.

Are there any grounds for optimism? As ever, the fate of a hapless being rests in human hands. In parts of Ireland it has been noted that some disappearances seem unrelated to the spread of mechanisation and the conversion of hay meadows to silage. During the 1950s, Corncrakes bred in wet meadows dotted among the bowl of hills surrounding Belfast. The habitat still exists but the birds faded away around 1980 (NMK). No hard reasons have been forthcoming and educated guesses point at misfortunes befalling the bird on migration or in its African wintering grounds. Yes, a lot can go wrong for a waif that embarks on an annual round trip of almost 15,000km to savannah grasslands south of the Equator. However, in response to beneficial management in Scotland, numbers have increased and a reintroduction scheme in East Anglia has tasted success when members of a new generation migrated to Africa and returned to breed.

MOORHEN
Gallinula chloropus

MOOR IS A CORRUPTION of 'mere'. Country people prefer Waterhen, which is apt. Moorhen and Coot are frequently confused. They share size, habitat and basic colour scheme. Coots have lobed feet and are mainly found on water. Moorhens have gangly, separated toes, better adapted for treading shorelines. Unlike Coot, Moorhen comes in Technicolor. The back is brown and the body slate blue. A chalky line delineates the flanks and the bill is vermilion with a vivid yellow tip. The bird swims with a peculiar pumping action, rhythmically cocking its tail to reveal white undersides.

Pugnacious throughout the year, rivals spar like kick-boxers. As well as a sharp *pik*, a harrumphing *kurruck* is a trademark (also heard from migrants passing overhead at night), suggesting the caller has burped or been stood upon. Territories are vigorously defended from March to autumn. During winter, owner-occupiers tend to remain nearby and squabbles are suspended, only to resume in spring. Chicks are black with red waxy foreheads and bills. Weaklings are abandoned or killed. The remainder receive TLC and, in heavy downpours, parents build platforms to provide a safe refuge in the event of flooding. Juveniles are brown with dull bills that soon hint at grown-up colours. Although well capable of flight at sixty days, close family ties keep young and old together for another month. Offspring have an extraordinarily high survival rate, up to 100 per cent in one study (Wood 1974). Unlikely as it may seem, migrants from Scandinavia reach Britain and a Scottish youngster was trapped at Copeland Bird Observatory.

The Moorhen's amphibious lifestyle has paid dividends. The species is widespread across all continents except Australia.

Until well past their first birthday, youngsters lack bright bill colours and their plumage is less than immaculate – they are teenagers, after all.

COOT
Fulica atra

FEW IDENTIFICATION CHALLENGES are as uncomplicated as Coot. Subjects are slate-grey except for a white frontal shield attached to an ivory-coloured bill. In flight, a narrow white border along the inner trailing edge of the wing is revealed. Take-offs require a taxi run, revealing grey-green feet with lobed toes and yellow-green legs. The back is rounded and the head angled forwards and nodded. Swimming birds are frumpish and famously aggressive. Some defend territory throughout the year. The male, abetted by the female, initiates sorties. Rivals patrol menacingly with heads down and wings arched, uttering burping clucks. They also emit a piercing nasal note that resembles a high-pitched piston. Jonsson (1992) likened the sound to 'a light bulb dropped on to a stone inside the reeds'.

Coots are aggressive and defend territory throughout the year, patrolling with the menacing air of a vigilante. Particularly pugnacious partnerships defend more habitat than they need, limiting occupancy of small lakes to just one pair.

Diet consists of vegetable matter, including grass and algae. Feeding techniques extend to clumsy dives. Outside the breeding season the bird is social. On European wetlands, dense wintering flocks can pass for a shadow or stain. Nests, typically a floating pile of dead reeds anchored to submerged vegetation, are constructed as early as March. Occasionally, zealous male housekeepers add mouthfuls of soggy stems and roots to the structure, burying eggs and causing hatching failures.

Chicks are born with a bald crown surrounded by a frill of orange fuzz. Parents sometimes kill offspring by repeatedly striking them on the bald spot. Perhaps they are able to assess the availability of food or the fitness of individual chicks, taking drastic action to ensure that only the fittest survive. Juveniles are smoky grey, grading into white on the chest, neck and throat. By early autumn, juvenile body plumage is replaced. Black appears, although some grey flank feathers remain. The bill becomes white. It is possible to see an age-related difference in the shape of the frontal shield. Viewed head-on, adults have wide-topped shields that taper to a waist where they meet the base of the bill. On a black head, the acute angle between the shield and bill base resembles pince-nez. On young, the shield is not yet fully developed; at no point is it wider than the base of the bill. It is more of a blaze on the forehead, much like that found on a horse.

Thompson (1849–52) was aware of migration in response to hard weather: 'In Ireland, where the winters are less severe than in Great Britain, these birds remain constantly about their summer quarters unless hard frost sets in, when they are driven for a time to the sea coast. At such times they appear in Belfast Bay in considerable numbers. A flock of Coots feeding at the fall of the tide on the eelgrass banks is a very entertaining sight from the bustle that prevails: that they may be seen in all attitudes, and running about with great, although awkward, activity.'

Despite being part of park life, vagrants have reached Iceland and Newfoundland. Fliers look ungainly with flailing wings and dangling feet, an inelegant appearance shared with Moorhen, Water Rail and Corncrake. All are related and renowned for intercontinental flights, most of which seem random rather than any form of true migration. Practically every oceanic island, however remote, has at some time been the home of an endemic rail. Once established, pioneers became quite distinct from their faraway forebears. Over time, many also became flightless. Oceanic islands function as evolutionary test tubes but suffer from unstable ecology. Unique species, once forged, are vulnerable to outside influences. In the last two centuries humankind's livestock and pets and associated pests have wiped out more than a dozen island forms of rail and brought others to the verge of extinction.

Unlike Grey Herons, Cranes fly with an outstretched neck and have a 2m wingspan. Despite such major differences, Grey Herons are called Cranes (or 'heron-cranes') by older country people.

CRANE
Grus grus

CRANES, it seems safe to say, were a part of Ireland's lost landscapes. There is no need to dig deep into the fossil record: the soldier-sized troubadour of bogland was around until the late Middle Ages. Although commemorated in Gaelic place names containing the word 'corr', an explanation for the bird's disappearance is hard to come by. The usual dispiriting conclusion seems inescapable – that habitat loss and hunting tolled doom. Or, as suggested by D'Arcy (1999), might the harshness of the Little Ice Age in the years around 1650 have caused extinction? Irish Cranes were probably resident, habituated to life across the soggy heart of the country. North European populations are unable to withstand winter freeze-ups and have evolved annual escape routes that thread them in majestic lines all the way to Iberia, North Africa and across the Bosporus. Conveniently for a heavyweight flapper ill-adapted to long sea-crossings, most of Europe can be traversed overland. Just as the continent's Little Egret has conquered Ireland, swelling numbers of Cranes are stirring thoughts of a return to former haunts.

In the autumn of 1979 two birds, thought to be adolescents and two or three years old, arrived at Horsey on the Norfolk Broads. Others joined them over the winter, but only the original duo remained beyond the spring of 1980. They paired up and first attempted to breed in 1981. Nesting continued, albeit with few young produced, until 1997. By then, maturing offspring – and possibly some new immigrants from Europe – boosted the nucleus. By the early years of the new millennium, two pairs bred in Yorkshire and three other pairs were successful elsewhere in East Anglia. In 2010, the population was fifty strong and comprised thirteen or fourteen fecund partnerships that produced eight fledglings. Meanwhile, in various eastern districts of the UK, non-breeders held territory in suitable habitat and a pair may have bred in Caithness (Stanbury & UK Crane Working Group 2011). Clearly, recolonisation is feasible and the birds are doing it for themselves, albeit greatly assisted by conservation bodies, land managers and landowners who came together as an umbrella – the UK Crane Working Group.

Enter, in 2006, the Great Crane Project. Not content with nurturing nature's own efforts, this organisation released twenty juvenile Cranes into the Somerset Levels in August 2010 and added more in 2011. Such restocking of national avifauna has become a surrogate for real conservation. With talk of 'rewilding' cutaway bogland across the Irish midlands, there is hope that Cranes, like our resurgent Great Spotted Woodpeckers, might return to the mended wilderness under their own steam, rather than being repatriated by PR zealots who fill the ears of a gullible public with warm pink fluff.

OYSTERCATCHER
Haematopus ostralegus

Pushed off shoreline feeding grounds by the rising tide, Oystercatchers congregate at roosts – preferably on an island – to nap and preen in safety. All birds know the meaning of 'me time', especially as they cannot afford the luxury of proper sleep.

Birds' bills grow imperceptibly. Oystercatchers that specialise in probing, rather than hammering through the tough shell of a mussel, develop a tapered bill.

When adult Oystercatchers moult into courtship plumage they lose wintertime's white hoop around the neck. Those that retain it during the breeding season are marked out as immature and fail to attract a mate.

OYSTERCATCHERS ARE UNMISTAKABLE – piebald plumage, carrot-like bill and stocky pink legs with the texture of starfish. In winter a white hoop encircles the neck, retained by non-breeders as a badge of immaturity. Loud, far-carrying *d'leep, d'leep* cries fill the air wherever they gather. Ireland's estuaries serve as wintering grounds for populations breeding in Iceland and Scotland. In addition, Faroese Oystercatchers formed 15 per cent of those caught for ringing at Belfast Lough (IF) and have also featured in ringing catches on Lough Foyle and Strangford Lough. Few, if any, European Oystercatchers are believed to winter in Ireland (Ruttledge 1966). Pairs breed at low density along rocky coasts, especially on islands. The skirl of alarm unleashed at intruders is intense. When the trespasser backs off, the bird lands in triumph and continues piping, its ire seemingly redirected at the ground.

While some probe for earthworms in grassland, mussels are a mainstay. Thinner-billed females stab the shell's hinge to prise it apart, whereas males hammer a hole straight through the shell wall. Bill length increases, gradually becoming more pointed, coinciding with a change from coastal feeding on molluscs to probing in grassland for earthworms and leatherjackets.

Pairs live long and mate for life; they also remain faithful to their breeding site. Unmated and immature birds face long waits to find partners and territories. Some start to breed and hope to succeed; others queue for a quality domain. Gaps may not appear until the wannabe territory holder is twelve years old. Oystercatcher pairs, unlike other shorebirds, feed offspring for up to two months. During this time youngsters learn, by copying, parental feeding techniques. Among beleaguered ground-nesting shorebirds, the bird is holding its own. Pairs seek out predator-free islands and mainland breeders use a combination of guile and aggression – sitters sneak off early long before danger threatens and then unleash a tirade of alarm at the intruder, followed in the last resort by mobbing. In England and Europe, canny others have spotted the sanctuary of flat rooftops, beyond the climbing ability of ground predators.

RINGED PLOVER
Charadrius hiaticula

Ringed Plovers lay four pointed eggs. They taper at one end, allowing them to fit closely together and permit the adult to cover all at once. Once the first-hatched chick dries, it prostrates itself under the parent. Within hours, siblings join it and the family is led away by parents, fearful that prying eyes might have noticed proceedings. Until they fledge, faith is placed in the chicks' camouflaged down and parental injury feigning, designed to draw potential predators away.

DESPITE PLUMAGE bedecked with hoops and bright orange legs, Ringed Plover livery is effective camouflage when viewed against sand or gravel. Large eyes and a short bill source prey by sight rather than probing. A few clockwork steps are followed by a pause. Occasionally a foot is extended and trembled against the ground. The habit is easily missed and reserved for substrates covered with a film of water, such as the edges of pools. Lapwings do likewise. What is its purpose? Prey is associated with the thin layer of mud and detritus that covers underlying sand. Research using a vibrating replica of a foot (Osborne 1982) proved that stationary nematode worms began to move after a bout of trembling. The opaque nature of the substrate and the water covering it make detection difficult until foot-trembling increases the visibility of quarry.

Ringed Plovers can be encountered year-round. Migrants destined for Iceland and Greenland pass through in spring and autumn, while others, probably from Scotland and Scandinavia, arrive to spend the winter. A bird ringed on migration at Belfast in August 1972 was recovered in Morocco in June 1976. All manner of bare ground is used for nesting. Lilting, yodelling calls accompany a slow butterfly flight at close to ground level. There is virtually no nest; a neat garland of flat-sided broken seashells or pebbles suffices. If an intruder approaches, one of a pair commences an injury-feigning performance worthy of an Oscar:

Ringed Plovers, two adults and (left) juvenile. In common with many juvenile shorebirds, upperparts plumage is delicately edged, suggestive of lace. The virginal plumes are soft and are soon replaced a more robust coat of plain-edged feathers.

anxious calls, crippled demeanour and a 'broken' wing. The wretch hobbles away. The urge to follow is irresistible. Having conned the visitor, recovery is instantaneous and the actor exits, stage left.

The standard call is a plaintive, slightly tremulous double-note delivered in a minor key: *too-ip*. Flocks startle easily but quickly settle. When searching for food, each defends personal space and reinforces territorial rites by chanting *t'weet-it, t'weet-it, t'weet-it* (depending on pitch, *t'woody, t'woody, t'woody*). The phrase has a rolling, clockwork rhythm. Because faith is placed in an ability to blend against backgrounds, a shrewd approach can secure close views, especially if an observer avoids looking in the bird's direction until the subject relaxes, duped into believing that it is not the centre of attention. Juveniles, which often form a significant proportion in autumn flocks, are beautifully patterned. The larger feathers of the back and folded wings have pale fringes that suggest lace. Youngsters have all-dark bills, mustard-coloured legs and an incomplete breast band that is only narrowly conjoined in the centre – rather than an unbroken black hoop. It is possible, when scanning through autumn parties, to detect singletons or small groups that are a tad smaller and darker. Such petite individuals breed in the Arctic and migrate to coastal wetlands in Africa, effectively leapfrogging parochial populations.

GOLDEN PLOVER
Pluvialis apricaria

A SUMMER VISIT TO ICELAND will invariably have, as a backing track, the plaintive pipe of Golden Plover. Having passed the winter with us, they arrive in unison on the breeding grounds. Before they quit our shores, nascent finery emerges in March. As April advances, increasing numbers of black, white and gold mannequins stand out. Squadrons adopt a range of profiles from Manta Ray (a spherical vanguard trailed by a ribbon of followers) to the V of a wave of bomber planes. Slowly the formations change shape. Birds jockey for position and the lead changes. Away from the front, wind resistance is reduced and studies reveal that heart rate drops when one bird tucks in behind others. Constellations twinkle high overhead like numberless black stars. With so many aloft, the strain of deciding when and where to land seems to paralyse whole battalions, which circle endlessly. Eventually a twister of scouts reconnects with the ground and a procession descends along an invisible escalator, thickening in numbers and eventually forming a brassy carpet.

Golden Plovers love space, especially flat landscapes beneath wide open sky. Because they feed less on shoreline habitats and more on fields, their routine is unrelated to the rising and falling of the tide. The voice is wistful and haunting. Flocks break into a chorus of 'sea shanty' melodic yodelling. During spring, calling intensifies, and is copied by Starlings. Robert Burns knew the sound and commented that he could not hear it 'without feeling an elevation of soul, like the enthusiasm of devotion or poetry'.

Handfuls nest on uplands in Ulster and Connacht. Formerly, they bred more widely, even on hilltops overlooking Belfast. Thompson (1849–52) wrote: 'Within the last very few years, when much attention has been given to the draining of mountain bogs, a change [decrease] has taken place with regard to our beautiful Golden Plover.' Loss and damage to bogland continues to hit them hard. Damp habitat supports insect larvae, vital for growing chicks. Drainage desiccates the habitat and destroys the cranefly breeding factories upon which chicks rely. If affected by dry summer weather, larvae production all but ceases. For chicks born during the following year's breeding season, there is no food.

Quantitative information on the fortunes of the remaining numbers breeding in Ireland's uplands is scant. These days, upland is no longer a quiet fastness immune to change. Far from it. Afforestation, overgrazing, turf-cutting, wind turbines, pipelines and power lines continue apace, in many instances without any apparent regulation or cognisance of the impact they inflict on habitat and wildlife, never mind the disfigurement of wilderness. Along with such visual intrusions comes more insidious baggage. Not only does extensive afforestation of moorlands result in the displacement of birds from formerly suitable breeding grounds, but predation on nests may also be an important issue locally, especially where young plantations harbour more predators. Ravens, Hooded Crows, Magpies and foxes have been given new 'forward bases' from which to operate, and extra rations to boot – sheep carrion. What chance do Donegal's remaining sixty to eighty pairs of Golden Plovers (Cox *et al.* 2002), the country's breeding stronghold, stand?

The Posh and Becks of plovers. The less black female undertakes the lion's share of incubation duties. Freckled plumage boosts her camouflage.

Above: Downy chicks are exquisite in a fluffy coat of gold and grey. By mimicking the background, the cherub is all but invisible. How many millennia were needed for the bird to evolve such perfect disguise? Inset: Resting on an Irish headland after an autumn flight from Iceland, a Golden Plover preens plumage and contemplates its next move. Iberia perhaps?

Left: Waiting for a ride home. Parked during late April on reclaimed land near Belfast, these Golden Plovers are fully revved up to breed as soon as southerly winds speed them to Iceland.

Winter flocks unpeel themselves from the sky and plane to earth. Tightly ordered ranks and gold-stippled upperparts can, on bare ground, suggest a stony boulder field rather than living birds.

GREY PLOVER
Pluvialis squatarola

Grey Plover's winter plumage epitomises the season: grey, drab and watery-eyed.

GREY PLOVERS are exclusively coastal, even preferring to roost close to the water's edge rather than commute to detached high-tide quarters. Lone, big-eyed hunters dot sandy shorelines or mud-sand estuaries and stalk marine worms by lunging at breathing holes and extracting the reluctant victim in a Lilliputian tug of war. Non-breeding plumage is symbolic of winter: grey, drab and featureless. Grey Plovers are dumpy and so too are Knots, which often share the same habitat. Both lack eye-catching features and look rather anonymous, right down to a shoulderless shape. Route One to identification is gait: Knots probe systematically; Grey Plovers stop, start and peer, in the manner of all plovers. Black axillaries, the area of the underwing equivalent to a human armpit, are distinctive in flight. Summer plumage, black-fronted and silver-grey above, is sensational but is seldom seen except on migrants freshly returned from the Arctic in August. The voice is a plaintive three-syllable whistle. The call was recognised by Belfast Lough's nineteenth-century wildfowlers, who named the shorebird 'Whistling Plover'.

LAPWING
Vanellus vanellus

Wings of lapis lazuli; ink obsidian for an eye. For sure the artist has to be no less than Salvador Dali.

AS SHOREBIRDS GO, Lapwing is avant-garde. Males have the longest head plumes and, during courtship, an air of bravura. In breeding plumage, the front of the face, chin and throat turn completely black, as if the bird has sneezed into a bag of soot. On females, the forehead is flecked with white. Following a post-breeding moult, all develop a black and buff visage, and a shorter crest. Big, obsidian eyes bestow remarkable vision. In winter, feeding is mainly nocturnal. The gait is halting, the eyes locked in a forwards stare. Often one foot is trembled. To a worm this feels like the drumming of heavy rain, which jolts the prey out of its burrow and – fatally – into view.

Sociability and peevish calls are the norm. Flocks fly in wavering, strung-out packs. The combination of floppy wingbeats with black-and-white underwings suggests the twinkle of tickertape. Migration routes are east–west, rather than north–south. Unfrozen pastures in Ireland and Britain are the winter home of many thousands of European kin. Exceptional flocks have been estimated at 15,000 (Spencer 1953) and 35,000 (Parquin 1955, in Cramp *et al.* 1977–94). Immigrants from as far away as the Russian steppes reach Ireland, testament to a primal urge to vacate areas covered by snow or gripped by frost. Such movements are normal when severe weather occurs after the ordinary season of autumn migration. In attempting to escape from cold, stragglers occasionally carry on out to sea, swept along by east winds that develop when bitter conditions prevail. Singletons and flocks occasionally make landfall along the eastern seaboard of North America. Fourteen were found, mostly in Newfoundland, between November 2010 and February 2011. For an earlier transatlantic flight, Witherby (1928) analysed meteorological charts and calculated ground speed in a prevailing easterly airflow at 150km per hour and felt that a transit of 3,000km could be made in less than twenty-four hours. Our few remaining breeding birds are far less well travelled. After wintering elsewhere in Ireland, Britain or southwest Europe, they

Above: Cold weather hits Lapwings hard. Flocks stream west in the hope of finding unfrozen ground. In desperation – and encouraged by a fool's gold tailwind – they carry on out to sea, leaving an icy Ireland in their wake. Some reach Canada, but most meet a watery grave.

Left: Raffishly handsome, Lapwing plumage changes colour with the light.

Like most shorebird chicks, baby Lapwings emerge from the egg within hours of each other. Because the birds are born to run (and hide), legs are more important than wings for the first three weeks of life.

return to territories in early March. Their tumbling displays and exultant rasping calls symbolise freedom. The spring sky is their stage and the first clutches of four speckled eggs are laid in the closing days of March. In favoured areas, several pairs breed in near proximity and scramble en masse to drive off intruders. Once chicks hatch, they peck instinctively and soon develop a knack for ambushing earthworms, beetles and arthropods. Within a week some practise foot-trembling (AMG).

Irish breeding populations have been devastated. Hillis (2009) states: 'Although still a widespread breeding species, Lapwing is seriously declining; its population decreased from 21,500 to 3,200 between 1991 and 2002, i.e. by 85 per cent (Lynas *et al.* 2007).' Although the list of woes is long, none is irreversible. But time is running out. For Northern Ireland, Partridge and Smith (1992) published a population estimate of 5,250 breeding pairs during 1985–87. By 1993, perhaps fewer than half survived. An important population on Rathlin Island crashed due to uncontrolled predation by crows and introduced

ferrets. Due to wanton environmental destruction by state-sponsored schemes, numbers were decimated in the drainage of the River Blackwater catchment in Tyrone and adjoining parts of Monaghan. By the end of the 2010 breeding season, the most optimistic estimate for Northern Ireland stood at 250 pairs.

Across Britain and Europe, the picture is similar. Data gathered from twenty-five countries covering the years from 1980 to 2009 shows that numbers have dropped by 52 per cent; in Britain, the breeding population decreased by a further 22 per cent between 2009 and 2010 (Risely *et al.* 2011).

Among a host of countryside changes, drainage and the conversion of permanent pasture to silage have deprived the birds of the close association they once enjoyed with farming. Lapwings frequently nest in arable land, where spring-sown fields offer suitable breeding conditions for a short period. Spring-sown crops have been replaced by autumn-sown crops, which are almost useless breeding habitat. Unlike cereal fields, root crops are more open and provide the birds with access to the ground.

Above: Breeding habitat in the making. On a number of wilderness reserves across Europe, wild but placid Tarpan Horses (Konik ponies) achieve a perfect balance of large grazing animals, birds and habitat – reservoirs of wildlife equivalent to Noah's Ark. The photograph depicts a scene at Portmore Lough, Antrim, where an innovative warden established a small herd, imported from the Netherlands' huge Oostvaardersplassen reserve in Holland.

Left: Lapwing populations are beleaguered. Suitable breeding habitat is in short supply and, except on offshore islands, foxes find and consume many eggs and young. Isolated in increasingly tiny breeding oases, entire colonies can be deprived of a new generation by the work of a solitary fox or feral cat.

In the Netherlands, maize fields are used by almost half the breeding population. The increased use of large agricultural machinery destroys many nests. In Sweden, 43 per cent of 870 clutches were lost in this way (Berg *et al.* 1992). Insidious changes in the web of life on farm fields adversely affect the intrinsic food value of pasture. Increased use of pesticides causes a reduction in the amount of available food (Hudson *et al.* 1994). Fungicides, seed-dressings and other chemicals diminish earthworms; herbicides strip food plants of insects upon which chicks feed. Deep ploughing and successive crop rotations, boosted by chemicals rather than manure, further reduce the biomass of earthworms and other soil invertebrates.

Pasture has a higher invertebrate biomass than cultivated fields. A decline in mixed farming – which enabled the birds to nest in spring crops and then move chicks to adjacent pasture – has also contributed to Lapwings' woes. Autumn-sown crops are too tall in spring. Silage is boosted by inorganic fertilisers and then cut early, destroying nests. On farmland, key invertebrate groups have declined since 1980 (Campbell *et al.* 1997). Carbamate pesticides and the molluscicide methiocarb have been shown to have a toxic effect on earthworms (Edwards & Bohlen 1996), the main food for Lapwings. Marginal fields are drained, using better technology, reducing the water table and so impoverishing them for earthworm foragers like Lapwing, while in uplands, sheep walk is less suitable than cattle-grazed ground.

Once breeding attempts are embarked upon, predation is generally the most significant cause of nest losses (Teunissen *et al.* 2005). The chief nest predators are crows, foxes and feral populations of North American Mink. Research in Great Britain and Europe proves that predation is the main reason for breeding season failures (Trolliet 2000). Dwindling populations become even more vulnerable through isolation: because they are tied to fewer sites, predators have better chances. Nocturnally, foxes blight many nesting attempts, as do feral cats and badgers. Incubating birds can drive off daylight raids by Magpies, until eggs hatch and chicks disperse. In former strongholds, such as the Shannon Callows, overwhelming numbers of Hooded Crows systematically scour breeding habitat.

Doubting Thomas conservationists should note a study (Schroeder *et al.* 2008) on an island (Wangerooge) along Germany's Waddenzee coast, which linked immigration of breeding Lapwings and Black-tailed Godwits to the location where, although the habitat was similar to mainland sites, the range of predators was smaller. Results showed that the birds were attracted to Wangerooge because they identified the area as safe. Yet at Belfast Harbour, breeding shorebirds were foredoomed to fail by the abandonment of predator control by the RSPB, which led to the collapse of a unique assemblage of nesting Lapwings and Redshanks. Basic protection was not afforded and offers of help from local industry were ignored (AMG). Curiously, this inaction flew in the face of RSPB's acceptance that scientific evidence proves a link between declines in ground-nesting shorebirds and the uncontrolled activities of generalist ground predators such as foxes.

KNOT
Calidris canutus

RUSSET BODY PLUMAGE is a hallmark of shorebirds that share Arctic breeding grounds. Knots shed winter grey and develop copper-coloured underparts. Adults pass through our latitude in July, still clad in midnight-sun tuxedos, resplendent but destined to vanish quickly. Mostly, we see sombre offspring with upperparts characterised by scallop-shaped feathers grown in unison, a virginal coat of brocade. The physiological strain of growing so many at once means that the feathers are small and somewhat flimsy; they flutter in a breeze. Robust wing feathers are kept for longer – until past the time of the bird's first birthday. All ages have short, straight bills and olive or mustard-coloured legs. On breeding adults, leg colour darkens appreciably. Thousands spend the winter on Strangford Lough's extensive mudflats. Abundance does not necessarily make them conspicuous. The larger the numbers, the more tightly packed the flock. Feeding groups move like marching ants and jab, grasping tiny molluscs not much bigger than a grain of sand. Rapid bill-tapping movements appear to act as a sensory guide to what lies below the surface. Thompson (1849–52) recorded nocturnal feeding: 'Many are killed [by wildfowlers] at night, when they apparently feed more than by day, both in darkness and moonlight. Shooters are drawn to their vicinity by their singular chuckling. A person, hearing the call one very dark night in October, sought them with a lantern, holding the light side towards them, when they admitted his approach within a few feet, and did not take wing, but ran before the light as he advanced.'

Above: Knots nest at extremely high latitudes, mainly between seventy and eighty-five degrees. Greenland and northern Canada are home to those that come our way in autumn. In spring, breeders skip Ireland and travel via western Norway to Iceland, then on to Greenland.

Below: Scaly plumage is a hallmark of juveniles. Young Knots are supercharged for migration. After quitting polar latitudes in August, several that staged in England in early September reached coastal wetlands in equatorial Africa less than a week later. From Britain, they flew 6,000km, covering around 800km per day.

SANDERLING
Calidris alba

SANDERLINGS nest in a circumpolar arc, some breeding just five degrees from the North Pole. Home is a carpet of mossy vegetation pock-marked by numberless pools where the days are long but summer is short. The mating system varies between areas and possibly from year to year. Some pairs are monogamous; other females lay a succession of clutches and leave incubation duties to their lone-parent husbands. Our wintering population breeds in northeast Greenland, from where the journeys of marked birds tell a fascinating story. Not surprisingly, most migrate via Iceland. Those destined to overwinter in Ireland are faithful to individual strands over successive winters. Among them are restless souls heading for winter quarters along sun-kissed beaches in Africa. Transit passengers have come from Mauritania, Ghana and Walvis Bay in Namibia.

Away from northern climes, the bird lives a predictable life that follows just one rhythm: the tide. The strategy is simple – run like hell along the water's edge, sprinting ahead of waves, then turn to probe the backwash for prey. A regularly snatched item is a painfully thin, opalescent worm that is extracted from its burrow like a sliver of glass. Flocks synchronise and resemble clockwork toys. At full pace leg movement is a blur. Frozen by a camera shutter, both feet can be seen to lift off the ground simultaneously. With no waves to chase at low tide, alternative feeding strategies are pursued. Busybodies pick frenetically among pebbles and algae, or toss dry seaweed for flies. Others emulate off-duty surfers and find a quiet stretch of beach to nap until the tide turns.

Sanderlings are similar in size to Ringed Plovers, with which they share the shore. Except in breeding plumage, they gleam silver and ghostly white, with a black sequin eye. In autumn, fresh-plumaged juveniles hit our latitude. While some mingle with adults, it is not unusual to stumble across singletons and small parties consisting exclusively of this age class. Shiny and new in August, the upperparts are blazed with bejewelled fretwork. Come September, spangly juvenile feathers are steadily replaced by silvery grey. Calls are clipped and squeaky, encoded syllables that sound like *wick … wick*. Distribution matches strands; 'Stranderling' would be an apt name.

One encounter made a lasting impression on Thompson in 1832:

> On 5 May, a warm, sun-bright day with blue sky overhead, I saw this species to much advantage from horseback. The grey attire appeared like Dunlins in winter plumage, but the season of the year indicated that this could not be. A pocket telescope proved the species. As they were all perfectly motionless, several with their heads beneath their wings awaiting, with exemplary patience, until the ebbing waters would uncover their feeding grounds, they together formed the prettiest and most innocent-looking group of birds I ever beheld.' (Thompson 1849–52)

For any who despair at shorebird identification, Sanderling is a no-brainer. Not only are they white-headed during the time they spend with us, they also have a trademark run.

Fledged in the Arctic, a juvenile Sanderling cannot afford to hang about. Evolution has programmed the novice to undertake a solo maiden flight lasting up to 100 hours. Canadian youngsters probably reach western Ireland in a single hop. Then most are off again – next stop Africa.

LITTLE STINT
Calidris minuta

LITTLE STINTS are seldom seen, which has more to do with rarity than stature. They are tots, smaller even than Dunlins, their usual companions. Being a pixie is no impediment to flying the world. The bird is a sun seeker, shifting from tundra to hot climes in Africa, Arabia and the Indian subcontinent. In autumn, small numbers of juveniles stray west and make brief refuelling stops on muddy wetlands. Size is a good clue to identification, but not diagnostic. A North American species – Semipalmated Sandpiper – is confusingly similar. Irrespective of plumage considerations, Little Stints walk with a bobbling gait. At times, the demeanour borders on hyperactive. If the mite is pausing before picking (in the manner of a plover), rather than employing a mincing gait, you might have stumbled across a Semipalmated Sandpiper. Keep watching! As recently as the early 1980s the challenge of clinching identification without trapping the bird was deemed impossible. Then along came Lars Jonsson's wonderful paintings, which blew away the confusion (Jonsson and Grant 1984).

Little Stints have their lookalikes, but attention to gait cuts through the confusion. The sparrow-sized shorebird feeds by combining a tiptoe action with rapid bill movements. Most prey – tiny and invisible to the human eye – is picked off the surface rather than probed.

CURLEW SANDPIPER
Calidris ferruginea

BREEDING IN SIBERIA and wintering in the tropics, Curlew Sandpipers are true globetrotters. They occur sporadically with Dunlins during autumn migration. Although just a little larger, they are regal with a longer bill used for methodical probing – often belly-deep – rather than fast jabbing. A former name was Pygmy Curlew. All ages have a white rump, a useful distinction in flight. Migrants are, in most cases, immaculate juveniles with stylish scalloped upperparts and a line of mascara through the eye topped by a bright, flaring supercilium.

Charles Darwin famously declared that because a male Peacock's unwieldy tail flew in the face of his notion of the survival of the fittest, it made him feel sick. What would he have made of the incontestable beauty of a juvenile Curlew Sandpiper? Maybe nature has another rule – survival of the beautiful?

PURPLE SANDPIPER
Calidris maritima

PURPLE SANDPIPERS live unobtrusive lives on seaweed-covered rocks just above the water's edge. Because they do not feed at night – prey is located by sight, not speculative probing – short winter days are hectic and complicated by tide and rough weather. Crashing waves force birds to leap, and although they resettle quickly, disturbance impinges on foraging. Gastropods are procured from different parts of the shore, including habitats above the high-tide mark, wetted by sea spray. Dogwhelks and winkles are swallowed whole and ground up in the gizzard. Feare (1966), in a study at Robin Hood's Bay, North Yorkshire, calculated that over the course of five hours' feeding, one bird consumed 4,600 snails. Turnstones, always opportunists, are often nearby. The character of the two is very different. Turnstones are athletic, bustling feeders. Purple Sandpipers are sedate: crouching, probing and sometimes scuttling like mice. During

naps, the bill's colourful base is swaddled among a cloak of grey. Bright mustard legs find a match among yellow-peppered lichen on boulders and serve to harmonise rock and bird. The voice is husky and not unlike the word *weet!* repeated in a short series.

A shrinking violet lifestyle led to the species being described as 'little known' by Thompson (1849–52). The name is not inaccurate, although the purple sheen is hard to discern except close up, when feathers high on the upperparts gleam mauve or lavender. Research (Corse & Summers 1999) points to British and Irish wintering birds being further travelled than previously thought. Those nesting on mossy plains in Iceland were assumed to be 'ours'. Not so. Iceland, it seems, is used as a staging area and winter home for breeders from Greenland and Canada. Others from the eastern Canadian Arctic migrate through Iceland and continue to Europe, including Ireland (Boere *et al.* 1984).

Although the Purple Sandpiper's overall appearance is not dissimilar to other shorebirds, lifestyle choice makes it unique. It inhabits rocky coast and shuffles, rodent-like, around the edge of boulders and outcrops encrusted with seaweed and molluscs. Tameness is another attribute. The combination of confiding demeanour, slate-coloured plumage and 'blind side' presence on rocks hide many.

DUNLIN
Calidris alpina

Top: adults in breeding plumage; middle: winter plumage; bottom: autumn juveniles.

During winter, Scandinavian Dunlins occupy a huge sweep of estuaries from Morocco to Ireland. Thirty-two birds trapped in winter on Belfast Lough between 1975 and 1980 were of northern European origin. They were sourced to Russia (one), Finland (six), Sweden (nine), Norway (five), Poland (six), Germany (two), Denmark (two) and the Netherlands (one). Conversely, the majority of southbound adults in July, and juveniles in August and September, hail from Greenland, Iceland and Scotland. For them, journey's end is the African coast from Mauritania southwards.

Breeding dress is acquired in spring. Ashen winter livery is replaced with a copper-brown back, hoary head and – an instant giveaway – a black belly patch. Wintering birds depart before they acquire breeding colours. They probably track east and fatten up on estuaries around the shores of the North Sea, most likely in the Netherlands. After a lag, fresh waves of migrants in breeding plumage appear during late April and May. Returning from Africa, they are bound for destinations northwest of Ireland, although small numbers breed in bogs and wet grassland in Connacht and western Ulster. Because circumpolar breeding grounds are slow to shake off the grip of winter, those nesting furthest north come last. Come mid-July, black-bellied adults head south. Not yet moulted, they are still bedecked in nuptial plumage. By August, ginger-headed juveniles are in the majority. Whitish tramlines separate back, shoulder (scapular) and wing plumage, and a measles-like rash of blackish spots peppers the flanks, a foretaste of adulthood's black belly.

With a judicious approach, youngsters can be tame. A detailed look reveals some rounder, plain grey feathers nestling in a sea of arrowhead-shaped, ruddy plumage. The grey feathers tell of changes afoot. Like deciduous foliage, the russet tier will be dropped during autumn. By November, bright brown juvenile feathering is gone, replaced by a whey look. The change affects adults too. All are returned to ashy colours for winter. Blandness does, however, emphasise character. Dunlin is a yardstick species against which less common shorebirds should be gauged. Concentrate on the face. Irrespective of age and season, the visage is plain. A beady dark eye – resembling a bullet hole – stands out because surrounding plumage is unremarkable. Voice is distinctive but grating rather than pleasant, except for a delightful bubbling trill on breeding grounds. The call, given in flight, is a rolling, scraping *schritt*. It has a rasping quality, trailing to an asthmatic wheeze as the bird recedes.

COMMON SHOREBIRDS do not come any smaller than this. Dunlins are ubiquitous on soft coasts and, at migration times, muddy shorelines around lakes. They are titchy worker ants, probing mudflats with fast stitching movements of a slightly curved bill. Watch carefully and you will discover that jabs are made in a direct line. Winter flocks feed and fly in unison, leading earlier writers to refer to them as Sandlarks. Bill size varies between sexes and geographically separated populations. Those breeding in northeast Greenland have the shortest bills, dwarfed by long-billed individuals from Russia. Based on bill length, body size and plumage type, it is possible to look at flocks of spring migrants and know who is going where.

RUFF
Philomachus pugnax

NOT ONLY are the sexes different sizes, they also have different names, males being Ruffs and females often known as Reeves. Males are as big as Redshank; some females are scarcely larger than Dunlin. Each is long-necked with a pear-shaped head and shortish bill. Body shape can, in a flash, switch from compact and dumpy to tall and statuesque. They perambulate with gusto. The gait is shoulderless and, when the head is held in the same plane as the body, a hump appears in the back. Often a little fan of plumage protrudes from the hump, like the end of a cape. On the wing, flight action is relaxed on broad wings that deliver long, gentle glides. Fliers look large. Late in spring, just prior to returning to breeding grounds, males grow a spectacular ruff and ear-tufts. The appearance is seldom seen here and the plumes are grown rapidly. To make way, neck plumage is shed, producing a scrawny base from which pendant finery emerges. Juveniles provide the bulk of our sightings. Migrants, some from as far away as Siberia, favour short grass habitats along wetland fringes. Most pass in August and September, although a few remain for the winter. Youngsters have neatly scaled upperparts and come in variable hues from rich honey-brown to blanched khaki. Winter birds, almost always males, turn grey and develop 'sheepskin nosebands'. The species is silent – enigmatic to a fault.

Males are famous for developing an elaborate 'ruff' of plumes around the head in the breeding season. Such a sight is rare in Ireland, where most encounters feature juveniles, which pass south in autumn. They too are remarkable and no two look the same. While size and colour intensity vary, aspects of shape and gait always say 'Ruff'.

JACK SNIPE
Lymnocryptes minimus

'JACK' MEANS SMALL, bordering on a titch. For a delightful poppet to be saddled with such a patronising name – surely coined by shooters when they noticed the smaller quarry – is an insult. Our winter visitors arrive in late October. One ringed in [then] Czechoslovakia on 29 April 1978 was shot near Banbridge, Down, in January 1980. When wisps of snipe are flushed from splashy cover, a Jack Snipe usually stays put. Instead, it will rise at the last minute from rank dry grass nearby. The bird is famous for sitting tight and has been stepped upon on more than one occasion. Flight is weak and fluttery, but more direct than Common Snipe. Singletons pitch in not far ahead and are silent unless accompanied. Where more than one are flushed they mumble *gitsch*, quieter than the whirring wingbeats that accompany take-off. Although brief, a flight view is usually good, since the bird is close. Look for a short bill. The wings are blunt, in shape recalling a game bird. Close to dusk, daytime stowaways emerge from tussocks and wet clumps and teeter into life by bouncing up and down. The bizarre, 'walk like an Egyptian' gait may be a means of maintaining a camouflage facade. Plumage is a habitat-matching collage that outshines Common Snipe's palate of colours by including green and purple: Jewel Snipe?

Jack Snipe are mighty midgets. The breeding range extends from the eastern Baltic to Siberia, which the diminutive skulker quits and migrates to winter quarters located in a vast arc from Ireland to Zimbabwe. Others winter in Asia.

COMMON SNIPE
Gallinago gallinago

DESPITE UNCEASING EFFORTS at concealment, a day in the life of a Common Snipe can be revealed. Daylight hours are passed among vegetation that matches plumage. Nirvana is mucky ground pockmarked by hooves that serve as trenches. Feeding probes are punctuated with a halting gait and movements are robotic. If startled, the body is pressed into the ground, or squatted in water. To disguise outline, the bright ginger and white tail is arched over the body to suggest an inanimate object. Only at dusk does the bird drop its guard, zigzagging into flight and calling a raspy, drawn-out, tooth-sucking *skutch!* The call elicits a response and is joined by a salvo from others hiding nearby.

Breeding territories encompass all manner of damp ground. However, nests are usually located among drier grassland. In early spring, 'drumming' flights commence and may be heard by day or night. Displaying males rise steeply and then dive, twisting and turning. The outermost pair of tail feathers spread, producing a bleating noise – vaguely recalling the 'baah' of a spring lamb – as air rushes through narrow feathers designed to vibrate and generate sound. When not tumbling and drumming, territorial males sit on a prominent perch and broadcast a completely different note, this time produced by conventional means. The proclamation is a rhythmically repeated *chip-ah, chip-ah, chip-ah*. Several 'chips' are given before the bird falls silent, starting up again after a pause. Huge numbers of Common Snipe breed in Iceland and many shot birds are ringed. The data makes interesting reading, although it scarcely atones for needless deaths. Those nesting in western Iceland travel mainly to Ireland, whereas those from the country's eastern half head for Scotland. Not all our winter visitors come from Iceland; some originate in Scandinavia and Russia.

Common Snipe feed in wet ground. The bill is driven face deep into mud. Once immersed, 'angling' jerks suggest that deep probes are being made. Often the bird takes a few steps, then tries again. Worms are located by touch and sucked whole out of burrows. Normally the bill stays put. The upper mandible is slightly longer than the lower and, if needs be, it can flex to manipulate prey. Another image of a Common Snipe – with the bill visible – appears on p. 14 (bottom left).

WOODCOCK
Scolopax rusticola

Woodcocks are shorebirds that live in forest undergrowth. To escape danger, broad stocky wings with rounded tips allow them to explode into flight, then jink and swerve.

EVEN IF YOUR VIEW is of limp remains, seeing plumage that has evolved to resemble woodland floor is captivating. The phantom does not move until dusk. During daylight it presses itself into shadows and remains motionless, unblinking if spotted. Most forage on grassy pastures. Cowpats attract worms and are hotspots. Nerve endings in the bill feel for soft tissue and prey is grasped by flexing the tip of the upper mandible backwards: rhynchokinesis, a perennial Scrabble winner. Telltale signs are clusters of holes the size of knitting needle points. Frozen ground creates feeding difficulties and large numbers undertake temporary evacuations across the Irish Sea or to the coast. Based on a sample trapped for ringing during the Big Freeze of December 2010, none was underweight. Displacement is temporary. Of 100 present on snow-covered Killard Point, Down, on 26 December 2010, almost none could be found next day following a rapid thaw (CN). Due to the bird's unfortunate status as game, many are shot. Recoveries confirm that winter visitors come from Norway and further east. Shooters claim that nocturnal travel takes place at low altitude, leading to heavy casualties when migrants encounter adverse headwinds and high seas. The first full moon in November is reputed to be the catalyst for a rapid transit from Scandinavia. A Woodcock ringed on the Dutch coast at Friesland on 15 November 1999 was shot four days later at Kenmare, Cork; a flight of 1,000 km.

Satellite tracking is proving revelatory. In winter 2009 two were caught and fitted with transmitters on the Isle of Islay, Scotland (see www.roydennis.org). The first popped across to Norway; the other, nicknamed Askaig, completed an odyssey to the edge of Siberia. It crossed the North Sea to Lübeck in Germany, then turned northeast and was on the Swedish island of Öland by 4 April. On 7 April it reached the east coast of the Baltic, in Latvia. From here it shifted northeast into Estonia and appeared to settle. Was this home? Not even close! It emerged that two weeks of minimal movement in Estonia was to permit refuelling. Flights resumed, taking it beyond the longitude of St Petersburg and then Arkhangelsk. Not until 24 May did it reach breeding grounds equivalent to the latitude of Alaska and the longitude of Iran.

During the 1988–91 survey years for the production of *The New Atlas of Breeding Birds in Britain and Ireland* (Gibbons *et al.* 1993), 179 grid squares in Ireland were found to contain breeding Woodcock, a reduction of 64 per cent on the previous atlas survey covering 1968–72 (Sharrock 1976). Roding birds patrol low in the sky, following a regular beat and croaking. The croak is followed by a high-pitched, air-escaping-from-a-balloon *tizzick*. Back and forth he goes, flying straight and fast, with heavy, owl-like wingbeats. Meanwhile, his mate is ensconced on the ground. During daylight she slowly rotates her sitting position to ensure that her head faces away from the sun, for fear of large eyes glinting and giving away position. Chicks leave the nest as soon as they are born. If danger threatens, the parent evacuates offspring by air, rising without a murmur and clasping the cargo with either bill or foot.

To facilitate vision on all sides without moving a muscle, the eyes of a Woodcock are located, Dalek-style, close to the top of the head.

BLACK-TAILED GODWIT
Limosa limosa

IT IS NOT OFTEN that the fortunes of a rare and beautiful creature change to such an extent that it becomes familiar even on urban green spaces. Among shorebirds only Curlews are taller, although there is little chance of confusion since Black-tailed Godwits have straight bills and, in flight, boldly patterned black-and-white wings and tail. Come April, adults moult out of winter drabness and acquire decadent brick-red chests and backs spangled with flame-orange and sable.

The bird winters on estuaries and coastal wetlands from Ireland to Morocco. In spring, adults stream north to Iceland. Ringed and colour-banded birds provide a fascinating insight. Although breeding and wintering quarters are the axes determining the birds' universe, within these limits an individual has many choices. Pairs separate and winter in different countries – Portugal and Ireland being two – before trysting in Iceland. Some adults settle in a limited wintering area and follow a sedentary existence; others are restless and flit from Lincolnshire to Hampshire, on to Liverpool and then across the Irish Sea to Ireland. Once here, itchy feet trek up and down the east coast from Dublin to Belfast and Cork. Remarkably, the same itinerary may be followed annually. Less colourful immatures, too young to breed or acquire showy plumage, remain with us during summer, enjoying a gap year. By August, southbound juveniles start to arrive, each maiden flight a solo effort; parents went south days or even weeks before. Across the back and wings, juveniles have tortoiseshell plumage that, along with bright cinnamon necks, contrasts with a pale belly.

Black-tailed Godwits wade and probe for worms and midge larvae in water, soft mud and grassland. When an abundance of food has been located, individuals pack close, within stabbing distance. The result is bill swordfights and a rising and falling babble known as 'shuckling'. In areas where they are used to people, flocks can be viewed well enough to discern structural differences between the sexes. Males are smaller, shorter-billed and shorter-legged than the truly gangly females. While normally fairly calm, alarm periodically sweeps like a wave of suspicion over a feeding pack and all stand erect. In that moment they appear statuesque, a forest of knitting needles. A snap decision to fly is executed by a flurry of wings and a near vertical take-off. Calls accompany departure, a salvo of *quick, quick, quick* – an onomatopoeic means of remembering the sound? A lean look pervades the flight silhouette. As well as a long bill, stick-like legs project well beyond the tail (see p. 13, bottom right, in 'Under the Hood'). Bar-tailed Godwit, while similar in shape, has shorter legs that do not project.

Because the outer third of the bill is crammed with touch-sensitive cells, the probing range equates to the distance that the bill (and sometimes the face) is shoved into mud. Feeding birds often do not see what they swallow when they pulse the head back and draw up dinner between the mandibles. Possibly a wise decision.

By April, a male Black-tailed Godwit's hormones have created a masterpiece. The bill has flushed yellow and blistering hues adorn freshly minted plumage across the head, chest and scapulars. Yet the folded wings are grey and tatty – but good enough to carry the bird home to Iceland. Proof that function and decadence join forces in courtship.

From left: adult male in breeding plumage; centre, juvenile male; right, first-winter female. Bill length is longer in females.

BAR-TAILED GODWIT
Limosa lapponica

BAR-TAILED GODWITS feed along firm mudflats and sandy coastlines, neither of which is popular with Black-tailed Godwits. They have a fine, pared-off bill tip, which curves gently upwards, like an upturned nose. The bill is driven deep into mud or wet sand to probe for lugworms and other invertebrates. Often, as it inserts the bill, the bird twists it sideways. Bar-tailed is shorter-legged and slightly smaller than its more elegant sister species, with plain wings and no black tail band. Nevertheless, identifying a lone bird is tricky. Winter field marks are a textured back pattern on Bar-tailed Godwit, due to each feather being dark-shafted, and a prominent supercilium that kinks upwards behind the eye. Crown plumage is streaked, producing a wet-combed look; on Black-tailed Godwit it is plain. Head-on, Black-tailed Godwits have a diffuse dark shadow vertically bisecting a grey chest – the inescapable analogy being a cleavage line. On a snoozing Bar-tailed, the breast is bisected horizontally by a gorget. The commonest flight call is a doubled-up low toot, not dissimilar to the cartoon voice ascribed to the Roadrunner character. Large gatherings perform spectacular aerial revolutions, diving at angles close to vertical when spiralling down to land.

Most of the world's Bar-tailed Godwits nest inside the Arctic Circle. Thanks to satellite tracking, phenomenal migratory stamina is being revealed. Those wintering in New Zealand breed in Alaska. The birds await the arrival of northerly tailwinds and then depart south, flying non-stop over the Pacific for around four days to reach antipodean winter quarters. Our Bar-tailed Godwits presumably make equally impressive long-haul flights to Lapland. Departures commence in March and all fly to the Dutch coast where they moult into breeding plumage. We rarely see them in roaring rufous except in July, when southbound

Distinguishing Bar-tailed Godwit from Black-tailed Godwit in winter plumage is not particularly easy. Across the upperparts, Bar-tailed plumage is streaked and mottled, akin to Curlew, whereas Black-tailed Godwit is relatively plain (see p. 152).

adults pass through en route to West Africa, where many winter. Juveniles follow on the cusp of August, those in the vanguard arriving simultaneously with juvenile Black-tailed Godwits from Iceland. On some muddy shorelines, the two can be seen probing side by side. A remarkable dissimilarity is found in the fact that the slightly smaller Bar-tailed Godwit has flown three times further to reach our latitude.

A juvenile Bar-tailed Godwit freshly arrived in Ireland in early autumn. With the nearest breeding grounds in the Arctic Circle of Finland, the youngster has already travelled far. Bar-tailed Godwits replace Black-tailed Godwits in northern habitats. The two are separated by the world's belt of coniferous forest. Bar-tailed breeds on Arctic tundra, Black-tailed on temperate marsh and meadow.

WHIMBREL
Numenius phaeopus

SOUND RATHER THAN SIGHT is the key to detecting this smaller relative of Curlews. Passing flocks are in a hurry and scarcely pause to feed. Calls ring out from overhead – a stuttered yodel of six or seven repeated whistles, easily imitated. A good rendition can entice strays to check out the impersonation. By July Iceland's breeding population is on the move again, this time drifting south less frenetically and heading for wintering grounds in Africa. Migrants like to join ranks of Curlews and godwits. In build, they are more compact, including the bill, which is shorter with a discernible crook midway along its length. A short-billed look is obvious in flight when, bizarrely, the bill can look straight. Curlew bills are longer, especially in females and, overall, their curvature is smooth and gradual. Compare the thickness of the bill tip with the base. The bill of a Whimbrel is relatively uniform; Curlew bills, except when juvenile, taper to a fine point, clearly narrower than the girth at the base. Moreover, Whimbrels have a chocolate-coloured cap divided by a light median stripe. In comparison, Curlew heads look lighter and less contrasting, although beware some with a narrow crown stripe. Still, problems remain: many pass overhead, curtailing comprehensive examination and loners dozing among Curlews tuck the bill among back plumage. Fear not: darker upperparts and a whiter belly are useful steers. Sifting for a young Turk among gatherings of old gentlemen Curlews is rewarding – the prince is demure and dashing. A few spend the winter with us, poking quietly for molluscs and crabs among rock pools and seaweed.

Above: Structure and flight pattern are broadly similar in Whimbrel and Curlew. While sometimes difficult to discern, a Whimbrel's stripy head pattern is distinctive; most look 'capped' and the bill is more sharply downturned than a Curlew.

Below: 'Heard before seen.' Every May, lyrical calling from flocks of Whimbrels fills the air over Ireland's western coastal districts. The melodic whistling is not just utilitarian: migrants are bursting to breed in Iceland and full of joie de vivre.

CURLEW
Numenius arquata

CURLEWS HAVE the air of old gentlemen and move sedately, like an anglepoise lamp brought to life. Coming in to land reveals a degree of ungainliness. They plane downward, hoist the wings to create drag, and run a short distance to become stationary, a procedure mimicked by a human parachutist. Size and long legs make recognition straightforward. The bill's shape is not accidental; the burrows of mudflat-dwelling worms are also long and angled. On land, the long bill is used to probe for earthworms or buried insect larvae. In flight a dark wing hand contrasts against mealy upperparts, while a white rump and finely barred tail suggest the rear-end profile of an immature gull, an analogy reinforced by size and a tucked-in neck. Most of the plumage suggests the colour and texture of weathered hessian rope. White feathering encircles the eye, a Polo mint in a sea of fawn. Because a proportion of Curlews show a narrow pale crown stripe, confusion with Whimbrel is possible.

In early spring, most quit estuaries and damp inland fields and migrate to breeding grounds in Scotland, Scandinavia (two killed on Strangford Lough came from Finland) and even further east; some in Lincolnshire hailed from Arkhangelsk on the Russian shores of the White Sea (AL). Thanks to a transmitter fitted by the Highland Wildlife Foundation, a year in the life of one female has been revealed. The bird was trapped on 31 March 2009 at the Beauly Firth in northeast Scotland. A flurry of signals received around dusk on 17 April amounted to strong evidence that she was up and away, possibly accompanied by a breeding partner. Through the early hours of 22 April she crossed the Norwegian mountains and arrived on the shores of the Baltic, in Sweden. Helped by a tailwind, speeds of over 100km/h were achieved. Until May the bird settled among coastal fields, moving north in small hops, before crossing to Finland. By 4 May she reached breeding grounds consisting of meadows and hayfields near Ruukki. Egg laying and incubation take one month and chicks are left in the care of the male roughly ten to twenty days after they hatch. Sometime in late June she left Finland and was relocated at the southern tip of Norway. On 1 July a signal was received from close to Mintlaw near the Aberdeenshire coast; four days later she touched down at the Beauly Firth. The breeding odyssey lasted a mere eleven weeks. Home, it could be argued, is really Scotland.

In Ireland, small numbers breed over a dwindling supply of upland fields, bogs and remote lake islands. During the period 1988–91, an estimated 5,000 pairs bred throughout the Republic of Ireland (Gibbons *et al.* 1993). Sixty sites were resurveyed in 2011. Only six held nesting pairs. The national population estimate stands at 200 pairs, a catastrophic decline of 96 per cent. What happened? Writing in 2011, Anita Donaghy of BirdWatch Ireland cites moorland vanishing under conifers, bogs cut over by machine, and marginal hill land drained and ploughed or abandoned and covered with rushes and scrub (Donaghy 2011). As habitat becomes fragmented, Curlews become vulnerable to

Above: A juvenile Curlew, fresh-feathered but with a bill somewhat shy of fully grown. Nowadays, few of the youngsters that appear on the coast in August boast a 'Made in Ireland' sticker. Local populations have nose-dived. Breeders have been purged by a cocktail of woes blighting bogland and hill ground; wild places once epitomised by the bird's bubbling song.

Facing page above: Curlews are gregarious and come together to rest and preen when feeding grounds are covered during high tide. Tawny withered grass offers perfect camouflage. Although seldom taken by Peregrines, dozing birds have much to fear from foxes. Night roosts are in shallow water, across which no quadruped can launch a surprise attack.

Facing page below: An aura of romance surrounds the Curlew. Its stirring call represents a narrative that sums up mud, water and sky – a skirl that betokens wilderness. Increasingly, it sounds like a lament.

predation. Foxes, succoured among conifer plantations, and a galaxy of crows make short shrift of clutches and offspring. Boosted by sheep carrion, Ravens have increased greatly across upland and were reckoned to be 'more than casual egg-eaters' by Derek Ratcliffe, a celebrated field biologist. North of the border, the situation is equally bleak. Surviving sanctuaries include islands in Lough Erne and the wilder Glens of Antrim, which held twenty-six pairs in 2011. In at least one – Glenwherry – predator control to protect Red Grouse has, despite being opposed by the RSPB, provided local Curlews with a lifeline.

COMMON SANDPIPER
Actitis hypoleucos

THIS IS A PRETTY SHOREBIRD with special qualities; the mundane name sells it short. For a start, it is not particularly common. Winters are spent in the tropics. By late April migrants are back and bobbing with tremulous uncertainty along lakeshores, coast and banks of moorland streams. They perch on stones and pick along wet edges. The tail pivots and the head jerks, keeping time with a spring-sprong gait. The ballerina is skittish and flies off quickly, accompanied by a ringing *see wee wee*. Once breeding territory has been established, proper song commences – an oscillating musical twitter. The verse is animated yet sweet; imagine the sound of a security alarm designed for a doll's house. By the middle of July, loners and family parties move to seashores prior to departure. When disturbed, flight is low and over water. Beats are stiff and come in short bursts on outstretched wings, as if quickly opening and closing an umbrella to shake it dry.

Right: Normally famed for a horizontal rather than upright stance, this juvenile is reacting to the presence of a stalking fox. Vigilance is ingrained. Because young shorebirds have independence thrust upon them as soon as they fledge, they are born with a full set of wits.

Adult Common Sandpiper in breeding plumage. Hotfoot from Africa, males waste no time in advertising for a mate. In a dramatic aerial display, the bird circles overhead and delivers a high, pulsating trill, fluttering its wings and describing a wide, heavenly loop. Yet under normal circumstances flight is 'seabird low'.

GREENSHANK
Tringa nebularia

GREENSHANKS ARE catwalk material. Their elegant stature and gait exude an air of shorebird royalty. Wading belly-deep along the edges of channels, they stride actively and occasionally dash around in pursuit of tiny fish. Aquatic feeding habits mean that the diagnostic leg colour – pickled cucumber green – is often hard to see. In winter, several hundreds occur in a thin nation-wide spread. At this season the bird is ghostly pale below and bank manager grey above. On the wing, a V-shaped white rump links to a whitish tail and the bird delivers an emphatic, ringing-in-your-ears *tew-tew-tew*.

Migrating adults with black-speckled breasts pass through in July, followed by juveniles sporting the neatest 'wet-combed' plumage of any shorebird. Small numbers breed on Scotland's Hebridean islands, with more in the Flow Country, but most hail from Scandinavia and are bound for Africa. Next time you watch a documentary featuring big game around a watering hole, keep a sharp eye out for a Greenshank dashing out of the path of a waddling hippo. It could be Hamish from Harris.

Shank (lower leg) colour separates Greenshank from Redshank. To boot, Greenshanks have grey-toned upperparts and a 'walking stick' slightly upturned bill.

REDSHANK
Tringa totanus

REDSHANKS are jack-of-all-trades shorebirds with subdued plumage brought to life by vivid orange-red legs, hence the name. The standard flight call is two notes – *tee yew* – but the terminal note is often spun into two or three repetitions: *tee yew, yew, yew*. Iceland's Redshanks winter with us, whereas our own breeding population has undergone a catastrophic decline, brought to the edge of extinction by a pincer movement of wetland drainage and predation by crows, foxes and introduced North American Mink. Traditional sites were marshy fields, often alongside Lapwings. Redshanks conceal themselves under a bower of grass and sneak off silently when danger threatens, proving that they can keep quiet when it suits them. Displays commence with the first mild spell of the New Year. With relish, males ring out *klu, klu, klu, klu* ad nauseam. At the same time, would-be husbands curtsy around potential partners, bill angled down and wings upraised, climaxing in a puppet-on-a-string airborne extravaganza on shivering wings. Reaching the azimuth of an arc, the bird glides forwards and repeats the show in a yo-yo progression. Winter visitors feed mainly on tiny mud-snails and worms. Redshanks are seldom still as they pick, probe and wade across mudflats, coastlines and fields. The size of the prey is minute, causing the bird to feed for many hours and even at night, influenced by tide cycles. In darkness the bill is opened and sieved from side to side to feel for prey. Nowadays, some patrol amenity grassland and, in parks regularly frequented by humans, appear less timid – until passers-by pause for a closer look.

Forever striding along at an even pace and pecking rhythmically in mud, the bird sees everything in the neighbourhood and is a loudmouth. Piqued alarm notes rally all and sundry. To bolster clarion calls, a striking wing pattern ensures that a warning is flashed.

Juvenile Redshanks are more brown-and-beige, with yellowish-orange legs and profusely dotted upperparts. Migrants arrive in August and frequently wrong-foot observers who cannot believe that the humble Redshank can be so sublime.

Wearing the expression of a man about to be hanged, a Redshank oozes distrust at human approach.

On estuaries, the range of prey available to shorebirds is reflected in bills and legs. Surface-probing Knots are short-billed and short-legged; amphibious Bar-tailed Godwits are long-legged and long-billed; macho-billed Oystercatchers tackle tough shells impregnable to others; orange-legged Redshanks are middlemen (all four of these species are in the photograph). All feeding is governed by the tide. High water is down time and a chance to rub shoulders with the neighbours.

TURNSTONE
Arenaria interpres

TURNSTONES eschew mudflats, preferring rock and wrack. Stones and limp piles of seaweed are overturned as skirmishers pick and poke. A low centre of gravity and a jemmy-bar bill bestow real strength. Small stones are not so much turned as tossed. Loose rocks up to the size of the bird itself are heaved aside to check for prey. When crashing surf does not drown acoustics, the clinking sound made by a squadron flicking pebbles recalls the patter of hail. Where wind-dried kelp gathers along storm beaches, ensembles shoulder their way through tossed sheaves, rolling kelp into tumbleweeds and snatching dislodged creepy-crawlies. Turnstones are the Starlings of the shore; indeed, the two armies frequently join forces. On North America's Great Lakes, migrants bound for the Arctic stop off at tern colonies and devour clutches. If disturbed, feeding parties tend to sit tight and hope for anonymity, dogged in the belief that their slate-spangled raiment disguises them. It usually does. When flight is inevitable, they dash off a stuttering volley of metallic *tu* notes.

Turnstones migrate huge distances and nest within fifteen degrees of the North Pole. Summer plumage is acquired in late spring and replaced during August. Consequently, the finery is generally only revealed in the Arctic, although early southbound migrants are still in party dress. Breeding birds are largely white-headed, their upperparts braided with flame orange, a far cry from winter humdrum. Ringing recoveries and sightings of colour-banded individuals indicate that our wintering population is derived from Greenland and northeast Canada. Some travel on to winter quarters along sun-drenched African coasts. In both 2009 and 2010, a bird tracked from a tiny (1g) geolocator completed a 27,000km round trip from Australia to Alaska. A juvenile ringed on the German North Sea coast was shot next day on the Atlantic coast of France, 850km southwest. During a fortnight at sea up to 400km west of Ireland during August 2009, migrants were seen flying low over the ocean in rough weather but passing high overhead on fine days (AMG).

For those lucky enough to visit the Arctic, the sight of our very own 'common or garden' Turnstone in full breeding plumage is a revelation.

Juveniles possess pristine, albeit sombre plumage. Travellers freshly arrived from the Arctic, because they have not encountered humans before, are often extremely tame.

Not only are Turnstones sociable during feeding bouts, sometimes they co-operate and team up to flip over objects too large for one bird alone.

GREY PHALAROPE
Phalaropus fulicarius

MOST BIRDWATCHERS struggle to see this species; some struggle to pronounce its name (*fal-a-rope*). Grey Phalaropes are birds of the ocean. Although they are shorebirds, they have largely abandoned land and, somewhere along an evolutionary journey, developed lobed feet for swimming. Feeding movements are extraordinarily fast, quicker than a feather wafted in an eddy of wind. They spin around, this way and that, in constant motion. Greenland is the source of waifs that pass our way in autumn. Rough weather temporarily deflects some close to the coast, chiefly juveniles embarked upon maiden flights. Finding that they have run out of ocean, some switch to feeding in sheltered bays. Others soldier on past headlands; indomitable blips buzzing along in the troughs between white-capped waves. During autumn, migrating Turnstones, Sanderlings and Dunlin also scurry past among choppy waves, but none is at home there. Only a Grey Phalarope will opt to settle on the water, glide like a cherubic shearwater or 'accelerate and decelerate' in a peculiarly variable groundspeed that, no matter its pace, seems stuck in low gear. When the world's oceans teemed with large whales, Grey Phalaropes attended the leviathans, landing on backs and divesting skin of parasites, oxpecker-style, a habit still witnessed on wintering grounds in the Roaring Forties.

Among shorebirds, the Grey Phalarope takes things to the limit. Entirely maritime outside the breeding season, it migrates from wintering areas strung over the southern oceans to breed within the Arctic Circle. Nicknamed 'galebirds' by coastal inhabitants in eastern Canada, most approach the shore only when swept along by storms.

ARCTIC SKUA
Stercorarius parasiticus

THINK OF SKUAS as marine birds of prey, although they usually stop short of harming their victim. There is no need – they simply want its dinner. They chase and panic a tern or Kittiwake into disgorging fish. Hence predator (technically, skuas are termed 'kleptoparasites') and prey are inextricably linked. Over recent years the disappearance of shoals of small fish in northern waters of the North Atlantic has led to catastrophic breeding failure among many seabirds. As a result, many Arctic Skuas are also failing to breed.

Four species of skua nest on tundra and pass our latitude on migration. Identifying them is a challenge. Even experienced birdwatchers can make multiple guesses in attempting to name a passing singleton, with one attempt supplanted by the next when impressions of size and flight become better refined as the target approaches. Two rarer species, Long-tailed and Pomarine Skuas, tend to slip past at sea and are hard to track down. Arctic Skuas loiter closer to shore, and between hunts they idle off the coast, waiting for passing trade. Hotspots occur where fish concentrate, such as Lough Foyle and Dundrum Bay. Patterson (1880) describes a scene from Belfast Lough that, except in the manner of its conclusion, can still be witnessed today:

[Arctic Skuas] are only to be seen here in the autumn, August and September, and into October. When shoals of fry come into the lough in large numbers, larger fish and birds

If a Peregrine were deprived of the acceleration provided by stooping, it might find that the Arctic Skua is its match as a speed merchant in level flight.

accompany them, and then it is that our beautiful bay looks its best. Its waters are full of fish; its surface covered with Razorbills, Puffins and Guillemots, and the air above peopled with gulls and terns. The skua singles out a bird that it observes to have been successful in fishing and, swooping down upon its unfortunate victim, pursues it relentlessly until the bird casts up part of its food. This accomplished, the skua, after picking up the dainty morsel, flies quietly away. The attention of one of the Bottle-nosed Whales, some of which are generally in the lough on such occasions, will now be attracted; and he generally puts an end to the fun by swallowing half the ball of fry at a mouthful.

Arctic Skuas bear some resemblance to gulls, but their dark, kelp-brown colouring and sleek lines hint of an altogether different way of finding food.

GREAT SKUA
Stercorarius skua

ALSO KNOWN AS BONXIES, a Norse name used in Shetland, Great Skuas are heavy, stocky and mean. The bird is a nomad, travelling hopefully and ranging far and wide in search of victims from whom it can steal food. Reputation is sufficient to cause panic, even if the bully is in a benign mood. Migration details are well known thanks to ringing. Chicks depart in August and pass rapidly south. Some have been recovered at the end of August on the coast of Morocco. Southward movement by juveniles continues throughout the winter and small numbers cross the Equator. Until they are old enough to breed – at age four or five – home can be anywhere from the Mediterranean to equatorial waters or the Grand Banks of Newfoundland. Adults tend to winter less far south, mainly between the Southwest Approaches and Iberia.

Hallmarks include brilliant white wing flashes, a hooked bill and sharp claws on webbed feet. A novel but worrying habit is the deliberate dislodging and capture of juvenile Kittiwakes from nest ledges. Non-breeders loiter off the coast from July onwards, often scavenging around fishing boats. Peak numbers occur from late August until the middle of October, when adults and the year's crop of juveniles track south. By November all have departed. In spring, passage involves mainly adults that pass north off the west coast of Ireland, rather than entering the Irish Sea.

In evolutionary terms, this is a new kid on the block. Its ancestral home is in the subantarctic, where four related species occur, two of which perform annual trans-equatorial migrations. Founders from the southern hemisphere established a breeding outpost in Iceland and then Shetland. Over a relatively short time period, perhaps only a few thousand years, northern hemisphere colonists evolved into a distinct species, although retaining a striking similarity to southern ancestors. The bird's fortunes were boosted when trawlers began gutting at sea and wastefully discarding unwanted fish.

Above: Given a choice between being knocked senseless and possibly killed, most seabirds jettison food and make a hasty escape from a piratical Great Skua.

Below: Great Skuas converge on seabird colonies to breed. For centuries, the world population was comparatively small – largely due to persecution – and restricted to Iceland, the Faroe Islands and Foula, one of the Shetland Islands. Thanks to decades of protection in Scotland, fortunes have changed and several pairs now breed in Ireland.

MUDDLED BY MOULT?

BIRDS DO NOT BREED when the food supply is at its best. They reserve the period of greatest abundance for the year's largest single moult – the replacement of plumage on the head, body and wings. This occurs after breeding and most juveniles moult at or around the same time. Moult is necessary because, as plumage wears, it reduces insulation and affects powers of flight.

The first feathers to be shed are the innermost primaries, and the last to regrow are the outermost primaries or the innermost secondaries. In the meantime, all other wing and body feathers are replaced. An orderly sequence is followed. Primaries can be numbered according to the order in which they are moulted, starting with the short innermost to the long outermost, usually the tenth primary (see 'Under the Hood', p. 12). The process is so energy-demanding that it cannot coincide with other activities such as breeding or migrating. Chaffinches were found to use 25 per cent more oxygen during moult (Newton 1972). Because food is usually plentiful in late summer, many adults moult then. At the same season, fledged youngsters undergo a partial (post-juvenile) moult, replacing their first generation of 'soft' plumage, much of it grown while still in the nest. Large flight and tail feathers, and the biggest wing coverts, are kept for another year. Adults, for whom moult can last twelve weeks, feel vulnerable. They turn incognito, as best they can, by becoming silent and secretive. Adult songbirds avoid long flights and skulk in cover. Moulting Wheatears have been observed feeding hastily, then retreating underground inside rabbit burrows (AMG). Hormones switch metabolism from breeding mode to plumage production. The skin becomes heavily vascularised and growing feathers are encased in a protective pin-shaped sheath connected to the blood supply. As the feather emerges, the sheath shrinks. When fully grown, the feather hardens and its blood supply ceases. Technically, it is a dead structure, although scrupulously maintained until the next moult.

Curlews exhibit a standard countenance from one moult to the next, although juveniles are shorter-billed than adults (see p. 156). Neither Rome nor Curlew bills were built in a day. Many species do not moult 'like for like'. Young Robins are speckled (see p. 271). When they moult in summer they acquire a red breast for life, male or female. Other species synchronise moulting head and body with the onset of breeding condition, and then change in late summer: in other words, they moult into breeding plumage and then moult out of it. Black-headed Gulls are largely white-headed during winter (see p. 171). Early in the New Year they moult head and body plumage: the body remains white, but chocolate-brown feathers create a hood. Once nesting is over, new plumage reverts to white. Finches and buntings attain breeding plumage without moulting. Their trick is to allow abrasion to expose underlying colours, thereby changing appearance without having to grow new plumage. In autumn, male Chaffinch has a two-tone buff-and-grey crown and nape. In preparation for courtship, the colour changes to bright slate-blue. The tip of each feather is weak, and wears off. The process is gradual throughout the year but accelerates in early spring, when an estimated 7 per cent of the feather tip disappears in a month (Sokolowski 1969).

What is the secret of understanding the variation of immature gulls, which look as if they were designed in a rage and dressed in a tempest? Essentially, they are teenagers going through moult phases. Until adolescence is over and they resemble parents, they are shunned as breeding partners. Blotchy plumage is analogous to acne. Black, white and grey form the palate of adult plumage. By definition, a large gull with some brown feathers will be immature. With each moult, the aspiring grown-up acquires a more mature look, and not just in plumage. Eye and bill pigments change, as does leg colour in some species. Young gulls are dark-billed and dark-eyed, whereas adults have brightly coloured bills and, in larger species, pale 'goat' eyes. Youngsters age on a sliding scale. Eyes lighten gradually, bills develop insipid colour and speckling disappears as a final generation of unblemished feathers becomes established.

In essence, once a *juvenile* moults its head and body plumage (for most, towards the end of summer) it embarks on a personal road to change. This begets the epithet *first-winter*. Fast forward to the following spring. When it moults again, at roughly one year old, it undergoes a makeover to *first-summer*. Next, in autumn, a root-and-branch moult of head, body, tail and wings reclassifies it as *second-winter*. In Black-headed Gull, second-winter plumage is adult-like. In effect, adolescence is over. Common Gulls retain residual signs of immaturity for one more year; *second-winter* is succeeded by *second-summer*. Adulthood is reached following another complete moult in autumn, when the bird is two and a bit. Large gulls make the same progression but their tariff is even longer: a Herring Gull's transition from dun to divine takes four years (see pp. 177–78).

Winter is the best time to regard immature gulls. Sublime filigree plumage can be enjoyed rather than regarded as some kind of identification challenge. Come spring, sophomores approaching summertime birthdays are a mess. Signs of moult are everywhere. Dog-eared plumage, mirroring a well-thumbed hymnbook, has been defiled by wear and bleached by sunlight; and missing feathers complicate matters. Older immatures, exhibiting elements of adulthood, are more easily identified. For all age classes, attention to size, shape and structure is an alternative guide. For example, bill structure is diagnostic in Great Black-backed Gull. While plumage has its uses, it is not the only recognition tool.

Depending on the size of the species, gulls take between two and five years to progress via a series of moults from adolescence to breeding age. Common Gull, depicted above (top row), morphs into an adult in three years, by which age it has replaced the large feathers of the wings and tail three times and body plumage six times. (L–r): fledged juvenile (summer); first-winter (autumn to spring); second-winter (one year older); adult winter (two years of age or older); adult breeding plumage. Note the deterioration in feather condition between juvenile and first-winter plumage. On the first-winter, except for the emergence of a grey 'saddle' and sufficient fresh facial plumage to make the bird pale-headed, all other feathers have been retained. Several effects of wear can be seen, especially across the wings. Worn plumage looks frayed and less colourful. Light-coloured feathers wear more quickly. Dark feathers contain melanin (blackish pigment) that actually strengthens the feather.

Moult progression in Starlings (bottom row) is easy to see. Juvenile feathers on songbirds are typically weak, so most shed them within weeks of fledging but strangely do not moult their main flight or tail feathers as adults always do. Thus, they have to manage with 'economy class' wing feathers for well over a year. Whether the juvenile plumage is similar to the adult (for example, crows) or different (for example, Starling and Robin), the moult always involves all feathers on the head and body. On close inspection, worn and faded virginal feathers are discernible on many one-year-old birds. In fact, Starlings are an exception because they undergo a total moult, including wings and tail.

Especially in July (second from left) juveniles in the throes of active moult combine the foreparts of a mousy fledgling (far left) with a rash of spots – a foretaste of adult-like winter plumage (third from left). Moult progresses headwards. By October young and adults are, to all intents, indistinguishable. Come spring (far right) adults lose spots and flaunt wonderful 'lacquered' plumes of emerald, cobalt and purple. These become visible when the covering of obscuring spots wears off. The older the individual, the longer the shag-pile breast feathering.

KITTIWAKE
Rissa tridactyla

IF YOU WANT TO experience onomatopoeia in action, visit a Kittiwake colony. The moniker is uttered incessantly by nesting pairs and others riding gusts along cliff-faces, dangling like puppets with crooked wings and splayed feet. Nests made from flotsam are attached to hair-raisingly narrow ledges. By trampling, the bird cements a foundation onto a protuberance. Chicks are equipped with claws for clinging. They are also remarkably placid, which reduces the risk of tumbling to a watery grave. To test instinct, researchers exchanged Kittiwake young for those of ground-nesting Black-headed Gulls. Within minutes, the Black-headed Gull chicks stepped from the ledge and fell (they were saved by safety nets). Rather than being fed by a parent regurgitating food at their feet, young Kittiwakes thrust deep inside the adult's mouth. A wide black band across the nape of juveniles is believed to serve as an appeasement mark that reinforces passivity.

Youngsters are dramatically different from adults. A striking combination of black, white and grey creates a zigzag pattern. Adults have a hi-vis lemon-yellow bill shaped like a carving knife, and short black legs. The legs are set somewhat close to the tail, affecting the bird's centre of gravity and producing a sentinel stance. Grey upperparts glow with a faint bluish light and black wedges across the end of the wings make the tips look as though they have been dipped in ink. Unlike other gulls that have black wingtips, adult Kittiwakes lack white marks within the black plumage at the wingtip. Moreover, the shade of grey separating the inner wing from the wingtip is silvery. Especially at distance, this catches the eye and may be more distinctive than the black wingtips, which are lost against the background of a dark sea. A Spitfire wingtip shape is best appreciated in overcast light.

During autumn, most disappear out to sea. Colonies are reoccupied in early spring. Troupes of adults bedecked in immaculate plumage appear like snow flurries from grey expanses of ocean. Irish Kittiwakes fan west, and ringing recoveries of chicks from Great Saltee, Wexford, tell a story of youngsters exhibiting wanderlust across a huge bailiwick from the Bay of Biscay to the Grand Banks of Newfoundland, or into the Davis Strait between Labrador and Greenland. By the same token, youngsters from Arctic Russia have been found here during the breeding season. Much empirical data has arisen through the slaughter of breeding seabirds in Greenland. Ours are among the dead. On migration, large numbers are compressed inshore by inclement weather. Battling high winds, they fly in roller-coaster arcs. Rather than being distributed randomly, they pass in 'lanes' and form up in flocks. In less turbulent seas they travel briskly with a distinctive rowing action, staying aloft but with the head crooked, on the lookout for food.

Left, three birds: adults in breeding plumage; centre and far right, juveniles; second from right, adult winter. Youngsters retain juvenile plumage until the following spring.

BLACK-HEADED GULL
Chroicocephalus ridibundus

ALL PLUMAGES show a dazzling white slash across the forewing. In breeding plumage the bill is wine-coloured, not the black-tipped bright red that it becomes in winter. Juveniles are startling. Drenched with fawn, chestnut and ginger, it is hard to believe they are the same species. During summer, a moult of head, underparts and most of the upperparts, amalgamates youngsters among hordes of adults. The transformation still leaves distinctions, principally the retention of some brown, juvenile wing coverts and a black tail band.

Black-headed Gulls are noisy: a hint of its cackling voice is given by the *ridibundus* (laughing) in its Latin name. Ubiquity masks peregrinations by a wanderer whose breeding range stretches from Iceland to Siberia. In February 2010, approachability permitted reading ring details of two at Antrim Marina on the shores of Lough Neagh. Both were born in Lithuania in 2006 (NMK). Black-headed Gulls on islands are opportunists, sometimes settling en masse where none bred before. On inland wetlands, breeding stations sometimes vanish inexplicably. The loss of large colonies on lakes across Connacht was attributable to predation by American Mink. Concentrations on the Copeland Islands disappeared for a different reason, almost certainly egg theft by humans.

All gulls lured by the prospect of a free lunch at landfill sites run the risk of contracting botulism. Individuals in the throes of the malady – which is fatal – are sometimes found in suburbia, cowering on the ground. They present a variety of symptoms, some consistent with having a broken wing. In truth, the bird is in the grip of an advancing paralysis. Neville McKee describes the mode and potency of the disease:

Botulism is a curious disease. It is not an infection by a microbe and is not infectious in the normal sense. The species responsible for bird deaths is *Clostridium botulinum*. Its spores are widespread and, if conditions become suitable for them to grow, the spores germinate and multiply rapidly. Botulism only thrives in water or juicy food that lacks oxygen, a circumstance that can occur readily in still bodies of fresh or brackish water in warm weather. The water has to have a stew of food in it – dead bodies of animals, a doomed fish shoal cornered in a drying pool or lake, a bloom of algae in the end stage, or overgrowth of water plants in the process of rotting. Many species of bacteria and other microbes decompose the surplus organic matter and, in the process, absorb all available oxygen. Oxygen from the air will not be able to diffuse into the water through the scum that typically blankets such water bodies; hence those bacteria that started the rotting process cease to be involved in decomposition once the oxygen is used up.

Botulism slashed gull populations after boom years in the latter part of the last millennium. Warm weather, foul water and waste food proved to be a lethal cocktail.

Eventually the stew is populated by anaerobic bacterial species – including C. botulinum. As C. botulinum proliferate, they exude a powerful toxin into their surroundings. If this is water (as in a rock pool) or even large lake, the water becomes poisonous to drink. Where the mass of bacteria grows in a carcass or in a sealed black plastic sack of waste food (especially meat-based) on a rubbish tip, the toxin diffuses through all of the contents of the sack. Gulls at rubbish tips that tear open the sack inadvertently eat food that is full of toxin. The toxin is a neurotoxin, affecting the nervous system. It first shows in the bird's legs making it unsteady, as if drunk. Then it spreads to the wings, which flop, suggesting that one or both are broken. Next, the entire body becomes paralysed leaving only head movement. The head droops, coining 'rubberneck' as a term for this stage of the disease in North America. Within a day or two, the victim dies.

The disease cannot spread as an infection because the bacteria are not of themselves poisonous. Rather, the toxin that exudes from the bacteria causes death through paralysis. Generally only the primary consumers of the original source of contamination will become ill and die. An exception occurs when flies eat the food source. Birds that feed on flies in large quantities can build up a lethal dose of the toxin in their own tissues. (NMK, pers. comm.)

(L–r): five adults in head moult transition to breeding plumage. The left-hand bird has almost acquired a full brown hood, tabbing the date of the montage as March. Until they are one year old, youngsters (far right) are orange-billed and retain brown, speckled coverts on the forward edge of the wing.

MEDITERRANEAN GULL
Larus melanocephalus

MEDITERRANEAN GULLS are on the march. In little under half a century the mainstay of the world population, centred on the Black Sea, has shot up from 31,000 pairs in 1946 to a staggering 319,000 in 1993. The species pushed west in a blitzkrieg colonising movement, founding new populations from Hungary to the Netherlands. In Britain, since the first pair bred in 1968, a manyfold increase has occurred. In 2000, the first Irish nest was found on Blue Circle Island in Larne Lough, although County Wexford has subsequently emerged as the epicentre of Ireland's small breeding population. Despite nesting in parts of the Mediterranean, the bird's status there is still that of a winter visitor. In 1950, when it was rare in northwest Europe, the bulk dispersed from a single site in Ukraine to winter off the east coast of Spain. Its fortunes seemed so tenuous that in 1960 Dutch ornithologist K. H. Voous said: 'It now possesses only a very limited distribution range with an unmistakeable relict character, and is probably in the course of becoming extinct.'

Everything changed when the main colony was protected. This led to an upsurge in the numbers wintering across Europe. It was here that sporadic breeding attempts started, often in mixed pairs with Black-headed Gulls. As expansion continued, it became possible to witness the evolution of migration routes. Pioneers from Italy and Hungary chose to move west to Spain for the winter, whereas others began travelling northwest to France, Britain and Ireland. In Ireland, the species has become increasingly regular since the 1990s, although discovering one is always a surprise, like finding a bank note lying in the street. Peak totals coincide with passage movements and post-breeding dispersal from redoubts in Britain and northwest Europe. Juveniles, many from the Low Countries, arrive here in August and continue westwards, both overland and around the coast.

Earthworms in grassland, invertebrates on tilled land, as well as fish scraps and marine organisms, are consumed. Originally regarded as coastal, many are detected inland. They are not especially site faithful and few can be staked out. A glimpse of head and bill poking out from a crowd is all that is needed to clinch identification. The bill has a wonderfully thick, blob-shaped tip and is held in a drooped position, as though heavy. Black-headed Gull serves as a yardstick for overall size: the script reads 'slightly larger'. In reality, Mediterranean Gulls are bulky, square-headed, fat-necked and long-legged. Furthermore, the broad wings are actually shorter than those of Black-headed Gull. In flight, the bird's silhouette is sunken-necked and the action is stiff and mechanical, with shallow wingbeats. The gait is a confident strut; individuals throw their weight around. The voice is distinctive. It scarcely sounds like a gull cry. Utterances are frequent only in spring – in winter the birds become mute – and a single *kyow* is delivered. Some liken the note to the word 'cameo'. In fact, it is easy to imitate and, if the counterfeit is good, the real thing may approach.

Mediterranean Gulls are medium-sized and take three years to reach adulthood. Breeding plumage is magnificent: coal black head, saffron-tipped lipstick-red bill, thick white banana-shaped crescents astride the eye, and a silver back bleeding into snow-white wingtips. At the end of summer, the hood is lost, replaced by a mask. During winter, all ages share the same head pattern, comprising a dark smudge in front of the eye, fanning out behind to link with 'bandit' ear-coverts that peter out as a zone of peppery stubble over the rear crown.

At rest, the back pattern of first-winters closely matches Black-headed Gull. Most are detected on head pattern and bill shape. In flight, the wing's variegation becomes important. Perversely, it can suggest a similarity to first-winter Common Gull. Several differences apply, one being gleaming white underwings, further enhanced by blackish primaries and a clear-cut dark bar along the wing's trailing edge. Between the two dark regions, the inner primaries are pale, almost translucent. Two-year-olds come close to matching adults, except for a variable amount of black at the wingtip. The black can encircle white and produce 'pearl spots'; on others it is restricted and suggests brush strokes, sometimes with a hooked terminus like a hockey stick. All ages are different, yet none disappoints. Indeed, a two-year-old Mediterranean Gull is one of the most exquisite birds on the planet.

Facing page. Topmost pair of small images: juvenile Mediterranean Gull (left) with, for comparison, juvenile Common Gull (right). Upper middle: two first-winter Mediterranean Gulls (dark upperwing pattern contrasts with clean back and underwing coverts). Lower middle: adult with breeding plumage hood (left) and second-winter (far right). Perched in foreground: adult Mediterranean Gull in winter plumage (left) and second-winter (right). Perched out of focus in background: adult Black-headed Gull (lower middle) and (upper middle) adult Mediterranean Gull.

COMMON GULL
Larus canus

COMPARED TO genuinely 'common' gull species, such as pushy Black-headed Gull or Herring Gull, this species is a shrinking violet. The legs, in proportion to comparatively long and streamlined wings, look short. Youngsters are distinctive and sport tricoloured upperparts consisting of a grey back, brown wings and blackish wingtips. In flight, a grey saddle and black-banded white tail catch the eye. After their first fifteen months, they moult and begin to resemble adults, although signs of immaturity persist for another year. Adult livery is pleasing. Legs and bill are lime-yellow and during winter the bill dulls and develops a dusky band. The upperparts are rain-cloud grey; two big white blobs positioned close to the wingtip fuse together and stand out as a roundel.

Although present throughout the year, numbers ebb during summer when adults repair to breeding redoubts on low-lying islands, either offshore or in large freshwater lakes. Many migrate northeast to breed in Scotland or Scandinavia; youngsters from as far away as Finland winter in Ireland. Scottish colonies have declined; mink and burgeoning numbers of foxes exact a heavy toll. Some colonies here have increased, possibly due to the relocation of Scottish breeders. A tenfold rise has occurred on the Copeland Islands, where a 2009 survey recorded at least 900 pairs (GH, SW). Strangford Lough held at least 400 pairs in 2009; a figure also regarded as an increase (HT). Significant colonies also exist in Connacht. A chick ringed at Carrowmore Lake, Mayo, on 4 June 1983 was retrapped twenty-five years later at Lough Gill, Sligo.

A wide-ranging winter distribution encompasses farmland and amenity grassland, where strangely hushed flocks search for earthworms. In spring, Trappist vows are abandoned and a musical yelping *keeh* is used both singly and in a rolling, lilting series that builds to a short crescendo. Common Gull is silver-tongued with a trademark 'canine' voice, commemorated in its Latin title.

Top: adults in breeding plumage; lower left, adult winter; lower right, first-winter. Behind lower right: adult Ring-billed Gull. Invariably, the eponymous black bar on the bill of a Ring-billed Gull (on birds aged two and older) is clear cut, vertically flat-sided and bounded fore and aft by the same yellowish shade. Common Gulls, except in breeding plumage (top left) also exhibit bill bands of varying intensity and constitute a trap. However, their 'ring' is closer to a dark zigzag and is almost always bounded by a limey base and – a different shade – insipid yellow across the bill tip. Note the differences in the extent of white fringes to the grey upperparts: on Common, bold white along the margins of both scapulars and tertials; on Ring-billed, the tertials are more narrowly edged with white and the scapulars are grey. Common Gulls are depicted in flight in 'Muddled by Moult?' (p.167).

LESSER BLACK-BACKED GULL
Larus fuscus

Left: Herring Gull, first-winter, to compare with similar age of Lesser Black-backed Gull (centre). The key means of distinguishing between youngsters is the paler group of five inner primaries on the wing of Herring Gull. Perched birds can be problematic. For such individuals, a sight of the wing pattern may be the only safe way to reach an unequivocal identification. Right: adult in breeding plumage (lower); two-year-old in spring (upper). Despite Lesser Black-backed Gull being equivalent in size to Herring Gull, to all intents and purposes, its outward appearance reaches maturity in three years, not the protracted four or five taken by Herring Gull. It is therefore less variable in its immature phases. The grey shade of upperparts is somewhat variable. In addition to minor differences in plumage saturation, prevailing light exerts an influence. In this montage, all shades are 'natural' and have not been adjusted.

LESSER BLACK-BACKED is the large gull that went off to modelling school. Its silhouette is streamlined; in many ways it is the dashing, good-looking migratory equivalent of Herring Gull. Southerly airstreams propel them here in March. Most spend the winter between equatorial Africa and Portugal. Irish birds have been recovered in Morocco, such as a chick ringed at Scaddy Island, Lough Neagh, found at Essaouira on 12 October 1980. Some overwinter, chiefly along the south coast of Leinster and Munster and around the shores of Lough Neagh. During autumn, Icelandic Lesser Black-backed Gulls pass through. In

Fit to grace a postcard, adult Lesser Black-backed Gull is a divine creature. It is possible to discern the contours of hidden musculature. Large breast muscles attach to a deep keel on the central breastbone to generate flight, best achieved by cutting down bulk. For this reason, birds' bones are hollow. Lesser Black-backed Gull, because it migrates every bit as far as terns, is magnificently streamlined, yet its sublime styling is under-appreciated. Especially, no bird illustrator 'sees' those elegant legs.

the course of a fortnight spent along the edge of Ireland's continental shelf during August 2009, migrants were encountered daily (AMG). In addition, Scottish birds travel southwest to Ireland. Results from solar-powered GPS tags attached by the BTO to nesting birds in Suffolk in 2010 and 2011 revealed insights that probably chime with journeys made by Ireland's breeding population. Autumn departure proved to be a leisurely affair until the onset of a cold snap prompted lingerers to depart. Almost all flew out to sea and traversed the edge of the Bay of Biscay before hugging the coast of Iberia to Africa. Morocco served as a winter base. Some stayed put, but others ranged far and wide, clocking up 12,000km and moving up to 1,450km further south to Mauritania before returning. In March, all turned back towards Britain. Northbound journeys were fast and direct. Some retraced the autumn route, while others made a beeline across central Spain and northern France to reach the south coast of England.

As with Herring and Great Black-backed Gulls, this species went through a boom period in the past half century. Recent declines have been attributed to a combination of factors, from a reduction in food waste at landfill sites to outbreaks of botulism. During its purple patch, the rate of increase was phenomenal. At Walney Island off the Cumbrian coast, a mixed colony of Herring and Lesser Black-backs shot up from 700 pairs in 1950 to 18,000 pairs in 1965. In recent years Lesser Black-backs have started to nest in high-rise downtown Belfast, swooping for scraps among the city's built environment.

Adult upperparts are slate-coloured rather than truly black. Great Black-backed Gulls have upperparts that are almost a full black. Herein lies a warning. Books are wrong to suggest that there is clear water between Lesser Black-backed 'slate' and Great Black-backed 'soot'. Judging shade on lone individuals of either, especially in flight, is tricky. Structure helps, as does wingtip pattern. Great Black-backed Gulls have white-tipped primaries that create 'whitewash' at the wingtip, although adults have less white visible during the final stages of regrowing new primaries in autumn. On Lesser Black-backed, no more than two small white ovals nestle among much black.

Lesser Black-backed is a fraction smaller than Herring Gull. Leg colour of adults is egg-yolk yellow; all ages of Herring and Great Black-backed Gulls have pink legs. Identification of juvenile and first-winter Lesser Black-backed Gulls is tricky. Great Black-backed Gull is not a stumbling block – for one thing, size and build distinguish – but Herring Gulls can throw a spanner in the works. Indeed, the difficulty seems to arise from a tendency among young Lesser Black-backed Gulls to pass themselves off as Herring Gulls, rather than vice versa. For Lesser Black-backed, look for sepia-tinted upperparts; sometimes the same shade concentrates on the ear-coverts, creating a mask. Because the species has evolved to travel far between breeding and wintering quarters, many retain juvenile plumage into winter. Herring Gulls, on the other hand, shed most juvenile plumage in late summer. Consequently, in autumn and early winter, there are often differences in back patterns. In flight, identification is more assured. Young Lesser Black-backs have uniformly dark primaries. On Herring Gull, the inner primaries stand out as a paler block.

HERRING GULL
Larus argentatus

Refuse tips formerly attracted gulls in great numbers. Waste food was easy to scavenge. Nowadays, edible refuse is covered immediately and the birds are successfully discouraged by a variety of means. Approachability led to a much better understanding of identification and the discovery of a new species to science – Caspian Gull *Larus cachinnans*. For some, including the author, dumps were shrines of learning and the occasional provider of hall carpet.

HERRING GULL is the standard large gull around our coasts and, during winter, inland. The Latin name contains the word *argentatus*, meaning silver – a reference to the back colour when fully adult. Additional characters are pellucid pink legs and a buttercup-yellow bill with a red spot on the angle of the lower mandible. The red spot is claimed to be an aiming mark for chicks to tap and stimulate a parent to regurgitate food. Adults are cold-eyed. In spring a fleshy ring flushes yellow and orbits the eye, hence the term 'orbital ring'. The bony shape of the head sculpts a pensive, furrowed look. As well as a wistful 'sound of seagulls' vocabulary, territorial pairs bark a scolding cackle. A variant, often heard when sussing out a potential feeding opportunity – a gull on a rooftop, sizing up a slice of bread in the street below – is a machine-gun chatter, along the lines of *ga, ga, gagga*. Full-grown juveniles whine. Some hang around the apron strings until they are nearly one year old.

Mainly resident, the bird nests in loose colonies on cliffs and marine islands. Almost anything is eaten. For years, the bird benefited from human activities, gobbling discards around trawlers and scavenging on landfill sites. Then avian botulism, a scourge of rubbish dumps, killed thousands, halving Britain's population between 1970 and 1988. Recent estimates (Seabird 2000 census) chart further declines, with a mere 6,325 pairs remaining in Ireland. Breeding numbers crashed on the Copeland Islands from around 3,500 pairs in 1982 to no more than 300 in 2006.

Adults are long-lived, some reaching fifty. Recruitment of fecund youngsters is a slow process, taking up to seven years. Occasionally, couples skip a season but resume reproduction the following year. At the end of the breeding season, all plumage is moulted, including the wings and tail. Incipient changes are noticeable in flight. For a time in autumn, the wings show two generations of feathers. Old stock is frayed or missing; replacements are short, like milk teeth, until they reach full length. On a sharp photograph it is possible to itemise moult. Working inwards from the long, outermost tenth primary, you can mimic a dentist: 'Primaries 10, 9, 8 old; 7 and 6 missing; 5 and 4 short and partially grown; 3, 2 and 1 all new and fully grown.' Note that growth begins with the short innermost and travels outwards towards the wingtip. The same applies to the tail, but is reversed across the trailing edge of the wing. Despite exchanging new feathers for old, by Christmas the wing looks the same. The same cannot be said of the head. Here, a fresh suit of grey-brown dappling makes the head 'dirty'. Come spring, snow-white feathering reappears. Hormonal activity linked with the onset of breeding condition enriches the blood supply reaching the legs, bill and bare skin surrounding the eye. The net effect is deeper colour saturation. The legs gleam pink, bill hues deepen and the fleshy orbital ring swells after months of near invisibility. Before attempting to identify immatures, it will help to read 'Muddled by Moult?' (p. 167). Youngsters present a sliding scale of plumage from 'speckled dun' to 'unkempt grey'. In essence, the changes needed to metamorphose a juvenile into an adult require two annual moults over five years. That makes ten plumage changes: small wonder that the variation is bewildering.

Bottom row, left: Lesser Black-backed Gull, juvenile, for comparison with juvenile Herring Gull (right). Middle row, lower: first-winters (both were born during the preceding summer). Middle row, upper: each bird is one year older than the first-winter below it. During the course of the year, they moult and change appearance. In effect, they are teenagers. In Herring Gull and most large gulls, adolescent plumages defy a clear-cut classification. Top row, right: a moulting immature (photographed in July) reveals its first set of emerging adult primaries. By October it will closely resemble an adult, although minor details, such as dark primary coverts, will indicate that it is still one year shy of maturity. Top row, left: adult in breeding plumage, photographed in late winter, when adults moult new head and body plumage and hormones flush the bill, legs and bare skin around the eye to emphasise colour intensity.

Bottom row, left: juvenile. Bottom row, middle and right: first-winters. Differences from juvenile are minor and do not alter wing or tail patterns. Middle row, lower: two-year-olds. Middle row, upper: three-year-olds. Upper row, left two birds: three- or four-year-olds. Beyond two years of age, it becomes increasingly difficult to be certain of age-class until adulthood is reached. Upper row, right: adult in winter (non-breeding) plumage.

ICELAND GULL
Larus glaucoides

WINTER IS THE SEASON to look for this elegant inhabitant of Greenland – which is where, despite the name, Iceland Gull breeds. The numbers that reach our latitude are regulated more by weather and trawler activity than any deep-rooted migratory urge. In late December 2011 northwesterly gales originating in the Denmark Strait (between Iceland and Greenland) swept record numbers towards windward coasts of Europe. In early 2012, at least 300 were discovered in Ireland. Most were juveniles, the age class most imbued with wanderlust. Youngsters arrive in port tucked in behind a nautical Pied Piper spewing discards. Rubbish dumps and sewerage outfalls are also an attraction – or were. Over recent years hotspots have vanished. Landfills have closed or become gull-unfriendly. Coastal outfalls have been 'cleaned up', leading to the eradication of not only clouds of dip-feeding gulls but also blooms of seaweed, abundant marine organisms and a bounty of wildfowl exploiting the enriched food chain. By turning off the tap of human by-products, an entire community has had its benefit cheque withdrawn. Iceland and Glaucous Gulls are sister species, distinct from other large gulls but not from each other. Iceland Gull is a tad smaller than Herring Gull. Glaucous Gull is larger, bulbous and front-heavy with piggy eyes and a hefty hooter that, on youngsters, is bright shell pink with an inky tip. Although just 'one dress size' smaller, Iceland Gulls appear demure, by dint of (at rest) a longer-winged silhouette and a 'peacenik' pigeon-style bust. Unlike Glaucous Gulls, that are prepared to 'mix it' with the riffraff of Herring and Great Black-backed Gulls, Iceland Gull behaviour is comparable to Kittiwake – quietly dip-feeding and minding its own business.

Ghostly paleness, soft wingbeats and hailing from northern latitudes synonymous with ice and snow make Iceland Gull a bit special.

GLAUCOUS GULL
Larus hyperboreus

A CERTAIN INCONGRUITY attaches to the name. Adult plumage consists of just two colours; white predominates, save for a shawl of pearly grey across the back and most of the wings. The shade has a glacial lustre, although the bird's title is coined from the Greek word *glaukos*, meaning 'bluish-green'. Like other large gulls, adult raiment takes about four years to develop. Juvenile plumage is buff or sandy but steadily blanches paler until, approaching its first birthday, the adolescent looks like an albino. Iceland Gull matches Glaucous Gull in plumage but not stature. Care is needed to distinguish the two (see Iceland Gull account). Glaucous Gulls occur all around the Arctic and breed as close as Iceland. Some venture far from native seas. Among a wintry melee of squabbling gulls a ghostly stranger is easy to pick out. A stirring rhapsody, written by a Mr Gray (Patterson 1880), captures its essence:

The Burgomaster Gull [Glaucous Gull] is associated in my mind with at least one picture of a wild sea. I witnessed some years ago a terrible tempest raging, spreading destruction and death: sea and sky were mingled in one dark, drizzling mass, and all else blotted out save a foreground of rocks, on which the broken waves were crashing with the noise of artillery, and from which clouds of spray rolled landwards like wreaths of smoke from a battlefield. Against the background of sea and cloud there appeared a Burgomaster Gull and a small band of kinsmen – the snow-white parts of their plumage appearing like specks on the pitch-like tint.

Above: Telling Glaucous and Iceland Gull apart is a game of percentages. Identical plumage reduces the process to evaluating structure. Even size is irrelevant on a lone bird. Compared to its equivalent in Iceland Gull (p. 180) this young Glaucous Gull is smaller-eyed and bigger-billed: both 'runner-up' qualities.

Below: Ponderous and pale, most winter Glaucous Gull stragglers are fawn-coloured youngsters. Although slightly smaller than Great Back-backed Gull, a Glaucous Gull has presence: a battleship in comparison to the smaller frigate of Iceland Gull, its sole confusion species.

GREAT BLACK-BACKED GULL
Larus marinus

THE NAME IS A HINT; this gull is a titan. Yet *Larus marinus* (marine gull) tells a different story. The bird is a nomad, appearing from nowhere when food becomes available in the wake of trawlers. Canadian Great Black-backed Gulls have reached Britain and some European breeders trek south to Africa. One ringed in Iceland reached Copeland Bird Observatory.

Pairs prefer to nest in splendid isolation; prized sites are strategic overlooks with a 'Who's the king of the castle?' look written all over them. The beast has a malevolent mien. The bill's shape – blunt and fat, yet sharp – is ferocious. At rest the rictus glints red, like a boxer's bloodied grimace. Pugilistic attributes extend to a thick neck, sluggish gait and gruff bassoon voice. The wings are broad and less pointed than other large gulls, making girth wide at the tip. In silhouette, flying birds are bombers, not fighter planes. Pairs, if they decide to turn into killers, wreak havoc. At Skomer Island off Pembrokeshire, as many as 3,000 Manx Shearwaters were slaughtered in a single breeding season. Puffins are turned inside out.

Adult plumage is striking. However, confusion is possible with Lesser Black-backed Gull, which can look just as satanic in certain lights. On an airborne Great Black-backed, the shape of the wingtip is 'full' and splattered with white, like dabs of spilled emulsion; the wingtip of Lesser Black-backed Gull has one, two or 'one and a bit' miniature white ovals. Ageing follows the same steps as in other large gulls, described in 'Muddled by Moult?' (p. 167). Once sooty-black plumage develops across the upperparts of immatures – generally when they reach three years of age – recognition is fairly straightforward.

Despite a larger size, youngsters bear a superficial resemblance to Herring and Lesser Black-backed Gulls. Young females are less solidly built than males. Clues to identification are monochrome plumage, purged of warm brown. First-winters have ebony bills and tail patterns that speak of much white and little black. Unlike Herring and Lesser Black-backed Gulls, the tail band is narrow and rudimentary, typically consisting of frilly black 'onion rings', thickest in the centre. Regard the wings. The sweep of the trailing edge looks close to uniform. The inner five primaries are barely paler. In contrast, the rump, uppertail coverts and basal half of the tail are whitish. Yes, there is dark flecking on, especially, the uppertail coverts, but this does not detract from a predominantly white-reared look.

Top row, left: adult pair (less heavily-billed female at left); middle: first-winter; right: two-year-old. Middle group (except flying bird at lower left): adults. By late summer, when these adults were photographed, sooty wings and backs have faded slightly. As a result, dark plumage has a brownish cast. The adult pair (above) was photographed in December. Following moult in late summer and autumn, fresh upperparts are blackest in winter. Bottom left, perched: juveniles; in flight (above juveniles), first-winter.

UNCOMMON GULLS

(IN SKY)
LITTLE GULLS
From left: two first-winters (black zigzag across upperwing, contrasting with white underwing); centre: two adults (plain upperwing, extensive sooty underwing); right: near-adult (black remnant close to wingtip indicates final stage of immaturity).

(OVER SEA)
SABINE'S GULLS
Left and upper: juveniles; right and lower: adults. The upper of the two adults is moulting out its slate-coloured breeding season hood.

GULLS ARE GREAT EXPLORERS. The ocean holds no fear and the wake of ships may provide scavenging opportunities until a pilgrim sights land. This scenario, as well as the vicissitudes of weather that may provide wanderers with a free ride over great distances, bring rare species to our shores. **Little Gull** *Larus minutus* is a toy. The titch breeds across freshwater lakes stretching from the Baltic to northern Asia and winters at sea from Sierra Leone to the Mediterranean and the Southwest Approaches. Handfuls migrate over Ireland and hundreds winter in the southern Irish Sea, normally out of sight of land. Like sparks from a wheel, a few stray from an established orbit and grace coastal wetlands. The now defunct fertilised waters of sewerage outfalls were formerly a haven. Ergo, a delightful species that was always scarce has become a rara avis.

Sabine's Gull *Larus sabini* is oceanic except for a brief spell during the Arctic summer when adults track north from the Roaring Forties to nest in Greenland. When attempting to find the Northwest Passage, James Clarke Ross and Dublin-born Edward Sabine shot several specimens of a 'small unnamed gull' that they found with Arctic Terns in northern Greenland in July 1818. Through this act the species became known to science, but its trans-equatorial movements were not fully understood until thirty were fitted with geolocators in 2011 (Stenhouse *et al.* 2011). On average, each clocked up 32,000km in a round trip to the Benguela Current off Africa's Namibian coast, staging along the way for six weeks in the Bay of Biscay and west of Iberia. Come April, they headed north quickly, covering 800km per day to reach fishing grounds off Senegal, Mauritania and Morocco. By May, warm climes were abandoned and northbound migrants did not halt until they hoved to among ice floes skirting Greenland. If Edward Sabine were alive today he would probably be amazed to hear that small numbers pass within sight of Ireland each autumn, deflected inshore by blustery winds. All ages flash white triangular central wing panels, bounded by black outer wings and a raincloud-grey (adult) or scaly brown (juvenile) back. Juvenile Kittiwakes constitute an identification hazard, especially when seen at long range. Practice is hard to come by and a distant yo-yoing dot may be all there is to go on. Because of a blunt wing hand, juveniles have a distinctive flight action. They progress with a somewhat laboured Lapwing rhythm. Adults cruise more powerfully, with an Arctic Tern beat.

A waif from North America may choose to spend the winter here and commute back and forth across the North Atlantic to breed. **Ring-billed Gull** *Larus delawarensis* has done precisely that. The stranger is styled along similar lines to Common Gull. Most attach to gull hotspots where easy pickings, such as bread handouts, are available. Ring-billed Gull is truculent. In stature, it combines some of the bulk of Herring Gull in the smaller frame of Common Gull, from which plumage details and bare part colour are subtly different. Deciding what is indicative of Ring-billed Gull, rather than part of the range of variation shown by Common Gull, is tricky. For that reason it is best to concentrate on a few diagnostic features. Staked-out adults are usually well known; most return over successive winters. First-winters are tough to identify. For them, tail pattern differences are inviolate: grey-washed, somewhat variegated, and never matching Common Gull's crisp black band on a snow-white ground. Adult Ring-billed Gulls are pale-eyed, an echo of Herring Gull rather than damson-eyed Common Gull. Beware the inappropriate eponymous name. While the real McCoy has an unmissable black hoop slashing across a canary yellow bill, adult Common Gulls also develop a dusky band for the winter. It is narrower and tends to be backed by greenish, rather than clear, yellow. Nonetheless, a de facto 'ring' is present. Adult upperparts are pearly grey and reduce the contrast of the white arc (tertial crescent) separating the grey back from black wingtips. Other distinctions await discovery by a careful observer. A personal favourite is the lightweight quality of Ring-billed Gull's fan of three grey, bleeding into white tertial feathers that cloak the base of the wing. Even in the faintest breeze they flutter gently like a prayer flag. Common Gull tertials remain sleeked down.

LITTLE TERN
Sternula albifrons

The Little Tern feeds close inshore or over lagoons and creeks behind beaches. Bad weather during the nesting season can thwart fishing activities and an unseasonable gale may wash away clutches. People and predators are a further headache. Despite all, Irish breeders are faring well, thanks to unstinting protection at key sites.

LITTLE TERNS look stunted, a titch with a curiously large head on a puny body. Tiny legs and a whirring wingbeat complement a Lilliputian stature. Wing action is much quicker than other terns, although the wings are equally slim and tapered. Unique among adult terns in breeding plumage, the forehead is white, not black, and the bill is daffodil-yellow with a black tip. The voice is squeaky and fast – a Sandwich Tern on helium. Little Terns feed close inshore and dive among breaking surf. Shelving shorelines of gravel or endless cobbles represent Nirvana. Because the bird likes to nest on strands and shingle ridges, its breeding haunts are often subject to disturbance in summer. People and birds do not mix. Kerry's only mainland breeding colony, close to Lough Gill, did not survive human intrusions during the 1970s. Happily, the birds had the good sense to move offshore to Illauntannig, one of the uninhabited Magharee Islands, where they were also spared predation by foxes, although butchery at the jaws of North American Mink is a constant worry. Small colonies occur on inhabited islands too, such as Tory Island, Donegal, and Inishmaan, one of the Aran Islands. Both are unprotected and visitors can unwittingly wander among clutches of eggs and minute fluffy chicks. Overhead, parents become frantic and noisy – a sure sign to backtrack and leave at once. Until the early 1980s a handful bred at Magilligan Point, Lough Foyle, and occasionally on inaccessible small beaches along the Lecale Peninsula. As chronicled by Thompson (1849–52), Little Terns formerly nested in some strength in Down. Thompson quoted Templeton, who considered them 'as common as *Sterna*

hirundo [Common Tern] … on the shore at Lecale.' Colonies also existed on Strangford Lough and on the long strands of Dundrum Bay.

Nowadays numbers are concentrated along the Louth and Wicklow coasts at sites guarded by BirdWatch Ireland. Beach areas are roped off and dotted with courteous requests to stay clear. Better than that, coteries of volunteers and staff from BirdWatch Ireland are in attendance to explain the need for their efforts and, of course, are delighted to let you see the birds with binoculars and telescopes. Their role is around-the-clock and becomes far more demanding at night. Four-legged predators could wreak havoc and are deterred; so too are daytime raids by crows. Despite every good intention, high tides may sweep away the colony's seed corn of eggs and young. Such was the fate of sixty pairs at Kilcoole, Wicklow, in June 2012. A northerly gale backed east and, driven on by a spring tide, crashed waves above the traditional high-tide mark. Eight nests survived but were devoured by a swirl of Hooded Crows and Magpies.

In July, a few – presumably migrants from western Scotland – pass along the shores of Belfast Lough. During August, adults and offspring up sticks and head for rich fishing grounds along the coast of West Africa. There, they mingle with the European population, many of whom breed, not on the coast, but inland along lakeshores and stony river shoals. As with other terns, youngsters stay south until they are one year older and capable of breeding.

SANDWICH TERN
Sterna sandvicensis

It is easy to become blasé about Sandwich Tern. First to return from Africa in spring and last to leave in autumn, they are a regular sight around the coast. Yet, when prospectors started to breed in 1850, they were lauded as the fairest tern of all.

Unlike other terns, Sandwich Terns are in no rush to migrate. At the end of the breeding season groups of adults and juveniles (centre) explore all parts of the coast, often heading north and west rather than gravitating south. Probably, they are acquainting themselves with potential fishing areas and alternative breeding sites. All terns are inveterate house-hunters. Because Sandwich Terns dilly-dally, they begin to moult and look decidedly 'wintry' before the last leave in October. A few even remain all year.

SANDWICH TERNS are piercingly noisy. Their strident *keerrick* draws attention. The call is uncannily reminiscent of the sound of dental amalgam being crimped into a tooth. In late summer, juveniles accompany adults and add a whimpering *sree* as a vapid accompaniment to its parent's freely given, grating proclamation. All ages head for the coast of equatorial Africa, although some venture further, notably a chick ringed in Wexford on 9 June 1989 that rounded the Cape of Good Hope and eventually died in December near Durban, on the shores of the Indian Ocean. A chick from Carlingford Lough lived until the age of twenty-two before meeting its end in Senegal.

Perhaps Sandwich Terns do not find the trek north too demanding, since they arrive a month earlier than other terns, and are also the last to leave in autumn. Small numbers have begun to spend the winter inside the relatively sheltered waters of Strangford Lough and along the seaward coast of the Ards peninsula. Another nucleus winters in northern Galway Bay. Dives are forceful, splashy and untidy; plunges are often initiated from a fair height. The species is colonial but individuals travel widely, making them a ubiquitous sight on the coast. Tracking results during the summer of 2010 revealed that some breeding at Groomsport, Down, travelled to Scotland to fish. Breeders at Lough Erne, Fermanagh, fly 20km to the coast before foraging; others follow the line of a dual carriageway to commute between Strangford Lough and the Irish Sea off north Down (AMG). Nesting islands are raucous and notoriously messy. As a result, some sprout luxuriant vegetation that envelops the colony. Once youngsters find their feet, they band together in roving packs.

Not only is Sandwich Tern larger than other species, it is also the whitest. The bill is ebony, tipped with yellow, and the tail is short. There is a tufted crest and the black cap moults rapidly out of breeding plumage, producing, as early as June, a white forehead peppered with black. Juveniles have black 'Chinese character' squiggles across the back and wings and short, largely all-black bills. The bird is a relative newcomer to Ireland. Its occasional presence was detected first around the shores of Belfast Lough, thanks to a series of records published by Thompson (1849–52). 'The fowler who killed this bird [in early September 1839] saw fourteen. He and another person on a dredging vessel remarked that, from its deck, they could have brought down the terns with whips. On 23rd September 1844, an adult was seen at the quay of Belfast where, perched on one of the mud-lifting scoops, it admitted of very near approach.' Breeding was first proved on Rockabill in 1850. Demonstrating that rarity adds to attraction, Mr Watters, who made the discovery, stated: 'Its flight is exceedingly beautiful, outrivaling even that of the buoyant Roseate Tern by its sudden turns and rapidity.' By 1900 colonies were on several parts of both the east and west coasts of Ireland.

COMMON TERN
Sterna hirundo

COMMON TERNS lead lives divided between two hemispheres. After over-wintering in the Southern Hemisphere, pairs either meet up on migration or arrive separately at colonies and wait for each other. One couple returned to the same nest site for seventeen years until the death of the male. Chicks never forget where they were born, a fact made even more remarkable because youngsters remain in southern latitudes for two years before returning home.

Calling and stylised body language replaces fighting in courtship battles. A bent posture, with body and bill pointing down, signifies an unyielding attitude. A bill pointed skywards means 'I concede.' Males prepare for the arrival of females by vying with each other in Top Gun duels, spiralling high, then gliding to earth and staking a territory. Happy couples harmonise in flight, ballet style. They sway, sideslip and float in unison. Unmated males cruise with a mouthwatering fish as a courtship gift, the equivalent of a bouquet of flowers. Courting birds parade. The male performs a clockwork foxtrot; drooping a wing is about as romantic as he gets. Having found a mate, he sticks with her – almost literally. Rather than sit side by side, he often perches on his partner's back and remains there in a copulating position, suggesting guard duty (AL). The couple go off on honeymoon, during which the male feeds his partner fish. Walnut-sized eggs are laid on different days and month-long incubation begins when the clutch is complete, ensuring that chicks hatch at roughly the same time. Eggs are heated against a brood patch of bare skin and periodically rearranged for comfort. A strange ritual marks nest changeovers. When one adult departs, it tosses a piece of detritus within reach of its nest-bound mate. Bit by bit, the sitting bird gathers the material around itself, garlanding the nest and, depending on the building material, transforming it into a turret. Chicks learn fast. They break out of the egg by using a short-lived 'egg tooth' (actually a blob of calcium) located on top of the bill. Then, like a parachutist unfurling from a foetal position, the baby unpacks itself and dwarfs the shell from which it emerged. It calls and dries in minutes to become a teetering ball of fluff. Adults switch from hunting larger prey and bring in tiddlers fit for a newborn. Diet is varied and opportunistic. A galaxy of small fish is caught, as are crabs, shrimp and, over fresh water, airborne insects. Youngsters learn to fish by copying a parent, and then set off alone on the most hazardous journey of their life. Evolution has programmed them to fly south until their migratory instinct subsides. Touchingly, they observe the rotation of the stars in the night sky over the colony, thus calibrating an innate GPS.

Terns require nesting islands safe from predators. The absence of islands on Belfast Lough meant that none bred, in contrast to adjoining populations safely housed on redoubts on Larne Lough, Strangford Lough and the Copeland Islands. The construction of wooden-floored islands on a coastal lagoon on Belfast Harbour Estate, and broadly similar rafts at Portmore Lough, bore fruit and attracted almost 300 pairs. Crucially important is the provision of a loose, malleable substrate that is capable of being sculpted by the birds; cockleshells are ideal. Fencing to exclude predators, chiefly nocturnal swimming foxes, is vital. Gulls and crows are normally 'batted away' by breeding birds. The success of artificial tern islands has been a rare highlight among Northern Ireland's beleaguered bird populations. Protection is not a science and the subjects are sentient beings – just like us. Yet, over recent breeding seasons, Belfast nestlings have been sacrificed to a watery grave through invented health and safety guidelines preventing experienced volunteer staff from constructing shell-pile refuges adjacent to colonies. Such minor work had been routine. For a significant number of errant chicks the shell-piles offered succour where they could be fed until fledging.

Adult Common Terns have a smart livery of bright red bill and legs, black cap and silver-grey back and wings set against a gleaming white breast. Alas, such a generic description will not distinguish Common Tern from Arctic Tern. Even their voices are similar, although Arctic Terns have a 'sharper' soprano delivery. At mixed colonies, visual differences sink in comparatively easily. Airborne, Arctic Tern bounces and its flight suggests the weightlessness of a shuttlecock. The tail is long with flexible tips that slightly exceed the wings at rest. Both have red bills. On Common, there is a black tip. On Arctic, the red shade is deeper, there is no well-demarcated dark tip and the bill is a spike, albeit slightly curved, like a plunging dagger. Arctic is dome-headed and somewhat neckless, yet its hindquarters are streamlined, sparking a skewed impression of a bulbous front attached to a stretched rear. Arctic can look white-cheeked with a snowy whisker dividing black cap from nimbus-grey breast. Leg length can be a useful distinction when both settle in mixed flocks. Common is longer-legged. Arctic's shorter legs can, depending on pose, look 'miniaturised' and too small for the body.

As summer advances, wear affects wing plumage by abrading the grey bloom (radii) of the primaries. When this happens, more of the feather base (rami) is revealed. On Common Tern, the rami are darker, close to blackish. As some outer primaries darken, an eye-catching contrast becomes established against pearl-grey inner primaries. By August the effect is striking. A dark outer cluster (comprising five or six feathers) butts up against a 'clean' inner group. This feature has been explained in terms of a difference in age between the two groups of primaries (Hume & Grant 1974). Those on the outer wing were claimed to be older – moulted at an earlier stage during winter and therefore darker through longer exposure to wear – than those on the inner wing. Therefore, by comparison, the inner group are fresher and their paleness is a manifestation of less wear. Such an argument falls down: wear does not darken feathers, it blanches pigment

Small details can go a long way in marking out juvenile Common Tern as less endearing than juvenile Arctic Tern (see p. 193). A sliver of white butts against the underside of the eye; the blacker face of juvenile Arctic Tern is prettier. Common Tern wings are murky and, across the trailing edge, grey secondaries create a frame. On Arctic, the secondaries and some adjoining coverts are gleaming white. Rump colour is a further distinction: grey on Common Tern; snow-white on Arctic Tern.

through exposure to sunlight, while environmental factors, such as wind laced with salt or sand, abrades edges (NMK). On the other hand, constant abrasion chafes overlying grey radii and exposes sooty rami. The feather, meanwhile, is fully serviceable. Moreover, the inner primaries are always pale – and never darken. Through summer, the loss of radii exposes the underlying (darker) rami found exclusively on the outer primaries, thereby establishing greater contrast. On a preening bird, the effect of one feather partly overlapping and 'protecting' another can be seen. Intact, unworn radii below the overlap are paler. By late summer most birds have lost radii and show a piebald wing. Across the darker group of outer primaries, the innermost is sometimes the blackest, because it was grown first and its radii have been abrading for longer. On Arctic, all the primaries are uniformly pale, appearing silver-winged both at rest and in flight. Underwing patterns are helpful. On Arctic, a charcoal rim highlights the trailing edge of the primaries, as though drawn using an eyeliner pencil. Common Tern has a broad diffuse shadow in the equivalent part of the wing.

Different criteria are needed to distinguish between juveniles. How do you convey beauty that, in the eye of the beholder, is more perfect in one species than another? At rest, Arctic has a panda face. Close views show an almost all-black bill and, within a few weeks of fledging, close to monochrome plumage. Common differs in having a buff forehead and a ginger or cinnamon tone to the upperparts. On Common, light plumage impinges above and below the eye. The effect is vulpine; Arctic, on the other hand, is a pixie. In flight across the upperwing, Common Tern has a prominent dark bar along the leading edge of the inner wing. The upperwing is well patterned but bright white is missing. The trailing edge of the inner wing is a tad darker than the grey shade across its centre. Hence, the trailing edge *is not white*. To boot, the rump and uppertail are distinctly off-white, verging on pale grey. The underwing falls short of gleaming whiteness and is traversed by a diffuse grey band along most of the trailing edge of the primaries. A flight view of Arctic Tern, say on an autumn seawatch, reveals a gem. While the leading edge of the upperwing is dusky and analogous to the same dark region on Common Tern, the effect is rather different. On Arctic, the duskiness bleeds rapidly into a grey shawl *contrasting with white tips to the greater upperwing coverts and all of the secondaries and inner primaries.* The upshot is a Persil-white 'rear wing' connected to a white rump. Take time to enjoy juvenile Arctic Tern. Flying into autumn winds, the poppet has an indomitable air and a fashion model narrow waist. The realisation that it plans to be at the edge of the Antarctic by Christmas is mind-boggling.

On log: Common Tern (left) and Arctic Tern (right). Middle lower: Common Terns flying with fish and perched. Middle upper: Arctic Tern. In sky: Five Arctic Terns among flock of Common Terns. Three Arctics are highest of all; another is the penultimate lowest. In addition to wing pattern differences (see species accounts) the wings of the Arctic Terns are narrower. The image captures a nuance of wing shape not normally discernible in moving flight: on Arctic Tern, the outer wing (hand) is skinny and somewhat hooked.

ROSEATE TERN
Sterna dougallii

Roseate Terns just about live up to their name. The pink tinge is no more than a blush. In the glare of sunlight it all but disappears.

A THEORY SUGGESTS that Roseate Tern was originally a tropical species that expanded into temperate latitudes. The bird's untidy plunge-dive is indicative of snatching fish from the clear surface waters of tropical seas. In evolutionary terms, the bird is 'older' than Common and Arctic Terns, prompting thoughts that it – or an ancestor – was the template from which others diverged. Formerly, dozens nested in Carlingford Lough, Strangford Lough, Larne Lough and on the Copeland Islands. These days, Northern Ireland has been all but abandoned. The epicentre has shifted to the barren island of Rockabill northeast of Dublin. Here, around a thousand pairs return each May from fishing grounds along the African coast. Choice of locale is idiosyncratic. Breeders choose to mingle among conurbations of tern brethren and conceal two eggs in, preferably, a dark hollow. Thronged with nesting Common Terns and swathed with banks of luxuriant Tree Mallow, Rockabill represents nirvana, especially since BirdWatch Ireland installed nest-boxes in serried rows on specially built terraces. Vegetation control, rigorous protection and scrupulous monitoring have produced terns in spades. Indeed, the mother ship is becoming an exporter of colonists seeking Lebensraum.

In preparation for courtship, adults grow a brace of lance-like outer tail feathers. In flight the twin prongs form a lyre, reminiscent of a skate's egg case. Breast plumage acquires a rosy 'baby girl' suffusion, hence the name. Cloudy weather boosts saturation and generates a candyfloss effect. Compared to Common Tern, the torso is spindle-shaped and the wings are narrow. In travelling flight, wingbeats are fast yet shallow, as though stuck in low gear. Common Tern exudes a steadier grace. Nevertheless, in point-to-point comparisons of both, Roseate is faster. The legs are just shy of vermilion, deep orange rather than red. In May, the bill is ebony. By June, orange straddles the base of the upper mandible, with a separate 'asymmetric' spillage at the base of the lower. During August, colour reaches maximum extent and covers about one third of each mandible. Non-breeders, presumably younger adults, are almost entirely black-billed and noticeably orange-legged. The bill is extraordinarily long and narrow; with both mandibles open, it evokes Edward Scissorhands. For breeding plumage adults, no-brainer distinctions from Common and Arctic Terns include chalky upperparts and minimal contrast between the upperparts and rump.

The flight call – *choo-vik!* – is unmistakeable. Even among the din of other species, a caller stands out. The note is a jab: a

If the Roseate Tern were a car, it would be a Lamborghini. Compared to other juvenile terns, the youngster too has something of the look of a stretch limousine. Young Roseate Terns sport a more complete cap than juvenile Common or Arctic Terns and look vaguely hooded. Except for smaller size, they resemble a Sandwich Tern of equivalent age.

short, sharp shock. Variation in speed of delivery lengthens the skirl to *kerr-ick* (reminiscent of Sandwich Tern) or shrinks it to *k'vik*. A wider vocabulary is used at breeding sites, including a raucous squawk similar to Jay; a high-pitched 'supersonic' whine redolent of a ricocheting bullet; and a 'pneumatic drill' clicking alarm, standard mobbing patois among terns.

Roseate Tern was discovered through the perspicacity of Dr McDougall, who realised that, among terns breeding on the Cumbrae Islands in the Firth of Clyde in the summer of 1813, several defied identification as Common or Arctic. His surname is commemorated by *Sterna dougallii*. Galvanised by the prospect of unearthing the species in Ireland, William Thompson paid a visit to the Copeland Islands on 1 June 1827:

One of these, a low, flat, rocky islet, but with short pasture affording food to cattle, is a chosen breeding ground of the terns, and either from these birds or gulls having formerly frequented it, bears the name of the Mew Island. Immense numbers of terns were flying around us, uttering their wild cry as we passed between the Mew and Lighthouse Islands. Poised beautifully in the air with their wings wafting or beating to maintain position, they looked keenly for their finny prey, which was obtained with the speed of an arrow. I could distinguish the Roseate Tern when on the wing from Common and Arctic Terns by its colour and by its note, which resembles the word crake, uttered in a hoarse grating key. (Thompson 1849–52)

Rather than registering the normal flight call, Thompson's *crake* perfectly describes the agitation of piqued adults. Subsequently, he had to stomach the near-annihilation of the colony. 'So incessantly are the poor birds robbed of their eggs, that our boatmen stated they can never bring forth their young until the time of hay-harvest, when the people are too much occupied to molest them. The birds themselves, too, suffered much this year [1833]. A party butchered not less than 50, of which about a dozen were the Roseate, and all were afterwards flung away as useless.' As a footnote, he added: 'Mr Knox, in his most pleasing *Ornithological Rambles in Sussex*, mentions a person having a peculiar breed of dogs, which he successfully trained to hunt for the eggs of terns and Lapwings. It is to be hoped that the breed has become extinct, never to be renewed.'

ARCTIC TERN
Sterna paradisaea

Arctic Terns see the world at its best, nesting in one sunlit empty quarter, the Arctic Circle in summer, then trekking to spend the winter in similar weather in the Antarctic: the bird that put G in GPS.

WAYS OF TELLING Arctic Tern from Common Tern are discussed under Common Tern. Lifestyle comparisons reveal further significant differences. Arctic Terns breed no further south than Britain, with most of the world's population nesting in a vast sweep across the Arctic. Once daylight shortens after midsummer, the bird sets off for Antarctic seas to fish in round-the-clock daylight. When winter becomes summer at the opposite end of the earth, roughly half of the Antarctic thaws. Little wonder that its seas teem with life. Each autumn a variable number of youngsters pass offshore. Alas, due to gull predation, pitifully few are offspring from Irish colonies. The largest, up to 800 pairs on the Copeland Islands, have been unsuccessful for six successive seasons (2006–2011). Single-handedly, just one pair of gulls ate fifty-five clutches. Whither tern protectors?

Mew Island, the smallest and outermost of the Copeland Islands, was where, on 11 June 1827, William Thompson discovered breeding Roseate Terns. This was sensational news, yet on the very same day he also discerned a further species 'undescribed in any work on British birds, it was unknown to me, and believed to be an ornithological treasure, for its specific difference from *S. hirundo* [Common Tern] was at once apparent' (Thompson 1849–52). The vision was Arctic Tern. Basically, Thompson thought that he had found a new species for science. Upon conducting research, his excitement was tempered when he traced another European description from seven years earlier, credited to Naumann, a German. The bird had been registered in the scientific archives as *S. macrura*. Translated, 'macrura' means long-tailed. But things did not end there. In due course an older specimen came to light. In 1763, Pontopiddan, a Dane, had assigned *S. paradisaea* to a similar specimen. His description

was poor. Nonetheless, in accordance with the rules of scientific nomenclature, his title was eventually given precedence and it has stuck. What's in a name? Pontopiddan's choice was inspired – Tern of Paradise.

Because the species is social, migrants tend to arrive and depart en masse. Fishing activities often involve a hovering, plunge-diving swarm. Time in the northern hemisphere is short. To cram in wooing a mate and rearing young, corners are cut. Compared to Common Tern, courtship rituals are less elaborate, eggs hatch after a shorter incubation, and chicks imprint on the first adult they see. A sense of urgency is pervasive. If the timetable does not run smoothly, late clutches and unfledged chicks are abandoned; the need to fly south is paramount. Fat reserves are laid down in preparation. Deposits were measured on a sample of fifty adults feeding off the Greenland coast (Salomonsen 1950). Nearly two thirds were fat, some exceedingly so. Analysis of fifty-eight recoveries of juveniles ringed in Greenland (Lyngs 2003) showed that they moved rapidly offshore and embarked for the edge of the continental shelf west of Europe. By October, the vanguard had reached Namibia. Once in South African waters, they lingered until Christmas, when many rounded the Cape of Good Hope and entered the Indian Ocean. Thereafter, recoveries ceased.

Although somewhat speculative, Salomonsen (1967b) described winter movements as follows:

> After leaving South Africa, the terns are drifted east by the strong westerlies in this area (The Roaring Forties), reaching the Antarctic pack-ice belt somewhere between 30–110 degrees east. This movement is completed before the moult

Proof that youngsters earn their stripes is the sight of small parties battling into autumn headwinds off western Ireland. Adults are nowhere to be seen and have probably crossed the Equator. Offspring are dainty as a fairy and airy as a butterfly. An inky skullcap and snowy hind-wings light up the nymphs as they dance over the waves.

of the remiges [flight feathers], which adults initiate in late December; juveniles about a month later. During October to March, concentrations of Arctic Terns have been found in the eastern Antarctic and in the Amundsen, Ross and Weddell Seas. In March, the pack-ice is reduced to its minimum size and the ice-edge is now within the continental zone of easterly winds. Many terns, perhaps mainly adults, then move westwards to the Weddell Sea area from where they start their northward spring migration. Others, perhaps mainly young birds, may circumnavigate the Antarctic continent.

In fact, the vast majority of youngsters remain in southern latitudes until they are two years old, enjoying a well-deserved gap year. When the Antarctic freezes, they track north and follow the initial phase of adult migration, halting around Chile and South Africa. Some continue north into equatorial seas and a few keen individuals keep going until, by July, they reach Ireland. Given their age, they look unlike their parents. In the new millennium, researchers in Greenland fitted geolocater tracking devices and followed adult Arctic Tern migration all the way from the Arctic to the Antarctic and back. Departing in August, they headed for a specific zone of the North Atlantic about a thousand kilometres north of the Azores. Next stop was along the coast of West Africa, where the migration stream divided. Some hugged the African coast south, while roughly half swept west past the Cape Verde Islands and continued until they reached the ocean off Brazil, whereupon they resumed a southerly course. Following a winter spent in the Weddell Sea, they turned around and, timing departure to coincide with southeast tailwinds blowing unchecked from a continent beginning to freeze, began to track north in March. Rather than adhering to the route that brought them south, they traced a gigantic S-bend with its pivotal point straddling the Equator. Basically, the birds went northeast from the Antarctic to the Equator, but northwest

once north of the tropics. The reason for detouring several thousand kilometres towards the Caribbean was to derive advantage from prevailing winds. They know that it is more energy efficient to fly a greater distance pushed along by favourable breezes than to stick to a straight line and encounter capricious headwinds.

One ringed in Down on 29 June 1941 was recovered in the same place ten years later. Others ringed in Ireland and Britain reached Australia on at least four occasions. A chick ringed at Copeland Island on 10 July 1989 was picked up dead 15,270km away at Bunbury, Western Australia on 15 November 2001. Assuming that it followed a conventional migration route and travelled east after rounding South Africa, it probably clocked up in excess of 25,000km.

In less than a month, down will be replaced by feathers and the baby will be off, leaving the northern hemisphere in its wake before rounding the Cape of Good Hope in the latitude of the Roaring Forties. A few get swept along by the strong westerlies and end up in Australia. In recent decades, massive breeding failure has blighted colonies around northern Britain. A lack of sand-eels meant that no young were raised. Overfishing is bad enough, but human use of the catch as fertiliser and cat food is unforgiveable.

COMMON GUILLEMOT
Uria aalge

Ashore, Guillemots waddle; the prostrate tarsus and posterior position of the legs restrict mobility. In flight or swimming under water, the feet stick out behind and serve as rudders. The stumpy tail limits manoeuvrability and probably explains the bird's rather wooden flight path – a straight line with a turning circle little better than that of a bobsleigh.

GUILLEMOTS take communal living to extremes. There is no nest and a single egg is incubated on top of feet by swaddling it against warm bare skin. Brooding adults cram against each other in tenement lines on narrow cliff ledges; others huddle on open-topped stacks where they can land more easily, even if that means knocking neighbours out of the way. Immediately after 'gathering itself', the new arrival stands bolt upright and gapes, a gesture signifying appeasement. Adults forage up to 80km from colonies. Breeders consume 90 per cent of caught fish and rear a chick with the remaining 10 per cent. Food, invariably a single fish, is carried lengthways inside the mouth. Back in the colony, random feeding by unrelated adults is frequent. After about three weeks, still partly grown and unable to fly, chicks jump. Losses through mishaps or predation stand at 17 per cent. If junior survives the leap, it acquires a foster parent. The baby begins diving and fishing for itself in just over a week. While accompanying its apprentice, the adult moults. This explains the common sight during summer of a partially grown youngster alongside a flightless adult. Juveniles call a lot, reinforcing the bond with its carer. The sound, a repeated whinny similar to territorial calls of Ringed Plover, can easily be heard from shore at up to a kilometre away. Adult voices are a low grumble and gave rise to the North American name 'murre'.

In breeding plumage Guillemot is chocolate-brown with a sinuous head fused to a stiletto bill. Thick-necked Razorbills, always a confusion risk, are inky black and have a broad-sided, white-striped bill. During winter, Razorbill's blackness is less unique because, following moult, Guillemot plumage is slate-coloured. Nevertheless, by practising on airborne groups containing both species, it soon becomes apparent that Razorbill is 'ebony and ivory' to Guillemot's off-black and off-white. Razorbills are slightly smaller. They can look stumpy, a by-product of the bill's blunt shape. Guillemot's dagger bill chimes with a javelin-shaped body. Behind the eye, white plumage is partly bisected by a comma-like black squiggle. Razorbill has a black domino encapsulating the eye. Because Guillemot is almost tailless, it is feet, not tail, that protrude in flight. On Razorbill, light plays a trick and throws the underbelly into shade, simultaneously striking white plumage riding high on either side of the stern, which shines brighter than Snow White's teeth.

Mankind has inflicted a series of disasters on auks in general. Woes include overfishing, direct killing of nesting birds, oil pollution and bycatching in nets. During autumn 1969, at least 20,000 Guillemots washed ashore around the coast of the northern Irish Sea (Furphy *et al.* 1971). Peak mortality coincided with the climax of moult and the onset of gales. Thousands were washed ashore, weak and dying. Virtually all were renewing flight feathers. Fifty were analysed and contained high levels of polychlorinated biphenyls (PCBs, widely used in the chemical industry). While not directly responsible for the massive scale of fatalities, it is likely that PCBs were a contributory cause, a tipping point that spelled death when residues may have overwhelmed birds whose metabolism had been weakened through a combination of moult and a failure to find food in rough seas (refer to Fulmar account for an example of potentially similar debilitation from accumulated toxins). During the 1970s and into the 1980s, an estimated 20,000 Guillemots and Razorbills drowned annually in fishing gear in Galway Bay. Nowadays, there is a concern to comprehend the reasons for breeding failure at many seabird colonies, especially bordering the North Sea. Climate change has been voiced as a factor driving the reduction of food. Triggered by sea temperature rise, zooplankton move north (or sink deeper) to find cool water conditions. Without zooplankton, larval fish starve, and the implications for seabirds are obvious. Several recent breeding seasons have been blank. Around our coasts the situation is not yet bleak.

Guillemots are gregarious. Territory size is dictated by the distance an incubating bird can reach while incubating its single, exceptionally large, pear-shaped egg. When bumped, the egg pivots around its axis, preventing loss through rolling. Guillemot eggs are highly variable in colour and pattern; variety might prevent mix-ups by jostling parents.

During winter, white cheeks and a dagger-shaped bill distinguish Guillemots from Razorbills.

RAZORBILL
Alca torda

IF COMMON GUILLEMOT is Tweedledee, Razorbill is Tweedledum. The two have much in common, including breeding in colonies, although Razorbills nest singly in rock crevices that are occupied before swarms of Guillemots pack out nearby ledges. During courtship the bright yellow gape is flashed, in the same way as Black Guillemot flashes a vermilion mouth. In summer the upperparts are black velvet. Look closely and you can discern an ox-blood veneer, restricted to the neck. Like other auks, Razorbills fly low over the sea with the body held level. Skinny, paddle-shaped wings means that airborne progress is high energy – all work and no gliding. Speed can be an impediment. Approaching breeding cliffs, incoming pilots struggle to brake. Around and around they go, splaying their feet and fanning a spiky tail. They lack manoeuvrability and landings usually require several attempts. Finally, decorum is restored and new arrivals stand upright and are the essence of sartorial elegance. As early as late February large rafts assemble on the sea during calm weather beneath nesting cliffs. A few come ashore to check out favourite lairs but most raft together in Conga formations and murmur a protracted frog chorus. To dive, wings thresh the surface and the bird upends and pivots underwater. Auks, as a general rule, do not spring before submerging. Beneath the waves, feet serve as flippers, aided by wings that, half-open, pulse through the water with a laboured beat. Research into the fishing habits of birds off Lundy Island in the Bristol Channel discovered that 90 per cent of dives were oriented towards the sun, suggesting that the direction of light could affect their ability to detect prey (Cayford 1981). Breeders did not travel far while rearing chicks and mainly fed within 15km of the colony. Young Razorbills have stubby, Jackdaw-like bills, which take two years to reach full size. Offspring, during their first winter at sea, migrate further than adults. A wealth of ringing data from Great Saltee, Wexford, documents dispersal to Morocco, Spain, France, Holland and Denmark. Many winter in the southern North Sea and in the Southwest Approaches, while small numbers enter the Mediterranean through the Straits of Gibraltar.

Razorbill in breeding plumage. In profile, the bill appears broad sided and blunt. Change perspective and it is transformed into a wafer designed to snatch and clamp fish.

Razorbills in winter plumage. Unlike Common Guillemot, there is a proper tail and all plumage areas are either solid black or solid white. On Common Guillemot, hair-like dusky streaks blemish otherwise white underwings and flanks.

GREAT AUK
Pinguinus impennis

GREAT AUK was originally known as Penguin; the title survives in its Latin name. The term may be derived from two Welsh words: *pen* (meaning head) and *gwyn* (white). Certainly, this description is consistent with the large white face patch. Formerly, English-speaking sailors knew the bird as Penguin. During the nineteenth century some of the same sailors arrived on subantarctic seas, where they once again encountered curious seabirds with black coats, white chests and wings reduced to flippers. What name would they give them, other than one they already used?

As we, the birdwatchers of today, stand poised to be judged by generations yet to come for a failure to halt the disappearance of breeding Lapwings and Curlews, it is nauseating to reflect on the fate of the Great Auk, the flightless Dodo of the North Atlantic. Had the bird not been bludgeoned to extinction by our forebears, it would still be around – a metre-long giant, paddling around these shores during winter and, no doubt, discussed as an identification pitfall liable to be confused with Great Northern Diver and quite possibly Cormorant. Field guide texts might caution, 'Best distinguished by colossal, blunt-ended bill and extremely low centre of gravity while swimming.' Except nobody knows if the bird had a low centre of gravity or, indeed, how it moved. There is no reason to think that it did not travel at speed with flying-fish leaps and plunges, just as Penguins still do. Moreover the bill, when viewed face on, was wafer-thin.

Great Auks bred around the rim of the North Atlantic and needed sloping promontories to scramble ashore. For millennia, they were hunted and venerated by native North Americans who regarded them as a food source and spiritual symbol; a Golden Goose. Bones were interred with the dead and occasionally a cloak made from skins was furled around a corpse. European settlers exercised no such restraint. An immense colony in excess of 100,000 pairs on Funk Island off the coast of Newfoundland was eliminated for the sake of the rich oil that the birds accumulated just beneath the skin. As oblivion loomed, curiosity value put a price on the head of any that remained. The last was killed in June 1844 on the island of Eldey off Iceland.

What of the bird's Irish connection? Ussher and Warren (1900) quote correspondence from Robert Lloyd Patterson:

In 1740 the Rev. John Gage purchased the island of Rathlin. He died in 1763, and though he did not reside in the island he occasionally visited it. A short paper in his handwriting was found many years ago, giving an account of some of the birds which he had observed frequenting the island. As well as I can remember he mentioned a great number [of Puffins, Guillemots and seagulls] and a large fowl bigger than a goose, which he supposed to be a Penguin.

Bone remains have been found at White Park Bay, Antrim;

Image is a Photoshop montage.

Waterford has a more intimate link. J. H. Gurney (1868) provided details, repeated with some minor additions in Ussher and Warren (1900).

The capture occurred close to the cliffs between Ballymacaw and Brownstown Head. Mr David Hardy, who observed the bird swimming about the locality, referred to it as a penguin. A fisherman called Kirby captured it without difficulty. It showed so little suspicion that sprats thrown to it enticed it near the boat, when it was taken in a landing-net, and appeared to be half starved. This was stated to have occurred in May 1834.

The captive was purchased ten days later (having been force-fed potatoes and milk) and held for four months in Horetown, Wexford. Dr Burkitt purchased the body and presented it in 1844 to the Museum of Trinity College, Dublin. The specimen still exists. Infinity tolls from the words of Thompson (1849–52), who has left us this cliffhanger:

I have little doubt that two Great Auks were seen in Belfast Lough on 23 September 1845 by H. Bell, a wildfowl shooter. He saw two large birds the size of Great Northern Divers (which were well known to him) but with much smaller wings. He imagined they might be young birds of that species until he remarked that their heads and bills were 'much more clumsy'. They kept almost constantly diving, and went to an extraordinary distance each time with great rapidity.

BLACK GUILLEMOT
Cepphus grylle

DISTRUST IS PASSED DOWN through generations. Along parts of the west coast of Ireland, Black Guillemots are wary to this day. Thompson (1849–52) hints at why: 'Mr Robinson informs me that [Black Guillemots] are generally wild and would not admit the approach of a boat within sixty yards without taking flight. When pursued, they always flew towards the open sea. By keeping to the sea-side of them while in the bay, they were obliged to fly within shot of his boat, from which he killed fifteen.' 'Mr Robinson' was in fact the Rev. G. Robinson. In Bangor, thanks to protection by North Down Borough Council, breeding birds have suspended their fear of people and endeared themselves to all.

Winter plumage is greyish white, crenellated with dusky fretwork like an aged lithograph. The flight feathers and tail remain black at all times and contrast with white wing panels. As early as January, adults blacken and return to breeding sites. Visits are random and conducted between fishing trips. Groups jostle on the sea and out of this 'club scene' pair bonds become established. Synchronised diving and underwater pursuit are part of the courtship ritual. On the surface, males swim around females, calling repeatedly with the sound and rhythm of a squeaky bicycle wheel, all the while displaying a brilliant red gape. Both birds nod, cock their tails and pirouette. Wing flapping is harmonised and if one flies, the other follows. Two eggs are laid and chicks do not leave the nest, hidden in a cavity, until fully fledged. Black Guillemots are resident and outside the breeding season move comparatively short distances offshore. In November, during gales blowing onshore and churning feeding areas into froth, large numbers (up to 800 in four hours) have passed north off St John's Point, Down.

Above: Synchronised swimming, bowing and calling form just part of delightful courtship antics. In some coastal harbours confiding pairs can be watched chasing each other underwater, their high-speed zigzagging betrayed by white panels on wings that beat like flippers.

Below: Unlike other members of the auk family, Black Guillemots do not migrate. Nonetheless, with a dramatic plumage change and a feeding shift to deeper water, they are much less conspicuous during winter.

LITTLE AUK
Alle alle

LITTLE AUK, the smallest auk breeding in the North Atlantic, nests in millions among scree and rock faces along the northern coast of Greenland and in Spitsbergen. Colonies are dense and, as with Puffins, the nest site is a chamber safe from predators. Variable numbers percolate south. The trick is to know when and where to look. The titch feeds close to the surface and dives to catch zooplankton, not fish. Rough seas make accessing prey difficult and the best policy for finding clement waters is to fly downwind. When a winter storm originating off Greenland tracks southeast, our chances are good. The most reliable site is Ramore Head, Antrim, but wrap up warm!

What does a Little Auk look like? If one were blindfolded and handed one to touch, the dimensions – small size, stubby bill and longish wings – would suggest Quail. Open a field guide and the impression erroneously conveyed is of stunted wings. Wing strokes may flicker like an old black-and-white movie, but the bird is a strong flier and its wings are not an afterthought. Distinctive manners include crash-landing rather than settling on the sea and, when afloat, a frumpy pose with partially spread-eagled wings dragging in the water, the owner resembling a bill-less Razorbill. Airborne, the underwing is dark and – a critical distinction from winter-plumaged or juvenile Puffin – with a white trailing edge.

The diminutive Little Auk wears the formal black-and-white garb of most of the auk family, albeit with a sparrow-like bill.

PUFFIN
Fratercula arctica

PUFFINS ARE CELEBRITIES that have managed to keep details of their private life secret. Like Swallows, they disappear completely in late summer. New research using data loggers is proving revelatory. *Mirabile dictu*, Irish breeders cross the North Atlantic and winter in a vast bailiwick stretching from Maine to southern Greenland. Ironically, Puffins from northern Scotland have been discovered wintering west of Ireland.

Most of the bill's triangular shape and colour is due to a wafer-like outer sheath. In winter, the sheath drops off, leaving a much smaller bill that is dark at the base. It takes five years for a full set of ridged, coloured bands to develop. Based on the number of grooves, it is possible to tell two-, three- and four-year-old birds apart. Portraits capture birds with mouths crammed full of gleaming fish. The first to be caught is pressed against the upper mandible and held there by the tongue and backward-pointing serrations along the bill. Except for the need to ferry food to a chick, there would not normally be an opportunity to see how many are stockpiled. The record stands at sixty-two! Sand-eels, sprats and fry make up the bulk. In winter, diet switches to zooplankton and squid.

Puffins are members of the auk family, a group of seabirds that includes Guillemot and Razorbill. Each has paddle-shaped wings that act like Penguin flippers under water. On average, dives are between 10m and 20m and prey is captured from dense schools. Every individual in a group of ten monitored for nearly two weeks regularly made deep dives of up to 70m. Dives lasted around thirty seconds but could extend much longer, up to two minutes. One made 184 dives in 80 minutes, coming to the surface for an average of only 3 seconds. Nesting burrows are excavated or commandeered from rabbits. To avoid predators, colonies are located on offshore islands or steep headlands that boast grassy slopes underlaid by soft soil. Tunnel length is longer than the reach of a human arm. Just one egg is laid. Based on the return rate of marked individuals at colonies, as many as 96 per cent of adults survive from one year to the next.

Colony attendance is irregular. Before coming ashore groups assemble in rafts. In light airs, most are discouraged from flying. However, stiff breezes create pillows of wind conducive to wheeling. Especially departing from colonies, pilots are remarkably nimble. The feet are clamped together, and fluttering wings outstretch as the bird holds itself like a dismounting gymnast. Adults with food quickly disappear down burrows. Al fresco gatherings are a hotchpotch of peer groups. Two-year-olds come ashore only during the chick-rearing period and do not enter burrows. Three-year-olds arrive earlier and inspect burrows but do not occupy them. Four-year-olds assume tenancy of any vacant burrows and remain inside for long periods without breeding.

Puffins score top marks for display antics, at times involving several jesters. Bill rubbing, synchronised bowing and a rolling side-to-side 'funny walk' are commonplace. Yet courtship leading

Puffin parents look the same and share incubation duties. Changeovers occur below ground: the departing adult takes a quick peep before launching into flight. Take-offs quickly turn into 'Eddie the Eagle' glides. Like a ski-jumper allowing gravity to do the work, the bird clamps its feet together, hoists its wings and flutters them to control descent to the sea.

to pair formation takes place on the sea at the beginning of the breeding season. After June, most postures are greeting ceremonies. Offspring have the longest fledging period of any auk and are fed by the parents for about seven weeks. By the end of July they disappear under the cover of darkness. Around the same time adults become flightless and moult. The seabird city that is the western extremity of Rathlin Island is chockablock with auks. Although there are Puffins, numbers are small and inaccessible. To see them close, a visit to Skellig Michael in Kerry or Great Saltee in Wexford is an experience not to be missed. At Skellig Michael, birds call from burrows underfoot; their voices sound like a revving motorbike or rumbling tummy. At St John's Point, Down, small numbers fly past in June and July. In flight, the dumpy silhouette, especially a blunt front, is characteristic. Puffins are small, even smaller than a Black Guillemot. In flight the underwing looks dark and there is no white trailing edge on its upper surface.

Facing page:

Top: Puffins find blustery winds fun. Calm days put the onus on the flier and incoming pilots ferrying fish to cliff-top burrows do not hang about. Buffeting wind, on the other hand, provides uplift and resistance. Like bees over clover, the multicoloured gymnasts hover and peer at unsteady human admirers.

Bottom: Puffins may be gregarious but unease from one can cause mass panic. Big feet provide propulsion during deep dives and are used for steerage and braking in flight.

ROCK DOVE
Columba livia

Above: Few parts of Ireland's coastline retain Rock Doves that are untainted by inbreeding with feral pigeons. This individual, part of a homogenous wild population on Inishbofin, Galway, portrays the subtle hallmarks of an ancient genetic lineage: a gently rounded head, slim and longish bill, and small 'pads' at the bill base (not quite joined when viewed head-on).

Below: Feral pigeons are descended from Rock Dove; a 'human-engineered' derivative arrived at through centuries of domestication and selective breeding. When mutants interbreed with wild ancestors, native Rock Doves are lost through swamping. Such has been the fate of most Irish Rock Doves. Counterfeit feral pigeons still hark back to an original appearance. On this lookalike specimen, signs of impurity include a bulbous forehead and a stout bill base with enlarged 'padding'.

PITY THIS SPECIES, for it is one of a handful of birds on earth that could become extinct through inbreeding. Through being domesticated, Rock Doves begat feral pigeons and racing pigeons. Ledges in dark sea caves are used for nesting and 'paper dart'

displays on V wings are charming to watch. Soporific purring would surely be highly regarded, were it not for the sound having become mundane over centuries, even attracting mild derision: 'a soft strangling sound like a pigeon' (Keillor 1991).

When humanised offspring go bush and look for a mate among unadulterated wild populations, their skewed plumage and structural imprint sullies Mother Nature's pedigree, and hybridisation between 'natural' and 'humanised' spawns a mess. Undiluted, immaculate wild kin exist only in parts of the west coast. Alas, even here, motley counterfeits – chiefly errant racing pigeons – arrive. While some move on, others stay and interbreed. In so doing, they pollute both the species' genome and natural sea cliff range. Off the coast of Connemara, the island of Inishbofin offers an opportunity to scrutinise a pristine wild flock. The real McCoy is rather fetching; in many ways more beautiful than commonly believed. Compared to even the most lookalike derivatives, Rock Doves are bluer overall. The head is more petite and, fittingly, 'dove-like'. The bill is longer and thinner, and the white or pinkish-brown 'powder puff' pads located on the top of the bill base are smaller. On feral pigeons, the pads are larger and often coalesce.

The demise and creeping extinction – through genetic death by a thousand cuts – of a beautiful bird is appalling. Contemporary identification texts push the subject under the carpet by suggesting that no clear water exists between Rock Dove and those feral pigeons that resemble wild stock: 'feral pigeons come in a wide variety of plumages, including a type that is identical to the "pure" [*sic*] ancestral Rock Dove.' (Svensson *et al.* 1999). Van Duivendijk (2010) is slightly better: 'Within populations of Feral Pigeons individuals occur which are (almost) identical to wild Rock Dove.' In its otherwise impressive online photo library, BirdGuides (www.birdguides.com) has abandoned any attempt to afford a proper identification steer to *Columba livia*, which is unceremoniously merged with the genetic detritus of feral pigeon, even though examples of pristine Rock Dove (for example from the Outer Hebrides) are among featured images. Untainted populations could be protected, not through costly habitat management but by removing feral pigeons, which arrive and become habituated among wild brethren. Irrespective of provenance, both Rock Dove and feral pigeon are easily caught when enticed with grain.

STOCK DOVE
Columba oenas

STOCK DOVE was the nineteenth-century precursor of Collared Dove. Kennedy *et al.* (1954) state: 'The first Stock Doves detected in Ireland appeared in Down in 1875, although Moffat had reason for believing that it was known as a winter visitor in Wexford previous to that date.' By the early part of the twentieth century colonists had reached all corners, except Kerry. Its ecology here seems somewhat different from Britain, since it is not as closely tied to woodland and feeds in open country, particularly where grain crops are sown. Eggs are laid in cavities and the nest is basic – a flimsy trestle of vegetation – or absent. In eastern Ulster, rabbit holes are utilised, as is the labyrinthine underworld of gorse (whin) bushes and rushes, among which dim cul-de-sacs serve as nest chambers. In the stately woods of Clandeboye Estate, Down, pairs habitually nest in trees, typically in recesses left by heart rot or a fallen bough. In western Ireland, cavities in wallsteads are commonly used, although tree-nesting occurs too (JW). In England, nest-boxes are accepted, provided they have a small entrance hole (9cm diameter). In a three-year study in Oxfordshire, almost the sole cause of nest failure was abandonment following visits by a predator (Robertson 1991). Twenty per cent perished for this reason; the main predator was Grey Squirrel.

Commencing around the late 1980s, the bird has declined markedly, although immigration still delivers singletons from overseas. In 1973, two thirds of all surveyed 10km squares held breeding pairs. In the same year, a loose flock of 395 birds was present on the North Slob in Wexford. In 1970, an early morning drive of 60km from Ardee to Dublin tallied 200 encountered in small parties along the roadside (TE). The birds were picking up grit or gathering spilled grain. Throughout the year, Stock Doves feed mainly on weed seeds, foraging over fallow ground, ploughed land and cereal stubbles. Favoured food plants are Wild Mustard, Knotgrass, Common Chickweed and various species of *Brassica* and *Chenopodium* (such as Fat-hen). The switch to autumn sowing has broken the association between the emergence of annual weeds and spring tillage. The lack of a comparable decrease in Woodpigeons during the same period suggests a specific change blighting Stock Dove. A reliable redoubt is the largest of the Copeland Islands, possibly where the species first bred in Ireland. Here, grazing by rabbits and sheep maintains a short sward, facilitating the growth of prostrate weeds that, on permanent pasture, are allowed to complete their annual cycle and produce seed.

Woodpigeon is Stock Dove's ugly sister. Shyness is embedded in Cinderella's demure looks and timid behaviour. The eye is dark cherry-red; the pale bill yellow-tipped. Gait and take-off are hair-trigger fast. Blunt wings generate a brisk action, without the noisy clatter and flailing wingbeats of Woodpigeon. An out-of-context singleton could be misidentified as a nippy shorebird, possibly a Golden Plover, or a bird of prey. Airborne, the plumage is bland,

a blank canvas. The head, back and upperwings are blue-grey and the body and underwings ashy. A delight is discovering, on a satisfying look, that the smothering of emerald and purple on the neck gleams mother-of-pearl. The wing pattern consists of an encircling dark frame, leaving a grey, hollow centre. Once the pattern is appreciated, flight identification is straightforward. Voice, like the species, is unobtrusive. The male's bassoon 'great ape' coo is at odds with a gentle visage. His muffled, inhale–exhale series of *woe-ah, woe-ah, woe-ah* increases in pitch and intensity with orgasmic frisson.

The greatest Irish concentration occurs on the Copeland Islands, Down, probably where the first colonists bred. At least twenty pairs nest in rabbit holes. Across Britain and Europe, Stock Doves utilise holes in trees, a practice followed in parts of Ireland when the bird was commoner.

WOODPIGEON
Columba palumbus

Juvenile Woodpigeon. Youngsters are weaned on crop milk produced by both parents. Milk supply is limited and only two squabs can be reared at a time. But then the parents start again and crank out offspring throughout the year. At rest, juveniles are grey and featureless. The eye and bill are dark and the neck lacks white.

Woodpigeons are disliked by farmers. Commercial crops are palatable to them – cereals, brassicas and all manner of green, ripening shoots. Despite shooting, the bird remains common as a result of a prolonged breeding season. Across suburbia, it is increasing. Woodpigeons used to be wary and were never regarded as garden birds. Nowadays they are a regular sight under feeders, hoovering up spilled titbits. Clover among lawn grass and ubiquitous ivy berries (available through late winter and spring) are other favourite foods.

IF WOODPIGEONS WERE PEOPLE their XXL silhouette would be charitably dismissed as big-boned. They are born plump. Yet, clambering among small branches, the bird can be remarkably agile and will even hang upside down and outstretch its neck to crane for food. Canoodling and side-by-side snuggling come naturally to a species that appears to be genuinely affectionate. However, Humpty Dumpty is noisy, clattering into flight if unexpectedly spooked. A walk through occupied woodland generates a snowplough effect; the racket of departure is a good guide to identification. Wings are used to generate vocal effects. As part of courtship and asserting turf rights, they are clapped together high over the back. Impresarios perform steep-sided undulations, climbing to the top of an arc with bustling wingbeats, and then gracefully gliding down. Nests are minimalist, a trestle of twigs through which it is often possible to discern two white eggs. Incubating adults are tight sitters and a protruding tail can be scrutinised from below. The feathers are paint cards for thunderclouds. Each is a grey tricolour. Yet, from above, the tail appears bicoloured: dark slate in a broad terminal band, diffusing into battleship grey across the base.

Adults dine on weed seeds, berries (especially Ivy and Elder), grain, clover (plucked segment by segment, leaving the stem intact on the plant), green roots, emerging foliage and nuts such as acorns and beech mast. Nowadays many associate with arable farmland and have grown attached to feeding on cereals. A staggering 8 million have been shot in Britain in one year. Diet forms a basis for crop milk, produced by both sexes and used as a supplement to wean chicks. Emancipated from a reliance on adult food to rear young, breeding can take place at any time. Juveniles lack a white neck brooch. Airborne, the diagnostic white 'new moon' wing band is unmistakeable and is common to both young and old. At rest, the same mark is reduced to a white knuckle.

The presence of large winter flocks led to a widespread belief that immigration occurs, especially from Scotland. Kennedy *et al.* (1954.) stated: 'It would appear, from the results of ringing, that most of our immigrants are of continental origin, for most Woodpigeons bred in Britain are sedentary. One marked in Northumberland in 1944 was found in Tipperary in November 1945.' Subsequent recoveries of ringed birds from Europe include one from Denmark in Laois, and another from the Netherlands in Cork. Data quoted in Cramp *et al.* (1977–94) indicates that almost 90 per cent of adults and 70 per cent of first-years are subsequently reported within 40km of their ringing site. In fact, Scottish birds are the most sedentary, with a mere 20 per cent of all ringed birds moving more than 8km.

Woodpigeons possess a rumbling-tummy voice. Equally, you could argue that they sound gagged. Five notes are delivered, with a change in emphasis occurring at the second note, which is of longer duration: *do-DOOOH-do, duh-duh*. However, there is a fly in the ointment. The long *DOOOH* is not uttered when the bird delivers its first stanza. Ironically, you may not appreciate its absence as the initiation of calling is unpredictable and comes out of the blue. Watching the performance is fascinating. The sides of the neck are inflated to generate a supply of puff and the wings pump in time with each note. The opening phrase serves as a warm-up and is followed – with more gusto – by two or three complete five-note series. The end of the composition seems to be a lottery governed by how much puff is left and typically tails off in a one-note whimper – a full stop. Cooing by one bird often sparks a response from a neighbour. Most callers are probably males, although females sometimes also call and their voices are said to be softer (Klinz 1955). Except in autumn, vocalisations occur in all seasons. Confusion is possible with Collared Dove, which can often be heard calling simultaneously. Collared Dove's triple-noted *hoo-HOO, hook*, as well as consisting of fewer notes, is higher, clearer (less muffled) and delivered with a somewhat faster tempo; the triplet also bears similarity to a losing team soccer fan's down-in-the-mouth chant of *U-ni-ted*.

COLLARED DOVE
Streptopelia decaocto

The Collared Dove found that, by spreading west and colonising Europe, there was a gap to be filled in the garden bird workforce.

ORIGINALLY FROM the Indian subcontinent, Collared Doves reached Turkey in the sixteenth century and had penetrated Bulgaria by the 1900s. The middle years of the twentieth century signalled a blitzkrieg. Collared Doves bred in Norfolk in 1955 and five years later launched across the Irish Sea, nesting in Bangor, Belfast, Dublin and Fermanagh. An adult ringed in May 1988 at Copeland Bird Observatory, and found dying in Wexford six months later, provided proof of wanderlust. During the late 1970s and early 1980s, flocks were commonplace. Especially in May, small expeditionary forces are still encountered on islands and bleak peninsulas along the western seaboard, looking for Lebensraum. Pilgrims appear on Inishbofin, Galway, treeless Rathlin O'Byrne west of Donegal, and on Sherkin Island, Cork, where breeding occurred for the first time in 2010 (JW). Annually, some reach Iceland.

With a tolerance of humans – although never becoming tame – the newcomer has occupied a niche in suburbia, particularly where leafy gardens provide cover. Blackbird has gained a big brother. Living on seed, fruit and berries, the bird is an opportunist and will pretty much take whatever is on offer. Crop milk is manufactured to wean chicks, freeing adults from the chore of laboriously bringing a succession of small food items to the nest. Milk amounts are limited, so only two chicks can be reared. Laying dates in a colony at Dornoch in Sutherland ranged from 16 April to 7 September (Macdonald 1976). Incubation time is a fortnight and juveniles fledge in three weeks. As many as five broods are hatched in a season and, like rabbits, juveniles are capable of breeding within months, not years.

Juveniles lack the white-bordered half-moon neck collar, although they acquire a narrow version in a matter of weeks, once they undergo a post-juvenile moult of body feathers. Youngsters also have more textured upper parts; each feather has a pale rim.

The legs and feet of all except fresh juveniles are wine red with whitish scaling. The effect is not fetching; it resembles psoriasis. Redeeming features include a beautiful ruby-red eye and delicate lavender-grey tints on the rump and, seen in flight, across the middle of the wing. Surprise lurks in the unexpected nature of the tail pattern. When shuffling low, closed feathers are grey-brown but fan and flash white on take-off. The effect is truly extempore.

A three-note signature, *hoo-HOO, hook* (the middle note being emphasised) can be confused with Woodpigeon. Occasionally, only the first two notes are broadcast, *hoo-HOO*, sparking a different similarity, this time to Cuckoo. Calling birds perch on rooftops, television aerials and telegraph poles, often early on fine sunny mornings, when their monotonous reveille disturbs slumbers. Inflation, bagpipe style, of neck-side air sacs is a necessary preliminary. These provide puff. How many calls per fill of air? Sequences of between six and a dozen 'triple coos' are normal. However, twenty-five have been recorded (AMG). As an added element in courtship display, callers launch steeply into flight and then glide earthwards. As they ascend, the wings are beaten rapidly. The angle of climb and frenetic wingbeat bring to mind the motion of an undersea swimmer heading rapidly to the surface. An eerie 'steam locomotive' wail serves as a contact note and is given at rest and in flight.

Decaocto (meaning eighteen) commemorates a connection to folklore. A legend came to the attention of Frivaldszky, a Hungarian naturalist, and in 1838 he applied it when naming the species. The story relates how a poor maid was servant to a hard-hearted lady, who gave her as wages no more than eighteen pieces a year. The maid prayed to the gods that she would like it to be made known to the world how miserably she was paid. Thereupon Zeus created a dove, which proclaimed *deca-octo*. Perhaps the original pronunciation was *dec-OCT-o*, a better rendition of the sound?

CUCKOO
Cuculus canorus

Given their cloak-and-dagger antics, Cuckoos are sneaky. Even a calling bird can be hard to pin down. 'While I am lying on the grass, thy twofold shout I hear / From hill to hill it seems to pass, at once far off, and near' (Wordsworth).

IN FLIGHT, Cuckoos resemble a badly rehearsed falcon. The wings are rakish and the tail is long and loose with a white-fringed, diamond-shaped tip. Wings are held horizontally and the flight action consists of brisk, down-flicked beats. The bird seems driven. It gives the impression, probably accurate, that it wants to move on before the local inhabitants know who is in their midst. Well known yet seldom seen, migrants arrive from Africa in the second half of April. Only adult males produce the eponymous call. Females make a different sound, reminiscent of Little Grebe's whinny.

Males are sleuths: the metronomic calling says, 'Over here, dear – I have found a nest for you.' When his mate arrives, she lifts one of the host's eggs in her mouth and replaces it with her own, dextrously squirting her egg into its diminutive home. The process is completed in less than ten seconds. Her egg must be a reasonable match. If not, the host will spot it and attempt to pierce the eggshell and eat the yolk. When deception is successful, two problems remain. First, the egg must be capable of hatching after a short incubation, similar in time to that of the host's ill-fated brood. Second, the addition of an outsize egg might exceed the host's ability to cover the enlarged clutch against the warm skin of the brood patch. Both issues are circumvented, either by pecking the host's clutch to ensure that none hatch, or removing some eggs to improve the chances of incubation efficiency favouring the Cuckoo's egg (Davies 2011).

The embryo has a short incubation time, which gives it a head start. Although blind, the newborn feels for eggs or chicks and heaves the doomed cargo overboard. Foster parents never abandon the survivor because they assume it is their own, duped by begging calls that mimic the departed babies and a gape colour to match. The chick fledges in late June or early July. To begin with it is still fed insects by besotted parents, even though the increasingly Gulliver-sized offspring forages for itself and seeks out hairy caterpillars, a poisonous food supply unavailable to other birds. How does a Cuckoo know it is a Cuckoo? Most birds do not recognise kin from birth but learn who they are through imprinting and association with their parents and siblings. Quite how juvenile Cuckoos work out their true identity is a mystery. One possibility is that the imprinting process is delayed and only triggered in winter quarters when the youngster hears a species-exclusive call from adult Cuckoos. Such a 'password system' has been discovered in other brood parasites, such as Brown-headed Cowbirds in North America (Hauber *et al.* 2001). A juvenile ringed at Copeland Bird Observatory on 18 July 1992 was picked up dead in the Netherlands ten days later. Data from five adult males electronically tagged by the BTO in Norfolk in 2011 charted earlier than expected departures (www.bto.org/news-events/news). Four departed from East Anglia in June, the fifth in early July. Each moved quickly to staging areas in northern Italy, southern France and eastern Spain. By early July, one reached North Africa. During late October the first crossed the Equator, overflying rainforest to reach winter quarters in the savannahs of southern Congo-Brazzaville. By December all were in the same region, despite following disparate routes and spending hugely differing times in staging areas along the way. Some followed a western itinerary around the Mediterranean and through West Africa; others headed due south over the central Mediterranean and traversed the Sahara before pausing for weeks in Nigeria.

A recent sharp decline is puzzling. An equivalent decrease in Meadow Pipits, the chief host, seems likely to trigger a domino effect. On the other hand, changes wrought by agriculture may have drastically reduced the supply of caterpillars that are the mainstay of both adults and young. Garden Tiger Moths, whose hairy caterpillar is popular prey, have dwindled. Thompson (1849–52) noted that, upon dissection, Cuckoo stomachs were coated with hair. He assumed that the lining was natural. However, under a microscope, the hair was identified as belonging to the larvae of the Garden Tiger Moth. Mild winters, which permit fungal attacks on moth pupae, have been cited as potentially affecting food supply; as has drought in Africa. This harks back to a similar erroneous apportioning of blame for the vanishing Corncrake. All birds need to produce new generations. It behoves us to look first under our own noses rather than thinking that we are not the problem. Reminiscing about glory days for farmland birds in Down, J. S. Furphy twice encountered juvenile Cuckoos being fostered by Yellowhammers between Rostrevor and Kilkeel. 'Now there are neither' was his dispiriting conclusion.

Juvenile Cuckoo with Meadow Pipit. Is all the fuss worth it? Despite cheating and not rearing its own young, the Cuckoo still has a lot of work to do. Nests of host species have to be found and a single egg deposited in each. Timing is everything. The Cuckoo's chick needs to hatch ahead of its adopted siblings in order to heave them out of the nest. Much can go wrong and not all surrogate parents are fooled; some attempt to peck a hole in the alien egg to prevent it hatching. To try and thwart such a tactic, the egg is thick-shelled. Smart thinking, but why did the Cuckoo; start the arms race in the first place?

BARN OWL
Tyto alba

Barn Owls are skilled rodent hunters and associate with farmyards, uninhabited outbuildings and 'headlands' (rough pasture around field margins). Like many farmland specialists, their population has crashed as agricultural practices become ever more efficient.

ON THIS SIDE of the Irish Sea, Barn Owls are strictly nocturnal and specialise in pouncing on mice, young rats, shrews and occasionally beetles. They have a heart-shaped face; a product of two concave facial discs positioned either side of the bill. Facial feathers are stiff and amplify faint noise. The bird itself is noiseless, thanks to soft-fringed wings. To help pinpoint prey, the ear openings are asymmetric. This lopsided positioning causes a slight time lag in sound transmission, giving the owl a bearing on the location of prey. Males choose mates, an unusual attribute in pair formation, which are selected on the basis of the quantity of black peppering among back plumage. Offspring from such mothers have been shown to be less prone to parasites and have a stronger immune system. Pair bonds last a year and couples separate and live alone after breeding.

Thompson (1849–52) stated: 'The White or Barn Owl is the most common species [of owl] and takes up its abode in towns, as well as in country districts.' When cereals were widely grown as part of a mixed farm, traditional practice was to tie sheaves of reaped corn, oats or barley and put them in stooks to dry before threshing the heads to extract grain. Spilled seed ensured a supply of rodents. A farmer near Lisburn recalls seeing an extended family of thirteen perched on a beam in a hay barn, watching for mice shouldering through the straw below (Faulkner & Thompson 2011). Today, few remain. Healthy, holding-their-own densities survive in Kerry and Limerick, thanks in part to additional prey in the form of Bank Voles and a recently established non-native species, the White-toothed Shrew. Monitoring the breeding activities of Ireland's remaining Barn Owls has revealed differences from British populations. Very few nests are in holes in trees – most are in buildings; breeding territories are significantly larger; nesting occurs a month later; and second broods are unheard of. Young are reared, not by both sexes, but mainly by the female.

Why are Barn Owls in trouble? Food availability is one reason, especially when you consider that one owl needs to catch around 1,000 dinners per annum. Rodents live among vegetation; fields of short grass are, effectively, deserts. It matters little whether the shortness is due to mowing, reseeding, silage production or overgrazing. Rough, long grass harbouring rodents may be available but is often restricted to roadsides where quartering birds, which patrol just a couple of metres off the ground, can be struck and killed. The inclusion of grassy banks along the sides of new motorways in those parts of the Republic of Ireland where Barn Owls still occur has led to a high mortality. Six birds found dead along the M8 in north Tipperary in April 2010 (*Irish Examiner*, 18 July 2010) were killed by lorries, probably through suction displacing the lightweight birds into harm's way. Such carnage is not new. Studies in the Netherlands showed that Barn Owl populations had been virtually wiped out along motorways with grass embankments. A survey in England found that 72 per cent of Barn Owls flying near major roads were likely to be killed. Concerned about the situation in the Republic of Ireland, the NPWS enlisted help from planning authorities, who have agreed, among several measures, to establish woody plantations along dangerous stretches, thereby discouraging the birds from hunting.

Mice and rats are poisoned around farm buildings and rural settlements, and many owls succumb through secondary poisoning accumulated from their prey. In the past, Warfarin was a common ingredient in rat poison. While an owl that ate a stricken rodent might suffer temporarily, it could recover. As rodents developed a tolerance to Warfarin more lethal poisons were introduced, slaying owls and raptors unlucky enough to catch affected prey. A lack of nest sites is another potential problem. Newer metal barns do not provide large cavities or hidden chambers. Moreover, across rural areas older houses are renovated or demolished, frittering away nest sites and a semblance of pastoral heritage. In the past, farmers saw the good that the bird did. For excellent practical advice the website of the UK's Barn Owl Trust (www.barnowltrust.org.uk) is indispensable, especially if you own some land. Although the species hunts over a range of terrain, from overgrown ditch banks to grass-entangled young tree plantations, the common denominator is long, tussocky grass with a deep litter layer. Rodents commute along concealed runs and live in chambers within the 'thatch' that develops at the base of stems. Doing nothing and preventing grazing can create the right habitat in as little as two years. Fields cultivated to the edge become life-free zones. Autumn-sown crops mean there is no winter stubble; the only time a standing crop offers shelter for rodents is just before harvest. Modern farmland is a mosaic, the key elements of which are autumn-sown cereals, sheep walk, dairy pasture, rye grass monocultures for silage and commercial even-aged stands of trees adjoining sanitised fields. Crops of potatoes and, especially, orchards are sprayed relentlessly. Mars would be an only slightly more alien habitat for owls and other wildlife.

LONG-EARED OWL
Asio otus

WOODLAND is at the heart of Long-eared Owl's distribution. By day, the bird roosts among dense timber, emerging after dusk to hunt for rodents over adjoining open ground. Examination of pellets reveals bills of songbirds too; the sleuth snatches victims from their beds. Bats also feature. Long-eared Owls are indubitably stealthy. Seen in car headlights, the underwing is pale and looks whitish, suggesting a Barn Owl. The flight style is wooden. The wings beat stiffly in a halting manner, as if the bird is an untested prototype. When prey is spotted the bird turns in a flash, as though it has just struck a window. They breed in old deep nests, usually those vacated by crows. Males proclaim a single, low-voiced *hoo* in late autumn and again in early spring. While the note carries up to half a kilometre, it is understated and uttered infrequently. Unless the air is still, no calls are made. Accompanying the performance is a wing-flapping display, resembling a butterfly swimming stroke. The wingtips buffet each other below the line of the body, producing a percussive whump.

Large young beg audibly. Their *peee-ee* sound is likened, accurately, to a creaking gate.

During winter, several come together and roost communally. Dense foliage is sought for shelter and concealment. Lairs are often among conifers, but a thick growth of trunk-swaddling ivy will suffice. An unknown number of migrants arrive from Scandinavia. Influxes of transient Norwegian birds pass through Scotland's northern isles during autumn. One ringed on 30 December 1985 at Kirkwall in Orkney was retrapped two years later in early March at Castlebar, Mayo. Analysis of the sex ratio of southbound migrants at Fair Isle Bird Observatory in Scotland showed most to be female (twenty-eight out of thirty-six), whereas the majority of thirty-six accidentally killed in Norway in winter were male (Overskaug and Kristiansen 1994). This suggests a sex-related difference in the distance of migratory movement.

Feathered tufts suggest ears and are raised in an attempt to say 'Boo!' Cat-eyed, the bird glares a warning. Actually, it is all for show and unless you back off the owl will flee.

SHORT-EARED OWL
Asio flammeus

SEEN WELL, Short-eared Owls are striking. Their eyes are molten gold, made cat-like and sinister by the sooty plumage that surrounds them. Although there are isolated instances of breeding, mainly in Ulster, most are winter visitors. In discussing diet based on pellet analysis, Fairley (1975) discovered that Field Mouse, House Mouse, Pygmy Shrew, Rabbit and birds amounted to 24 per cent of prey, whereas young rats accounted for 76 per cent. Demonstrating opportunism, Short-eared Owls along parts of the Dublin coast singled out roosting Starlings and Greenfinches. Once again, pellet analysis gave the game away (JR). Damp scrubby meadows, sand dune systems, heathery expanses and uncut fields of tussocks are favourite haunts. Upland bogs and drier habitats within salt marshes are also frequented. Unkempt prairie beside rubbish dumps, with a surfeit of rats, represents nirvana. During the 1980s, up to nine wintered at Belfast's main municipal rubbish dump. Hunting often commences before dark – put simply, once rodents stir, so do the owls. During the day, they sit tight, sometimes down rabbit holes.

Unlikely as it seems, many Short-eared Owls are long-distance migrants. Ringing recoveries show that birds hatched or nesting in Scandinavia and Central Europe travel further than those breeding in northern Britain. Although scarce, crepuscular habits mask an accurate picture of winter abundance in Ireland. This bird flew in from the sea off Galway.

Abroad with sufficient daylight to discern detail, caution is needed to distinguish between the two 'eared' owls. Both fly on stiff wings with exaggerated slow wingbeats. Short-eared Owl has a prominent dark wingtip and white trailing edge, best appreciated on a topside view. Heavy mascara around the eyes says 'mad cat' rather than 'wise owl'.

NIGHTJAR
Caprimulgus europaeus

When darkness falls, the Nightjar stirs and opens huge eyes that sit in sockets occupying almost half of the skull. Unlike owls, Nightjars locate prey by sight, not sound. Superb vision espies moths and an enormous mouth, fringed with bristles, scoops supper in a twisting, darting flight.

MEET THE MASTER OF DISGUISE, a chimera incarnate. In outline and plumage a reposing Nightjar mimics a decaying stick complete with lichens and peeling scales of bark. If spotted, it prostrates itself with a rigid, outstretched neck, or sinks the head into the body to reinforce comparisons with a discarded lump of wood. Meanwhile, huge obsidian eyes remain shut lest they give the game away. Previous generations of country folk were familiar with its fondness for hawking moths. Because it swooped for prey around livestock, it was reputed to suck goat's milk and was christened 'Goatsucker' in England. In Ireland, its eerie nocturnal churring led to the name *Tuirne Lín*, meaning 'spinning wheel'.

Nightjars winter in Africa and breed over a vast region from scented Mediterranean hillsides to forest heaths and bogs in Scandinavia. Formerly in Ireland they favoured open scrubby woods and moor. Conifer plantations of young trees were also used. Possibly the birds accepted them as part of the scenery in areas that were traditional haunts before afforestation. Across Ulster they occurred sparingly in many areas; Fermanagh amounted to a stronghold. In Britain a widespread decline began in the early part of the nineteenth century. Factors driving the demise have defied explanation. During the years 1968–72, the years of the first breeding birds atlas (Sharrock 1976), a skeleton breeding population still existed in Ireland and Nightjars were recorded in ninety-three grid squares throughout the country. By 1988–91, that number was down to eleven, with only three cases of confirmed breeding. Although churring birds were reported elsewhere, the sound probably belonged to night-singing Grasshopper Warblers.

In Britain, the bird has bucked the trend of decline. In 2005, the population was estimated at 4,500 churring males, an increase of more than one third since 1992. Dedicated heathland restoration schemes in southern counties, particularly Dorset and Hampshire, have facilitated re-establishment. However, developments in northern England have been even more encouraging; by 2011, large afforested areas of North Yorkshire had become home to approximately 500 pairs. Nowadays, operators consider the bird's needs and a mixture of clear fell, young growth and mature standing and lying timber is provided. In some parts of Leinster and Munster similar developments have attracted an embryonic cluster of pairs. Given sympathetic forestry practices, the *Tuirne Lín* may yet return to enliven the night with sound.

SWIFT
Apus apus

Aloft most of the year, Swifts still require the services of their legs to cling to vertical surfaces and access a potential home. Needle-sharp claws act like grappling hooks capable of supporting the bird's weight even on smooth walls. Incapable of feeding on the ground, Swifts catch all their food in flight. When feeding young, insects are amalgamated into a food ball (bolus). Three centimetres in diameter, the completed bolus forms an obvious bulge in a hawking adult's mouth.

FIFTY MILLION YEARS AGO a Swift fluttered and fell to a watery grave in a tropical sea that has since become part of Germany. Preserved from decay in oily sediments, it was embalmed. Descendants of the fossil still arc like black bolts of lightning across the sky. Imagine that, a prototype so flawless that further evolution has been unnecessary! What are its secrets? 'Wing morphing' is one. By cupping wings close to the body, speed is doubled. At night, cruise control is engaged and the bird glides asleep, safe in its universe. Over Lough Neagh, hatching clouds of midges rise like smoke, and Swifts hover above the insect soup, gulping mouthfuls. It is believed that some commute from Scotland to partake in the feast. A long-winged shape limits manoeuvrability: however, the wings have a remarkably short humerus (forearm) and rotate like oars, facilitating rapid changes of direction. In this way the bird can deviate to one side or another and snatch insects off its line of flight. Consequently, it is a fallacy to suggest that the bird merely flies through the air trawling with an open gape. In flight, insect hunters listen to the hum of prey, avoiding wasps and stinging bees that emit a distinctive buzz.

The phantom's only connection with terra firma has become its Achilles' heel. To breed, Swifts are reliant upon finding a cavity of exclusive size. Nests are made from airborne material cemented together with saliva. Having adapted to inaccessible nooks and crannies found at rooftop height – gaps under tiles being a favourite – many have become homeless. Worse, adults may batter themselves to death in vain swoops to enter blocked-up former nest holes. Each year fewer find breeding places in a refurbished, uPVC landscape. Since the Second World War, building regulations require apertures to be fitted with grilles preventing access. In effect, new buildings are Swift-proof. Moreover, summertime renovation of older property has crushed occupants to death. In the Low Countries, it is illegal to renew a roof without providing a cavity or a purpose-made hollowed-out brick. In England, local authorities are taking steps to help. In Ireland, iniquitous health and safety legislation has been invoked as a justification for ignoring the birds' plight. Nonetheless, concerned citizens have fostered colonies on the walls of their own homes, safeguarded others on public buildings and persuaded Tesco to finance the construction of a nesting tower at Crumlin, Antrim. Indeed, an opportunity exists for every church in the land to install a nest-box, invisible if necessary. To help, visit www.swiftconservation.org or www.saveourswifts.co.uk

When they are on the wing it is impossible to differentiate between the sexes. To us, they even sound similar. Perhaps pair formation takes place during winter? No, at this season they are nomadic, unpaired and – the mystery deepens – completely silent. Kaiser (1997), by using his own ears and powers of observation, noticed that some birds perform a duet. He established that females are the higher-pitched sex and drive away rivals from the vicinity of nest holes. Antagonistic behaviour is based on voice recognition. If an unmated bird seeks to use a nest site as a roost during bad weather, it is tolerated if it remains silent. Males arriving to feed young with a full mouth of insects, and therefore incapable of calling, are attacked by sitting females, ceasing when the speechless husband manages a muffled version of his call.

Parents cannot afford to travel too far from their nests. Weather and availability of flying insects are inextricably linked and cold snaps or summer downpours produce famine conditions. When shortages occur chicks halt growth and fall into a kind of persistent vegetative state. In miserable weather roosting adults do the same. 'On being touched, [adults] appeared to awaken, but remained docile and dozy for several minutes before apparently recovering and leaving' (Walker and Rotheram 2011). Caught insects are moulded into a ball. When feeding young, the sphere is large enough to alter front-end silhouette, making the head club-shaped. A 'bug burger' brought to feed young in Antrim contained: chironomids (non-biting midges) 25 per cent; aphids 18 per cent; psyllids (sap-sucking insects) 11 per cent; lonchoptera (spear-winged flies) 11 per cent; beetles (mostly surface-crawling water-beetles) 11 per cent; and others (hemiptera bugs, bees, wasps, sawflies, ladybirds) 24 per cent.

Sites are jealously guarded. Even after the young fledge and leave the nest, adults remain. Post-breeding overnight stays and daily visits of up to five weeks have been recorded. 'House-sitting' is necessary because adolescents arrive in midsummer. They fly close to openings and attempt to pop inside. A vacant, undefended home could be commandeered. When a desirable residence is located its whereabouts is remembered and, during a winter spent south of the Equator, thoughts of a 30mm hole in faraway brickwork make a tiny heart flutter.

Swifts are long-lived, some surviving into their twenties. Maiden flights are momentous events. If grounded, false starts can be fatal. In the week before fledging, juveniles switch from a sedentary lifestyle to continuous flight. Rookie pilots slim down for take-off; dieting burns off fat stores built up as insurance against bad weather during parental feeding. At all costs, the lift-to-drag ratio has to be right. A few miscalculate and, because they are too heavy, flutter to earth. If found uninjured, they should be kept overnight and released from a height next day.

New buildings and regulations that apply to the refurbishment of older property amount to a death warrant for Swifts. Ted Hughes' lines – 'They've made it again / Which means the globe's still working, the Creation's / Still waking, refreshed, our summer's / Still all to come' – sound worryingly hollow. At least Tesco is listening. Why not every church in the land? Swifts screaming around towers have been depicted in paintings since the Middle Ages.

KINGFISHER
Alcedo atthis

Left: Kingfishers were reputed to dive with their eyes shut, having made a prior positional fix on small fish from a perch or by hovering. However, not only do they keep their eyes open but they are able, thanks to a flexible retina, to compensate for the change in refraction between water and air.

Right: Where tangles of willow sweep over clear water, a motionless Kingfisher can remain undetected unless caught by sunlight. Iridescent back plumage illumes a rosette of chestnut-orange and cobalt-blue.

'DID YOU SEE THAT?' A bolt of turquoise zipping low over water suggests a UFO made of light. If forewarned by a dog-whistle call, prepare to be enthralled. The decadent dart is found along clear, sluggish waters. To find finny prey, perches are essential, and the elimination of trees and bushes from riversides deprives the Kingfisher of operational bases. Moreover, breeders require vertical or overhanging banks – those sloping away from a watercourse are not normally chosen. Mechanical grading removes nest sites or renders them unsuitable by leaving a sloping angle. Burrows approach a metre in length and incline at thirty degrees towards a bulbous chamber. With few exceptions the hole is located within half a metre of the top of a bank, secure from the risk of flooding. Pairs live separate lives outside the breeding season, then merge territories and occupy a chamber defended by the male throughout the year. Young remain in the dark until they can fly. Families contain up to five chicks and, if a regular supply of small fish is available, a second brood is raised. The nesting season is long – from March to July. Almost three quarters of nests produce fledged young. Allowing for subsequent fatalities, this means that there are sufficient new recruits to repopulate streams and rivers after losses during severe weather. Ringing recoveries tell of localised dispersal; one bird ringed at Portmore Lough, Antrim, reached Coleraine. During winter some switch to estuaries and dine on shrimps and marine fish. Life span is relatively short; ringers rarely catch individuals older than three. Central European populations migrate to the shores of the Mediterranean and French Kingfishers winter in Spain. In October 2011, a Polish migrant reached Essex.

GREAT SPOTTED WOODPECKER
Dendrocopos major

Above: No nation on earth appreciates the beauty of the Great Spotted Woodpecker as much as the Irish. Having been without them for millennia, it is a surprise and delight to welcome the new colonists (photograph taken abroad).

WHO WOULD HAVE THOUGHT IT? Although numbers are small, it seems that Ireland is in the process of being colonised by Great Spotted Woodpeckers from Britain. Breeding was first proved near Downpatrick, Down, in 2007. Two years later an astonishing eight pairs were located in Wicklow (*Wings*, BirdWatch Ireland, Winter 2009). Accepted wisdom held that the Irish Sea was an insuperable obstacle to colonisation, forever ensuring that we were outside the ken of several sedentary birds found just across the water. From time to time Great Spotted Woodpeckers arrived during winter, a likely season for temporary visits of Scandinavian (or 'Northern') *Dendrocopus major major* that periodically irrupt from across the North Sea and stray west. Northern populations possess a short, stout bill: a consistent feature of immigrants. In 1968, an invasion year, one shot and another trapped in Ireland possessed Scandinavian biometrics (Flegg 1971). However, one shot in 1959 at Crom Castle, Fermanagh, proved upon measurement to be a longer-billed British Great Spotted Woodpecker. Over how many years did occasional pioneers from Britain hint at things to come? Kennedy *et al.* (1954) state that bones found in caves in Clare might provide evidence 'connecting it with a former fauna'. Could woodpeckers have vanished with Ireland's once extensive deciduous forest? It is hard to conceive of habitat destruction on a scale so vast that scarcely any sizeable block of mature woodland was left standing. Tragically, though, such oblivion did befall Irish woods, and it is quite feasible that an indigenous population could have been made extinct through habitat loss.

Writing about the disappearance of Great Spotted Woodpeckers from northern Scotland, Sharrock (1976) states, 'Early Scottish writers mentioned the species as breeding in the remnant woods as far north as Sutherland during the seventeenth and eighteenth centuries. By the early nineteenth century, the bird had apparently disappeared [from Scotland] and much of England north of Cheshire and Yorkshire.' Things have changed. By 1900, settlers spread west from the Firth of Forth; thirty years later they had reached Argyllshire and penetrated through Inverness-shire to Sutherland. From 1995 to 2007, the Welsh population more than doubled; and since 1994 strays have regularly reached the Isle of Man, probably breeding in 2005. Irish colonists seem, therefore, to have been spawned by pincer movements using short sea crossings – from southwest Scotland to Down and from Wales to Wicklow.

In Britain, several factors helped fuel expansion. Reafforestation provided new habitat while Dutch Elm disease created a boon of food, such as larval and adult invertebrates. Some began to visit gardens where a year-round supply of dietary supplements such as fat balls and peanuts could be found. Taken together, a tipping point occurred that allowed the population to expand. Critical mass was reached and scouts on this side of the Irish Sea

Left:: All woodpeckers are adapted to climbing vertically. Four hooked toes face both ways to provide maximum purchase, aided by a stiff tail that serves as a prop. The bill is stout and sharp for flaying bark and a long sticky tongue flicks and attaches to insect larvae lurking in bark cavities. Ingeniously, the tongue's operating muscles wrap around the skull and connect to just one nostril in the bill – the bird breathes through the other during taps and hammering.

found what they needed. Although many trees are non-native, some natural regeneration and enlightened replanting of oak woodland enticed the would-be colonists to stay. During the eighteenth century, landowners decided to re-timber their estates, many bemoaning the loss of the original forest. Between 1766 and 1806, the Royal Dublin Society encouraged tree planting and 25 million trees were established. Tracts of some of these woods are where today's Great Spotted Woodpeckers breed. The arrival, nay return, of Great Spotted Woodpecker is not without some irony.

Males have a red cockade on the nape and juveniles have red crowns. Adult females (featured in both images) lack red on the head. An undulating flight that ends with the target clamped against a trunk is diagnostic. Listen out for a sharp, strident *tchick!* somewhat recalling an agitated Blackbird. Drumming out a tattoo against bark proclaims territorial rites and the pre-breeding drum-roll can be heard from late February to early April. A rapid rain of bill taps against a sounding board, usually a dead branch, produces the sound. Both sexes drum. The sound – 'like hitting an inflated thin rubber bag with one's finger' (Clowes 1931) – lasts just over a second and is audible up to 500m away.

CHOUGH
Pyrrhocorax pyrrhocorax

THE BIRD IS DISTINCTIVE in many ways, just one of which is a loud, twanging call that rends the air and dies; an explosive starburst, memorable but gone in a puff. Phonetically, the note can be transcribed *chow!* Michael Viney (in *The Irish Times*, 18 September 2010) coined an analogy for the half-shriek: 'It was September, silence on the hillside, broken only by corner-boy cries of Choughs.' Apparently, 'chough' was originally spoken as 'chow'. Even without sight of the bright red bill and feet, mannerisms are a giveaway. Choughs are restless children and walk like drunken sailors. The upper half of the leg is tightly black-feathered and, against the bright red lower half, suggests that the bird is wearing black legwarmers. Noisy acrobats constantly talk in class and have fidgety habits such as flick-knifing the wings open and shut. Flight is punctuated by a skyward jerk, a preamble to a roller-coaster glide. The action is elastic and the bird appears to crest a set of invisible skateboard ramps, the splayed primaries evoking the spokes of an umbrella blown inside out. Airborne pairs or small groups sway and swing like charred paper, yet progress is rapid, with no dilly-dallying.

Commencing in Wexford, then wrapping continuously west around the coast as far north as Donegal, Choughs occupy a niche in the Atlantic-dominated landscapes of the Celtic fringe. Their airborne presence is on a par with a speech bubble, and on foot they evoke an artist's signature in the corner of a stirring panorama. In Down, they formerly occurred around the shores and islands of Strangford Lough and in the Mourne Mountains. Three were seen over the slopes of Slieve Binnian on 21 October 1966 (JSF). Hard facts explaining disappearance are hard to come by. Perhaps farmers unwittingly shot the insectivorous peacenik of the crow tribe. In Cornwall, traps set on grassy cliffs to catch rabbits slayed many Choughs in the early 1900s. Was this repeated here? The talkative comical crow was a popular pet in north Wales and nests were robbed. Maybe pairs along the Mourne coast lost young for a similar reason. Trade routes were well established between here and north Wales. Dr J. D. Marshall (Armstrong 1944) summarised status on Rathlin Island in the early nineteenth century.

Deeply slotted wingtips bestow Choughs with a mastery of the turbulent airflow rising along cliff faces.

In the month of July, I found them everywhere associated in large flocks, at one place frequenting inland situations, and at another congregated on the seashore. They had just gathered together their different families, now fully fledged, and were picking up their food (which consisted chiefly of insects) either on the shore, in the crevices of rocks, or in the pasture fields. I found them frequenting the corn and pasture fields in even greater numbers. Collectors offer such tempting sums for their eggs that many nests are robbed and the contents sent off by post. To the islanders the sum obtainable for a clutch is great wealth. I have known a stormy altercation at a dance when one man accused another of taking eggs he had intended to steal himself! Happily there are some men who are incorruptible. With one such I clambered down a cliff at night to visit a Chough's nest, which he took care to know nothing about when with other islanders. The young got away successfully. Other crows may outclass the Chough in mischievousness, the Raven in intelligence, but in appearance as well as in habits he is the gentleman of the family. It is in keeping with a world in which refinement is often despised, that the handsome Chough should be fighting a losing battle against invasive, ubiquitous vulgarity, whether in the shape of Jackdaws or men.

The account spotlights the avarice of collectors. Before land-use changes affected habitat in the latter part of the twentieth century, might greed have been the main reason for extinction across Ulster's eastern seaboard? An English egg collector regularly raided at least one breeding site at Malin Beg, Donegal, during the 1960s (FC). Right up to the last decade of the twentieth century the species remained in good heart on Rathlin until most were deliberately shot. Since 2009, single pairs have resumed breeding on the island and on the adjacent mainland.

Choughs are dependent on farmland for most of their food, taking large numbers of leatherjackets (the larvae of craneflies) as well as the larvae of dung flies and dung beetles. The fauna of cowpats provide nutritious feeding at those times of the year when leatherjackets are unavailable, chiefly in winter and early spring. When cattle are wintered indoors, Choughs are deprived

The Chough is a dwindling species restricted to wild western districts. Baffling declines peg back numbers in terrain that formerly held many more. In Wales, nest-boxes have boosted numbers. Certainly curious, a pair has visited the illustrated 'des res' on a Connemara cliff.

of cowpats. Awareness of this fact has led, in parts of the bird's Scottish breeding range, to management agreements to out-winter cattle.

Concern has arisen over the effect of injecting cattle with Ivermectin, which doses livestock against nematode parasites. An environmental side effect could be a reduction in the developmental stages of some dung beetles and flies that are sensitive to Ivermectin residues (Dimander *et al.* 2003). Moreover, Ivermectin may impoverish soil-dwelling populations of nematode worms and possibly leatherjackets. However, Barth *et al.* (1993) reported no significant difference in total numbers of soil nematodes in cowpats from cattle treated with Ivermectin when compared with non-treated animals. Still, mystery surrounds recent declines across Connemara and possibly other parts of western Ireland. Adults exist but breeding activity is at a low ebb. No tangible deterioration has affected habitat, but some problem is afoot. On Inishbofin, Galway, local people formerly witnessed sizeable flocks of Choughs feeding in the vicinity of the island's cattle. Those days are gone. Between 2007 and 2012, Inishbofin's two remaining pairs, and occasional roaming bands that visit, have shown no interest in associating with (injected) cattle or cowpats.

Of thirty-three feeding incidents analysed from Ireland in the 1982 breeding season (Bullock *et al.* 1983), 60 per cent involved leatherjackets as likely food items, 24 per cent ants, 12 per cent beetle larvae, and 9 per cent spiders. One notable incident involved Choughs feeding alongside gulls, Rooks and Oystercatchers on adult Chafer Beetles *Phyllopertha horticola*, hatched in large numbers from machair (maritime short turf) in early June. Good feeding habitats must have some bare ground or vegetation short enough to allow digging access. Dune grasslands can be crucial feeding sites in winter and lie adjacent to beaches, some of which accumulate wrack deposited by gales. Tidewrack also constitutes an important winter food resource. Shorehoppers *Orchestia gammarella* and larvae of Kelp Fly *Coelopa frigida* are the main prey (Bullock 1980). Sometimes improved grass is used for foraging; arable land is not used at all. On the Scottish island of Islay, grazing Barnacle Geese create ideal feeding conditions of short turf enriched by droppings. Habitat needs were further refined by a study based in north Wales (Whitehead *et al.* 2005). The birds chose short, grazed swards where invertebrate prey is likely to be most accessible. Most sward heights were less than 7cm; the optimum was 2cm. Where

livestock had abandoned traditionally grazed cliff tops or slopes, encroachment by scrub and bracken rendered the habitat unsuitable. At 'micro habitat' level, stock boundaries consisting of stone-faced earth banks (known as 'cloddiau' in Wales) proved to be important. Bank faces were grazed but not trampled by livestock, and the easily accessible shallow soil meant that the ground was eagerly inspected on a regular basis. Through agri-environment schemes, many cloddiau in Chough breeding territories have been earmarked for protection.

On the Calf of Man, farming ceased in 1958 when it became a bird observatory. Then, there were thirty Choughs, including ten breeding pairs. With livestock removed, short-grazed pasture turned rank and bracken took hold. Numbers declined and only four pairs attempted to breed, all unsuccessfully. In 1969, Logthan sheep were introduced and, a decade later, numbered 100 ewes. Chough numbers rebounded and in 1982 eight pairs raised a total of twenty-two young. In contrast, Choughs disappeared from Cornwall during the late nineteenth century when dairy farming went through a boom period and coastal grasslands were converted into arable fields and managed pastures for cattle. Uplifting news is that Irish Choughs have spearheaded recolonisation. DNA evidence confirms that the nucleus of a new Cornish population came from Ireland. In north Antrim, coastal pastures have been 'improved' and cliff-top fencing segregates reseeded fields from formerly grazed slopes that revert to bracken or scrub, delivering a double whammy to foraging needs. Bare earth and soft, crumbly cliffs are important, and the National Trust has instituted habitat improvements along those parts of the Causeway Coast footpath within its bailiwick. There is hope. There are healthy populations in Donegal and on the Scottish island of Islay, from which new colonists may yet be drawn. Perversely, offspring from a breeding outpost on Rathlin could gravitate to peer groups on Islay or Donegal. Studies of ringed Choughs in north Wales have shown that adults lead youngsters away from coastal sites and into upland areas where they form roving bands with other family groups and non-breeding birds. The same activity has been observed in Kerry (Gray 2005) and around Glencolmcille, Donegal (AMG). Parents then return to home ranges for the winter, leaving independent young to fend collectively. Feeding and roosting together through autumn and winter, older hands help indoctrinate the new generation.

SPECIES ACCOUNTS

MAGPIE
Pica pica

The late James Fisher, an eloquent and indefatigable advocate for conservation, wished that Magpies could be reduced to a level that would make the species an interesting rarity.

MAGPIE'S LATIN NAME is an onomatopoeic representation of its machine-gun rattle that contains an irritating excess of affected anguish. The rhyme that begins 'One for sorrow, two for joy' has lost its relevance. The land is overrun; a plague has descended. Unwittingly, we have shifted the balance in the bird's favour. Rural areas, suburbia and town centres – all are occupied at enormous densities. Across a universe of farmed countryside, animal feed, carcasses and a range of edible detritus are consumed. Our ubiquitous road network provides an abundance of roadkill. Each morning, chattering undertakers patrol thoroughfares looking to scavenge. Born bold, Magpies are cocky and fearless. In Britain, numbers have increased by 112 per cent over the last thirty years, making them the thirteenth most commonly seen bird in gardens. In Ireland, the scale of increase is greater. Controversy surrounds the bird, as some refuse to acknowledge the destruction it inflicts on songbird populations. Evidence from the Game and Wildlife Conservation Trust's farm at Loddington, Leicestershire, found that at keepered sites where the Magpie population was controlled, songbirds flourished. The RSPB refuses to accept these findings, claiming that there is no convincing evidence to show that Magpie predation is a conservation issue for songbird populations, and that the failure of nests of potentially vulnerable songbirds did not increase during the period of rapid Magpie population growth in the 1970s and 1980s. The RSPB's report on the predation of wild birds in the UK (RSPB 2007) states: 'The number of birds in the population will increase between the beginning of the breeding season and its end. For the population to remain stable between years, a large number of birds must die (the "doomed surplus") between the end of one breeding season and the beginning of the next.' This statement is balderdash.

The RSPB prefers to hide behind a fog of research findings that purport to be definitive. Few are. Unscrambling the gobbledegook is not easy. One study (Paradis *et al.* 2000) has been held up as holy writ. It demonstrated that it is possible to have a particular density of Magpies across habitats occupied by songbirds that, although they lost eggs and young due to predation, were not diminished. Not mentioned is a subsequent study carried out in the Czech Republic (Salek 2004):

A three-year experimental study with artificial ground nests was carried out in a highly fragmented agricultural landscape in southern Bohemia, Czech Republic, to examine whether population density or spatial distribution of active Magpie nests contributes to the pattern of predation on dummy nests. Out of the total of 335 dummy nests with a known fate, predators robbed 126 (38 per cent). Nests placed closer to active Magpie nests were predated significantly more than distant nests in two out of three years under study. Moreover, the distance to the nearest active Magpie nest was found to be the most obvious factor affecting nest predation risk.

Bleeding-heart liberals have leapt to the defence of Magpies and sage words have been pooh-poohed and virtually ridiculed – such

A three-year study in the Czech Republic found that Magpies discovered and attempted to destroy almost 40 per cent of songbird nests in their territory.

Monitoring of the destruction inflicted by Magpies on songbird nests found that size matters. Mistle Thrushes are large enough to deter murderous raids. For smaller species, resistance is futile.

as those of Bruce Campbell (Campbell and Watson 1964): 'Magpies feed mainly on insect grubs but, like other crows, will eat a great variety of food and are dangerous to young birds and eggs.' The theory invoked by conservationists is that songbird victims rally and second broods counterbalance initial losses. Magpies time the hatching of their own brood to coincide with the presence of songbird nestlings. Serendipity is not involved; robbers execute systematic early morning hit-and-run raids when most of us are still asleep.

Neither the effect of a high density of Magpies on songbirds nor the effect of predation on individual species has been scrutinised in any detail. An interim report of a study (Adderton 2003) into the impact of Magpies and other crows on the nesting success of hedgerow passerines in Northern Ireland states:

Changes in agricultural practices over previous decades have generally had a deleterious effect on numerous species of bird in both population size and range. However, populations of corvids have increased substantially. Consequently, they have been implicated in the decline of some passerine species through egg and nestling predation. Work to date has focused on Magpie and Hooded Crow predation on the nests of Blackbird and Song Thrush. During the 2003 breeding season, forty nests, situated in hedgerows of different types, were monitored in order to calculate nest survival and identify predators. Thermal data loggers were utilised to accurately measure the time of nest failure and understand how the

quality of the hedge can affect survival by influencing adult incubation behaviour. There is strong evidence to suggest that many nests are lost to corvids, although other factors may play an important role in governing nest survival. Hedge management, especially the cutting regime, can influence the concealment and accessibility of nests and inadvertently facilitate the discovery of nests by other predators [for example, domestic or feral cats].

In particular, Spotted Flycatchers appear to be paying a high price at the hands of Magpies. Removing them and crows from flycatcher breeding territories led to the reversal of a decline (Stoate & Szczur 2006a, 2006b). This fact has received next to no publicity, yet Spotted Flycatcher's seemingly inexorable demise has been extensively talked up and blamed on a range of intangible factors, from global warming to habitat changes in Africa, whereas the bird winters in a huge arc within which no other species has yet shown a comparable decline in European breeding grounds due to 'problems in Africa'. Clandestine Magpie control in Northern Ireland has benefited songbirds, albeit in pitifully few areas. Among monitored results was a doubling in the number of breeding species in one area of mixed farmland. At another site, a Sedge Warbler population quadrupled and produced eighty fledged juveniles. Before control, nearly all young had fallen victim to Magpies and Hooded Crows. Rather than proclaim this good news, those involved feel like members of an underground movement.

'Based on regular visits, it strikes me that Spotted Flycatchers are still common in the remote western fringes of Scotland, particularly on offshore islands, where Magpies are scarce or completely absent' (NMK, pers. comm.). This image, taken in the years before the bird became so reduced in numbers that it gained admission to a 'protected' list (a hollow euphemism) cannot be taken nowadays – because nest photography is illegal. In essence, this is a good thing. Yet green zealots have gone too far: 'Note that photographing ANY bird species in Ireland [and, apparently, in Northern Ireland] on the nest requires a licence [from the government]. To do so without one is actually illegal' (BirdWatch Ireland website, March 2012). This approach smacks of an iniquitously broad-brush and extreme health and safety attitude. Who is going to prosecute the tourists who admire and snap the tame nesting seabirds on Skellig Michael or Great Saltee, possibly among the last bastions of unfettered access to and enthralment with wild nature? David Attenborough (2009) bemoaned the same mindset: 'Collecting many kinds of natural objects is now forbidden by law. For very good reasons, it is illegal to collect birds' eggs or pluck wild flowers, nor is it allowed on many sites of geological importance for a child without a permit to go in search of fossils, as I once did. And I worry about that. For it seems to me that the collecting impulse was responsible for stimulating an interest in natural history and ultimately giving people a love and an understanding of the natural world. Maybe some of us will be able to translate that passion to accumulate material objects into an equally satisfying way of collecting photographic images of birds and butterflies and dragonflies and wild flowers. I hope so.'

It appears that the species is a recent arrival and that, until Ireland's forests were chopped down, it lacked a niche. Thompson (1849–52) stated: 'Smith, in his History of the County of Cork, published in 1749, remarks that the Magpie "was not known in Ireland seventy years ago, but is now very common."' In 1772 Rutty observed: 'It is a foreigner, naturalised here since the latter end of King James II's reign [1685–1688].' Based on receipts held in the Northern Ireland Public Record Office of payments for vermin by a Grand Jury in Antrim between 1727 and 1758, a total of 4,459 Magpies were killed, probably mainly by gamekeepers (Price & Robinson 2008). Furthermore, Thompson (1849–52) recorded:

This bird has increased and multiplied to a goodly extent in Ireland. The intelligent and trustworthy gamekeeper at Tollymore, Down, the seat of the Earl of Roden, informed me in September 1836, that having ranged the country for many miles around the park, he, by robbing their nests, shooting and trapping them, destroyed in one half year 732 birds and eggs.

Ussher and Warren (1900) add: 'The Magpie, thus introduced, spread rapidly, and is now to be seen everywhere through Ireland, except in the barest moorlands.' The use of the phrase 'thus introduced' may have been intended as a figure of speech, or used by the authors to imply that the process of colonisation was begun when, according to Robert Leigh of Rosegarden in Wexford, 'Under a dozen [Magpies] ... came with an easterly wind [and made landfall along the Wexford coast] in 1684.' The notion, parroted by many, that Ireland was colonised by means of a one-off event seems fanciful. It is more likely that, following influxes in autumn, founders arrived naturally. Barrington (1900) refers to migration at Hook Head, Wexford, on 18 October 1893: 'Magpies very numerous close to the lighthouse, probably 150–200.' Nowadays the sight of autumn flocks is not uncommon around coastal extremities. At least 500 arrived over Cape Clear Island, Cork, on 16 October 2010. Probably, most were post-breeding flocks of Irish provenance.

Primarily a resident of mixed deciduous woodland, Jays feed on acorns wherever they become available. Birds from a wide area converge to gather them. Coniferous trees are second best, but acceptable in some cases – pine seeds are palatable.

JAY
Garrulus glandarius

Jays are strikingly coloured. Intelligent and not averse to plundering the eggs and nests of other birds, they are not popular in some quarters. They are also in demand for another trade: their fretwork of bewitching azure wing feathers (mainly primary coverts) is used for fishing flies.

'YES, IT'S A CROW, Jim, but not as we know it.' Parodied lines from *Star Trek* apart, Jays are everything that other crows are not – they are colourful. If nest-thieving habits were not a stain on character, the species could be embraced more wholeheartedly as a dazzling novelty in woodland and large leafy gardens. Thompson (1849–52) never saw a live wild Jay in Ireland: 'I am not aware of the existence of this bird either now, or for a long time past, in the north of the island, although there are many districts apparently well suited to its abode.' He quotes Dubourdieu (1812), who wrote about birdlife in Antrim: 'The Jay was much more frequent before the woods at Portmore were cut; it is still however to be met with about Shane's Castle, and other woods at the borders of Lough Neagh.' In Thompson's era – the first half of the nineteenth century – the species was tied to the remnants of Ireland's once ubiquitous oak forest and occurred in a discontinuous belt straddling protected woods in private hands in Cork, Kerry, Tipperary, Kilkenny, Kildare and Dublin. Perhaps a few held on in large estates in Ulster since, in the twentieth century, nuclei still existed at Shane's Castle, Antrim and Tollymore, Down. Thompson was unable to cite a reason for the scarcity of the species. However, one of his correspondents, Mr Yarrell, speculated that an Irish statute from the reign of King George II (1727–1760) that offered a payment for the heads of Jays, Magpies and other crows led to decline, since 'numbers [of Jays were] killed in consequence of this reward being offered'. In the latter part of the twentieth century gamekeepers appear to have become less zealous, or the birds reached a critical mass that fuelled a breakout from largely private demesne woodlands. Especially since 1980, they have become a familiar garden bird where extensive plantations of tall trees adjoin suburbia.

In autumns when acorns are plentiful Jays make hay, carrying up to eight at a time in the gullet, throat and bill, and burying them up to several kilometres from the parent tree (Vera 2000). Small acorns are ignored. Usually several band together and estimates talk of thousands of acorns being transported. Chettleburgh (1952) documented the total removal of an acorn

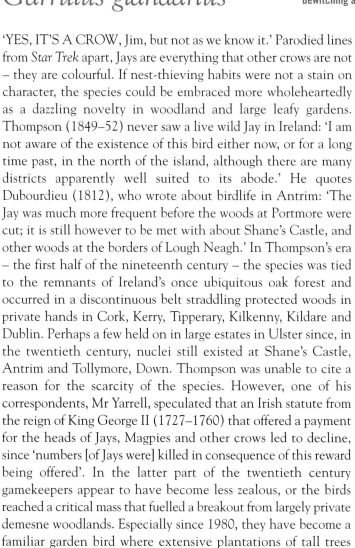

crop between September and November. Activity peaked during October and transport flights filled the working day. By mid-November, thirty-five birds had buried an estimated 200,000 acorns, each secreted separately and pushed or tapped into the ground. During the course of the year almost all of the cache were found and eaten. When seedlings appear, the bird hauls up the plant, exposing the acorn, which is then peeled and fed to youngsters. Bossema (1979) demonstrated that adults select seedlings on the basis of green stem colour, signifying that the acorn is not yet decomposed. Conversely, green-stemmed oak seedlings not buried by the bird survive untouched. Jays also eat wasps: prey is seized and its rear abdomen bitten hard, rupturing the insect's poison gland and nullifying its sting. The wasp is then eaten without further precautions (Goodwin 1952).

The main cry is a harsh squawk: *skaak!* The style of delivery invokes an accusatory tone, as though the bird is narked and yelling 'What?' Other calls include a cat-like whine and occasional mimicry (Buzzard's mewing call is often faked). Jays are stealthy and slip quietly through cover. A gaudy patchwork of colours makes surprisingly good camouflage. When seen as a moving silhouette against a tracery of branches, they cavort like small agile primates. Flight action recalls the butterfly swimming stroke; round wings arc forwards to provide laboured, somewhat jerky, propulsion. On the ground, bounding hops and tail cocking are standard. The vinaceous body colour of Irish populations is reputed to be deeper and darker than those in Britain. Further distinctions are said to include 'forehead and crown darker with broader black streaks; back of crown and nape usually considerably more tinged blue' (Witherby *et al.* 1938–41). Immigration has never been proved, so Hibernian stock may possess unique inheritable characteristics. On the other hand, Jays that flew in off the sea at Brown's Bay, Antrim, in late October 2005 (AMG) and near Ardglass, Down, in November 2009, may indicate overseas immigration. Perhaps this accounts for the origin of the ostensibly 'relict' population near the coast at Tollymore, Down?

JACKDAW
Corvus monedula

JACKDAWS are party animals and possess a mischievous streak. Gangs of youthful non-breeders have been observed taking it in turns to fly repeatedly through the air space above tern colonies, provoking the terns into giving chase; other groups, possibly of a similar age, have been seen diving at dense flocks of roosting Golden Plovers for no purpose except to cause panic (AMG). Jackdaws have complex social networks. Pairings are arrived at which can elevate the status of an individual, such as a low-ranking female who marries well. Clan members are emotionally attached to buddies, not necessarily of the opposite sex, and preen each other's plumage and huddle together as protection against wind, rain and cold. The species is brainy and captive birds are excellent talkers. Inherent craftiness may explain why the bird does not waste time over nest construction. Sticks are dropped down holes until a blockage is formed. If this process is too taxing, a shortcut is to steal material from the partially constructed nests of others. Watching the comings and goings at a colony is never dull. Headquarters include quarry faces riddled with holes, abandoned farm buildings or landmark trees whose girth and age provide cavities where branches have snapped off or rot set in. Sites are occupied year round. For humans living within earshot, the neighbours are noisy, communicating with *chak* calls rather than caws. Should a Grey Heron or Buzzard inadvertently drift near Mission Control, troops are scrambled and the trespasser is hounded.

Jackdaws are short-billed and pale-eyed; the iris on some adults is silver, on others iceberg blue. Juveniles, until they moult into first-winter plumage during September, have a sooty appearance before grey plumage emerges on the nape and neck-side. In autumn they have dull, chain-smoker eyes. Iris colour undergoes a bizarre metamorphosis: 'When juvenile, tinged pale blue, at about a month old becomes dull brown and gradually changes to dull white and not pearl-grey until a year old' (Witherby *et al.* 1938–41). The wings are pointed, with neat ends and minimal splayed fingering. Flight is fast, at times acrobatic, and aerial groups are capable of fast synchronisation – impressive, but not Starling perfect. Lone, direct-flying individuals can suggest other identities, such as a pigeon, shorebird or bird of prey. When showing off or chasing away intruders, the bird rejoices in phases of fast daredevil flight, as though vying for Top Gun status.

An unknown percentage of Jackdaws are immigrants from Britain and continental Europe. Among them are a few whose origins can be deduced by the presence of a fairly bold, silvery neck collar. Classic individuals originate from the eastern Baltic and have been termed Nordic Jackdaws, although similar populations are found in Turkey. The true scale of migration is masked by the fact that many continental visitors – even from western Russia – are identical to local Irish stock. This state of affairs was observed by examining the make-up of travelling flocks in Estonia in April 2010 (AMG). In common with Hooded Crow, Jackdaws are prone to partial albinism. A not infrequent example is a symmetrical white band across the base of the primaries on both wings, producing a pattern reminiscent of Great Skua. Because crows tend to be sedentary, it can be possible to follow the survival of well-marked individuals, which are accepted as flock members without prejudice.

Cackling right up to bedtime, Jackdaws join Rooks at winter roosts. Both are early risers and are up and away before daybreak.

Quintessentially a jack of all trades, the Jackdaw's social networking and varied diet have led to a population surge since 1970. Over 100,000 pairs now breed in Ireland.

Baltic Jackdaw. Not previously suspected of travelling here from overseas, a new realisation (backed up by minor plumage distinctions, including a frosty collar) accepts that, like winter-visiting Starlings, some come from the eastern Baltic and Russia. Photograph taken in Estonia.

ROOK
Corvus frugilegus

Above, left: Rooks need tall trees for nesting and grassland in which to feed. With a face like a trowel, larvae and insects are grubbed from the soil. Farmers approve such actions, but less so the bird's ability to dig up and eat young cereal shoots.

Above, right: Until its first birthday, a young Rook has a black-feathered face and its bill structure is yet to attain the 'dagger' proportions of adulthood. During its first autumn and winter, the expression is more like a Hooded or Carrion Crow.

Left: At the end of the breeding season, shabby matt black feathering is replaced with a new coat of fresh plumage, burnished with violet.

ROOKERIES COME ALIVE early in the New Year. If a 'caw chorus' was played to a human subject under hypnosis, they would probably conjure up an image of a latticework bedecked with shaggy-winged crows busily engaged in ferrying sticks to treetop nests hung like black pancakes against a colourless winter sky. Some colonies in century-old trees are as old as the timber. Minor repairs are needed after storms. Ironically, the great gale of 7 January 1839 obliterated Rooks more than rookeries. In its aftermath, 33,000 corpses were counted along lakeshores in Westmeath (Thompson 1849–52).

Pared down to almost one syllable, the cry of a Rook is *ka*. Plumage is shot with 'Sinatra blue' and deep purple. Waddlers let it all hang out, loose-winged and baggy-trousered, with 'knees' hidden beneath a ragged cloak. A large part of the diet is composed of grubs and the larvae of insects injurious to crops. The banana-shaped schnozzle functions as a digging fork. Unfeathered, naked skin in front of the eye permits a clear line of sight to the bill tip. Youngsters have fully feathered faces with a bill lacking the full taper of an adult, risking misidentification as Carrion Crow. Helpfully, their silhouette combines a trademark peaked crown with a Concorde 'broken nose'. Put

another way, the head and bill profile of a young Rook has lumps and bumps; that of a Carrion Crow is smooth and curvaceous. Scrutiny of the gape-line reveals another point of difference. The rear corner of the gape is discernible on Rook but cloaked by feathering on Carrion Crow. In flight, the centre of a Rook's tail is bulbous.

The species displays remarkable social cohesion and breeds, roosts and feeds together. Before Rooks take off en masse to snooze among arboreal architecture, pre-roost gatherings pepper fields like black rain. Near Cultra, Down, thousands congregate at the side of one of Northern Ireland's busiest roads, the A2 between Belfast and Bangor. Where do these birds come from? Surprisingly, many spend the day on the far side of Belfast Lough and commute across a wide expanse of water. Normally, with wings shaped for flapping, not gliding, crows shun marine crossings. By flying low, wingtips almost brushing the surface, the birds effectively reduce drag, provided they stick to a height lower than the amplitude of each stroke. In essence, the wind-flow around the wing is 'squeezed' between bird and water and acts like a pillow of air, buoying flight.

CARRION CROW
Corvus corone

Once a young Rook has been excluded from the identification process – not an easy task – an all-black crow has to be a Carrion Crow. Raven, while also utterly black, is much larger.

Carrion Crow is copying Collared Dove in expanding its range westwards. Colonists tend to be loners that, on failing to find a breeding partner of their own kind, pair with a Hooded Crow, a sister species. Offspring from mixed marriages are not uncommon in eastern Ulster (where most Carrion Crows are based) and resemble a 'dusky' Hooded Crow.

CARRION CROW is ubiquitous across England and Wales, and south of the Great Glen in Scotland. A gradual expansion into the breeding range of Hooded Crows in western Scotland has been ongoing since the 1980s. It would appear that a quiet invasion is taking place rather than a full-blooded blitzkrieg. Through time, relationships forge and mixed pairs, involving a Carrion Crow interbreeding with a Hooded Crow, indicate that plumage differences are no impediment to assimilation. Many hybrid progeny resemble a swarthy Hooded Crow. Isolated Carrion Crows, associating with Hooded Crows, are an increasingly regular part of the scene along those parts of the Irish coast facing Scotland and Wales; no doubt the departure points of wanderers-cum-colonists. Hybrid offspring do not seem to travel far and none has penetrated west of Lough Neagh, although mixed pairs have been seen at Lough Shark, Armagh, and Banbridge, Down (JSF). As yet, there has been no authenticated record of a breeding pair of pure Carrion Crows on this side of the Irish Sea.

Until one year of age, young Rooks fail to develop a pale bill base, which constitutes an identification pitfall. (Means of safely distinguishing juvenile Rook from Carrion Crow are described in the Rook account.) Sometimes flocks of 'Carrion Crows' are reported, typically in autumn. Groups of adolescent Rooks often travel together. Because all in the party have a dark-faced countenance, they are blithely misidentified. Soon the report passes unchecked into the mass media. Does it matter if observers make mistakes? Yes, it does. Data used by O'Donoghue, Cross and O'Halloran (1996) to review the status of Carrion Crow was, through no fault of the authors, heavily infused with erroneous reports. Recorders are supposed to uphold standards. Wearisome sloppiness means that a mapped distribution for the species (Gibbons *et al.* 1993) is wrong. Luckily, information published in Copeland Bird Observatory's annual reports is reliable. An exemplary summary for 1955 to 2005 reads:

Carrion Crow is primarily a spring visitor but also occurs occasionally in autumn. During the first two decades, only one or two on a few days annually, but sightings have steadily risen over the last three decades [1975–2005]. There are now from 10 to nearly 100 'bird-days' annually in April and May and up to 30 in autumn. The biggest days have been in April, the maximum 26 on 22nd April 2000. It has been postulated that the zone of hybridisation has now moved into Ireland, taking in about a mile breadth of the Ards Peninsula. The Hooded Crow could be entirely replaced by the Carrion Crow over the next 200 years in both Ireland and Scotland. (www.habitas.org.uk/cbo)

In early September 2010 a flock of twelve Carrion Crows arrived and spent one day at Copeland. Calls were heard that, with just a little practice, safely eliminate Rook as a contender (NMK). Such rigour is refreshing. Post-2005 observations by careful observers have confirmed a tendency for autumn migrants to winter on the Ards Peninsula and to return as a flush of migrants in early April, via the Copeland Islands, towards the Galloway coast of Scotland. In 2011, fifteen were present on 9 April, outnumbering the local Hooded Crows. Both date of passage and the occurrence of small bands indicate that immatures were involved. Breeding adults occupy territories in late winter and, by April, should be nesting.

HOODED CROW
Corvus cornix

Coastlines are favoured, yet mudflat-dwelling Hooded Crows tend to be dismissed as scavengers. In reality they are searching for mussels. Unable to hammer open the mollusc like an Oystercatcher, they drop shells from a height on to the nearest hard surface. Concrete piers and railway tracks bear witness to their ingenuity.

Looking like a Dickens character, Hooded Crows are not fussy about where they find dinner.

HOODED CROWS (known as Grey Crows in most rural districts) get a bad press from farmers and keepers of game. Undoubtedly, they are shrewd opportunists and will finish off a sickly or unguarded lamb. Where there is an abundance of nesting birds, for example at important breeding refuges such as the Copeland Islands, just one pair can do enormous damage. Across overstocked farmland and along roads that provide them with flattened fauna, numbers are sustained at densities higher than would be sustainable in a 'balanced' natural environment. By way of proof, crows are scarce in the woods and farm fields of the eastern United States and Canada. There, dead fauna are eaten by Turkey Vultures that locate carcasses by smell. Across Ireland, Hooded Crows seem most at home along the coast. 'Shellfish Crow' or 'Shore Crow' would, in fact, be an apt alternative title. The bird is a beachcomber and uses roads, boulders and railway lines as hard surfaces upon which to drop mussels and winkles and crack them open. Pairs tend to be solitary and communal roosts are uncommon. Where winter food supplies are plentiful, gatherings occur among woodland or on rocky hilltops offering a commanding view. A roost containing 200 was reported at Ballyworkan Moss, Armagh (Deane 1954). There is practically no evidence of immigration. A chick ringed in June 1940 at Carnlough, Antrim, was recovered in the same area nine years later.

Close up, the bird is not unattractive and has an intellectual face with an inquisitive slumberous eye and a machete-shaped ebony bill whose owner has a diffident, wary walk. Ever watchful, individuals act as sentinels and alarm when a bird of prey appears. Next time you hear a grating *grrik, grrik, grrik*, look up. Chances are that one or more Hooded Crows will be mobbing a Sparrowhawk, Buzzard or infidel Raven. Hooded Crows are jealous of trespassing rivals. Perched Buzzards, especially if the raptor is mantling a dead rabbit, are subjected to tail pulling and truculence. Magpies often join in. Hooded Crows sound sullen. Three to five notes are cranked out in a metronomic, drawling rhythm: *kaaa, kaaa, kaaa*. The call attenuates like the *baaa* of a lamb. Rooks, in contrast, utter an unslurred *ka*. In flight, fingered wings look ragged; progress is flappy and somewhat unsteady, a far cry from the jauntiness of Jackdaw or power of Raven. A whitish patch at the base of the primaries is not uncommon, and sometimes extends into a pale wing-bar. During summer, youngsters are strikingly piebald. Pale 'deep pile' plumage has a buff or mauve glow. In late summer adults moult. New plumage on the wing coverts, chest and throat has a cobalt hue.

RAVEN
Corvus corax

UNIFORM REGALIA – the sinister black severity of a biker's leathers – coupled with a machete bill and shaggy throat distinguish the monarch of crows. In flight the folded tail is spool-shaped and juts out further behind the wings than the protrusion of head and bill. The tail's diagnostic profile shows best overhead. The wings are long with vulturine, deeply slotted primaries. Wingbeats are powerful yet elastic. Ravens love to soar and cruise at altitude. Sunny days initiate energetic high-level circling, with copious wingbeats and calling. With each croak the bill opens, revealing macabre mandibles. Gruff sound bites come from cheerleaders – maybe a rallying cry to exchange information about food whereabouts? Human certainty of avian motives is lacking. Ravens may not be the largest birds on earth, but they regard themselves as Mr Big. One stentorian squawk elicits supplication. In still air the whump of wingbeats carries for a kilometre. On the wing they tumble and briefly free-fall. Pairs passing overhead lock feet in a playful docking manoeuvre, further evidence of joie de vivre. A group was photographed taking turns to slide upside down along a snow bank. Nothing other than fun seemed to be at the heart of this activity. Pestering by lesser mortals is dodged by a nonchalant wing flip, resulting in a half-roll in which the bird pivots 180 degrees before righting itself.

The word Raven has remained virtually unchanged since its Anglo-Saxon transcription as *Hrafn*. Perhaps the moniker was, all along, onomatopoeic – a grunt that passed into written language. Estonian, an ancient tongue, gloriously invented *Ronk*, which is still in use today. Ravens make a variety of sounds from ghoulish squawks to sonorous croaks, guttural clucks and a gong-like *boing*. They summon each other with a *krack rack-rack*. A pet Raven kept by Konrad Lorenz (1949) learned to address him by name, making it 'the only animal that has ever spoken a human word to a person in the right context'.

In the 1950s, the bird's counting ability prevented a photographer – Eric Hosking – entering a hide when accompanied by a colleague, who acted as a decoy. The Raven was able to deduce that if two people went into the hide and just one emerged, someone remained. Only when a class of school-children was pressed into service was the counting limit surpassed. In North America, researchers at a nest were bombed with stones and footfuls of gravel.

Breeding age comes comparatively late in life and a wing-tagged Scottish male did not find a mate until six years old (Booth 1986). Although pairs stay together for life, widows quickly remarry. Communication is sophisticated and news of a bounty is transmitted quickly. Roosts act as an information exchange. Solitary pairs make a beeline to gather with others at easy pickings many miles outside their home range. Irish Ravens have been recorded commuting to north Wales to exploit a sudden abundance of food. In the Mourne Mountains in July 1995, 128 were counted feeding on a hatch of Tiger Beetles across Slieve Commedagh (AMG). Youngsters roam widely and may regularly cross the Irish Sea. A chick ringed at Ballycastle, Antrim in May 1987 struck wires and was killed in Suffolk in January 1988; another reared on the Copeland Islands in 1956 was found dead near Campbeltown, Strathclyde, the following March.

The caliph inhabits uplands and wild coasts. Most nests are located on inaccessible ledges beneath overhangs; others are concealed in trees. Cunning as ever, tree-nesting Ravens call little. Carrion accounts for most of the diet. Like wolves teasing and harassing herds of Caribou to single out weaklings, Ravens buzz groups of gulls or shorebirds in the hope of discovering the sick or lame. When discovered, the victim is attacked immediately and may be hurled onto its back and disembowelled while still alive. Is it any wonder that soldiers of yore came to regard circling Ravens as ill omens? Mounting evidence from Scottish gamekeepers and nature reserve managers, for example on Islay, points to Ravens being outright predators of shorebird chicks. On the small island of Inishbofin, Galway, rogue individuals among three pairs of Ravens – an unnaturally high concentration sustained by an embarrassment of riches of sheep carrion – have turned their attention to Mallard and Lapwing. In spring 2012, visiting birdwatchers observed the annihilation of several ducklings followed, over subsequent days, by the slaughter of Lapwing chicks. On how many other islands are nesting shorebirds imperilled by Ravens?

Largest of the crows, Ravens have little to fear. Adults, once they have a territory, stay in it all year and use the same nest sites annually – though they may alternate between locations. Young disperse over considerable distances but remain in contact with an adolescent peer group by meeting up at roosts where information is shared about food availability. Sheep densities across Ireland's uplands provide regular carrion and the population is probably at an all-time high (at least 2,500 pairs). In many ways a predator, rogue Ravens are a menace, a fact that dewy-eyed conservationists seem unprepared to acknowledge.

Ravens roll and dive in upcurrents over windy crags and sea cliffs, then hang in the sky like an extra in a Hitchcock movie. If disturbed near a nest site they resort to guile and race past below a passer-by, shrewdly hugging the blind side of intervening terrain. In direct, rapid flight, the wingtips become pointed, morphing their shape to resemble a giant falcon. Seen from above, black plumage has a bluebottle gloss. Youngsters, until they are several months old, are black with a hint of brown.

GOLDCREST
Regulus regulus

A miniaturised green flame of a bird, Goldcrests sound like a shrew that took singing lessons. Small size and a hovering habit allow access to cramped spaces inaccessible to larger insectivorous birds. Because of their puny size, Goldcrests have a virtual monopoly when it comes to gleaning insects from the underside of leaves and picking aphids from tree bark.

THERE IS A CERTAIN IRONY in the fact that Europe's tiniest bird seeks out the tallest trees. Goldcrests are insectivorous, an attribute that makes life difficult because, unlike seed-eating birds, they cannot store food in a crop. Consequently, they forage from dawn to dusk. Size is Route One to recognition. The titch hovers regularly; the wings blur but balled-up yellowish feet at the end of dark tarsi catch the eye. Tiny and compact with a near-invisible short slender bill, the mite is endearing and often indifferent to observation, especially when examining foliage and flitting from twig to twig. The Latin name *Regulus regulus* attests to distinctive head markings. A coronet of yellow, topped off with flame-orange in the male, is bordered with black. Both sexes have peppercorn eyes on a bland face and a drooping, Fu Manchu wispy moustache. Lispy calls shuttle together in a short series: *si-si-si-si*. It is easy to imagine 'a mouse up a tree' as the source. Song, if anything, is higher-pitched and lasts for several seconds, an impressive feat for tiny lungs. Depending on hearing range, it

may be inaudible. The construct is cyclical with a terminal crescendo. Rhythm and finale suggest a car ignition trying, but failing, to start.

Goldcrests pour over the North Sea in autumn, especially when anticyclonic weather establishes around Halloween or early November. This signals the onset of winter across Scandinavia. Westbound migrants have a tailwind for take-off. They follow a vector taking them southwest, confirmed by one ringed at Aberdeen on 22 October 1988, which flew 357km south-southwest and was retrapped nine days later at Copeland Bird Observatory, having averaged 40km per day (if it flew every day, which is unlikely). Although many are caught and ringed in autumn, almost none are re-trapped in spring. Perhaps they return by a different route or do not pause in coastal districts on migration? More poignantly, the species' winter mortality rate is high – most do not live a year.

BLUE TIT
Cyanistes caeruleus

Despite incontestably pretty looks, the human eye still fails to see Blue Tit plumage at its best. When seen in the ultraviolet vision of a female, the blue of a male glows even brighter. The deeper his lustre, the higher she rates him.

BLUE TITS are relatively unfazed by human presence. Many are borderline nosy, an attitude that allows close study of an engaging bossy boots. Chief among diagnostic markings is a dark 'spectacle frame' running through the eye; without it the bird would be white-faced. Airborne, a cigar stub head truncates in a wafer tail and the blob travels straight as a die. Blue Tits see ultraviolet light, which highlights the lustre of blue plumage. Females select mates based on the strength of ultraviolet reflectance. Most of all, they look for a glossy cap. Studies have revealed that the number of feather mites (tiny parasites that can impair health, although not cause death) affects the brightness of plumage. Heavily parasitised males look dull. As with Great Tit, the birds become brighter with each moult for the first three or four years of life. Urban-dwelling Blue Tits are scruffy. During harsh winter weather, hard-pressed rural cousins that move temporarily into built-up areas return sullied (Perrins 1979).

Although nests are concealed in cavities – or nest-boxes – with tiny entrance holes, safety is not guaranteed. Failure due to infanticide is not uncommon. A rival male looking for a mate will destroy a brood and then hope to woo the female, thereby spreading his own genes. Usually just one brood is reared and, within minutes of emerging into daylight, the family is led away. The vicinity of the nest is deemed unsafe, lest predators have been watching. Young are reared on tiny caterpillars and grubs. Larger caterpillars are carried singly because of the need to dispatch prey before feeding it to chicks – live caterpillars can bite. Even though a pair of Blue Tits may feed 10,000 caterpillars to a brood, a mature oak can harbour over ten times that amount. As the breeding season approaches, adults feed among opening leaf buds. This is where caterpillars and emerging larvae find their first meal of spring. 'Pussy Willow' flowers are rich in pollen and attract insects; Blue Tits eat both, pollen being a rich source of protein (Perrins 1979).

Less colourful than her husband, the female Blue Tit is chief architect. Some males are barred from entering the chamber and are obliged to pass building materials to the matriarch, only being allowed to inspect the oeuvre by peeping through the entrance hole. She does all the technical stuff – far more than simply picking the wallpaper. Compared to their woodland counterparts, clutch size is smaller in urban Blue Tits and fewer young survive, probably due to a shortage of suitable food.

Zealous gardeners who eradicate insect life at ground level generally do not extend the slaughter into tree foliage, so Blue Tit young do not starve. Except, that is, in commercial orchards – principally in Armagh, so-called 'Orchard County' – where relentless spraying results in famine conditions. Consider the following. First, from a chair-ridden B. J. Massingham in England, whose time was brightened by watching the journeys of parent Blue Tits between their nest and the apple trees in his orchard. He calculated that the brood received at least 1,500 meals each day, consisting of grubs of the apple blossom weevil and maggots of the Apple Sawfly. Next, Thompson (1849–52) attempted to dispel ill feeling:

> The Blue Tit often falls victim to unpardonable ignorance in this country in consequence of the injury it is supposed to do to fruit trees. When in the very act of saving the buds, by picking away from them the insects bent on their destruction, and which man himself with all his power could not destroy, this poor bird is savagely slaughtered. Thanks to Mr Weir we have some idea of the vast amount of good done by them in the destruction of caterpillars. This gentleman watched for seventeen hours and ascertained 475 visits containing caterpillars fed to nestlings. Sometimes they brought in a single large one; at other times two or three small ones.

Blue Tits are sedentary. Although youngsters disperse widely, neither they nor adults fly any distance out to sea. The species is rare on offshore Islands. Copeland Bird Observatory lies close to the coast and is connected by the stepping stone of Big Copeland, yet even here the species is not met with annually. A ringing study (Burgess 1982) indicated that females wander more widely than males in their first winter, a phenomenon also noted for Great Tit. This may be due to casual or evolutionary reasons – dominance by the slightly larger males over females, or preliminary searching for suitable breeding sites.

The repertoires of Blue Tit, Great Tit and Coal Tit are rich and varied, with fundamental notes in the vocabulary of one having parallels in the others, albeit at a different pitch or timbre. Are we deaf to a recognisable theme in Blue Tit vocabulary – a rolling vibrato? Unmistakable plumage spawned the bird's name. Had the species been a Plain Jane its voice might have earned it the epithet Tremolo Tit. A multipurpose coda 'trembles' into a quavery finale and covers everything from song to indignant blasts directed at us if we unexpectedly step into the garden. Phonetically: *tsee, tsee, tsu* followed by *h'h'h'heeeee* (or *hu'hu'hu'hu*). The climax hangs in the air, like a violinist holding a note or the stutter of a CD that has developed a fault. When a Sparrowhawk is spotted, initial *tsee, tsee* notes are emphasised as a specific warning. These notes become more strident and purer; the shuttled ending remains the same. A frequent 'B side' is a chiding *brrrr*, slurred – and slightly decelerating – and with the frisson of a motor revving into life.

Young Great Tits resemble adults but have yellowish cheeks initially bounded by a poorly developed dark border.

GREAT TIT
Parus major

IT IS OFTEN SAID THAT, when puzzled by a hidden chime coming from tree canopy, the source will be a Great Tit. The polyglot produces a bewildering array of notes. Individuals have a repertoire of phrases, switching from one to the other during singing bouts. Mobile treetop minstrels sound 'happy'. Bell-like and with the rhythm of a squeezebox, one trademark couplet is likened to *tea-cher, tea-cher*. The ditty resembles using a bicycle pump to inflate a tyre. Apt as this analogy may be, the same applies to the repertoire of Coal Tit. You can compare the two on www.xeno-canto.org. To facilitate fast searching, type in 'nr:' followed by the digits of the XC (Xeno-Canto) catalogue number. Recordings made in Northumberland by Richard Dunn demonstrate just how alike the two can be: XC 71454 (Great Tit) and XC 95058 (Coal Tit). In life, Coal Tit voice comes across as thinner and more nasal. In autumn a bouncy *chee, chee, chur'r'r'r'r* is often heard. As ever, the salutation has a confident feel. Unfortunately, Blue Tit sounds similar. Throughout the year paired adults and flock members who know each other use shorthand to keep in touch. One regularly heard note is *pink* and is exclusive to males, distinguishable by a black bandolier that runs the length of the chest and broadens behind the legs. Viewed from below, the black stripe resembles a slim egg timer: thin in the middle and bulging at each end.

Great Tits are large-billed. The beak is robust with a fat, 'B-pencil' tip. It is used to crack open hazelnuts, which are clasped between toes and struck repeatedly like a stonemason tapping with a chisel. Oak galls are split to access the grub inside. In flight, white outer tail feathers are a helpful feature to distinguish from Coal and Blue Tit.

Gompertz (1961) discovered that each male tends to have at least four songs, usually of different tempos. Contesting males tend to use the same type of song in vocal duels. If one changes, the other parries by copying the new sound. The more varied the song, the more appealing the singer to eavesdropping females,

Primarily insectivorous in summer, the Great Tit switches to seeds during winter, for which it forages on the ground. The stout bill, with a convex, bulging lower mandible, allows it to tackle larger food items. Hazelnuts are opened by being clamped underfoot and hammered, woodpecker style. Males are usually brighter than females with deeper yellow underparts, a glossy (rather than matt) black cap and a wider black breast-stripe, especially behind the legs.

hence the need for one vocalist to keep pace with the other. Adult males sing most intensively in spring. Neighbours know each other. When a newcomer moves through the area, potentially looking for a mate, established males call each other. Females listen in and play jukebox jury. If paired to an inferior chanter, she seeks out the superior impresario and mates clandestinely with him. In a classic study (Krebs 1982), several males were removed from territories. In some plots, loudspeakers were installed and song was broadcast. After eight hours all territories were checked. New males occupied only those territories that remained quiet. Begging calls of fledged young of all titmice are a familiar sound in woodland in high summer. Foliage resounds with sibilant *tzee-tzee-tzee* stammers. Gompertz (1961) claims that the begging notes of Great and Blue Tits differ: 'pitch variation of the Blue Tit is nearly always such as to end in one or more falling notes whereas the Great Tit almost invariably rises.'

COAL TIT
Periparus ater

Are we all victims of mass hallucination? Field guide depictions show the bill of the Coal Tit to be slim and tiny, allegedly an adaptation for feeding among clusters of pine needles, a shape that typifies populations east of the Irish Sea. In Ireland, Coal Tits are not fine-billed and possess a fairly robust bill, more suited for broadleaved woods.

COAL TITS have a black head with pale cheeks, a badger stripe on the nape and a smudgy black beard, blacker and more extensive in males. Cinnamon-coloured flanks are fluffed during cold weather. The rear crown conceals a ruffled crest, sometimes elevated like a Ku Klux Klan hood. There are two wingbars: that on the median wing-coverts is dotted, bringing Tipp-Ex to mind. The upperparts are grey, tinged with olive; cobalt fuses the crown (in males) and a lustre of mayonnaise – a yellower shade of pale – permeates the rear half of the cheek. Almost a quarter of all food is animal matter. Caterpillars and larvae are immobilised prior to being removed for storage and aphids are cached in pellet form, each pellet containing around two dozen insects, packaged in the bird's saliva (Perrins 1979). Attending garden feeders, the bird discards more than it can carry away, like a fussy shopper pawing over bric-a-brac. Indeed, much time is spent hiding food, rather than feeding. Seeds and pieces of nut are lodged among moss and soft substrates; some birds have a penchant for the compost of potted plants. Memory of where items are secreted is accurate. The downside to conspicuous industry is that nosy neighbours notice. Great Tits rob supplies throughout the winter.

Coal Tit is no stranger to terra firma and breeding sites are often at ground level. Blocked-up mouse holes become chambers lined with moss and dead grass – but not feathers, an adornment popular only with Blue Tit. After the breeding season, troupes join forces with other tits, Goldcrests and Treecreepers. Foraging as they go, all eyes watch for Sparrowhawks. Life expectancy is short, although one from Coleraine survived for nine years before being killed by a predator, probably a Grey Squirrel (KWP).

Thompson (1849–52) left a vivid account:

When in Colin Glen on 19 November, I saw Blue and Coal Tits in company with Goldcrests. All were clinging to the centre of the underside of Sycamore leaves, and describing a circle with their bills by picking with extreme rapidity all around them, during which operation their weight did not bring to the ground a single leaf, though all were sere and yellow. The Coal Tit feeds much at this season on the red berries of honeysuckle, carrying the berries one by one to a place of concealment.

A waspish minority glow primrose yellow on the rear cheek and neck stripe. Indeed, it has been claimed that the suffusion is unique and merits classification as 'Irish' Coal Tit: 'Mantle, scapulars and back strongly washed olive-buff; cheeks, ear-coverts, sides of neck, centre of breast and belly pale yellow or yellowish-white, not pure white; flanks and under tail-coverts yellowish-buff.' (Witherby et al. 1938–41). Mr Collingwood Ingram discovered yellow-washed individuals 'in the pine woods of Sligo' and news of the find was communicated to the world through an article published, not in a scientific journal, but in the Daily Mail (28 December 1910): 'New British Bird: Yellow Coal-Tit found in Sligo' (Dickinson and Milne 2008).

The case for status as an endemic Irish subspecies is undermined by the presence of similar individuals in parts of Wales (Witherby et al. 1938–41) and Scotland's Outer Hebrides. Furthermore, some Coal Tits in Ireland appear to be as white across the rear cheek as their British and Scandinavian counterparts. Although a few are probably migrants from overseas – three ringed in Europe have wintered in England (Sellersa 1984) – local family parties seen in September, when juvenile plumage has been moulted, show a range of rear cheek suffusion and constitute a spanner in the works. Perhaps diet accounts for the colouring? Carotenoids (chemicals that produce keratin) beget yellow, orange and red colouration in plumage. Birds manufacture these hues through consuming carotenoid-containing food. Yellowishness of titmice plumage has been studied in Great Tit (Slagsvold & Lifjeld 1985) and habitat-dependent differences were found in the colouration of offspring. Nestlings reared in a deciduous forest were yellower than those reared in coniferous woodland. When eggs were switched between the nests of two different habitats, the results were similar, indicating that differences were not genetic but related to food quality. Yellower nestlings received more caterpillars than nestlings that had paler plumage. Is it not plausible that such findings apply to Coal Tits?

Nonetheless, it is possible to detect a semblance of a geographical pattern with a general trend to yellower rear-cheeks (and more olive upperparts) in western districts. Feasibly, a similar phenomenon might apply in Scotland. The variable appearance of 'Irish' Coal Tit may amount to nothing more than a chimera influenced by the local environment; or might a gene exert an active influence? For the moment, all is theory. While admitting that his thoughts amount to shameless speculation, Neville McKee commented:

I suggest the yellow wash on the white plumage areas, and the green hue of the back, is due to a yellow pigment deposited in those feathers at the time of the annual moult. The basic back colour is, of course, blue-grey, but the yellow pigment changes the colour to a greenish tinge over the grey-blue background. Throughout the year, the yellow tinge gradually fades, almost certainly due to bleaching by ultraviolet light, until the tint turns white and greenish-grey becomes bluish-grey. For years I had thought that the reason for the paler birds farther east was because of fairly frequent invasions of Coal Tits from Scotland, which diluted the effect of the Irish 'yellow' gene. However, another hypothesis could be diet-related. Perhaps some mineral or dietary carotenoid is present in greater concentration farther west? (NMK, pers. comm.)

The situation is further complicated by minor variations in bill shape across Ireland (Perrins 1979). Bill thickness is slightly greater in western populations; those in eastern districts match British Coal Tits. Because a stouter bill tends to be associated with living in broadleaved woods, it is intriguing to ponder if, all along, an indigenous Irish Coal Tit existed?

Coal Tits, almost as a pastiche of diminutive size, have the highest voice of the capped tit tribe. Boring, whining tseu and tzee monosyllables serve as small talk between kin foraging in cover. During songbursts a nasal timbre is distinctive, even though many phrases find an equivalent in Great Tit's vocabulary. For Great Tit's tea-cher, tea-cher, tea-cher, read see-chu, see-chu, see-chu (or sittchu-sittchu-sittchu). Listen to the pace. Coal Tit is usually faster and not likely to draw an analogy to the 'kindergarten' feel of bell-like sounds that typify Great Tit. Like most resident songbirds, Coal Tits are stimulated by lengthening daylight and recommence territorial overtures in the first fine weather after Christmas. Simple the repertoire may be, but it is high fidelity that disperses New Year gloom.

WOODLARK
Lullula arborea

WOODLARKS graced parts of eastern Ireland until some time around the middle of the twentieth century. Across Europe the bird is sedentary in the milder west but migratory in the colder north and east. In Britain, the population has increased from around 250 pairs in 1986 to 1,500 pairs in 1997. The improvement is thought to be largely due to the availability of clearings in forestry plantations, created to benefit them. In Britain, East Anglian Woodlarks largely desert their breeding grounds in winter, whereas a greater proportion in southern England are resident on heathland and in the New Forest.

Realistically, Ireland's chances of being recolonised look slim. Could Woodlarks have been decimated when our woods were felled, with skeleton bands restricted to peripheral habitat that was eventually lost? Thompson (1849–52) regarded it as 'a resident, but very local species ... where the soil is warm, the country well cultivated and wooded'. He singled out parts of Antrim and Down as known haunts. A handful hung on in Wicklow until late in the nineteenth century and into the last century in Cork, where, perhaps prophetically, the bird was much prized for its song and 'greatly sought after by bird-catchers.'

Another latter-day absentee from Ireland. Woodlarks formerly had a patchy distribution from Down to Cork.

SKYLARK
Alauda arvensis

A FLICKERING SPECK in the blue, pouring out a continuous rhapsody that turns human heads heavenwards – that is how most people encounter a Skylark. Divas are difficult to see on the ground because they scurry and freeze. Occasionally one rises from a verge, revealing white outer tail feathers set off by a blackish tail. The bird undulates in flight, like a skateboarder cresting invisible ramps. Rippling calls serve as a pointer to overhead migrants. Cold snaps in Britain send pulses west, fleeing frozen or snow-covered land and travelling hopefully, in search of mild conditions and food. Barrington (1900), by collating reports from lighthouse keepers, provided a graphic account:

> An extraordinary rush at Copeland lighthouse on the night of February 20th 1890 is described by the keepers, Messrs E. McCarron and C. Hawking. Immense swarms of birds around lantern from 10pm to 4am: Skylarks, Blackbirds, Starlings and thrushes. The air was filled with birds. The balcony outside was completely covered with corpses; they were five or six deep. Numbers got through the cowl into the lantern. The lantern-glass was so much soiled, both inside and out, that eight buckets of water had to be carried up next day to wash it. A labourer doing work at the lighthouse gathered 200.

Winter stubbles used to provide sustenance for flocks numbering thousands. Breeding numbers have decreased drastically, both here and across Europe. The decline has been rapid and shows that huge areas of countryside have suffered massive environmental degradation. In 1970, around 75 per cent of the UK's cereals were spring sown (Donald & Morris 2005). That is, the cereals were planted in the spring, grew during summer and were harvested in autumn. After harvest, the stubble was left until ploughing in late winter. Nowadays, spring-sown cereals have been all but displaced by varieties sown in autumn. These higher-yielding, drought-resistant strains are harvested as early as mid-July and the next crop is planted as early as September. Research (Schlapfer 1988; Jenny 1990) has confirmed that Skylark densities are higher in spring-sown cereals than in varieties planted in autumn. Autumn-grown cereals, because they have been growing for longer, are tall and dense by spring, making it almost impossible for birds to access the crop. On the other hand, the sward height and density of spring cereals allows birds to penetrate lower, sparser vegetation (which, luckily, still conceals the nest). Proof can be found by looking at how tractor tramlines are used. Initially in autumn-sown cereals, nests are placed away from tramlines. Then, as growth thickens the crop, an increasing proportion of nests are constructed at the edge of tramlines, the only part of the field where access is feasible. In contrast, nests in spring-sown cereals are placed randomly within the crop. The effect on nest success is profound; almost all tramline nests are either found by predators or destroyed by

Above: Sometimes fat, sometimes slender, occasionally crested, typically shuffling – then suddenly statuesque. Skylark posture is multifaceted.

Below: Except across hillsides, sand dunes and districts where rough grazing preserves open sward, Skylarks have been purged from the Irish landscape. Silage production and the height attained by autumn-sown cereals in spring and summer (removing access to the ground for nesting and feeding) have driven out farmland's greatest bard.

Many birds whose plumage is sombre for the sake of camouflage appear to compensate by producing beautiful songs. Skylarks warble continuously, sometimes for up to ten minutes at a time: 'A press of hurried notes that run / so fleet they scarce are more than one' (George Meredith, 'The Lark Ascending').

wildbird cover – but there is little sign of sympathy. A low-cost solution is to manipulate the sward structure by deliberately leaving patches of ground unsown within the crop. Nicknamed 'Skylark plots' the patches (at a minimum, roughly 4m square) are created at a density of two per hectare by briefly turning off the seed drill. For convenience, the resulting plots are then treated in the same way as the rest of the crop. Although weedkiller can still be applied (to deter pernicious weeds), a glaze of sparse vegetation develops naturally, which provides ideal nest cover. In England, results from a growing number of participating farms indicate that, by providing undrilled patches in winter wheat, as many as 50 per cent more chicks are reared. The practice has been included as an option in agri-environment schemes.

Our remnant population moves south at the end of summer, possibly destined for France and Iberia. If they survive the winter, breeders arrive back in March. Nests are a cup of grass, usually hidden in a tussock. Single-handedly, the female weaves the structure and incubates. Eggs hatch in a fortnight, a remarkably short time. Juveniles scatter before they can fly. Seeds and plant leaves are eaten throughout the year, although adults switch to foraging for invertebrates (spiders, earthworms, adult beetles as well as their larvae and pupae) in the breeding season in order to feed small, soft-bodied prey to chicks.

When livelihoods connected people to the land, Skylarks were highly regarded as cage birds. Thompson (1849–52) leaves a recollection of bird-filled times, made all the more poignant by characterising the sentiments of the captors:

> Nowhere is the Skylark more sought as a cage-bird than in Ireland, and the song given forth right merrily from the little patch of green-sward within its prison, implying that it bears confinement well. But it is with regret that we see the lark, whose nature is to pierce the clouds when singing, so circumscribed. Yet we do not only think of the Skylark. To the poor artisan in the town, this bird is of great service by enlivening him with its song, associated with which in his mind are doubtless scenes in the country, the love of which is instinctive. The lark is treated with affection. The first walk of its master each morning, before the day's tasks begin, has for its object the providing of a fresh sod for his pet singing bird.

Because many Skylarks have been lost, generations of country people think that silence is normal in spring. The pleasure of being alerted by a symphony to look up and spot a lark tumbling notes from the blue vault of the sky has been lost. Does Shelley's description of the 'star of Heaven / in the broad daylight' count for nothing?

tractor tyres. Worse, birds nesting in tramlines are forced to forage elsewhere and tend to make only one nesting attempt, given the unfavourable environs. In spring-sown cereals, two broods can be raised. Sowing cereals in autumn means that most farmland is virtually devoid of seed in winter and any stubble that remains has been hoovered clean of surplus seed. Modern harvesters gather over 99 per cent of grain.

The ubiquitous conversion of hay meadows into silage fields has been a calamity. Traditional grass meadows were often cut just once, at the start of the breeding season, providing cover until young fledged. Modern grass crops are cut more frequently, perhaps every four weeks, leaving insufficient time for chicks to be raised. First cuts take place in May, when many young cannot fly. Studies in Switzerland and France (Eraud & Boutin 2002) found that harvesting destroyed virtually all nests in grass and spring-sown cereals. To boot, stock densities on grassland mean that sward height is short, leaving no tussocks. Livestock herds also trample nests. Changes to suit the birds can be made in agricultural practice – setting aside suitable nesting ground, leaving patches of seed in winter stubble or planting some

> Teach me half the gladness
> That thy brain must know;
> Such harmonious madness
> From my lips would flow,
> The world should listen then, as I am listening now.

SAND MARTIN
Riparia riparia

Seen head-on, Sand Martins have a wide gape for snatching airborne insects. Unlike Swallows, the tail has a shallow fork. Juveniles (far right) have bright edges to the wing and adjoining coverts.

APTLY NAMED BANK SWALLOW in North America, Sand Martins excavate a burrow up to a metre long. Artificial nesting walls, complete with chambers, have been constructed in some areas, including at the Ulster Wildlife Trust reserve at Bog Meadows in Belfast. For a living, the artisan catches insects over water. Sand Martins have dark underwing coverts, noticeable as sooty oxters connected to a brown breast gorget. The gorget has a messy lower border and a spur of dark plunges like cleavage into white breast. From above, look for a brown back sandwiched between darker wings. The lower back runs to sandy brown; some have pale foreheads and a masked face. A compact, short-tailed shape exerts an influence on flight style, which is direct and bustling, with less artistic merit than that of a Swallow. At times, frenzy grips flocks and the birds gyrate like finches.

A buzzing vocabulary comprises a single, repeated utterance along the lines of *bazz, bazz, bazz*; a doubled-up *ba-zup, ba-zup* (easily heard as 'rabbit, rabbit') and a pulsating shuttled *zz, zz, zz, zz* that recalls cicadas or the sizzle of an Irish Breakfast. Perversely, the panic-button call – *keeer* – is tern-like, although 'miniaturised'. It bears an affinity to the flight call of Siskin. Just one utterance begets a reaction. At a stroke, the colony is evacuated.

The extent to which second broods are attempted varies, but cannot be measured since birds change mates and even colony (Cowley 1983). Some females re-mate and leave a brood in the care of their first husband. In early autumn, southbound migrants join groups of Swallows and House Martins. Youngsters are exquisite and have dingy, finely streaked throats and smoky heads. The rump and upper tail-coverts are peppered with pale scalloping, and the wing and tail feathers are pale-edged. The three large tertial feathers cloaking the base of the wing remain until at least the following spring and serve as a guide to age, being buff-edged on juveniles.

There is a strong indication that, in autumn, Ulster Sand Martins cross the Irish Sea and make landfall in an arc from Lancashire to Wales. This is further north than populations travelling from southern Ireland, many of which cross to Pembrokeshire. Once in Britain, onward movements point to deliberate selection of a short sea crossing from southeast England to France. Many Irish birds have been trapped and released on the west coast of France. Tracking through Iberia, the birds cross the western Mediterranean and follow the coastal fringe of North Africa – or in some cases head south across the Sahara – to winter quarters along rivers and wetlands stretching east from the coast of Senegal to Lake Chad and the Niger inundation zone of Mali. Drought in Africa, particularly in the Sahel region, is believed to have been responsible for the crash witnessed in 1969, when only half the population returned. Spring migration is rapid; routes seem to be the reverse of those used in autumn. One ringed at Mallow in Cork in 1973 was trapped on spring migration on Malta on 28 April 1974, well east of the expected track. First-years arrive back a fortnight later than adults and breed within a few kilometres of where they were born.

SWALLOW
Hirundo rustica

SWALLOWS ARE A METAPHOR for migration and the return of spring. Whose heart does not lift at the sight of the year's first twisting overhead, like a spark from a chimney? The name is derived from old German meaning 'cleft stick', a reference to the deeply forked tail. Males grow long streamers to attract females (Moller 1991); those with the best kit are the fittest migrants, genetically endowed with the strongest immune system and resistance to parasites. In other words, quite a catch. To boot, tucked away in the middle of a twittering serenade is a short rattling note. It has a function on a par with the red cockscomb of a cockerel. Males with the feistiest rattle weigh more and browbeat rivals. However, success in attracting a mate is no reason to relax since marital unfaithfulness – and infanticide by jealous unmated suitors – is a constant threat. Husbands regularly visit the marital home and, if empty, emit false alarm calls. Males frequently cry wolf during the egg-laying period, when females are fertile and promiscuous, than during the incubation phase, when ovulation ceases. At least two broods are reared annually. Endearingly, young from one generation help feed the next. Juveniles lack long tail streamers and have cinnamon-coloured faces. Extended families stay together until autumn and sometimes depart en masse, assembling at vespers for a Last Supper gathering and not returning after dark.

In late summer, flycatching lessons are imparted to rookies in a remarkable game of Catch the Feather. The baton is caught and then released in an eddy of wind. Parked like fidgety jets overhead, a wannabe Top Gun pilot breaks ranks and gives chase. Once caught, the plaything is released and the next contestant swoops up to the plate. Similar behaviour has been noted in Tree Swallow, a North American species, albeit in a poem ('Feathering' by Galway Kinnell). The poet does not, however, allude to the taking-it-in-turns nature of the activity.

It is well known that Swallows winter across southern Africa. Less well known is segregation based on country of origin, 'all those of German origin, save one, are within 10 degrees of the Equator while all those of British origin, save one, are in the eastern half of South Africa' (Witherby *et al.* 1938–41). Many perish. One of the largest gatherings, estimated to contain at least 2 million, on the slopes of Nigeria's Mbe Mountains, is exploited for food. Each evening the birds congregate to roost in 3m-tall elephant grass. As they descend at bedtime, locals ambush them by hoisting a glue-covered 'chimney sweep' into their ranks. As many as 200,000 are caught and eaten locally or sold in nearby markets (*The Independent*, Monday 7 November 2011).

Above: The Swallow is one of the few birds that occur on five continents. An exclusively insectivorous diet means that, to obtain food throughout the year, northern populations must migrate before winter. Unlike other migrants, many of whom fatten up before departing, Swallows feed as they go. This forces them to hunt every day. Exhaustion overtakes many. Mortality can be as high as 60 per cent in adults and 80 per cent in young; prolific breeding offsets such losses.

Below: Cinnamon-faced juvenile Swallows await their next meal. Adults rear two or three broods each year. Most fledge successfully, but late chicks are in danger of being abandoned once migration instincts – and the need for parents to feed themselves – override domestic attachments.

The pleasure of having unblemished eaves is pretty feeble compared to the pleasure of allowing House Martins a chance to build a home and raise a family.

HOUSE MARTIN
Delichon urbicum

HOUSE MARTINS are master artisans. They gather mud from puddles and painstakingly mould upwards of 2,500 pellets into a gourd that solidifies in concentric bands. One layer acts as mortar for the next. The builders know what they are doing and vary the type of mud, bypassing some sources and flying far to get the right stuff. The chamber is lined with feathers and access is via a small top entrance. One thing that the adobe structure is powerless to resist is vandalism. Belfast International Airport committed an atrocity in 2010 when a thriving colony of fifty pairs was deliberately festooned with wire mesh to prevent the birds returning to renovate, rebuild, and replenish increasingly imperilled populations.

During 1973 and continuing in 1974, a major decline in previously healthy populations across parts of Scottish farmland was traced to a chemical (fentin hydroxide, brand name Tubotin) used in the control of potato blight. The compound is mixed with water and then sprayed on crops. A common occurrence was spillage from mixing tanks, with residue collecting in muddy pools in farmyards and corners of fields. House Martins drank and collected mud from the polluted puddles. Examination of nests revealed deaths on a massive scale; incubating adults were dead and showed grotesque distortion of the mouth, as though if dying in great pain. Some juveniles fledged successfully, thereby explaining the continued existence of colonies over subsequent breeding seasons, until the returning offspring succumbed to poisoning during the next season. In addition to outright nest destruction, does this explain declines here, particularly where potatoes are grown?

House Martins winter in Africa. Millions reach the continent's equatorial region, yet, remarkably, their winter whereabouts are a mystery. Limited recoveries include birds found dead in highlands in the wake of thunderstorms, killed by hailstones. Perhaps, like Swifts, the birds behave as storm-chasing nomads across the tropics? Evidence supports this conjecture and speaks of high-level foraging for insects over rainforest, notably in Congo-Brazzaville. A unique feature is a blinding white rump. House Martins have all-white underparts with a black-masked face and, visible in good light, a deep blue gloss across the back. On the ground, note the distinctive white 'furry' legs and feet. Flight is less acrobatic than a Swallow and – an echo of winter habits – the birds often ascend high to hunt. Calls are gritty and chirrupy, phonetically: *prrrt-prrrt*.

LONG-TAILED TIT
Aegithalos caudatus

The Long-tailed Tit is an odd man out, differing in appearance from 'capped' tits by a long tail, stubby bill and pink plumage.

WHO SAID THAT EVOLUTION lacks a sense of humour? The invention of Long-tailed Tit marked a high point in avant-garde. Linnaeus gave it a unique genus – *Aegithalos*, meaning purse, commemorating the appearance of its nest. The foundation is moss, poked into a cleft and held in place by gossamer wrapping. Steadily the inglenook grows into a dome; the artisans pay special attention to the roof and create a cushioned door whose elasticity seals the bird inside but yields for egress. To camouflage the edifice, an exterior coat of lichen is added. Perspicacious Jays watch and wait and predate some nests later. On average, ten eggs are cradled among a duvet of 2,000 feathers and a sitting bird holds its tail erect over its back.

Several supernumeraries attend an active nest but seek approval to do so. Helpers hover in front of the owners, who respond in like manner (Gaston 1973). The minstrels are tribal and do everything as a troupe. Roaming flocks consist of extended family. Parties move in surging waves through trees or along hedges, flicking movements of long tails creating the impression that the vegetation itself is twitching. One group of eight caught and ringed in Lincolnshire was retrapped 40km away. A sputtery *tupp!* is shuttled into a polysyllable that sounds like the word 'syrup'. The opera is accompanied by a mousy, lively *zee-zee-zee*. Sound precedes a cluster of acrobats twisting and tumbling through twigs, undulating in short unsteady flights and gathering up before crossing open ground, which they traverse in follow-my-leader drill. In winter, coteries form part of a galaxy, comprising Blue Tits, Great Tits, Coal Tits, Goldcrests and Treecreepers. Long-tailed Tits are insectivorous and peck in and around buds. Perrins (1979) discovered that hawthorn is popular in autumn, oak in midwinter and birch, maple and ash after the beginning of March. Some roving flocks incorporate gardens and attend feeders. Numbers fluctuate from year to year: as much as

80 per cent of the British population have been wiped out by freezing conditions, despite an endearing habit of huddling together at night.

In Thompson's day (1805–1852), Long-tailed Tit was uncommon. Perhaps harsher winters had the effect of suppressing the population?

The Long-tailed Tit is less known in the south than in the north, over which it is diffused, but not plentifully. When my observations on the species were published in 1838, it had not been met with in the province of Munster, but since that period has been met with there. Its distribution from north to south is now known. In the northwest of Donegal, it has been seen but very rarely. In Antrim it has been seen at Portglenone: from the latter place one was sent to Belfast as a bird never before observed. Its numbers would seem of late years to have increased considerably throughout the north, where the species occurred only twice to the late Mr Templeton. Within several miles around Belfast, in Antrim and Down, it has been met with where there is a sufficiently great extent of wood. It inhabits the plantations of the mountain glen, with their rocks and din of cascades. To meet with a family is always interesting, but they have particularly attracted my admiration when flitting over the waters of a river, and about the overhanging trees that border it. I have noticed them among alders and birches, and they appear about hawthorn hedges. The stomachs of four killed in January and March were, with the exception of two seeds in one of them, entirely filled with insects, among which the remains of minute coleoptera were in every instance discernible.

CHIFFCHAFF
Phylloscopus collybita

CHIFFCHAFFS effervesce an onomatopoeic, sprightly two-note ditty that pierces the air like a silver hammer. *Collybita* means 'moneychanger', an analogy to the clinking beat. Frustratingly, the singer is usually a dot clamped neck-achingly high to a treetop. The mite is dependent on mature trees and, in the breeding season, occurs in broadleaved woods and copses. During late summer tall scrub suffices, bringing one of the prettiest-faced warblers closer to eye level. By October, Willow Warblers have departed, leaving migrant Chiffchaffs as the only show in town. Originating from a vast swathe of northern Europe, they reveal a diaspora of coloration ranging from warm brown to cool olive. Most travel on to spend the winter around the Mediterranean. Tail-end Charlies stay put in Ireland and take their chances, eking out winter in thickets near water and hoping that insect quarry holds out until spring.

WILLOW WARBLER
Phylloscopus trochilus

HOLIDAYMAKERS FROM EUROPE enjoying winter sun in southern Africa are amazed when they hear Willow Warbler's cascade of lispy liquid notes. How can this be? Willow Warblers winter south of the Sahara and sing just before they trek north. The globetrotter is petite and lightly built, almost frail, with a watery stripe above the eye and a luteous wash atop a whitish breast. Arriving home in early April, pilgrims spread like a flood among bushy ground, preferably containing a few deciduous trees. Unfurling candelabras of willow filigree attract myriad insects and in turn this eponymous warbler. The nest, a dome of thatch, is concealed on the ground and constructed by the female on the cusp of May.

Woodland birds demonstrate a wide variety of adaptation, ensuring that competition for food is avoided. The trick is to find a successful niche. Chiffchaffs exploit tree canopy, gleaning insects, grubs and caterpillars from foliage. By staying 'up top' they keep apart from shrub-dwelling Willow Warblers.

The Willow Warbler's long-haul migration from Africa penetrates well-lit scrubby woodland as far north as the Arctic Circle. Time is tight. Males sing upon arrival and keep going until the young hatch. Only one family is raised before adults head south, leaving youngsters to follow at their own pace.

BOTH ARE SLIM AND GRACEFUL with a body size smaller than a Wren. Each gleans insects among foliage and is seldom still. Characteristic actions include twitchy flicks of wings and tail and vertical darts to seize prey spotted in silhouette on the underside of leaves. The duo is a challenge to tell apart. Voice distinctions are helpful, especially song (see below), aided by segregation based on choice of habitat when breeding. Chiffchaffs are shorter-winged than Willow Warblers. There is a measurable ratio – primary projection – that points up identification based on wing length. Alas, this is impossible to judge on a moving bird. Nonetheless, the longer wings of Willow Warbler chime with similar aspects of build, such as a stronger bill and flatter head. Chiffchaffs, by comparison, are dumpy. They are little guys, elves that would not look out of place on a Christmas tree. The bill is fine, outlined in dark around a pale core, and thin, with little girth, mirroring two straight lines coalescing to a spike. On Willow Warbler, the base of the lower mandible is bright, varying from yellowish to, especially in autumn, dilute orange.

Chiffchaffs consistently have dark or black legs. Their legs are spindly, thinner than matchsticks and with a narrower diameter than those of Willow Warbler. While the soles of the feet are mustard-yellow, discernible when toes wrap around a stem, the top of the foot is dark. Leg colour is cited as an important distinction from Willow Warbler. While true in almost all instances, knowledge of leg and foot structure is key. The tarsus is bony and cylindrical – in cross-section, an oval. Head-on, the shin is narrow and dark. Width is greatest from the side. The outer leg matches the shin's shade but blanches and becomes pellucid towards the rear, where leg shape alters and terminates in a narrow edge. Viewed from behind, the leg is both narrow and pale (typically, horn-coloured or watery yellow). Moreover, paleness fuses over the inner leg. Hence, on a perched Willow Warbler, leg colour varies depending on angle. Unlike the tarsus, the foot is fleshy, albeit sheathed on its topside by plate-like scales. Especially in autumn, many Willow Warblers exhibit yellowish bootees; some look yellow-footed.

During the breeding season, wear and colour fading affect plumage; adults gradually lose yellow pigment through exposure to sunlight. Following moult in late summer, new feathering brings out differences in expression. Willow Warbler comes across as sharp-faced due to an emphatic pale supercilium and dark eye-stripe. The supercilium tapers and seems longer behind the eye than in front; the eye-stripe is well defined. On Chiffchaff, the supercilium is shorter; the eye-stripe is blurry and forms a plain, blusher patch on the cheek (technically, the ear-coverts). Willow Warbler cheeks are diffusely patterned; at best stubbly, like five o'clock shadow. On Chiffchaff, two crescents frame the eye and make it pop, bringing the face to life. The lower is conspicuous and hard to miss. Willow Warbler has a narrow eye-ring, most discernible around the lower half of the eye; the upper half is subsumed by the pale supercilium. Despite lighter underparts, overall plumage impressions suggest that Chiffchaff is closer to uni-coloured: buff, khaki or olive-brown. Some tend to sandy, others glint honey-pine or nicotine on the side of the chest. Close up, look for yellowish striations on the chest, like dabs of hair gel. On Willow Warbler the chest is plain and seems lit from within by a saffron light, suggesting a yellow bosom. Once juvenile Willow Warblers moult into first-winter plumage, their underparts glow grapefruit yellow. Identifying such individuals is a no-brainer.

Chiffchaff's habit of dipping its tail is diagnostic. The action is rhythmic, a metronome keeping time, and accompanies shifts in foraging position. Momentary wing flicking may accompany the gesture and some are snappier than others. Willow Warblers jerk the tail in tandem with twitching the wings but tend to downplay movement; at times foraging action is almost wooden. Depending on mood, it is possible to encounter a Chiffchaff that is not disposed to flex its tail.

Ears as well as eyes are needed. In the breeding season Willow Warbler unleashes a flowing minuet. Males broadcast all day; the anchorman continues through dead afternoons when everything else has piped down. The composition is a tapestry run together in a cadence, no jumping or discordant notes allowed. Phonetically: *seep-seep*, *tie-tie*, *tay-tay*, *wirri-wirri-wee*. The terminal notes sound lazy, like a spinning coin losing momentum. Chiffchaff song is likened to *chiff-chaff*. The couplet is given in series but the connection is binary: *chiff-chiff*, *chaff-chaff*, *chiff-chiff*. The momentum evokes a pendulum. If close, you can discern a low, chiding *gurr … gurr* between verses. When diva days are over, wistful syllables replace arias. Thimbleful fragments are delivered through a partly closed bill. Willow Warbler is soft-spoken; its *hoo-eep* is tentative and easily counterfeited by whistling. Chiffchaff's plaintive note is inflected with an inquisitive frisson: *hweet*, *heep*, *tswee* or *swee-oo*. With each utterance, an imaginary question mark seems to hang in the air. Nothing beats listening to the birds themselves. Xeno-canto (www.xeno-canto.org) features many recordings. Typical examples include, for Chiffchaff, XC 26140 made by Stuart Fisher in Surrey in October 2003 and, for Willow Warbler, XC 75461 made by Volker Arnold in Germany on 9 April 2011. It is important to display the sonogram while listening (see p. 18). By referring to sonogram pattern, minor differences can be noticed. The trace of Willow Warbler's call is 'fuller', making it clear and mellow, and ends with a diagnostic change to a more rising pitch. Chiffchaff rises in pitch throughout its call. Without the aid of a sonogram this telltale difference is hard to appreciate.

Autumn migrant Willow Warblers and Chiffchaffs. All the images were taken in September or October. Top row: Willow Warblers. Individual (top right) is the least common type. Its pallid plumage suggests an origin in northern parts of Scandinavia or further east. Middle row, upper: left, Willow Warbler (commonest type); right, Chiffchaff (commonest type). Lower four birds: Chiffchaffs. Greyer individuals, such as that upper right of these four, tend to occur most frequently from mid-October onwards. Like pale Willow Warblers, they hail from northeastern Europe; some may originate from parts of Russia as far to the east as the Ural Mountains.

WOOD WARBLER
Phylloscopus sibilatrix

Among drifts of rustling leaves glinting green, Wood Warbler takes the same plumage shades available to other leaf warblers and turns them into Day-Glo colours. Then it sings – an astonishing, fizzing cascade, shouted by a slight chorister high among the boughs.

THIS, THE FAIREST OF ALL 'LEAF WARBLERS', is rare. The species shares with Willow Warbler and Chiffchaff the family name *Phylloscopus* (leaf-explorers). The song is a long and passionate trill, a panegyric to lofty cathedral woods. A mellow pipe is heard continuously during courtship. Even where widespread, as in parts of Europe, canopy-dwelling habits make Wood Warblers elusive. Among numberless green leaves lit by slanted light, a green, white and yellow brassard is perfect camouflage. Compared to its fidgety relations, the bird is less twitchy and scarcely flicks its wings and tail. Shape is often distinctive due to a habit of slightly drooping the wings, which show in silhouette apart from the body.

During the 1980s, several pairs bred in north Antrim at Craigagh Wood and Glenarm. Numbers dwindled through attrition of nesting attempts by a host of predators including rats, mice, Badgers, Red Squirrels and Jays. A Sparrowhawk killed an adult feeding young. A prototype predator-proof cage was designed and accepted by a nesting pair (NMK). Regrettably, the device failed to get official approval. It seems that no passion or desire to embrace innovation exists among those who claim to be protecting birds. Instead, a miasma of bureaucracy dogs the efforts of those who try to help. A tiny population does its best to hang on in Wicklow, although breeding success is unknown.

BLACKCAP
Sylvia atricapilla

Uniquely among warblers that occur in Ireland, Blackcaps differ between the sexes. Males are blessed with a spectacular, high-octane song. Females, on the other hand, are the glamour pusses.

BLACKCAP has become a summer and winter visitor, a unique combination for a warbler. In late summer, local offspring disperse within 25km of where they were born before disappearing south in October (Langslow 1979). Recoveries indicate a flight of around 800km to southwest France or northeast Spain. Here, trapping is still rife and many get no further. A juvenile ringed at Oxford Island, Lough Neagh, on 2 August 1992 probably staged in France or Spain before being shot while migrating through Morocco on 15 August 1994. Winter recoveries come mostly from Iberia and North Africa. In April a remarkable concentration occurs at the northern edge of the Sahara in Morocco and around the western Mediterranean coast of North Africa. Have these birds spent the winter south of the Sahara? By late April, breeding birds are back. During winter, European immigrants replace them and occupy suburban gardens. Numbers, distribution and arrival dates vary between years. Indeed, ringing recoveries confirm that some switch countries annually. One ringed at Corbally, Antrim, in December 1980 was killed by a cat in Nantes, southwest France in November 1981.

Nesting pairs frequent deciduous woodland replete with shrubbery. Males sing aloft, broadcasting over a wide arc. Getting a bead on the soloist is not easy. His head pivots regularly, throwing notes widely. He begins hesitantly. Then, after a momentary dalliance or pianissimo drop in pitch, full power is unleashed. As a rule of thumb, the song increases in volume and pace. The end comes abruptly, like phone credit dying in mid-sentence. The composition is fiery, lasting around five seconds. Sheer speed of delivery – Ferrari fast – provides a basis for recognition. Flamboyant high notes spark from a mellow tapestry, as though trying to construct something fine. A petulant, ball-bearings-knocking-together *tek … tek* alarm is given, both on breeding sites and during winter, especially when birds are close to a roost site. Wintering birds, just before they depart in early spring, start to mumble song (called sub song). In effect, they are tuning up and the compositions are unrefined rehearsals that lack gusto.

Despite being monotone, male plumage is far from humdrum. The black cap – a shallow ellipse that absorbs most of the eye – is bounded by an ashy nape. The upperparts are darker 'dirty' grey, at times with an olivaceous cast. The throat is silvery, swaddled by a dove-grey breast against which gunmetal flanks fade to white on the belly. Sometimes the undertail-coverts are fused with a hint of yellow. Ginger-capped females differ in more than just head pattern. They are brown-backed with buff, not grey, underparts. Females chose mates based on song, specifically the rate at which a male sings. Moreover, the chosen mate is not picked because he is a good parent. In fact, males are far from 'husband of the year' material and the best singers are often the worst chick-rearing fathers. Research shows that the song rate of successfully breeding males is higher than males whose nests

Suburban gardens have become a habitat in their own right. For every snaking avenue of bricks and mortar there is a corresponding corridor of planted trees, bushes and – increasingly – complimentary food. Not only have Blackcaps exploited this niche but also, through surviving the winter, successive generations have returned to breed across Central Europe and remodel their migration route to include Irish back gardens as a desirable winter residence.

failed through being discovered by a predator. Females realise that a male's singing intensity equates with his skills at nest concealment. In other words, she is prepared to overlook his parental skills if he can construct a safe, camouflaged nest.

Exactly where do our wintering Blackcaps come from? Enough have been ringed, either as nestlings or in winter quarters, to prove that they are not the offspring of local breeding pairs. Most hail from central Europe. Theoretically, they ought not to be here, since most from this region (Denmark, Germany and Austria) travel to Mediterranean countries. In short, the birds arrive by a quirk referred to as 'reverse migration' (Busse 1992). Taken as a whole, the total breeding range can be divided into three regions, each with a different standard direction for migration. West European Blackcaps fly southwest in autumn; central European birds fly south; populations breeding in Scandinavia fly southeast (through Balkan countries to the Middle East). Psyched up and ready to migrate, some miscue in tail winds that drift them in the 'wrong' direction. Instead of

arriving in balmy Mediterranean olive groves, they finish up in southwest Norway. Of those that continue, Iceland is the next stop. Many must meet a watery grave. Others sense that they are lost and make a conscious decision to reorient. By switching direction and 'seeing out' their genetically programmed urge to travel a set distance, they find themselves in Ireland. By accident, they have chanced upon a destination where the living is easy. This scenario, while it explained the bird's past status as a scarce winter visitor, no longer fits the scale of winter abundance. Put simply, some European populations evolved a new migration route. Analogous to programming a satnav, successive waves of survivors have committed route details to memory. And because the return flight to European breeding grounds is comparatively short, males from Ireland and Britain arrive ahead of southern wintering populations. Their offspring inherit the novel migration, the living proof of which we see in our back gardens in winter.

GARDEN WARBLER
Sylvia borin

THE BREEDING DISTRIBUTION of Garden Warbler is limited to riparian woods in Fermanagh and similar habitat stretching as a disjunct corridor along lakeshores in Monaghan, Cavan and Leitrim. In Britain, drier habitats are also occupied, including deciduous growth among conifers. Occasionally migrants in eastern Ulster sing in such places, suggesting that they are strays from Britain. Could it be that the felling of Ireland's forests restricted the bird to remnant tracts of inaccessible woodland? Through being forced, ancestrally, to retreat to the only available habitat, have Irish breeders become inflexible in their choice of habitat? Have they become addicted to moist, tangled woods?

Jonsson (1976) was the first to compare the song to rippling, running water: 'A babbling brook of clear notes and chattering but without the Blackcap's high fluting notes.' Nonetheless, Blackcap constitutes a perennial spanner in the works. Most songbirds are inspired to sample acoustic raw material issued by rivals and neighbours. Apprentices begin their singing career by copying their parents in the year of their birth but, upon returning to nesting haunts, refine their repertoire by listening to the local *Top of the Pops*. Hence it is easy to become confused by Blackcap's versatility. A consistent steer is a hesitant opening before surging to hit the high notes. The outpouring is flamboyant but comparatively short-lived; a firework that is spent in around five seconds. Garden Warbler, while equally rich, is uniformly busy. It is more sustained and the phrases are longer, up to seven seconds. The voice is 'burry' and the verse sounds as if uttered from inside a closed mouth (in fact, the bird's bill is only partially opened). Compared to Blackcap, there is homogeneity and a seamless start and finish. The effect can become monotonous. Warning calls, a trail of tetchy mechanical clicks, have the tempo of a child imitating a machine gun and rise in pitch like an alarming Blackbird. Distinctive plumage is notable by its absence. The body is pastel, mainly brown and beige, except on the side of the neck where dove grey sits like a soft cashmere scarf. For a warbler, the bill is short. The eye is partially encircled with a bulging white upper rim. Head on, the upper breast takes the form of a sandy bib, demarcated against a creamy belly. Both in disposition and looks, Garden Warbler is a shrinking violet.

Bizarrely named, the last place to look for this lover of woodland understorey is a garden. Bland looks – the species is podgy, short-billed and famously shy – cloak an operatic voice. Arguably, Garden Warbler is Ireland's Nightingale. Unfortunately, given a limited breeding range and claustrophobic habits, its vocal talents remain unappreciated.

WHITETHROAT
Sylvia communis

FOR THOSE OLD ENOUGH to remember how common Whitethroat used to be, the bird's fragmented distribution is a lamentable reminder of glory days. Before 1970 exuberant song was ubiquitous from scrub, thorny nettle beds, tangled railway embankments and sunlit wild hedges. Seventy per cent of the west European breeding population disappeared in 1969. The disaster was caused, it is claimed, by swarms of Desert Locusts that stripped foliage, fruit and flowers from vast swathes of nectar-producing bushes that provided pre-migratory fattening for northbound migrants staging in savannah from Mauritania to Chad. Millions perished and few made it home. Although numbers have since partially recovered, the species has been beleaguered by habitat loss. The 'reclamation' of scrub and marginal land, and the inexorable loss of insect life from hedgerows – now machine-cut to serve as stock-proof field

boundaries rather than living quarters for wildlife – have ousted many. Where topography renders operations ineffective, such as near the coast or on steep ground, luxuriant scrub and Whitethroats flourish. Hawthorn interweaved with briars and umbellifers are a magnet; the carpet of white blossom betokens a linen tablecloth bestrewn with food.

Whitethroats love a stage. Troubadours strike a statuesque catwalk pose with a raised crown and puffed-out white throat, as bushy as Santa's beard and sometimes fluttering like an errant tuft of cotton wool. A fizzy discourse is a bead to a svelte, willowy warbler, clamped imperiously or launching into flight, filling the airwaves while treading air like a puppet. Alarm calls are less easy on the ear; staccato *bazz … bazz* monosyllables suggest scolding Starlings. Wedding day pastels pervade the male torso of a morning-suited grey head and carnation-pink chest. Legs are 'dilute orange' and a twitchy tail is dark with white edges. Wings gleam russet. Resorting to argot, most of the wing coverts and tertials are rusty, so too the folded edges to the flight feathers. The eye-catching brown shade is present on females and juveniles too. By July plumage is worn to a nub, the tail reduced to a ratty appendage.

Left: A juvenile Whitethroat in autumn. Rusty wings, pale legs and a white throat distinguish the species at all ages.

Below: Animated, a singing male Whitethroat delivers Jumping Jack discourses; a two-second snatch of Bedlam. When the songster raises crown feathers and turns the throat to cotton wool, identification is a no-brainer.

GRASSHOPPER WARBLER
Locustella naevia

SHROUDED BY BRAMBLES and fashioned long, slim and sylph-like, this coy inhabitant of tangled undergrowth is hard to see. The upperparts are darkly striated in zip-fastener rows. During sinuous movements feathered symmetry is retained, like scales of snakeskin coiling in harmony. The eye is highlighted – but not encircled – by pale bangles. Soft mascara bisects a fawn face of shy grace. The pale throat ruffles during singing marathons and glows cream. At the same time, the body pulsates. The forecrown is capped, its pincushion of dark dots contrasts against an abruptly plain nape. The interplay of ambient light exerts a chameleon influence. Not only is the changeling dextrous, its plumage radiates the hues of surrounding vegetation. Clasped toes are pellucid pink and have the delicacy of a newborn's fingers. Flight views tend to be just long enough to notice a spear silhouette with a spool-shaped tail that, somehow, seems loosely attached. Favourite places include the luxuriant herbage of young forestry plantations or scrub along the drier margins of lakeshores. Reports of a mystery sound, prompted by the bird's whirring, stridulating insect voice, make their way into the postbag of environmental journalists every spring. Singing is prolonged during the hours of darkness and individual bursts can last a minute or more. Dawn and dusk, either ends of a nightshift soliloquy, are the best times to see the figment of the shadows. The reverie, while feeble, carries a kilometre in still air. Gilbert White (1789) penned a perfect portrait:

> The [Grasshopper Warbler] began his sibilous note in my fields last Saturday. The country people laugh when you tell them that it is the note of a bird. It is a most artful creature, skulking in the thickest part of a bush; and will sing at a yard distance, provided it can be concealed. I was obliged to get a person to go on the other side of the hedge where it haunted. Then it would run, creeping like a mouse, through the bottom of the thorns. Alas, it would not come into fair sight, but early in the morning, when undisturbed, it sings at the top of a twig, gaping and shivering with its wings.

Top: A mysterious bird that, but for its song, would be invisible to many and attract Holy Grail status. The head pattern recalls a Meadow Pipit, whereas body language says 'mouse'.

Below: Singers perch low and, if spotted, are often approachable. Detection is, however, complicated. The vocalist, bill open, turns its head from side to side, altering volume and pitch, thereby skewing assessment of position.

SEDGE WARBLER
Acrocephalus schoenobaenus

Sedge Warblers are nosy. An advantage of living in dense undergrowth is that an intruder makes noise. Abnormal sounds are checked out surreptitiously by scouts that sidle down vertical stems to investigate.

Richly patterned, a Sedge Warbler's creamy supercilium and bright ginger rump are as noticeable in flight as they are at rest.

SEDGE WARBLERS dwell in reedy thickets and overgrown ditches overrun with nettles, brambles, umbellifers and – in the west of Ireland – fuchsia. The silhouette is distinctive, a ball clamped near the tip of a stem. Chatterers are extroverts; at other times the mite is a secret stalker of insects. Occasionally one emerges into view and performs a 'bumblebee' song flight, discoursing and revealing a bright orange mouth. At rest, a sunken-necked frumpish pose is standard; precisely the sort of bad posture that would draw admonishment from a teacher. One singer incorporated alarm calls of Swallow, Blackbird, Blue Tit and House Sparrow in quick succession (AMG, JW). Tempo and vehemence suggest a grumpy typist hammering out a long letter. At times a disembodied switch from churring monologue to strident whistles prompts thoughts that two species are present in the same bush. A black-bordered crown is freckled and there is an unmissable creamy-white stripe over a heavy-lidded eye, encased in a furrow running to the gape. Through the interplay of light, the mouth exhibits a 'disapproving' rictus that curls over the lore like a mandarin's whiskers. Perched proclaimers permit a clear view of a bright cinnamon rump sandwiched between olive-brown wings. Across the upperparts, a bold pattern is

created by bright edges to three large overlapping feathers (tertials) that cloak most of the folded wing.

During the early 1990s intensive trapping at reed beds from Antrim to Senegal managed to piece together a fascinating picture of a savvy migrant using a series of sites as stepping stones. Sedge Warblers from Portmore Lough, the Shannon Estuary and Youghal headed across the Irish Sea. A few stopped off in Glamorgan, but most continued to Elm's Farm at Icklesham, Sussex. Others from Ireland were ringed in northwest France at Etang de Trunvel, Finistère. Presumably these birds flew directly south to Finistère – or did they visit Welsh or English reed beds en route? Journey's end for many was Parc National des Oiseaux du Djoudi in Senegal. Finishers started arriving from 25 October. Faithfulness to breeding sites has also been documented by recoveries at Portmore Lough. A chick ringed there on 6 July 1975 was retrapped in early August at Radipole Lake in Dorset and returned to breed at Portmore the following spring. More remarkable was the return to Belfast Harbour Estate, in May 2004, of one of two albinos to within a few hundred metres of where the duo fledged in 2003.

REED WARBLER
Acrocephalus scirpaceus

A Reed Warbler peers for insects on exposed sediment. The stalker is agile and can cling, feet apart, to adjoining stems, thereby doing the splits.

Reed Warblers time nest building with reed growth. Attached to stalks, a deep-woven cup slowly rises until it is suspended partway up tall stems. Hidden from view and swaying high over deep water, the structure is virtually impregnable.

REED WARBLERS are a summer soundtrack in reed beds of suitable size (tennis court or larger) in eastern districts and extend west to Cork. To become acquainted you need to visit between May and August. Song recognition is vital because the bird is a sleuth. Business requires it to sneak up on insects among reeds or glean them from the surface of water lapping among stems. Nearby willow bushes are patronised unobtrusively and frequently become favourite feeding places. Movements are sudden and clunky. Stems bend and a snout pokes out. Everything is streamlined – bill, body and tail are aligned in a javelin plane. Head pattern is minimalist. A pale furrow connects eye and gape. In essence, Reed Warblers have a sullen face that only a mother could love.

Other species dwell in the same 'dismal swamp', notably Sedge Warblers. Both are incessant singers. While some Sedge Warblers breed in reed beds, they generally stick to the margins and sing in bushes. If broadcasting from reeds, they are easy to see because they sit in view and perform song flights. Reed Warblers seldom sit up and never perform song flights. Moreover,

unless the reeds are growing in water, the habitat will not suit them. Common Reed *Phragmites australis* is the key. Wetlands that comprise Reedmace *Typha latifolia* (also known as Common Cattail or, erroneously, Bulrush) or Lesser Reedmace *Typha angustifolia* are ignored. The nest is a woven basket situated low down over water. The location deters predators. As reeds grow, they hoist the nest high among a forest of swaying stems, hence the need for a deep cup to provide secure lodging for chicks.

Our Reed Warblers are among the most northerly in the world and do not arrive until late April. They sing randomly throughout the day, clamped to a stem a short way from the tip. Foraging takes places mainly in the morning when insects are easier to catch, leaving males free to chant after lunch. The song, while guttural and with a somewhat stalling, lurching momentum, has a basic rhythm which is never disguised for long. The delivery is one-paced and lacks Sedge Warbler's range of high, pure notes interleaved with rough, scratchy passages. Attentive listening reveals a backbone of doubled-up notes: *chup-chup, chirk-chirk, charook-charook* and so on. During the breeding season, excitement lifts part of the performance, which acquires a grandiloquent feel. Ecstatic phrases are probably inserted to impress females. Males return first, space themselves out and use vocal powers to signal territory ownership to rivals. Basically, they are duelling. However, when females arrive, they enrich their song with extra syllables – by adding 'twiddly bits'. Females listen and discriminate between suitors; proof that a good singing voice matters.

Some remarkable data emerged from a long-term study in Jersey (Long 1975). From 1951 to 1970, 4,126 birds were ringed at St Ouen's Pond, where at least 100 pairs bred. Some were proved to have been present throughout as many as nine consecutive breeding seasons. Nest sites were marked and individuals were shown to build to within 1m of the previous year's location in a uniform patch of reeds. Recoveries showed that adults were faithful to the site and that migrants from elsewhere passed through. Locally raised juveniles showed less attachment to natal areas. The mortality rate for juveniles was twice that of adults, which is not surprising given the challenge of a return trip to Africa before coming home to find your first love.

WAXWING
Bombycilla garrulus

IT IS HARD TO BELIEVE that such an exotic bird – backcombed crest, black eye mascara, velour underparts and pearls on the wing – is a frequent winter visitor, albeit an erratic one. In Dutch the species is named Pestvogel, a connotation that likens its caprice to lemmings or locusts. North Americans invoke the epithet Bohemian Waxwing, a further testament to nomadism. Waxwings breed across taiga and are insectivorous during summer. With the onset of autumn, live prey vanishes and the mannequins switch to berries. When food is hard to come by, they head west and cross the North Sea. Like an Olympic torch doing the rounds, once the vanguard hits eastern Scotland, we can expect to be included in the itinerary, although where flocks settle is a lottery. Groups are driven by fervour and gobble, strip and leave. They are wide-mouthed and consume huge quantities of berries – more than twice bodyweight daily – for which they have an intestinal tract. Feeding bouts are intense

and purplish pavement stains act as a spoor. Just how many berries do they eat? In early 2001, 500 spent four months devouring cotoneaster berries in Belfast's city parks and housing estates. Based on counts made over several days, individuals consumed an average of 500 apiece. How many berries did the flock go through in the 100 days between Christmas and mid-April? The answer is around 25 million!

Adult males have the largest number of waxy tips and a herringbone assemblage of yellow and white edgings to the primaries. Youngsters possess few waxy tips and have striped, not herringbone-patterned, primaries. Calls serve as a dinner gong and are also used by flyovers seeking company. The sound is a trill, thin and mechanical, like a peal of silver bells. Seen in silhouette, airborne flocks can be tough to tell from Starlings. Rear-end distinctions help. Waxwings look hip heavy and their dense-feathered midriff sags like middle-age spread.

Do not be fooled. Despite the impression of huddling against the elements, Waxwing plumage is sumptuous and warm. Between bouts of berry guzzling, satin-breasted diners retire to high perches to nap before returning to where they left off.

TREECREEPER
Certhia familiaris

IF CHALLENGED to find a Treecreeper, the bird's habitat would be straightforward to locate – wide-girthed trees – but it is not a delicate denizen of the trunks. The feathery earwig is out there, somewhere among the boughs. Knowing its contact note speeds up the search – a high rippling *zzrreeee*, a piercing lisp that if heard once could be dismissed as a creaking branch. The quaver is a bead to a jerky movement disguised as bark and clamped like a fridge magnet. In a flash it swoops low and attaches to neighbouring timber. Be patient. Here it comes again, shuffling into view, the scimitar bill poking deftly into nooks and crannies for eggs, larvae and spidery prey. As it climbs, the tail is splayed and pressed tight. Each rectrice is broad-based with a spiky tip, honey-pine in colour. Trestle toes spreadeagle to give maximum purchase and thin translucent claws resemble petrified tendrils of chewing gum. The hooked hind-toe is enormous, much longer in adults than youngsters. Treecreepers struggle to perch horizontally. When travelling downwards they use reverse gear, rather than turning around. Profile views reveal a silvery breast and a wiggly white line above the eye. In flight a pale wing-bar is revealed. At rest, on the folded wing, the zigzag bar is shaped uncannily like the emblem of the SS.

Cryptic plumage instils confidence and the species is not shy, just mercurial. Thompson (1849–52) documents high jinks:

> Mr R Ball has known the Treecreeper to be captured by boys getting to the opposite side of a tree (at the base of which it commenced feeding) and making a random stroke with a hat or cap, at the place they supposed it had reached in its upward movement. On 4 June 1842 Mr Thomas Garrett brought me a specimen that he captured at Cultra, near Belfast. He remarked that, on being alarmed by a stone striking the trunk near it, the bird clung closely to the bark and remained motionless, not flying off until the hand is all but laid upon it.

Treecreepers roost in hollows excavated in rotten wood. Remarkably, since Wellingtonias have been planted, commencing in the mid-nineteenth century, the bird has learned to seek them out. Did a pioneer, copied by others, make the discovery? The bark has a cardboard quality and can be excavated to create a snug groove. Overnight, just the back of the roosting bird is visible, suggesting a cactus sprouting from fibrous trunk. Several scooped-out refugia are made to ensure that, no matter what direction the wind, a lee can be found. The understated song is poorly known. Although quiet, it is beautiful. Proper listening is made difficult by the singer seldom uttering the aria more than once in the same place. Performances tend to be restricted to March and early April. In pitch, not volume, it is close to Wren, but the arrangement is reminiscent of Chaffinch or Willow Warbler – a stream of silvery notes quickening to a chuckling crescendo.

Almost umbilically attached to bark, which they circumnavigate in halting spirals, Treecreepers ought to know the best places to nest. In reality, a suitable home is hard to come by. It needs to be a spacious chamber, completely hidden from view, with a tiny passageway for access. For this reason, the same residence is often used each year.

As feathers wear, they fade and blanch in colour. Adults moult after rearing young. Domestic duties are the last hurrah for plumage that has taken a battering through the previous year. The gingernut juvenile Wren is, for the moment, strikingly different in colour from its parent. However, following moult, the two will appear similar.

WREN
Troglodytes troglodytes

WRENS ARE NOT OUR SMALLEST BIRD, but they are the shortest, with a cocked tuft of a dozen tiny feathers for a tail. Thick soft plumage keeps the cherub warm and puny wings generate a whirring flight reminiscent of a big brown bumblebee. The Latin name is a giveaway to lifestyle. Wrens live low lives. Armed with a disproportionately big bill, they turn over stones, leaves and detritus in search of creepy-crawlies. Look at those legs! Comparatively, they are as strong as the hindquarters of a Kangaroo and are used for propulsion, like a sprinter rising from the starting block. If agitated, the limbs are fully extended while the owner stands tall, Meerkat style. Although almost ubiquitous – both mountainsides and small offshore islands are occupied – the species is most numerous where cover is thick and moist.

A vocalising Wren is the Edith Piaf of the understorey. Few birds sing louder or manage to cram as much racket into each burst, which lasts a full five seconds. On a woodland walk the accompaniment becomes Muzak, aural wallpaper, especially along territorial interfaces 'policed' by megaphone males. Bards sing open-mouthed and with such gusto that the stumpy tail sways from side to side. The effect is operatic. Within the composition there are distinct stanzas, seamlessly stitched together: *please, please, please – can I run, run, run – away with you, with you, with you?* In particular, listen for a burry quality to the song's mid-section. Alarm calls are very different: short and narky.

In North America, the species name is Winter Wren. That is the season when the bird migrates from Canada and fans south through the United States. Wrens actually migrate? Well, yes they do – even here. In the past, when lighthouses on barren rocks had keepers, migrants were frequently seen. Recoveries of English Wrens prove that some leave and go as far afield as southern France. Immigrants from Europe occasionally arrive across the North Sea, a staggering thought. One captured in Northumberland on 24 September 1998 had flown 900km from Sweden (Clark *et al.* 2000).

Pause; crouch; spring! A Wren's legs whiplash the mite into flight. Small, relatively stunted wings are little used during foraging. Nevertheless, the titch is capable of migration and some regularly cross both the North and Irish Seas.

Cold weather decimates local populations. Keeping warm is best achieved by sleeping together. In Norfolk in February 1969, in a standard nest-box, sixty-one entered through a two-inch diameter hole, mostly singly, although sometimes up to four squeezed in at once. The birds came and went in silence, arriving at dusk and taking twenty minutes to leave, mostly one at a time, next morning. Wrens are born quick, edgy and secretive. To begin with, youngsters are diffident fliers. Flights are short and some halt on the first available perch in open situations, something that furtive adults never do. Bright 'begging chick' yellow along the inside of the mouth is a badge of youth and soon disappears. On all ages, the brightest area is a ginger swatch on the upper side of the tail. During summer, when adult plumage becomes progressively worn and blanches, youngsters glow like gingernut biscuits. However, after a comprehensive moult in late summer, all look similar. A subtle age distinction is found on the under-tail coverts. On juveniles, rich brown with diffuse buff spots; on adults, cool tawny with distinct white dots.

STARLING
Sturnus vulgaris

STARLINGS ARE the avian equivalent of army ants. Moorland, dunes, pasture, seashore, manicured lawn – nowhere escapes a thorough poke. Synchronised bill-to-eye co-ordination is one of the reasons why the stormtrooper rules the world. That Björn Borg look and slightly mad expression are due to a head and bill designed like a gun sight. Next to Mick Jagger, the owner has one of the strongest sets of mouth muscles on the planet and the bill can open underground to lever out leatherjackets. In one action, splayed mandibles prise a peephole and eyes stare forward. The technique is clinical enough to part a sheep's wool and pick parasites from skin. Gangs of Goths scour the ground, conducting the equivalent of fingertip searches for hidden food. Certain worms occur in clusters. By pooling their effort, if somebody strikes lucky, everyone will be rewarded.

'Thus, they were first seen in 1838 on 23rd October, when they rushed past my informant at half-past eight o'clock in the morning, and continued passing in flocks as many as 200 strong until two o'clock in the day.' Although the prose sounds like H. G. Wells, the words were written by William Thompson (1849–52) and describe the great autumn immigration of Starlings witnessed arriving 'at a point of land where a river enters Belfast Bay about a mile from the town'. In those days Starlings were exclusively winter visitors. When two pairs bred in Belfast in the 1840s – one in the steeple of St Anne's Cathedral – local newspapers carried the story.

By assembling reports from lighthouse keepers, Barrington (1900) elucidated the nature of migration. Evacuations to the Atlantic coast were precipitated by the onset of freezing weather and snow. Some did not stop:

Throughout the winter, Starlings show a constant tendency to pass westwards, especially on every renewal of cold weather, and it is probably a result of this tendency that the west coast observations for November largely outnumber those for October. The flight in this direction does not always cease even when the Atlantic is reached. For example, on 31 October 1886, and again on the following day, we find the curious record of several thousand going west from Eagle Island, Mayo. When the cold becomes intense, great multitudes throng the western islands, and numbers perish there. In February 1895 the keeper on Clare Island, Mayo, reports: 'Starlings, Skylarks and thrushes came to island during the hard frost and snow this month, and mostly all died from hunger and cold.' Corroborative details are furnished from Samphire Island, Kerry, where Mr Dunleavy was then stationed. On 7 February, 'vast numbers of Starlings, Skylarks, Song Thrushes and Redwings' were noted going south all day, in heavy snow. Next day they were still going south: 'One continuous flight; they were all exhausted, and numbers of Starlings fell. It is pitiful to see the hundreds of birds dead and dying all about the island, particularly Starlings; the sea is also covered with them, and gulls feeding on them, although vast numbers of gulls have also died.

Foraging Starlings bustle and squabble. If startled, they vamoose in an instant. Hair-trigger reactions are enhanced by the bird's ability to swivel its eyes backwards. Potential danger is detected without wasting precious time raising the head.

Ireland has since been colonised and a large resident population is topped up in winter. One trapped at Belfast on 21 December 1975 returned to Latvia the following spring, where it was killed by a cat. Reinforcing the connection with the Baltic, a chick ringed in Estonia in June 1986 was caught and released at Larne in January 1987. In autumn, the great exodus from Europe peaks in October. In early March, immigrants return overseas. Before that, they lay on the best treat of winter. Like a tribe recognising secret ley-lines, waves follow predetermined routes and thicken themselves along telegraph wires. With dusk approaching and ranks swollen, a tipping point is reached and warriors circle in pulsating masses, patterned against a darkening sky, alternately whirring wings and then gliding. The swarm pivots and changes shape, its wheeling action changing opacity – one moment a pall of black smoke, the next a grey mist. In gathering gloom, gyrations are performed without a visible signal. The effect is mesmerising, as if a whole battalion marching in a parade had slapped rifles on to shoulders in unison – without the sergeant major uttering a command. Research has demonstrated that an ability to perform simultaneous manoeuvres is due to each bird keeping an eye on its neighbours. If one switches direction the ultra-rapid response is unanimous. Then comes the puerile and incessant chattering before lights out. Walking above crammed ranks huddled underneath bridges in Belfast is a noisy experience. Yet you have to admire the command structure. It is not clear who is in charge, but when that guy says 'shush!' thousands fall silent. As well as building ledges, roost sites include woodland, reed beds and holes in cliffs. A variety of explanations have been offered for the displays (Brodie 1976). Where there is a choice of overnight accommodation, such as over woodland, flocks may shift location or fragment into splinter groups. Hence aerial 'team building' may be a collective means of assessing the continued suitability of the previous night's roost site. High wind or attacks from predators precipitate changes in location. Although, numerically as a species, Starling is hardly on its last legs, the breeding population has crashed. In urban areas a lack of nest cavities in a tightly regulated building control environment has made both them and Swifts homeless. In rural districts Starlings spend most time on agricultural land searching for insects, populations of which have decreased drastically in the last thirty years. This could be the key to the bird's decline. Given Starlings' utilisation of dung pats for foraging, it is possible that increasing use of livestock medicines, such as avermectins, has contributed to food declines by reducing the numbers of dung-dependent invertebrates.

Above: Where masses throng and are panicked, the dusk sky booms when wings whump at once. Human passers-by convulse involuntarily, entering heart-attack country thanks to the power of sky-wheeling Starlings.

Right: After autumn moult, Starlings of all ages are bejewelled. Plumage detail appears painted by hand. Frosty white tips speckle the underparts. The upperparts are etched in bronze; the feather tracts resemble segmented armour plate.

The wing shape is unique and resembles the cold front symbol on a weather chart. On a mission and not hanging about, the wings are cupped against the body, sparking a bobsleigh resemblance. In winter, overhead flocks of thrushes look similar. Watch carefully and you might notice that thrush wings only half close between flurries of wingbeats. Youngsters have plain 'just fallen down a chimney' plumage (see 'Muddled By Moult', p. 167). During July, a rash of polka dots erupts across the belly. The result is a wilful paradox of spotted underparts and nondescript foreparts, as though body parts from two species were grafted together, Frankenstein's-monster style. The transformation is protracted. Not until October does the population become a homogeneous band of brothers; even then a few late-moulting juveniles retain remnants of a brown balaclava, furry in texture and incongruous as a dunce's cap. By April, male underparts are spotless (except the undertail) and burnished to an oily sheen. Fully revved for courtship, hopefuls pout a shaggy boa of lance-shaped emerald green (and some violet) breast plumes; the greater coverts share the same lustre. Dark Spanish eyes combine with a powder-blue bill base (hazel-eyed females have all-yellow bills, brighter across the distal half) and pink legs become more deeply colour-saturated. Breeding plumage males

in western Ireland have truly azure bill bases (wan greenish-blue in eastern seaboard populations) and strikingly long and pendulous breast feathers. Probably, such dandies are elder statesmen bestowed with the finest regalia. Offshore populations are longer lived and contain a larger ratio of males in excess of two years of age (NMK).

For a voice that is a mixture of bubble and squeak, Starlings pack a verbal punch. A common backing track is a burry rattle reminiscent of cardboard reverberating in the spokes of a bicycle wheel. Soloists become lost in soliloquy, reciting an endless absent-minded juggling gurgle, suggesting that something is stuck in the throat. The bird likes to echo the music of others. Impersonations include Curlew, Wigeon, Lapwing, Golden Plover, Common Snipe, Yellowhammer, Grey Wagtail, Bullfinch and Whimbrel. Forgeries are mastered in a flash. The opening salvos of Mistle Thrush and Blackbird in the New Year are copied and fashioned into aimless, albeit melodic, whistling. Telephone rings, reversing truck bleeps and unseasonal Swift screams are remembered and impersonated. Researchers who tried to tutor impresarios by playing them a range of songs failed. Defiantly, the artistes copied excerpts from the experiment, such as rotating tape recorder reels, transmission hiss and researchers' coughs.

DIPPER
Cinclus cinclus

White chest plumage would seem a handy means of locating a static Dipper. But not always: in a world of rushing water, black-and-white combinations amount to camouflage.

The Dipper is the only songbird that feeds underwater. The unlikely amphibian walks into shallows or stands, belly-deep, on a rock and, ducking the head, disappears. Immersed in the current it walks along the stream bed, flicking pebbles and winkling out larvae of aquatic insects, all the while pumping the wings to hold steady.

DIPPERS MAY BE SHORT AND DUMPY, but they know how to shift. Along rushing streams they fly low and fast, their progress marked by sinuous bobsleigh turns. It is easy to miss the whirring black blob, zooming past like an overweight, satanic Wren. Luckily they call frequently, a metallic *zink*, commemorated onomatopoeically in *Cinclus cinclus*. Both sexes sing a scratchy warble in autumn and winter, concentrated in the vicinity of nest sites under bridges or behind waterfalls. Pairs are single-brooded but some males are polygamous. The nest, a football-sized dome similar in design to a Wren's, is used and repaired annually. One near Banbridge, Down, has been in continuous use from 1954 to at least 2010 (JSF). Standing on a rock surrounded by a frothy current, Dippers cut quite a dash. A chestnut cummerbund of variable intensity borders a white paunch. The width of the band increases with age and males have brighter – more ginger – bands than females (SN). The bird strikes a sentinel pose and curtsies vigorously by flexing both wings outwards and down, reminiscent of a wet umbrella being shaken. The busybody plops into the current and hunts in gravel beds and whirlpools for stonefly larvae, snails and small fish. Fishermen swim with open eyes protected by an opaque white membrane, obvious when blinked. Larvae are extracted by battering their cases against rock. Pairs breed early; some clutches are laid in February. Because larvae are abundant in March – they are yet to hatch into adult insects – there is plenty of food for chicks in spring. Moreover, among windless wet ravines warmed by shafts of sunlight, extra insects can be gleaned by working surfaces near the water's edge, rather than plunging into the rippling rill. Formerly branded as consumers of fish ova, 548 were killed in one three-year period during the mid-nineteenth century in the Scottish Highlands. Upon dissection, no ova were found.

Along with populations on the Isle of Man and Scotland's Hebridean Islands, 'Celtic' Dippers form a homogenous subspecies, *C. c. hibernicus*, distinguished by 'crown and nape somewhat darker [than specimens from England and mainland Scotland] and rest of upper-parts decidedly so, tips of feathers being blacker and broader; under-parts with less chestnut-brown, colour being usually less bright and not extending so far down belly, which is black-brown, but this character though very obvious in a series is not so constant individually as darkness of upper-parts' (Witherby *et al.* 1938–41). Research into the genetic relationships of subspecies across Europe, which differ mainly in belly colour, showed almost no divergence in DNA, suggesting that, through isolation, minor differences in morphology have developed, whereas genetic lineage has remained the same (Lauga *et al.* 2005). Nonetheless, it is uplifting to believe that on this side of the Irish Sea we are blessed with a singular taxon that is a product of isolation and genetic drift, tantamount to a clean white sheet of creation. Yet, on examining live birds and digital images, there appears to be great similarity between populations in Britain and those here (AMG). Seldom is it possible to seek guidance from a fieldworker who has devoted most of a lifetime to an Irish bird. However, Ken Perry has done just that (Perry 1986). His elucidation confirming the distinctiveness of *C. c. hibernicus* is gratifying:

There is a difference [between Irish and British Dipper] in feather coloration, which is quite easy to see on trapped individuals. The brown shade of ours is both darker and duller across the upperparts, whereas the cummerbund width is broader and colour is warmer in British Dippers. Our birds also have finer legs, so much so that they require a smaller diameter in ring size. Based on tarsus thickness and duller upperparts coloration – a unique combination – a bird in the hand is eminently assignable as an Irish Dipper.

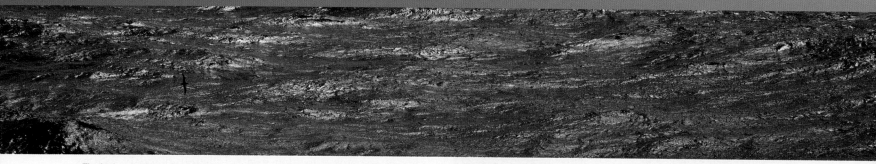

MIGRATION: A GLORIOUS STATE OF FLUX

The lanky speck is a Great Shearwater. Home is the Roaring Forties. Thanks to consummate powers of flight and a genetically inherited map of the Atlantic Ocean's wind patterns and seasonally abundant food supplies, the entire population embarks on an annual world tour.

BIRDS ARE AMONG the most mobile creatures on earth. Regardless of what lies beneath them, they can keep going for as long as they have the energy. They are blessed with the gift of quite rapid flight and remarkable orientation, a capability they use to migrate over long distances. For some, fact has outstripped fiction. Aleutian Bar-tailed Godwits fly non-stop for nine days from Alaska to New Zealand, a distance of over 11,000km. Indeed, many species experience perpetual summer by moving from one hemisphere to another. Securing food year-round is at the heart of this process and requires migrants to integrate knowledge of its availability at staging points straddling the globe. Those travelling furthest ready themselves by doubling weight. Some songbirds, Wheatear being one, embark on trans-oceanic flights lasting up to 100 hours. To make space for high-energy fat, they shrink non-vital organs, including the digestive system. Flying high in cool tailwinds, they are pushed along in thin air and breathe by reconfiguring the quantity of oxygen-carrying haemoglobin in the bloodstream. In effect, they become Clark Kent, changing into Superbird before taking to the sky. Sooty and Great Shearwaters, which pass through our seas in autumn, breed on remote islands in the Roaring Forties. Miniature data-loggers reveal that many fatten up on the Grand Banks of Newfoundland and do not eat again until they arrive off the east coast of Argentina. In the meantime, some will have passed Ireland in a day. Luckily, we still do not understand fully how they navigate, leaving much mystery and all the magic intact.

In our own backyard, feats of movement go undetected when we see members of a species throughout the year and assume that the same personnel are involved. Few birds are resident and the majority go in all directions at all seasons. During winter, most suburban Blackbirds hail from Scandinavia, the Baltic countries and beyond. Females and youngsters are the most migratory. Males are home birds but can be forced west in severe weather. Outwardly, local and foreign stocks look the same. However, by the end of February, a change occurs that can only be seen in the hand. Wannabe migrants have begun to deposit fat alongside chest muscle; the material resembles candle wax. The pilot, perhaps Russian and more than likely female, has refuelled itself.

Yellow-browed Warbler is a sprite from Siberian taiga. When cool autumn winds blew, its kin departed post-haste for tropical Southeast Asia; yet it trekked west to Ireland. Although as insignificant as a pea tossed into the Grand Canyon, the waif is not lost. It is an envoy testing the species' current range limits and powers of survival. If successful, a new migratory route might, in time, evolve.

It pays to remember, too, that migratory habits may change. Nowadays Blackcaps from central Europe are widespread in gardens in winter. What began as a novelty around forty years ago has become commonplace. Around the same time, Collared Doves crossed the Irish Sea and began breeding all the way west to the shores of the North Atlantic, a final push in a pan-European spread begun fifty years earlier. Intrepid parties of Bearded Tits have, since the 1970s, crossed the Irish Sea and settled to breed in reed beds in Wicklow, Wexford and Cork. So far, attempts at colonisation have been short-lived and have met with failure. Nonetheless, they prove that nature indulges in sweepstakes to attempt range expansion.

As an observation zone, our geographical position on the edge of the European land mass is immensely to our advantage. The region harvests a wide variety of migrants, including rare birds that are not lost but temporarily out of normal range. Infantry mostly comprises the young, a generation born to disperse and put out feelers for pastures new. Their occurrence allows us a share in the bird life of foreign lands. In autumn, witnessing a mite from Canada or Siberia snatching flies from dwindling foliage brings a sense of wonder at the restless urge that brought it here. Vagrants are far from spent genetic material.

RING OUZEL
Turdus torquatus

Ring Ouzel is the only thrush that is a summer visitor. Most spend the winter in North Africa. High-energy berries are a vital food source: from Bilberries and Rowanberries in Ireland to juniper berries in the Atlas Mountains. This migrant female is guzzling cotoneaster berries.

RING OUZELS formerly bred in virtually every Irish county. Ussher and Warren (1900) stated: 'I can find but four counties, viz., Meath, Westmeath, Longford and Armagh (which are not mountainous), from the avifauna of which Ring Ouzel can be excluded.' Older literature listed Ring Ouzel under the alternative title of Mountain Blackbird. Indeed, the bird inhabits most European mountain chains and nests all the way to the Arctic Circle. They spill south in autumn, filtering over high passes and occasionally alighting on coastal headlands. Migrants from Norway are deflected across the North Sea and handfuls stray west as far as Ireland. Waifs are elusive and seem to sense that they should not be here. Often presence is given away by stony 'takking', uncannily like the resonance of striking a rock against the surface of a frozen pond. Populations breeding in Scandinavia, Britain and Ireland are believed to winter in North Africa, predominantly in the Atlas Mountains, where they concentrate in large Phoenician Junipers *Juniperus phoenicea* and gorge on the berries. In fact, by excreting seed, the bird is one of the tree's main propagating agents. Recent studies (Ryall and Briggs 2006) paint a depressing state of affairs in parts of the Central and Eastern High Atlas. Although Ring Ouzels are still common winter visitors, all sites had damaged trees, ranging from removal of branches to total destruction. Browsing by goats had removed seedlings and local people chop wood for cooking, heating and building material. It is estimated that, at current exploitation levels, the remaining juniper forest is under threat.

Looking dizzily upwards at mist swirling above columns of grey granite brings home the grandeur of breeding haunts. Rock walls and scree act as a sounding board. The notes are reminiscent of a slow-paced Song Thrush: *pew, pew, pew … eve, eve, eve … choy, choy, choy.* Unless the singer is close, terminal 'chuckling' is inaudible. Getting a bead on the performer is maddeningly difficult. The silhouette resembles Fieldfare, not Blackbird. Airspeed is Exocet fast; sufficient to generate wind noise when passing overhead. The black-tipped bill is lemon, although Adonis males revved up to breed disport an orange-yellow bill. At rest there is a light panel on the folded wings, almost silvery on a proudly perched male. The breast's ermine crescent confers majesty, a Lord Mayor's chain of office. Roughly translated, *Turdus torquatus* means 'thrush with a collar'. The white arc is deep enough to divide head from body. Females are variable, their body colour ranging from dark chocolate to off-black; some are almost as white-collared as males. On first-winter females the breast gorget is absent although the underparts are etched pale, like the knitted furls of an Aran sweater. Thompson (1829–52) knew the bird well: 'In autumn, flocks eat the berries of the Mountain Ash … and are called Round-berry Birds. Ring Ouzels appeared in numbers like Fieldfares and Redwings among the Mounterlowney Mountains [Sperrins], Tyrone, in the last week of August in the years 1817 and 1818. Their resort was to some Rowans near a shieling at the extremity of a glen, where

six or seven have been killed at a shot as they were feeding on the berries.'

Migration details were provided by Barrington (1900), who analysed sightings and dead birds (lighthouse kills) supplied by keepers from 1881 to 1897: 'The Ring Ouzel's migration route is peculiar, the light-stations at which it occurs being nearly all situated either in the south, between Tearaght (Kerry) and Tuskar (Wexford), or in the northeast, between Mew Island (Down) and Inistrahull (Donegal). From the northern stations it has been noted on spring migration only; at the southern stations it is observed both in spring and autumn.' Barrington's data chimes with a small flood of migrants passing north in spring, followed by a sprinkling of autumn stragglers derived, presumably, from Scandinavia. By 1950 breeding had ceased in many former haunts and the bird was thin on the ground even in traditional areas (Kennedy *et al.* 1954). Within the next decade it had been lost from five more counties (Ruttledge 1966) and breeding in Northern Ireland was known from just two districts: the Mourne Mountains (four pairs estimated in 1952) and Fermanagh. However, this is probably a pessimistic representation – tracking down breeding Ring Ouzels is not for the faint-hearted or sedentary. Nevertheless, during the 1980s it became apparent that the population was crisis-ridden.

Speculation is a dangerous thing. If touted as holy writ, it can generate complacency. Well-meaning guesses can catch hold like brushfire and take on gospel status once passed through a mill of literature, dressed up with a quasi-sophisticated air. The alleged detrimental (to Ring Ouzel) expansion of Mistle Thrushes and Blackbirds into upland breeding habitat has acquired a King Solomon legitimacy and is still cited as a reason for the bird's disappearance, yet nothing untoward was discovered during a five-year study in the Pentland Hills of eastern Scotland (Poxton

Grazing by sheep has shorn much Irish upland of its natural vegetation. The island is a time capsule. Rowan, Silver Birch and heather survive, but the fragment is forlorn.

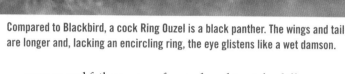

Compared to Blackbird, a cock Ring Ouzel is a black panther. The wings and tail are longer and, lacking an encircling ring, the eye glistens like a wet damson.

1986): 'Three Mistle Thrush nests were found in each of the first two years, but only one or two in the last four years. In one occasion in 1979 Ring Ouzels and Mistle Thrushes nested within 10–15 m of each other.' In 2011, a pair of Blackbirds nested within a hundred metres of breeding Ring Ouzels in Donegal and shared a grassy foraging slope where both species hunted earthworms (AMG).

While answers – and therefore a chance of solutions – may escape honest endeavours, it is galling to see gobbledegook obscuring valiant appraisals. The most recent breeding atlas (Gibbons *et al.* 1993) does not inspire confidence. A population estimate for Ireland is put at 180–360 pairs. This is wildly inaccurate. Almost predictably, climate change is trotted out as one culprit for the decline. Beale *et al.* (2006) suggest: 'Knowledge might allow management aimed at buffering the impacts of climate change on Ring Ouzels.' The article is written in the impenetrable patois of academia – jargon that excludes interested readers – and is waffle: 'Weather variables have changed over recent decades, with a significant increase in summer temperature [and] significant decrease in summer rainfall [in Britain and Ireland], and a non-significant decline in Moroccan spring rainfall. A model based on these trends alone predicted an annual decline in occupancy of 3.6 per cent (compared with an observed decline of 1.2 per cent), and suggested that increased summer temperatures after the main breeding period could affect the survival rates of adult and/or juvenile birds.' Meanwhile, in the Real World in Shropshire, a breeding survey carried out from 1994 to 2005 on an extensive upland plateau – the Long Mynd – charted inexorable loss and explained why the birds vanished. The report summary reads:

The population was stable throughout the 1990s at around a dozen pairs. This reduced to eight in 2000, three in 2001, two in 2002, and one in 2003. In 2004 only a single unpaired male returned, and only passage birds were seen in 2005. The species is now on the verge of extinction as a breeding bird in Shropshire. This population crash has, almost certainly, been caused by predation. A research project compared the success and failure rates of nests found in eight different study areas around Britain. The loss due to predation on the Long Mynd was far higher than that found in any of the other study areas. In practice, nest loss in Shropshire must be higher than that actually recorded ... the observed rate of nest loss correlated well with the observed rate of population decline. A study of feeding areas showed that there was no shortage of food on the Long Mynd, and this situation had not changed over many years. Several Ring Ouzels were colour-ringed. This demonstrated that the percentage rate of return of the previous year's birds was sufficient to sustain the population. Therefore, other causes of the decline – conditions in the wintering areas or on migration routes, such as shooting at migration 'choke-points' at high passes in the Pyrenees – can be discounted. The eleven-year breeding study shows that all other possible causes of decline can be discounted in this isolated population, except predation. (Smith 2004).

Predators increased on the Long Mynd for reasons that are all too familiar – a rise in the number of sheep and concomitant carrion, including Pheasant carcasses. Ground-nesting Curlew, Common Snipe and Teal were also hammered. However, looking at Ireland's historical record, it should be remembered that Ring Ouzels waned steadily. The bird was common in Thompson's day (up to the mid-1800s) and still widespread by 1900. By 1954 Kennedy *et al.* had noted a marked contraction. By 1966 Ruttledge (1966) reported that the situation had worsened. For want of better terminology, 'economic development' of upland habitats – newly planted conifer forests creeping upslope, their dense shadows overwhelming natural vegetation of Bilberry and heather – was scarcely a widespread phenomenon at this time. Yet, in many areas, the bird was already on the slide. Had something else changed? Yes: sheep had replaced cattle. Commencing somewhere in Central Asia, pastoral herders brought Blackface Sheep west as far as the Pyrenees. By the mid-1700s the Blackface was climbing through the Highlands and becoming synonymous with Scotland. The first flocks in Ireland

Mobile but scarcely able to fly, youngsters leave the nest and hide. Unless there is mature heather to screen them from predators, few survive.

Males are magnificent. Black velvet plumage showcases a snowy gorget. The flight feathers are silver-edged, producing grey – not black – wings in flight.

came with Scottish planters to Ulster and eventually spread west to Donegal. One of the first introductions to Ireland was in the mountains of western Mayo (Viney 2010). The Great Age of Sheep spread countrywide like an infestation of maggots, nibbling upland flora to oblivion. Steep terrain, high elevations and palatable woody vegetation (especially saplings and montane trees and shrubs such as Juniper, Rowan and Blaeberry *Vaccinium myrtillus*) are part of a herd's universe. Except where natural vegetation grows out of reach, it will be eaten and, through continuous grazing, never return. Estyn Evans (1951) describes the impact on the Mourne Mountains:

> Change was accelerated when sheep replaced cattle as the mainstay of the mountain economy from the end of the eighteenth century onwards. It is reckoned that six sheep can live in the place of one cow: this is the usual equation where grazing in common is practised. Indeed Harris (1744) gives the sum in the form of one cow or eight sheep. Not only do sheep bite more closely and indiscriminately, but also they are more mobile than cattle, and twenty-four pointed hooves do much more damage than four large hooves. Sheep have a depressing effect on flowering plants and shrubs, and indirectly on insect and bird life. They have reduced tree growth on the hill margins to a few stunted specimens of prickly thorn and holly. It is clear that the almost exclusive use of the Mourne hill pastures for sheep grazing is a fairly recent development, and that cattle were formerly far more important.

In England, Scotland and Wales, researchers galvanised with a sense of urgency have embarked on detailed Ring Ouzel studies. These days, one click with a mouse calls up a cornucopia of knowledge. Anyone can discover that breeders return in April and feed mainly on earthworms, beetles and all manner of insect larvae pulled from moist soil, generally grassland, often along wet flushes or in gullies containing streams or waterfalls. Tall heather conceals nests and acts as a safe nursery for juveniles awaiting parental food deliveries. If a territory contains ripening berry-bearing trees and shrubs then, *ipso facto*, the bird's needs are met.

Second broods are attempted and adults and independent young disperse and switch to a diet of berries, insects and earthworms. In Donegal, around ten pairs were located as recently as 2002 (Cox *et al*, 2002). A partial re-survey in 2011 produced happy news – several were still present (AMG). Recent Nothern Ireland data quoted in Wotton *et al* (2002) is largely guesswork. Worse is balderdash masquerading as fact, for example 'requires upland scree with associated bracken …' (Allen & Mellon 2010).

Fieldwork, including radio tagging, conducted in the Scottish Highlands from 1998 to 2007 summarised a study area decline from forty to fifteen pairs (Sim *et al*. 2008). It was found that productivity is influenced mainly by nest survival rates, not brood size or the number of breeding attempts. Predation was the main cause of nest failures. Fledglings were healthy and mortality rates were due to predation, not ill health or adverse environmental factors, such as impoverished habitat. The main cause of death was predation in the first four weeks after fledging. Of thirty-eight fatalities, 47 per cent were killed by raptors and 37 per cent by mammals. Deaths caused by birds of prey also feature among known fatalities in England's Peak District. Peregrines were the main culprit but information on the scale of predation is hard to come by – conservation organisations like Peregrines. Ironically, Watson (1972) felt that some pairs nested near Peregrine eyries to gain protection.

Due to sheep grazing spanning more than two centuries, much Irish upland has become unsuitable for Ring Ouzels. Where a suitable heather-grass mosaic remains, Rowans and berried shrubs (especially Bilberry, nestling among tall heather) may no longer survive. The berries, known as fraughans, were once so abundant in rural districts that great quantities were exported – some 400 tons in 1941. But the map in the *New Atlas of the British and Irish Flora* (2002) shows cavernous blanks where the shrub grew before 1970. In remote districts where needs are met, Ring Ouzels cling on in Donegal and Kerry. Even here, sheep are ubiquitous. Bilberries and Rowan seedlings are hard to find. Except on impossible ledges, sapling trees stand dead and petrified, their bark lacerated and stripped by rubbing. Overhead, sheep-following crows squawk and peer from sentinel crags, a sight as heart-warming as battery acid in a baby's bottle.

BLACKBIRD
Turdus merula

WISHING THAT commonplace were rare is a wicked thought. The reason for such perversity is not to malign but to draw attention to Blackbird song. Because it is ubiquitous, it is regarded by some as boring. Heresy! The medley is magnificent. It is *the* song of suburbia. An abundance of troubadours creates a remarkable wall of sound. Singing peaks during April, especially around dawn. The argy-bargy is all about courtship. Even in lashing rain, megaphone broadsides are launched in darkness, as through combatants are singing from the shelter of their beds. Females are fertile and territories are being defended or lost. In the affairs of birds, a male without domain is of little account. While land and conjugal rites underpin male song, its intensity varies. Some mornings a veritable eisteddfod breaks out, with each crooner at the top of his game. Gaps are shortened between verses and innovation is rife, with a variety of higher-pitched notes appended to each stanza.

The medley's bedrock consists of between three and ten syllables that appear to slide together – or skate – as a relaxed songburst. The caroller uses whim and spontaneity. Once you listen, you discover than the construct is never quite the same twice. A frequent characteristic is a rise in pitch, as if the voice has suddenly broken. On the coat tails of a full-voiced opening, the composition climbs in register and is 'crushed' into an undistinguished warble in which notes become thinner and tighter. Imagine wringing out a wet towel. After an initial flood, residue is released only by squeezing. Be aware that distance or listening from indoors muffled by double-glazing makes the rise in pitch difficult to detect. When heard as part of a Full Monty dawn chorus, the terminal 'twiddly bits' suggest that two species are singing: one rich and melodic, the other thin and raspy. Beware. Blackbirds are virtuosi. Performances are varied and it is crass to oversimplify their compositions. One size does not fit all. In reality, only the opening melody is 'compulsory'. After that, the soloist may – or may not – choose to improvise.

Alarm is raised in a wail of protest delivered as accelerating yelps that accompany an escape flight, the notes receding as the bird's silhouette does the same. A prescient *tchook, tchook, tchook* is frequently vented into a shrill *Eek!* proving that something is up, possibly a stalking cat. A shrew-like indrawn *zeeee* is sotto voce shorthand flagging up presence, as though the bird has just gone online. During winter, groups find themselves foraging in closer proximity than normal. A certain amount of internecine squabbling results – say in a garden where apples have been provided. Listen carefully. A back-of-the-throat *toot* punctuates proceedings, on a par with the clucking of contented hens or the peculiar electronic bleep made by supermarket tills. Starlings latch on to the sound and sample it.

A Blackbird on a lawn with its head crooked, allegedly listening for worms, is a familiar site. If interest piques, the head tilts and the bird lunges. Prey has to be extricated from a burrow and a brief tug of war ensues. Determination may lead to divots being gouged out. A vexing question remains: how did the bird spot the worm? The answer was supplied by research carried out in California using wild-caught American Robins, the North American equivalent of Blackbird (Heppner 1965). Investigators used an automatic noise generator, recorded noises made by earthworms and carried out elaborate tests with artificial wormholes offering the birds a choice of no worm, an odourless dead worm or a fresh specimen. The aim was to isolate the method of discovery: sound, smell, sensing vibration or sight? The conclusion was that only visual clues are used. Avian eyesight is remarkable, yet most species lack binocular vision and cannot freely rotate the eyeball. Hence, before striking, the bird crooks the head to obtain a positional fix with first one eye, then the other. When engrossed, Blackbirds prefer to walk rather than hop and, in an attempt to deliver a speedy *coup de grâce*, one foot often shoots forwards and rakes over the target area to try to snag prey by using claws. Earthworms venture close to the surface when soil is damp. Morning dew and wet weather, which potentially drown worms, constitute happy hours.

Because ivy berries are available in late winter and spring, they are a popular food. But not the seeds. These are spat out, explaining the propagation of ground-level ivy (JC). Unlike Song Thrushes, Blackbirds are noisy feeders in undergrowth. They sift through leaf litter by kicking it backwards. You can hear them. Piles of leaves mysteriously scattered over tidy lawns dumbfound zealous gardeners. Who would have thought that leaf-blowing machines jeopardise foraging habitat? But soil-dwelling organisms concentrate in the mould beneath leaf litter: blow away the leaves and the food source is gone.

Based on a study of bird kills at lighthouses and first-hand reports from keepers, Barrington (1900) shrewdly deduced information about the timing of immigration.

The period of densest migration for the Blackbird extends from 15 October to 15 November. The spring [emigration] does not begin until February, and is probably at its maximum about the middle of March. In autumn, the adult males are in a minority to the end of October, numbering only eighteen of a total of fifty; but throughout November and December they are equal in numbers to the female and immature birds together. In the spring movement, on the other hand, the males seem to predominate during the first fortnight of February, while after February 20 only two males have been received to fourteen females.

In other words, young and adult females, hailing from Britain and Europe, arrive first in late autumn. Adult males remain on overseas breeding territories until later, evacuating west only when cold weather bites – which explains why movements in

Top: first-winter female. Middle row: left, first-winter female; right, adult female. Bottom row: left, first-winter male; right, adult male (with exceptionally vivid bill).

the harshest weather contain a much higher ratio of males to females. Ringing confirms that Blackbirds from northern England and, especially, Scotland cross to Ireland for the winter. Norwegian Blackbirds also flood west, joined in smaller numbers by others from further east, including Russia. A male ringed at Carrowdore, Down, on 26 January 1964 returned to Latvia to breed. Proof that British (and no doubt Irish) Blackbirds sometimes up sticks and travel abroad comes from a female ringed in Essex on 13 May 1966 that was trapped at Santander on the north coast of Spain on 2 January 1968.

In summer, juveniles are ginger. For a few weeks, spotted chests demonstrate a thrush lineage. By late autumn, first-winter males are distinguishable. They have dull bills and brown-washed primaries contrasting with sooty body plumage. A careful look at the greater wing-coverts, which border the folded primaries at rest, reveals another subtle difference. Fresh adult (black) feathers adjoin older juvenile (brown) plumage. Because new coverts grow first from the inner part of the wing, the worn and more faded juvenile coverts are located on the outside. Brown-plumaged mothers and daughters look more alike. However, young females have dull, brownish-grey bills; matriarch bills are smattered with yellow.

FIELDFARE
Turdus pilaris

GOD WAS IN A FUSSY MOOD on the day he designed Fieldfare. The bird is affectingly elegant and multicoloured. The head is crisp grey, on some 'blue rinse'. Above the eye a light brow bestows a quizzical, headmistressy look. Black mascara smudges tight against a lemony bill base and braids into ticks spilling down the throat and coalescing in a black jaw. The centre of the throat is lit yellow, as though reflected from the bill, while a richer bronze glow drenches the chest before paling to a buttery hue on the flanks. Streaks, chevrons and chain-mail crescents are arranged in separate zones across the underparts. Spots, normally a thrush hallmark, are absent. Adult males have a black face, saturated ochre chest and breakfast-juice bill. The back is saddle brown and the rump and upper tail-coverts fuse together and form a block of grey. Airborne flocks resemble bomber command – maintaining an even keel, staying in formation and not yo-yoing. The flight is measured, even sedate. With each flick, the wings are raked back but not closed against the body. The resulting pose is reminiscent of a ski jumper. On the ground, assertive personages droop wings and strut with a puffed-out chest and ruffled rump. Males have blacker tails than females.

Fieldfares are winter visitors from northern Europe, arriving in flocks during October. Ringing confirms a mainly Scandinavian origin. Populations from central Europe and Russia head for France and Iberia. Nonetheless, a few end up here, such as one ringed at Dundrum, Down, on 30 December 1972 that was found dead in Moscow on 25 October 1974. Scandinavian individuals have been re-trapped over subsequent winters, indicating that they are faithful to wintering sites. If hard weather strikes, either in mainland Britain or on the near continent, migrants deluge west. Many enter gardens. Sweet apples (not cooking apples) are a favourite. Normally, flocks are distributed in open fields and along hedges. Haws are consumed ravenously; other birds swoop imperiously to the ground and work outwards from hedge bottoms, hopping a short distance, then crooking the head to peer for worms. Heather hillsides are dowsed for the same quarry. At dusk, they slink among areas of rough grazing to roost. Flocks chatter loudly. The sound hints of Magpie with a similar bossy frisson, recalling the scissoring action of hedge clippers. In contrast to Redwings, Fieldfares do not call while migrating at night.

Top: Noisy and aggressive, one Fieldfare will attempt to defend an entire garden containing more food than it could possibly eat. A raised tail is not an idle threat. The wannabe lawn master means business and will charge, peck and kick.

Left: Winter visitors from Europe, Fieldfares normally probe unfrozen pasture for earthworms and insect larvae. Cold weather drives them into hedgerows and gardens, where, until the ground thaws, they eat berries and fruit. Redwings are fellow travellers and most flocks of 'winter thrushes' contain both.

SONG THRUSH
Turdus philomelos

For once it is possible to use a cliché with conviction. Song Thrush does exactly what it says on the tin. The bird is born with an opera inside its head. The song is loud, clear and vivacious. Carollers perch proudly. On treeless islands pulpits are hard to come by; so any elevation will do, especially stone walls that allow the aria to echo.

SONG THRUSH is a shrinking violet. Usually solitary, it has an edgy look. Until it sings. The chest inflates and energises a coy bird. The head rocks like a gospel singer and the delivery has gravitas. Stanzas consist of one or several syllables. Each is repeated: *choy, choy, choy, chur-ee, chur-ee, chur-ee* and so on. It is Robert Browning's rapturous thrush that 'sings each song twice over'. It seems as if the star cannot wait to get going, for it launches into arias on calm days in the dead of winter. Ironically, the main contact note is an easily overlooked, self-effacing *zit*, akin to the final tightening of a nut when changing a car tyre. Analogous to the alarm of Blackbird, there is a similar accelerating burst: *chip, chip, chip, ip, ip*. But the salvo is tinny, a soprano version. In fact, Song Thrushes emit alarm calls infrequently and tend to fly off silently or employ *zit* as shorthand for 'exit stage left'.

Head on, the forehead and crown appear shield-like. The plumage is chestnut and stands out as a flat cap. Side on, everything changes. The cap shrinks, pegged back by the front of the supercilium that arches between eye and bill. The effect is a furrowed brow. Some show a sad face. Like the tears of a clown, dusky blotches radiate in two rivulets and fretwork darkens the cheek, emphasising a white ring behind a baleful eye. Across the underparts, a buttery yellow glow shines from within. Song Thrush and Mistle Thrush are our only spot-breasted thrushes. Yet their spots differ. Concentrate on the chest – not the throat – to assess the pattern. On Song Thrush, the markings are stealth bomber arrowheads that align like ribbons or teeth in a zip. Mistle Thrush markings are half-moon crescents and pepper the plumage randomly, a swarm of bees or black hailstones, merging and thickening at a hotspot on the side of the chest.

Although the bird is famous for dining on snails by cracking them open on a rock anvil, earthworms are preferred. Snails are eaten only when the ground has become baked or frozen and worms cannot be dug out. Davies and Snow (1965) monitored behaviour in Oxfordshire. They found that territories are not occupied regularly or consistently. Often, during the day, birds search for food over considerable distances. In one case a male fed almost a mile from home. In winter, both sexes defend individual territories, although most territory-holding birds are males. Those ringed as nestlings from the local district very seldom establish new territories there. This agrees with ringing data, indicating that young Song Thrushes disperse widely. Indeed, it suggests that winter influxes across Ireland are likely to contain a high proportion of youngsters. A few occupy territories consistently from year to year. Males, on average, remain longer than females. Even so, few stay longer than two years and about half disappear within a year. Augmenting males already holding winter territories, new males arrive steadily throughout winter. Females arrive in March, marking the beginning of the breeding season, then leave in July. Females are

Song Thrushes feed on the ground and rarely perch in hedgerows to pluck berries. Furtive by nature, the bird moves with short runs or hops and startles easily. Even then, it opts to be self-effacing and usually flees silently. Its chief contact note is a dry monosyllable, best remembered for being underwhelming.

fickle, moving around the neighbourhood and settling briefly in different territories.

Pairs are not faithful. In autumn and early winter, subdued song is heard from males that remain on breeding territory. Low-key song appears to signify presence and ward off newcomers. Virtuoso singing designed specifically to attract a mate is heard chiefly in February and March. Later in the breeding season, the most sustained song comes from those males that remain unpaired or have lost mates. Food is of four kinds: earthworms, snails, caterpillars and fruit. Earthworms were taken most often from January to June. Caterpillars are taken in May and June when they drop from trees and tall vegetation to pupate in the ground. The amount of feeding on earthworms is related to availability: during summer downpours they are avidly devoured, whereas snail hunting recommences in dry spells.

REDWING
Turdus iliacus

Two great rivers of Redwing migration straddle Ireland. In winter, Scandinavian populations come west; in autumn, birds from western Iceland fly over us in darkness, heading for France. Some break the journey and can be enjoyed in daylight. Evolution has built a bigger, bolder bird for the rigours of a long overseas flight. Many are swarthy and memorably blotched. When, later in the winter, European migrants pitch down, they look almost puny. Compare this Iceland Redwing with the European Redwing alongside the Song Thrush in p. 267.

LIKE VIKINGS, flocks of Redwings sweep down from the north each winter and embark on a campaign of pillage. They stick together, stripping haws from hedgerows and prising earthworms from burrows. Predisposed to restlessness, troupes feed intensely and bury themselves in trees or scrub. They panic easily; wings and tails recede over fields or rocket through the far side of tall hedges. Watch how they fly. Wings are held half open and the hand is flicked. A piercing half-shriek – *zeeeeeeip* – comes on suddenly, a trailing note that erupts from startled flocks (www.xeno-canto.com, catalogue number XC 25083, recorded by Neils Krabbe on 28 June 1982 at Oulu, Finland). In daylight, bird and voice can be linked. The same high stridor can be heard from the night sky in late autumn. The bird is tapping out a call sign and hoping for a reply. On the deck, a quiet yelp is used. The utterance has the intonation of fright at inadvertently sitting on a sharp object. Full alarm is an indignant burst, akin to the echoing taps of a hurled stone bouncing off ice. Song is reserved for faraway breeding grounds. But not always. As winter fades, flock members tune up. Normally songsters are concealed in bushes or tree crowns. The chorus is a discordant gabble reminiscent of Starlings.

Cold weather changes everything. Wormy pastures become ice-bound and suburban gardens with berried, ornamental trees attract refugees. Motivated by hunger, innate furtiveness is suspended and one of winter's icons reveals itself in close up: a small sharp-faced thrush with a stripy head and rusty flanks. At the height of the big freeze in January 2010 an estimated 200,000 descended on the Kerry coast. Here and elsewhere many died. In desperation, flocks flew out to sea. Several made it to eastern North America.

Redwings breed in Iceland and from Scandinavia east across all of Russia. Those in Iceland have been separated long enough to develop minor physical differences, notably greater size and swarthier plumage. They migrate southeast, a change that could not have come about gradually, as any direction from Iceland between southeast and the normal southwesterly direction of European birds would lead to a watery grave (Milwright 2002). Redwings from eastern Iceland tend to winter in Scotland and Ireland, and those from western Iceland tend to winter in France and Iberia. No Icelandic-ringed Redwing has been found outside Iceland before the beginning of October, but few remain there into November, when winter bites. Not only is autumn migration synchronised, it also harmonises with favourable northwest tailwinds. Optimum conditions occur following the passage of a cold front. At such times large numbers arrive on headlands and islands along the Irish west coast. Several have been recovered in Iberia and southwest France in October, some within days of being ringed, suggesting direct flights of about 2,400km. There is little evidence that Ireland is used as a significant staging post on the way south in October and November. It seems that those planning to winter in Iberia fly directly to western France and relocate to northwest Iberia later in the winter. European Redwings follow two major migration routes to their wintering areas, passing north or south of the Alps. Large numbers track along the North Sea coast; many from Fennoscandia make the open-sea crossing and disperse into Britain and Ireland. By November, populations from Finland and Russia are involved in a great westward exodus.

Our birds come, therefore, from both northeast and northwest. One ringed in Tipperary in January 1990 spent the following New Year in Portugal. Extraordinary flights are undertaken. Who would have predicted that a bird ringed in Antrim on 2 January 1977 would be retrapped in Perth, Scotland, the next day? Paradoxically, a few make spectacular longitudinal shifts between years. Multiple recoveries in Lebanon and Iran document individuals that, the year before, spent Christmas in Britain, France and the Netherlands.

Weak and starving, a Redwing (right) and Song Thrush (left) feed side by side. Territorial aggression is forgotten in severe weather. Huge numbers of thrushes died during the big freezes of two recent winters.

MISTLE THRUSH
Turdus viscivorus

MISTLE THRUSHES disport themselves like sergeant majors – upright carriage, chest thrust forward and a bit of a belly. The bird looks as though it has swallowed a tennis ball. Airborne, it powers along with deep beats, revealing white oxters and tail corners. When they are in a bossy mood the flight path can be direct and intimidating, accompanied by a machine-gun rattle. In winter, vigilantes guard individual trees laden with berries and drive off all comers, even flocks of Redwings or Waxwings. *Viscivorus* is contained in the scientific name and, translated, is a combination of *viscum* (mistletoe) and *voro* (devour). Aristotle mentioned the bird's fondness for berries in the fourth century BC. Mistletoe berries are an important food in Mediterranean countries where a red-berried species grows on olive trees.

Plumage is varied and 'cold'. The underparts look as if they have been peppered with black rain. The downpour must have been more intense at the sides of the chest, where a cluster forms. The back is stony grey-brown and feather groups are pale-edged (see 'Under the Hood', p. 15). Tracts of wing plumage resemble the texture of well-worn corduroy or driftwood. Mass hallucination among bird artists has led to Mistle Thrush being depicted with a solid, almost massive, head and bill. In life, both are relatively puny and almost serpentine.

Commencing on still days in January, territory-holders crank up the volume. The breeding season is nigh and the intention is to plant an early territorial flag. The phrases are short but nonetheless catch the ear of Starlings, who imitate them. During the breeding season, soloists are stimulated by approaching inclement weather and sing lustily before a lowering sky. Solemn verses, delivered in a controlled, mandarin manner, spawned 'Stormcock' as an epithet. Lone pipers like to perch high, often at the dizzying top of a sentinel tree. In truth, the song is tough to distinguish from Blackbird. One way to tell the two apart is tempo. Mistle Thrush diction comes in saturnine, lapping waves. Phrases are short and similar; vocabulary is limited. Soon a cloned, repeating pattern emerges. You could argue that Blackbird sings the words whereas Mistle Thrush speaks them.

The species was, apparently, unknown in Ireland before the nineteenth century. Thompson (1849–52) charted colonisation:

> The remarkable feature in the history of this bird, is its absence from the country until of late years, and its rapid increase from the period of its first appearance – an observation which applies to Great Britain as well as to Ireland. The first individual that I have heard of was shot by John Sinclaire about the year 1800 from a flock of Fieldfares at Redhall, Antrim. [Although, in an appendix, it is recorded that the bird was actually shot a few days before 3 February 1808.] In the counties of Antrim and Down, the Mistle Thrush was at first confined to the warm and richly wooded districts, but gradually spread from them over the plantations generally. Of late years it has inhabited those which stretch farthest towards the mountain tops.

In light of Thompson's concluding remark, the bird's original title of Mountain Thrush makes sense.

Left: Extrovert and brimming with confidence, Mistle Thrushes think nothing of hounding smaller birds from their feeding zones. During winter the bird can look big-bellied; probably the only species that could be told to lose weight. In reality, tubbiness is due to plumage fluffed out for warmth.

Below: The Mistle Thrush commences singing early in the New Year. Soloists perch high and prominently. The verse recalls a Blackbird, a reminder to source the sound and perhaps see a large lusty thrush in full voice rather than a more tuneful and melodic Blackbird.

SPOTTED FLYCATCHER
Muscicapa striata

Like a prodigal son, just when hope fades, the familiar face silently reappears. The Spotted Flycatcher is the last summer migrant to return in spring. Heavily reliant on flying insects, in sunshine it performs spectacular swoops and hovers but resorts to squirrelling forays through foliage in cold or wet weather.

Inset: A dead snag provides a perfect operating base from which to apprehend prey. Paired couples use a selection of 'his and hers' perches to avoid competition.

SPOTTED FLYCATCHERS, lacking striking features, foster a sober impression. Detail reveals a bib of streaks and a combed, sometimes raised, crown. The head can appear large, whereas the feet and tarsi are Lilliputian. The hawker is adept at catching flies, bees, wasps and butterflies. A favourite lookout may be used repeatedly and sentinels sit upright with the tail held downward. Indeed, poise and behaviour identify the bird more readily than plumage. Alternate flicking of one wing punctuates adroit, flamboyant sallies. Hovers are sometimes performed and, if close, bill snaps are audible. The song is humdrum, a feeble mix of squeaky piping and shrew-like whistles, punctuated by pauses. The call is a thin, hissy *zee*, to which a slapping *tuck* of alarm is added, sometimes repeated. The *zee ... tuck* combination is similar to the sound of a ring-pull being released on a can of soft drink.

Sunlit glades and streamsides in woodland constitute summer lodgings, alongside the leafy grounds of country homes, hotels and manses. Airy spaces overhung by canopy are key; bug-hunters need unfettered access to zoom-room. Snags are commandeered and homes constructed against bark (or trelliswork) from moss, cobwebs and grass. Youngsters have pearl-spotted upperparts, hence the name. Two broods are attempted, one in June with a second in July. Pairs are more likely to produce offspring in years when June weather is warm and sunny (O'Connor & Morgan 1982). This is a result of a greater abundance of flying insects. Davis (1977) found that the quantity of insects trapped in warm weather could be ten times higher than on cold days. In terms of 'catchability', prey activity is

important. To boot, balmy conditions free parents from devoting time to brooding nestlings during spells of cold or wet weather.

Spotted Flycatchers are long-range migrants, wintering across a wide band of Africa, from equatorial regions to Namibia. It is known that, of all Palaearctic–African migrants trapped at Saharan oases, Spotted Flycatchers have the smallest fat reserves. Under normal circumstances they have little difficulty in replenishing body fat by catching abundant flying insects. During droughts, insect life is reduced, with grave implications for tired migrants in need of refuelling. Commencing in the early 1980s, many breeding haunts have been abandoned. In the UK, there has been a 70 per cent decrease since 1975. What has gone wrong? In this era of state-funded conservation strategies, it is realistic to expect that efforts might be made to address the bird's plight. The UK has a Biodiversity Action Plan. Its lead partner is listed as the RSPB.

The action plan reads:

Current factors causing loss or decline. These are not well known, but may include one or more of the following. **1**: Weather effects. These appear to be important and could have population impacts if long-term climate change occurs. **2**: Drought in the Sahel region. This has been implicated in the declines of a number of trans-Saharan migrants. The Spotted Flycatcher passes through the Sahel region en route to wintering grounds in southern Africa. Changes in conditions in the Sahel or the wintering areas could be a

When fly-catching starts, it is pure burlesque. Between forays, performers do the equivalent of catching their breath by simultaneously flicking both wings, a useful identification trait. To obtain the calcium needed to produce eggshells, females consume snails and woodlice.

factor in the species' decline but no clear link has been established. 3: Changes in agriculture. Firm data on the importance of this for Spotted Flycatcher are lacking, but there is growing evidence that a range of birds found on lowland farmland are affected by low invertebrate availability during the summer. 4: Loss of nest sites. Many Spotted Flycatchers nest in large trees and there has been a large-scale loss of these in woodland, parks and hedgerows (especially following Dutch elm disease), which are favoured habitats. However, there are no quantitative data on the effect of these losses. (UK BAP 2010)

Can the action plan's analysis be believed? Proof is lacking? Given a huge winter range in Africa (one ringed at Cashel, Tipperary, on 23 June 1984 was found freshly dead on wintering grounds in Angola on 20 January four years later) and the fact that the bird's western Palaearctic–African migration strategy is shared by other species that are not suffering decline, such as Sedge Warbler and Grasshopper Warbler, perhaps answers ought to be sought more keenly at home rather than pointing the finger abroad? Many vacant former haunts are unaltered. But some of their inhabitants are new. In 1975 Spotted Flycatcher breeding habitats did not harbour Grey Squirrels, Jays or many Magpies. In Britain, Great Spotted Woodpeckers increased considerably in the same period. All prey on the eggs and young of songbirds. According to the RSPB's annual Big Garden Birdwatch, Magpies have become the thirteenth most commonly seen bird in UK gardens. In less than thirty years, they have increased by 112 per cent. On this side of the Irish Sea the scale of increase is considerably greater. A trial conducted by the Game and Wildlife Conservation Trust at Loddington, Leicestershire found that on keepered sites where Magpies were controlled, songbirds flourished. The RSPB refuses to accept these findings, yet endorsed other results from the same trial in a corporate review of the effects of predation on bird populations:

A study at Loddington in Leicestershire, run by GWCT, investigated the effects of removing Magpies and crows on songbird nesting success and population levels. Game management began in 1993 and involved a range of habitat improvements and predator control. Predation by crows was the main cause of nest failure, and nesting success of four out of six open-nesting songbird species was higher in areas with fewer corvids. In addition, numbers of five out of six songbird species increased following the start of game management. Thus, while crows probably did influence nesting success, it is unclear whether predator removal or habitat improvements (or both) were responsible for the songbird population increases. Although the Loddington study will continue for several more years before conclusions can be drawn, for the Spotted Flycatcher, at least, predator control may have been beneficial. Flycatcher numbers increased in woodland, though not in gardens, between 1992 and 2001 – the period of predator control – and declined after 2002 once predator control stopped. It seems that predation reduced flycatcher breeding success at Loddington, perhaps accounting for fewer breeding birds in subsequent years. The identity of the predators was unknown. (RSPB 2007)

Nest concealment is not Spotted Flycatcher's strongest suit. Research into mate preference in Blackcaps, which have increased spectacularly over the period of Spotted Flycatcher decline, showed that female Blackcaps prefer to mate with males whose song output indicates an ability to construct a better-concealed nest than a rival male (Michl 2003). If only Spotted Flycatchers did likewise. Worse, parents seem to be at a loss when it comes to defending a threatened nest; a far cry from thrushes, whose actions in defence of chicks were effective in deterring all but four attacks (out of fifty-two) by Jays (Weidinger 2009).

ROBIN
Erithacus rubecula

ROBINS EVOLVED to forage in the dim underworld of woodland. Big eyes, black as sloes, milk light from shade. Disturbance to the leaf litter by mammals is a godsend and probably explains the bird's watchful savvy in attending soil turners, from deer to gardeners. The species was officially known as Redbreast until 1952, when the British Ornithologists' Union formally accepted Robin. Plumage discussion is unnecessary, except to issue a reminder not to miss the short-lived appearance of mottled juveniles. By midsummer they undergo a dramatic transformation. Progressing from the belly and travelling headwards, spotty breast plumage is replaced with red (in reality orange-russet). A popular myth claims that the absence of red in juvenile plumage is designed to protect the apprentice against adult aggression. Since when did adults react to the red breast of an intruder impinging on territory, rather than simply the presence of the trespasser? Pugilism is often prefaced with a characteristic flight style. Going into combat, an irate Robin becomes a guided missile and flies straight, fast and hard. During short sallies, wing-whirr is audible; a cherub's wings purr loudly.

Both sexes sing and can do something that we cannot: they discriminate between male and female song (Hoelzel 1986). Sonogram analysis shows that the male voice is more complex. Gently soughing arias are poured out in short 'hors d'oeuvre' stanzas. Like snowflakes, no two are quite the same. If Robins went to school the music teacher would issue an admonishment: 'Shows potential but needs to develop.' No matter, the diva enlivens the bleakness of winter and is all the more beautiful for being a lone piper. In full flow, the grave silence between verses and the duration of the composition itself lasts about the same, roughly three seconds. Longer bursts are used in megaphone diplomacy between rivals. Duellists may be of either sex and territorial rights are at stake. Autumn migrants searching for settler's rights are 'sung at' by not-in-my-backyard locals reluctant to admit newcomers. Broadcasts are modulated with an open mouth yet sometimes emerge from a closed gape. Even with a gob stuffed with a wriggling worm destined for his mate, a show-off male can manage a bar of song. The commonest call is a metallic, irregular tick given in a short, hesitant series. The sound has a stalling momentum, similar to the click-stops of a rickety wheel of fortune halting at the winning number. When feeling edgy or alerting youngsters to danger, a high-pitched, almost supersonic *seeeh* is emitted. The intonation is whimpering.

The Robin in your garden during spring is probably not the one you saw there in winter. Ringing returns indicate that many Scottish Robins winter with us. A 1983 juvenile from Oban was killed in January 1984 by a cat in Lisburn, Antrim, while an adult ringed at Templepatrick, Antrim, on 16 January 1993 occupied a breeding territory at Kylesku in the Scottish Highlands. Spring fatalities from the Maidens lighthouse off Larne, Antrim, testify to the emigration of winter visitors.

Newly minted, a baby Robin is Bambi with feathers. In juvenile plumage, the filaments that form an air-catching surface on either side of the quill are reduced in number. Probably, in the exigencies of fast growth, it is better to have fewer plumes but a serviceable feather. The effect, nonetheless, is exquisite: the youngster's raiment resembles hazy gauze.

After a matter of weeks, lace-like virginal plumage is moulted and replaced with a more rigid coat. By autumn, young and old look the same.

In Victorian times, British postmen wore red tunics and were called 'Robins'. Cards delivered at Christmas began to feature the posties' namesake. Soon the bird's unshakeable link with the season was forged.

Breeding behaviour was worked out in the 1920s by J. P. Burkitt in his Enniskillen garden and carried to a conclusion by David Lack, who famously published *The Life of the Robin* in 1943. Burkitt used numbered metal rings as a means of distinguishing individuals, one of which was still alive eleven years later. He proved that what had been deemed courtship display, involving posturing with a puffed-out chest, was really aggressive behaviour. Data showed that three quarters of the winter population are males and that a large proportion of females leave the area. Lack, by following Burkitt's lead, was able to map breeding and winter territories, and study how these changed over time. Breeding territories, held jointly by a pair, were larger than those held in winter by individuals. Robins frequently trespassed into adjoining neighbourhoods in search of food. If spotted, trespassers were attacked. 'Inside their territories the birds sing, fight, display, and make themselves conspicuous; outside them they do not sing or display. They retreat if attacked, keep as inconspicuous as possible and, if disturbed, usually fly straight back to their own domains.' The outcome of a raid on a territory-holder by a territory-seeker was graphically recorded. 'The mated male was getting the worst of matters and had lost a great many feathers from his chin and one side of his face. After two hours he ceased to resist, and fled from the attacks of the newcomer. The hen took no part in the encounter and after a while began to follow the newcomer about as if he were her mate.' The vanquished male remained in the territory for two more days and was regularly harassed by the victor. The female and victorious male then raised a family together.

WHINCHAT
Saxicola rubetra

WHINCHATS FAVOUR UPLAND FIELDS and hill pastures, typically those containing Meadowsweet *Filipendula ulmaria* or mosaics of rough grassland with low bushes and tall plants, which are used as perches. Stone walls, barbed wire and fence posts are employed as lookouts. Like Stonechats, they sit on a topmost spray and peer, Kingfisher style, into the vegetation below. In a flash, the sentry drops to the ground and returns with prey, perhaps a beetle, its limbs still slowly turning like crabs' legs.

A summer visitor from Africa, breeders return in the latter half of April and the first clutch is laid in May. Nests are concealed in tall grass and a second brood is attempted in June or July. Warm sunny days ensure a plentiful supply of insects and ward against broods dying through exposure to rain. Territorial birds call regularly (migrants appear to have taken a vow of silence) and pairs and family parties stay in close proximity. Typical notes include a fizzy, somewhat drawn-out *chah* that has a 'deep fat-fryer' quality. *Teck* notes are intermixed in the repertoire. Compared to Stonechat, behaviour is less animated and wings and tail are flicked considerably less.

Thompson (1849–52) cited a preference for habitats off the beaten track, even around Belfast: 'across the base of the mountains and the adjacent fields, or low-lying cultivated ground, containing shrubby underwood. In no part of Ireland have I seen the Whin-chat numerous, and compared with the Stone-chat, it is very scarce.' Farmed landscapes have been drastically altered since Thompson's day. Insect-rich marginal land is fragmented and in short supply. In uplands, the conversion of luxuriant heathland to bowling green sheep pasture has obliterated wildlife. On adjacent moorland, overgrazing by sheep has exacerbated matters. In a few areas the species has been 'saved' by forestry plantations. When trees are young, less than a metre tall, the tangled understorey provides a treasure trove of feeding and nesting habitat. Saplings make ideal perches. Once the branches spread and form a light-excluding canopy, the habitat is lost. Luckily, due to rotational forestry operations, similar habitat may become available nearby and, when migrants return from Africa the following spring, they may be able to switch to similar habitat in the general vicinity. If not, the population is lost, seemingly for good.

Small but confident, Whinchats perch openly and are easy to locate among hill-foot country. A summer visitor from Africa, their numbers have declined sharply as hillsides and marginal land have been 'reclaimed' – tall herbs extinguished, wild thickets grubbed out and wet flushes drained.

Breeding pockets fare best across hilly districts extending north from Larne, Antrim. Damp upland fields, some replete with leggy Water Avens *Geum rivale*, provide hunting grounds for family parties. In the Republic of Ireland, Whinchats inhabit low-lying marshy meadows and old cut-away bog. Adult males in nuptial plumage are sensational. Their chests glow fiery apricot in sunlight, terracotta satin in shade, and are sandwiched between snow-white bellies and warrior heads. Some breeding males, possibly one-year-olds, are more muted. Females are somewhat dowdy; useful camouflage for incubation. Compared to Stonechats, the bird is lighter in colour. Diagnostic features include, at all ages, a prominent supercilium and twin white panels at the base of the tail. Although Stonechats have a variably pale rump, the tail is dark. Juveniles, once they moult into first-winter plumage, exchange baby-bird streaky upperparts for a pearly cloak.

STONECHAT
Saxicola torquatus

Stonechats have an affinity with fence lines and the tops of gorse (whin) bushes. In rural districts they are as cheery as Robins. Snow cover is their Achilles heel. Rather than undertake a long migratory flight in search of mild conditions, stalwarts hang on and hope for a change in the weather. When this does not happen, mortality is high and countrywide. Above: female; below: male.

Mannerisms and silhouette alone identity this poppet of perches.

STONECATS ARE ROBIN-SIZED and show equivalent confidence. Favoured haunts are places where nature has been left in peace – overgrown pasture tangled with pockets of whin and thorn, strips of tall heather and bracken behind fence lines or bushy gullies adjacent to spate streams. In ragged coastal districts tetchy twosomes patronize neglected fields, rough hillsides and sand dunes peppered with a few bushes and brambles. In all chosen habitats, they parachute into undergrowth, emerging from entanglements with a smorgasbord of flies, grubs, caterpillars and beetles. Sometimes an individual towers twenty metres or more and treads air to gain prey-spotting advantage from an aerial view, its action more hoverfly than bird. Each time the cherub alights, wings are flicked and the tail is quickly fanned (slightly to the side and up) accompanied by a high *wheet*, then a gravely *trak, trak* – accounting for the stones-knocked-together moniker of 'stone-chat'. Adults protect nestlings by emitting *whit* and *chack* calls when a predator is detected. They vary the two types of alarm depending on the location of the threat (Michl 2003). *Whit* calls suppress the loud food-begging calls of nestlings, so brood detectability is made more difficult. When they operate as decoys to distract intruders, parents use louder, more readily noticed, chack calls. The spring song is a quick-fire melody, a hissy jumble recalling the start of Skylark's rhapsody.

Stonechats are bigheaded, yet the tail is diminutive, fit for a Wren. In the breeding season, males combine a sooty hood with a white collar and rusty 'bleeding heart'. Females sport autumnal shades throughout the year and are light-throated in winter. By September, moult transforms males. In non-breeding plumage, they resemble females seen through smoked glass. Coppery wings distinguish Robin-like juveniles. Adults flash a ginger rump overlain with a thin scattering of dark ticks. Most males have at least a modicum of off-white at the core of the rump. A few possess a white handkerchief cradled between the back and folded wings (on the lower scapulars). While some pairs remain on territory throughout the year, during winter they seem thinly spread and somewhat nomadic. Youngsters disperse. Juveniles ringed in Britain have reached the Mediterranean. During autumn, migration is obvious in coastal districts of western Ireland. On Inishbofin, Galway, fifty-strong influxes have occurred. A nestling from Donaghadee, Down, wintered at Aylesbury, Buckinghamshire, and in the following spring reappeared close to where it was raised. Stonechats are susceptible to cold winters, when local populations may be eliminated. Population crashes can be offset by an ability to rear three broods, although only a comparatively small proportion make it to breeding age (Fuller & Glue, 1977).

WHEATEAR
Oenanthe oenanthe

Wheatears that breed in Ireland spend the winter in semi-desert, snatching large ground-dwelling insects across southern Algeria, Mali and Mauritania. Come March, Africa is forgotten and they fly rapidly north. By St Patrick's Day, the first males are back in soft Irish rain. If the sun shines, they leap high and rend the air with a fast scratchy warble.

THIS BIRD'S RADAR is world class, but a pain. Hair-trigger watchfulness suggests a simile – as wily as a Wheatear. Striking when perched, imminent departure is ingrained and the sentry shows you a disappearing white rump, like a galloping deer's behind. A black tail emphasises the snowy rear that in bawdy Old English was coined White-arse, reputed to be the derivation of Wheatear, a sobriquet that transcends vulgarity. Wintering in Africa, Wheatears are long-range migrants, specialising in snatching insects from short vegetation and bare soil, or swooping to conquer prey basking on sunlit rock. They hunt by eye, alternating imperious gazing with charging hops, high-speed Kangaroo romps that create the impression of running. Most occur in uplands where outcrops pepper short, cropped sward. In western districts and on offshore islands many breed on lower slopes close to sea level. The species breeds widely across virtually the whole of the Old World and in adjacent parts of North America where it is absent in summer only from the central Canadian Arctic. That said, nesting birds are spreading west around Hudson Bay, and it has been postulated that the gap may be bridged. The colonisation of North America has only occurred following the retreat of the last glacial period (some 10,000 years ago), yet all still migrate back to their ancestral Africa every winter. For Alaskan-breeding birds, this is a journey of 15,000km each way, making it the longest recorded passerine migration: achieved by a bird weighing only as much as four €1 coins!

On migration, ploughed or fallow fields, golf courses and coastlines are frequented. In keeping with an edgy personality, display flights are frenetic. Vociferous males launch into a steep ascent and shuttlecock back to earth, like a hat hurled aloft at a passing-out ceremony. A spread tail – flashing more white than is visible in normal flight – accompanies the performance. Song bursts are fast, brief and scratchy. Ad hoc mimicry is included. Impersonations are lightning fast and may be so tightly interwoven that they pass undetected. Sometimes an alarm call is sampled – borrowed – from another species and put to a similar purpose. Wheatears are unsung mockingbirds; their parrot skills are sophisticated and come close to perfection. However, the imitations, through being masked by interpolated 'chaotic' notes and enunciated sotto voce, can be missed. Bootlegs overheard on Inishbofin, Galway, include Chough, Swallow, Skylark, Dunlin, Ringed Plover, Arctic Tern, Red-throated Pipit and Snow Bunting. In almost all cases, only alarm calls were reproduced. Probably, Chough was copied from Ireland – but not necessarily overhead in the spring when first broadcast. In other words, the bird remembered the sound. By the same token, excerpts from Arctic Tern and Snow Bunting reprised by migrant Greenland Wheatears in Ireland in late April – before Arctic Terns return – constitute flashbacks to the Land of the Midnight Sun, components of vocabulary that amount to a scrapbook of the bird's travels. Flight calls of Red-throated Pipit reflect the soundscape of African wintering quarters. Ethnic notes fall into two categories. A dry flat *wheet*, quite like a half-hearted referee's whistle, has a ventriloquist quality. The caller defies location. A hard, stone-knocking *tak* provides help. The two sounds are linked arbitrarily. A typical combination is *wheet* (then a gap) *tak, tak*. Away from breeding areas, the silence of migrants is legendary.

Wheatears are mercurial migrants. After a half-year absence they pop up in the same spot, looking fresh and new as a morning newspaper. Where have they come from? Desert fatigues garb is no accident; in previous days this female (left) would have been in northwest Africa. Frayed wing feathers are a clue to age – around ten months. The songbird weighs little more than three €2 coins. In Ireland, breeders patronise stony hillsides with short coastal turf. Here, in May, locals rub shoulders with larger cousins that fatten up before departing for Greenland and Canada, a journey they complete in one hop. With a know-all face like a teenager, a juvenile (right) looks good to go. The tail and wings are immaculate. Once frail bum-fluff plumage across the foreparts is moulted, it will quit Ireland by night.

Females arrive in April and a single brood is raised from a nest concealed in a hole, which may be used from year to year, although not necessarily by the same birds. The literature suggests that a second brood is quite common. For example, from 1948 to 1953, 47 per cent of pairs on Skokholm Island, Wales, laid two clutches (Conder 1989). Observations on Inishbofin, Galway, have not detected second broods (AMG). Findings from a population at Clee Hill, Shropshire, from 1998 to 2009 found second broods to be the exception (Fulton 2010). The first juveniles fledge in late May, suggesting that clutches were laid at the end of April. To begin with, youngsters are not as cautious as their parents, who grow agitated. Whatever the reason, Wheatear breeding plumage has a short shelf life. By late June adults look dishevelled. Feathering is spent and, especially in males, the honey yellow that fused the chest in April is blanched to a small bib of flaxen yellow. Livery approaches monochrome. After young fledge, adults look to their own needs. By July they moult and are hard to find. Juveniles quickly shed speckled first-generation feathers. On the wing in late May and June, they are grey-bodied except for bright terracotta edges to the wing-coverts and fawn fringes to wing and tail feathers. As post-juvenile moult advances from the belly towards the head, the changeling acquires a Frankenstein's-monster look with a grey speckled head

attached to a beige body. The sight of a new generation is memorable but is eclipsed by the appearance of migrants passing north just as local offspring fledge.

Data on the mean dates of arrivals in Iceland was made accessible at the instigation of Finnur Gudmundsson, Director of the Icelandic Museum of Natural History (Boyd 2003). Two things stood out. First, initial arrivals were at least a month later than those reaching even the most northerly parts of Ireland. Second, the vanguard hit northwest Iceland first, six days before the mean for the southeast. Both facts point to the use of Ireland and western Britain as a spring staging ground for Iceland's population. More intriguing is the likelihood that, as the season advances, Ireland and western Iceland serve as stepping stones for Wheatears venturing overseas, even further northwest.

'Greenland Wheatear' defines longer-winged populations that breed in Greenland and Canada. Members of this boreal tribe exude enthusiasm. Seen in our latitude during May, they are manic, revved up and keen to get home. Rather than hug the ground and perch on low promontories, they zoom up onto rooftops, telegraph poles and overhead wires. Even when not pushed, they fly off and may not alight until well out of sight. Their underparts are a swarthy false tan. Amid blue-grey upperparts on males, there is a wedge of dun. Regard the cheeks.

In autumn, juveniles and adult females are similar; adult males look masked. Migrants flit ahead and reveal a gleaming white rump, the corners of which jut into a black tail. When spotted, perched individuals vault from walls and fence posts, as if to say 'missed again!'

Migrant males show brown flecking. On females, the upperparts are brown, not grey. On some, the exigencies of an epic migration prompt the retention of frayed wings and tails that have served nine months and clocked up over 10,000km. Although renewed annually – in late summer – they are scruffy.

Autumn recoveries suggest that Greenland Wheatears perform a non-stop crossing of the North Atlantic, making landfall in a great arc from western Ireland to southwest France and Iberia. Salomonsen (1967a) proposed that Wheatear populations breeding in Iceland and Greenland had evolved a transoceanic migration that takes advantage of wind associated with depressions. In autumn, by passing behind and south of low-pressure centres tracking over Ireland, a migrant's at-sea odyssey is boosted by northwest tailwinds. In spring, southeast airflows directed towards Iceland occur at the front of approaching depressions. For this reason, spring migration follows a more northerly vector, through Ireland and Britain. In late August, before starting, fat reserves are laid down. Based on studies of captive birds, Ottosson *et al.* (1990) found that the relative increase in the pre-migratory body mass of Greenland Wheatears was almost twice as high as that of Wheatears breeding in Scandinavia. September occurrences on the Selvagens, islands between Madeira and the Canary Islands, demonstrated that freshly arrived migrants had low weights – some almost half the estimated departure weight – symptomatic of having completed an airborne marathon (Lyngs 2003). Indeed, it was postulated (Thorup *et al.* 2006) that birds breeding in West Greenland and Canada may accomplish migration to their wintering grounds in West Africa in one direct, transatlantic crossing of more than 4,000km – a supposition that may well be correct.

In July 2010, light-level geolocators weighing 2g were attached to migrants departing from Baffin Island, Canada. They revealed breathtaking confirmation of a transoceanic flight: one bird managed to retain a geolocator all the way to wintering quarters in Mauritania and back. Leaving Baffin Island, the 25g songbird flew about 3,400km to its next location somewhere in western Ireland. It completed the journey in no more than four days – an average flying speed of 35km per hour. Although the flight path may have overflown southern Greenland, the bird was almost certainly airborne for the duration. Probably, it left with a tailwind. Based on studies at Helgoland, Germany, Wheatears are known to synchronise departures in a migratory direction with nocturnal tailwinds (Schmaljohann & Naef-Daenzer 2011). Just as amazingly, the return leg in spring involved a repeat performance. Departing from a location somewhere in western Britain or Ireland, it recrossed the same vast sweep of ocean to touch down in Baffin Island. Such mind-bending revelations add even more wonder to witnessing nine migrants fluttering in a strong headwind and rain around the *Celtic Explorer* at 53°33'N 14°38'E in the early hours of 23 August 2009 (AMG). The nearest land was the island of Inishshark, Galway, 300km due east. For well over an hour they circled but did not land. However, migrants resting like shuttlecocks on splayed wings have been seen taking off from glassy calm in the Bay of Biscay during August (AL). Mother Nature breeds a tough cookie.

DUNNOCK
Prunella modularis

The bill is slim and fine-tipped, designed to apprehend tiny soft prey. Therein lies a problem – feeding demands are constant, especially when rearing a family. Hopping is incessant and accompanied by a quick-fire tail flick. Stationary upright poses are not used to spot ground prey. Instead, Dunnocks hunch forward like a stressed typist.

SUBURBIA'S GREEN SPACES are a potpourri of different habitats, most of which exist in microcosm – a patch of trees here, a hedge there, and lawns and shrubbery in between. Some birds thrive in this manicured setting. Dunnocks occur at fewer than one pair per square kilometre in the New Forest, England, compared to thirty pairs per square kilometre among farmland and gardens in the English Midlands. The species name is derived from Old English *Dunn*, meaning grey-brown, a nod to a plumage collage that fits shadowy stems and leaf litter, although in spring wear turns grey to a superb almost-blue. Feeding action is vigorous and large feet are used to thrust vegetation aside and seize anything edible. Shuffling on the ground, the bird has a distinctive forward-leaning stance. Asymmetric flicking of just one wing punctuates movements. Calling is frequent – a hiss-loud *seeh*! The note is delivered in a high key and evokes an anxious disposition. Autumn migrants call early in the morning. If answered, the single note is doubled once an acquaintance is found. Another construct of the same fundamental sound is an accelerated, bouncy *he' he' he' heeh*. A short fiery song is delivered from a sunlit perch on the first fine day of the new year. Females sing to attract males, an unusual aspect in bird behaviour but less

surprising for Dunnock, given the matriarchal structure of the bird's breeding behaviour. The composition attracts unimpressive reviews in field guides, yet it is 'breathless' with no gaps or gear changes – just galloping gusto from start to finish.

The species feeds on small invertebrates. Collecting food is time-consuming, especially when rearing nestlings. To lighten the parental load, a female recruits more than one husband. Each male wishes to father the brood. This gives rise to sperm competition and one husband is openly favoured and made to feel dominant, while the other is granted clandestine mating access. Occasional chases and agitated calls are a sign that high jinks have broken out. The female deliberately plays one off against the other. Separately, and out of sight of the rival, the senior male regularly attempts to accompany the female and peck at her sexual organ (cloaca) beneath the tail. Small white capsules of sperm are stored here, which can be jettisoned if the female so wishes. She exercises power by demonstrably ejecting the sperm capsule of one male in front of the other – who is then granted conjugal rites. The winner is the female who acquires two male helpers. In fact, DNA fingerprinting shows that chicks within broods often have different fathers (Davies 1983).

HOUSE SPARROW
Passer domesticus

As early as February, love is in the air for male House Sparrows. They chirrup ad nauseam and the bill turns slate-coloured as a mark of breeding condition. If a female is caught watching, she is serenaded at close range and treated to a display of flamenco dancing: the suitor droops his wings and sets them a-quiver.

HOUSE SPARROWS ARE SOCIAL, and life revolves around a breeding colony, sometimes consisting of just a few souls. Sources of food are found by scouts and quickly tapped. Nous and alacrity are part of the psyche. A female surreptitiously shadowed a foraging Blackbird and seized worms from its bill when it peered fixedly ahead for fresh prey (AMG). Once settled in a colony, new recruits remain there for life. Youngsters do a certain amount of exploring, although ringing suggests that a sense of adventure is lacking, since distances scarcely exceed 30km. At Copeland Bird Observatory, where the species does not breed, migrants are uncommon, although formerly regular. From 1955 to 2005, sightings decreased from annual (1955–69) to rare (six records between 1969 and 1987) and, since 1996, none. These figures chime with an overall national decline, with a pool of fewer individuals performing nomadic post-breeding dispersal. A propensity to fly over the sea is, however, not completely anathema because a breeding population of roughly a dozen pairs on Inishbofin, Galway, largely disappears in late summer. Presumably, they fly back to the mainland, 5km across the sea. Elsewhere, vagrants arrive on remote offshore islands; several have reached Sable Island, 180km east of Nova Scotia, Canada.

In England, colour-marked birds dispersed to fields of ripening grain in July and August. By September, when the grain was harvested, flocks dwindled (numbers exceeded 500) and adults returned to respective colonies, whereas juveniles scattered across a home range within which all colonies were located. Individuals 'on a mission' fly high. Their demeanour is surprisingly rapid, almost powerful; so much so that their identity as humble House Sparrows could easily be doubted. One clue is a distinctive wingbeat, shared with Tree Sparrow. The wings whirr and become a total blur between brief shallow glides.

Males differ between the seasons. During autumn and winter the bill is buttery yellow and the black breast bib is smaller and less noticeable, through being obscured by pale fringes. In spring, particularly during March and April, males are at their best and exhibit shiny black bills and almost burgundy head plumage abutting a nimbus-grey crown. Cloudy cheeks yield to white around the margins of a black bib. Small print creates a grumpy look, particularly a thin furrow of pale that curls like a puckered brow from the eye across the top of black lores, and a white wisp behind the eye. Virtues of female plumage are unsung. In reality, she is fetching, especially in late winter and early spring. Seen

Sparrow respectively. Both species spread from their centres of origin with the advance of agriculture. The House Sparrow had probably been in England since Roman times.

Until autumn-sown cereals replaced those planted during spring, late-summer mobs of House Sparrows were commonplace across arable districts. As recently as the 1980s a drive along rural roads bordering harvested cereal fields was almost guaranteed to stir flocks picking spilled grain. Dense parcels rose as from a shaken rug and whirred into hedges, the grey rumps of males easily marking them out. Those days are gone. Moreover, arable crops are harvested so assiduously that virtually nothing is left in stubble or in farmyards. Annual herbs and grasses – debased by the term 'weeds' – are sprayed, removing insect food and seed from the food chain. Across towns and suburbs uPVC has blocked off nest sites. Garden pests are brought to their knees with pesticides, and urban front gardens converted from untidy grass (and food-rich dandelions) to inert low-maintenance fashion statements or paved lifeless parking spaces. It transpires that, although adults are able to eke out an existence, chicks starve to death. For the first fortnight of life, baby sparrows are weaned on small insects, aphids especially. Small caterpillars are also an important food. The creepy-crawlies are not there any more. Flowerbeds (House Sparrows peck the bases of flowers to get at nectaries) and garden hedges are fast becoming anachronisms.

Decline is a word in common currency. However, the picture is complicated and most farmyards still resound to the chirping of sparrows. Disease is a fact of life in all bird populations. By applying a basic knowledge of epidemiology, there may be a plausible basis for believing that illness is exerting an influence. Neville McKee conceived the idea, which applies in equal measure to Tree Sparrow:

My hypothesis is that disease is continually lurking, but wanes when the population is reduced by it. When it fades almost completely, numbers start to recover. As fresh progeny expand, they eventually come into contact with a core still carrying the disease. Alas the resurgent waves will, most likely, lack immunity. Ergo, the disease reappears and a downward spiral begins once more. Importantly, where the population is discontinuous, pockets survive through isolation or because, through time, they have developed better resistance. Given the parochial nature of House Sparrow distribution, new recruits may be slow to arrive – if they arrive at all. (NMK, pers. comm.)

alone and out of habitat, females generate puzzlement. The supercilium is eye-catching and harks of something rare. The eye sits in a porthole and sandy-coloured cheeks flush grey in a rear hotspot, an echo of grey-faced male plumage. Paralleling the change in male bill colour, her bill switches in late winter from yellowish horn with a darker, dusky pink tip, to neutral grey with, on some, a hint of mustard yellow across the base of the lower mandible. Both sexes occasionally fluff up rump plumage and link it with flounced flanks, creating an amorphous fawn petticoat. The appearance is cuddly, but somewhat dashed when the wearer begins rolling in dust to dislodge parasites. A certain paradox exists. Despite living under our noses, House Sparrows are nervous and feeding groups startle at the drop of a hat. If anything, their corporate antenna is more sensitive than that of Starlings.

How come House Sparrows live in association with us and do not have a 'natural habitat'? Denis Summers-Smith (1984) explains:

The next major factor in the history of the sparrows was the transition of Man from a hunter-gatherer to a sedentary agriculturist at the end of the Pleistocene about 10,000 years ago. The sparrows, preadapted to the seeds of grasses that were the precursors of the cultivated cereals (wheat, barley, rice), were prime candidates to exploit the situation. Of twenty species, 60 per cent show some association with Man, nesting in buildings, and feeding on cereal crops, scraps around houses and feed put out for domestic animals. The two populations best placed for this were the birds living in the Fertile Crescent of the Middle East and the Yellow River Valley in present-day China, the centres where agriculture originated: the putative ancestors of the House Sparrow and Tree

House Sparrows possess an encyclopaedic knowledge of feeding opportunities. Being resident and sedentary, it is imperative that they find food locally throughout the year. They have tricks up their sleeve. One habit that infuriates gardeners is a penchant for snipping crocus petals from opening blooms. The activity looks like vandalism, but in reality, the bird is probably checking for hidden insects.

By way of corollary, Bruce Mactavish commented on the discontinuous nature of a decline in parts of eastern Newfoundland, Canada: 'During the late 1980s, House Sparrows were abundant in St John's, Newfoundland. Then, inexplicably, they vanished. Sometimes a few reappear but do not prosper. Meanwhile, in isolated rural areas there are many healthy pockets, yet survival needs appear to be met for both groups, especially the widespread provision of feeders during winter' (BM, pers. comm.).

Thompson (1849–52) described the species as common throughout Ireland. Dig a little deeper, and his narrative is spellbinding and prescient:

This bird is in some places much persecuted by individuals who, knowing the injury committed by it on the grain-crops and in the garden, are yet ignorant of the great benefit conferred by its destruction of caterpillars. A sparrow-destroying order given forth in our juvenile days may here be mentioned. An old soldier, who had been in the Peninsular War, was, on that account, selected from the farm labourers as being, axiomatically, the best shot. With plenary instructions to destroy all sparrows, he spent day after day in going about the cornfields for the purpose of shooting them. The report of his gun was frequently heard, but no testimony in the shape of sparrows was ever produced. Whenever he saw that two or three sparrows had alighted together on the standing corn sufficiently near, which was by no means seldom, he fired at them. Often as he did so, not a bird fell, though how much of the grain was thereby sacrificed, we cannot take upon ourselves to say, for *it* could not be missed. The shooter would not believe that this result was owing to his want of skill, and more than once trampled down the grain to look for the imaginary fallen birds, which were in reality afar off rejoicing in their escape. When the wages of this sportsman, and the value of the ammunition he expended, together with the grain destroyed by him, are considered, there can be little doubt that the amount of damage that the sparrows could have done (and nevertheless did do) must be trivial in comparison. Many well-attested accounts have been published of the destruction of crops by insects, in consequence of small birds being destroyed for their pilfering propensities. When in France in 1841, I was made aware of a recent instance of this kind. In the fine rich district of Burgundy, sparrows had, some time before, been destroyed in great numbers. An extraordinary increase of caterpillars and other injurious insects soon became apparent, and occasioned such immense damage to the crops that a law was passed prohibiting the future destruction of the birds.

TREE SPARROW
Passer montanus

Tree Sparrows look dapper – Charlie Chaplin moustache, chocolate cap, white cheeks with black earphones. The sexes are similar and share incubation duties. In big brother House Sparrow, the female incubates alone.

TREE SPARROWS ARE SVELTE. The head is cocoa-coloured and the plumage deep pile; think of a fur hat. The juxtaposition of black, brown and white masks the position of the eye, emphasising a black-feathered 'pupil' on snowy cheeks. The voice is metallic and sudden: *chip!* and *teck!* notes pepper the vocabulary. In flight, a knocking *tet, tet, tet* is distinctive, reminiscent of impacting ball bearings. Breeders utilise narrow-entranced cavities, typically in abandoned wallsteads, though spacious nest-boxes are readily accepted. Male and female are similar. Juveniles have a grey centre to the crown and a duller black cheek spot. In winter, lookalike bands join finch flocks roaming weedy fields and stubbles for seed. Come the breeding season, insects are crucial for chick growth, and adults turn to marshy ground, especially ditch banks, for provender. Thompson (1849–52) wrote: '[The Tree Sparrow] appears in Templeton's *Catalogue of Irish Vertebrate Animals* "as a doubtful native"; but to my ornithological friends and myself is quite unknown. The species is only partially distributed in England and has not been found in Scotland.' Although Thompson's comment was accurate for Ireland, his remark about status in Scotland was wrong. Summers-Smith (1984b) states: 'It is not known when the Tree Sparrow first arrived in Britain and Ireland – the earliest record that I can find is for Scotland (Sibbald 1684), oddly

preceding that for England: a bird collected in Yorkshire in May 1720. The Tree Sparrow was present in the Western Isles and the adjoining west coast of Scotland from 1758 (even on St Kilda) ... though it had disappeared [from St Kilda] by 1930 [the date of human evacuation there].'

The bird possesses a propensity for sudden population bursts, often followed by contraction. Its history in Ireland is entirely in this vein. According to Ussher and Warren (1900), the first specimen came from Dublin. Breeding occurred (no population estimates are given) and by 1898 a Dr Patten remarked: 'The Tree Sparrow seems to be extending its range. This year I noticed double the number about Baldoyle, and I obtained a specimen from Crumlin (eight miles from Baldoyle).' Immigration continued and pioneers fanned west, leapfrogging overland and not halting until confronted by the North Atlantic, whereupon they put down roots on islands and headlands. The most remarkable record is that from the barren monolith of Blackrock, west of Mayo, where a pair bred among cliffs in 1939.

By the mid-1950s the species was in rapid retreat. Kennedy *et al.* (1954) stated: 'Although formerly the Tree Sparrow had well-established colonies, these have either ceased to exist or the numbers present are very small. Donegal alone seems to be where the bird maintains a precarious foothold, though even there it

Populations of Tree Sparrows periodically wane, then rebound. At times they disappear completely, dwindling to the point of extinction. The new millennium has, so far, witnessed unprecedented growth. During previous colonising bursts, pioneers virtually encircled coastal districts but failed to penetrate far inland. Not this time. Colonies have been founded in Armagh, Carlow, Laois and Kilkenny.

has decreased considerably.' By 1959 the species was deemed extinct. Its disappearance was not, however, matched by a concomitant decline in Britain. There, numbers grew. In 1960, migrants pushed across the Irish Sea. Five years later a staggering plantation of fifty-six colonies existed, mapped by Ruttledge (1966). Yeomanry had once again encircled the Irish coastline. A novel feature was the establishment of bases at Lough Beg and a handful of sites around Lough Neagh. Since then, fluctuations have occurred but, by and large, numbers in the Lough Neagh basin have not withered. Meanwhile, in Britain, the BTO estimated that, between 1970 and 2001, the population shrank by 94 per cent. Unpredictable as ever, a great renaissance began around 2009. During 2010, breeding strongholds prospered and, despite bitter winter weather, flocks numbering upwards of 100 roamed widely. Imbued with innate wanderlust, echelons subsequently pushed further afield. Echoing events not witnessed since the boom years of the 1950s, small flocks reached several offshore islands – but only along the west and north coasts. Rathlin and Tory witnessed influxes and parties arrived on Inishbofin, Galway in the spring and summer of 2011.

Population explosions are borne of adequate food supply and driven by fecundity. Collared Dove is a prime example. However, the vicissitudes of Tree Sparrow's boom and bust is far more puzzling. What is going on? Outbreaks of disease could underpin the cyclical nature of events (see the House Sparrow account, which outlines a hypothesis). By way of potential corroboration, dead adults have periodically been found in nest-boxes at Portmore Lough. All birds are afflicted by parasites that live on the exterior of the body (ectoparasites) or internally (endoparasites). There are several categories of endoparasite, including *Nematoda* (roundworms). Heavy infestations can kill. Larvae occur in the bloodstream and feed by affixing themselves to tissue walls. Evolution has produced organisms adapted specifically to certain groups of birds or to particular feather tracts or types of nest. This secret world ebbs and flows unseen. In some species, such as Blue Tit, pristine plumage serves as a bill of health, proof of a low parasite loading that confers mating advantage. Comparatively little is known of the machinations of birds' internal fauna except that, each year, microscopic armies of Davids fell an unknown number of Goliaths.

YELLOW WAGTAIL
Motacilla flava

2 May 1917 was a particularly black day in the history of the Yellow Wagtail in Ireland. Alas, it was just one of a series of breeding season killing sprees that undoubtedly led to the bird's extinction at the hands of well-heeled collectors.

FROM THE URAL MOUNTAINS all the way west to Wales this, the doyen of wagtails, is a summer visitor. These days, Ireland falls outside the breeding range. During the nineteenth century it was locally common, mainly along lakeshores in Connacht and Ulster. Thompson (1849–52) was aware of a breeding hotspot along the northwest coast of Lough Neagh, around Toome. On 3 August 1846 he saw ten birds (including juveniles) where the River Bann flows out of the lake, the exact place being described as 'the margin of the lake below the bridge [at Toome].' Ussher and Warren (1900) published details of a second concentration that was discovered along the southern shore of Lough Neagh. Robert Warren visited both areas sometime in the late 1800s. He reported:

> The Lough Neagh colony, so long supposed to be the only one, seems divided. I found the bird common at Toome Bridge, and thence along the Bann to Lough Beg, and again along the south shores of the lake in the counties of Armagh and Tyrone. The Armagh shore is a peat district, where turf-cutting is done extensively, and the nests are often placed beside banks or sods of peat, shaded perhaps by a plant. I saw one among oats under a thistle. Although the bird was abundant near the lake, I saw none at any distance from it; but it is stated to range inland in Armagh two miles, and to arrive about 10 April.

Writing in 1954, Kennedy *et al.* declared the species extinct:

> In the district near Lurgan known as The Montiaghs, where the Yellow Wagtail bred plentifully in the bogs, numbers

commenced to dwindle in 1922, and it was not long before a general decrease became noticeable in all the Lough Neagh haunts. Around Lough Beg a few were still breeding in 1942, but there too the bird was decreasing. In 1941 in an area that had been particularly favoured, not one was seen.

Reasons for the inexorable retreat are unclear. One factor that cannot be underestimated was the wanton collecting of adults, nests and eggs in the breeding season. This happened along the southern shore of Lough Neagh and may well have been repeated elsewhere in Ireland given the process that fuelled the slaughter – a frenzy of avarice to own a curio. The 'trophies' are in the Ulster Museum, complete with dates and locations. They also contain the names of those who killed them, the chief assassin being Herbert Malcolmson. 'Irish' Yellow Wagtail is no longer with us. However, vagrants sometimes occur and isolated pairs have bred. From 1956 to 1958 a small population became established at Belfast Harbour Estate among pools in wet grassland. Three pairs nested in 1958 and, based on plumage, originated from the breeding range of Ashy-headed (Yellow) Wagtail, which breeds south of the Alps, mainly in Italy. Occasional migrants are still drawn to the spot, designated a Nature Conservation Area by Belfast Harbour Commissioners. Ten years of habitat restoration – with plans to introduce Tarpan Horses (Konik ponies) gifted by a Polish nature reserve as part of a portfolio of measures designed to maintain wet meadows likely to attract Yellow Wagtails – have been left to wither by RSPB.

GREY WAGTAIL
Motacilla cinerea

A breeding resident of fast-flowing rocky streams, the Grey Wagtail also patronises slow-moving rivers if weirs or mill races create turbulent water attracting aquatic insects, the bird's main food. Absent from North America, the species' stunning appearance is well known among that continent's birdwatchers who, if visiting Ireland, put it at the top of a 'must-see' list.

THE NAME IS CONFUSING. Far more distinctive than 'morning-suit grey' upperparts is a lanky bobbing tail attached to a brilliant yellow backside. The legs are pale and rather short, bestowing a low centre of gravity. Flight is deeply undulating yet remarkably smooth: an airborne kangaroo. Calls signal an incoming singleton. The note is superficially similar to the *chissick* of Pied Wagtail but of superior cut-glass clarity, piercing and split into two emphatic halves: *jeet-jeet*. Home turf is rushing streams and ravines. In several cities – Cork, Dublin and Belfast included – Grey Wagtails occupy a lofty niche and snatch insects from gutters and undisturbed standing water on flat roofs. The song is a pleasant buzzing shuttle of stammered *zee* notes.

During winter, Grey Wagtails take up residence in habitats where water is the common denominator. Coastlines, especially at freshwater outflows, are frequently patronised. Pairs come together in March. Tyler (1972) found that 97 per cent of 699 nests were built close to running water. Bridges attracted 178 nests; other recorded sites included ledges in sheds, notably fishing huts; ledges in quarries; old ruins; drainpipes in walls; and the roofs of houses. Some nests are built close to those of Dippers and Pied Wagtails that live amicably in the same habitat. During courtship, the male hovers and dances like a puppet, flashing hi-vis yellow. Gradually, he turns black-throated, save for a thin white moustache. Two broods are raised and then the pair separate. Youngsters disperse widely, some reaching the Mediterranean and North Africa. Sociability is not a hallmark so, unlike Pied Wagtail, communal roosts are unknown.

PIED WAGTAIL
Motacilla alba

A WILLOWY BALLERINA pattering on tiptoe across the lawn, in a flash crouching low and lungeing after an insect nestling in the sward, then darting skywards in pursuit of airborne prey, is a familiar sight. Bizarrely, filling station forecourts are also patronised. The bird snatches flies from bare surfaces – concrete walls, pavements and the margins of muddy puddles – and has the knack of picking tiny grubs from loose earth of any sort, including rubble coated with a veneer of weeds. In wet habitats, Pied Wagtail is as likely as a Technicolor Grey Wagtail, though fast-flowing streams tend to be the exclusive preserve of the latter.

Accompanying a bounding flight, Pied Wagtail's *chizzick* call has a 'looseness' that is hard to put into words. To get a feel for the sound, try shaking a fistful of change. Sometimes the *zz* component may not be emphasised; a smoother *chi-chik* or harder *chiddick* transcription might be more apt. Occasionally the caller shifts to a higher key: *fizz-eep!* At rest, depending on mood, a wider vocabulary is used, among which is a cheery *T'is you!* The second syllable is variable and sometimes truncates to *T'is up!* In essence, Pied Wagtail is an incorrigible polyglot. Among the repertoire is supercharged twittering, directed at anything irksome from transgressing rivals to stalking cats or us if we wander over an invisible territorial line.

Outside the breeding season communal roosting is widespread. Well-lit street trees are popular. Famously, a London Plane tree in Dublin's O'Connell Street held 600 birds in 1930–31 and was used for six months of the year. By 1934 two trees held 2,000 and three were in use until at least 1950, by which year 3,600 were present (Kennedy *et al.* 1954). Although generally believed to be resident, Pied Wagtails disperse widely. Some wintering birds are Scottish, and Irish offspring reach Britain and Europe.

Populations breeding in Ireland, Britain and a sliver of the adjacent coast of Europe, are truly 'Pied' Wagtails. In full breeding plumage (acquired in early spring) males are the epitome of dapper and, for the only time in the year, the plumage is purged of grey. A black throat connects the chest with sooty upperparts. Adults of either sex disport a plaster of Paris white face and an honest eye. Juveniles have much grey on the forehead, a quizzical dark brow above the eye and softly speckled cheeks. In autumn, a lemon sorbet facial wash (indicative of new plumage) is present on many, irrespective of age. By October juveniles have moulted to become first-winters. Indications of age include plain grey upperparts and a smudged face with, compared to adults, less pristine foreheads and stippling on the cheeks. Crown and nape plumage is a mix of black and grey. Outside the breeding season, adult males are still predominantly black-backed and show broad white sides to the greater coverts, linking with the median coverts and forming virtually a panel. Females and first-winters show two less-connected wing-bars. Especially on adult males, the forward limit of the black crown cap barely extends past a point directly above the eye. Much white separates cap and bill, accentuating a nun-like face. First-winters are less angelic and have a mixture of cloudy grey or sooty plumage forward of the eye. Outside the breeding season, partnerships are commonplace. One of the pair may be a youngster and both individuals may be of the same sex.

Across Europe and in Iceland, the species goes under the title White Wagtail and has a different appearance, with a pearl-grey back and an almost white flank. Migrants cross our latitude in spring and early autumn, travelling back and forth between breeding grounds in Iceland to winter quarters in Spain and North Africa. They follow a more northerly route in spring, availing of southeast airflows blowing to Iceland. In autumn, northwesterly airstreams are utilised. In high plumage in late April and early May, adults are a fine sight. Males have snowy underparts and immaculate 'morning-suit grey' upperparts that contrast dramatically with a black crown and nape. In autumn differences are less clear cut. A winning combination is silvery-grey flanks with a grey, not black, rump. A preference for coastal habitats and lakeshores, and a tendency towards skittish behaviour are other useful steers. When disturbed, White Wagtails tend to fly high and vamoose: hallmarks of a revved-up migrant, rather than a pottering Pied Wagtail. Cleaner than average first-winter Pied Wagtails can be perplexing. Some combine homogenous medium-grey upperparts with what appear to be eye-catching pale flanks. In sunlight, grey flanks can blanch and take on a distinctly pale hue. Keep watching. When the bird is out of direct sunlight the flanks revert to smoky grey. Furthermore, the presence of an 'air-brushed' dingy grey wash on the side of the chest indicates Pied Wagtail. The chest sides on White Wagtail are pearl grey.

Black-and-white plumage and a bobbing tail make Pied Wagtail instantly recognisable. Seasonal changes affect the appearance of all. Moreover, distinctively patterned 'White Wagtails', migrating between southwest Europe and Iceland, pass through Ireland, mainly in April. Male Pied Wagtails are black-backed throughout the year; in spring they acquire a black throat. Females have grey backs and a somewhat smaller bib. Juvenile plumage is 'complex' with more patterning on the head and chest than either parent, and they exude a hint of brown. Smartest of all, White Wagtails have a clean back and sides. 1) juvenile, July; 2) first-winter, September; 3) first-winter (to show variation), October; 4) adult female in November; 5) adult female acquiring breeding plumage in March; 6) adult male in October; 7) adult male in breeding plumage, March; 8) White Wagtail, adult male in April.

MEADOW PIPIT
Anthus pratensis

Naming and locating all parts of Meadow Pipit plumage would amount to an end-of-term examination. Few species delineate feather tracts with such individualism, and all in the name of camouflage. A grid of pale tramlines and interlocking shadows are lost against bent grass and weathered heather. Frayed edges to the inner greater coverts and tertials (see Under the Hood, p. 12) also tab the feathers over six months old. The bird regrew these feathers in late summer, a clue that the photograph was taken in the following spring.

Variation in appearance arises through wear and tear. During the breeding season adults come to look grey. Technically, feathers are inanimate, lifeless objects, but the strain of raising a family wilts their outward appearance. For safety, youngsters leave the nest before they can fly and gradually moult speckled head plumage. By autumn both generations sport new – similar – coats. The colours are rich and seem to glow from within. October is Meadow Pipit's finest hour.

IF MEADOW PIPITS could hire a PR agent they might achieve stardom. Unsung 'little brown jobs' with a jaunty wagtail strut and a permanently startled face, they perform a derring-do migration over the eastern North Atlantic, upon which they cannot land. Each autumn, squadrons sweep south from Iceland, Scotland and western Scandinavia. Most do not stop, trekking on to France, Iberia and Morocco. Despite being disposed to emulate Amelia Earhart, flight style looks ineffectual – jerky and swishy – as though the bird is treading water. Calls accompany take-off, a variable salvo of lisping *seep* notes, commonly doubled or trebled, then reprised as a single call. Formerly, breeding birds were ubiquitous across lowland. Tangled grass is made for them. Spidery feet and a veritable *Guinness Book of Records* hind claw bestow an ability to walk through stalks and snatch craneflies.

Perched on overhead wires they appear to be wearing crampons (EK). Alas, wall-to-wall silage has extirpated the sprite from sterile, lifeless fields. The remaining strongholds are on moorland, bog, untamed edges of forestry plantations, and hillsides and coastlines too steep to cultivate or graze. Fencelines excluding sheep not only save nesting habitat, they also make perfect perches. Decline spells bad news for Ireland's Cuckoos, whose eggs evolved to match Meadow Pipit. In spring, courtship flights are spectacular. The performer sails aloft and, cup-winged, descends to the metre of a squeaky bicycle song-flight whose dénouement is a wiry, ecstatic flourish. The display of Rock Pipit is similar. Careful listening suggests that the stronger notes of Rock Pipit 'echo'.

ROCK PIPIT
Anthus petrosus

ROCK PIPITS poke among rotting seaweed for Sea Slaters, Kelp Flies and other creepy-crawlies that live in the intertidal zone or in habitats above the high-tide mark wetted by spray. On vegetated offshore islands, territories incorporate both field and shore. In Antrim and Down, numbers mysteriously declined during the early 1970s. Previously, small flocks foraged together; nowadays distribution is linear, spread out thinly at regular intervals. Disease probably explains the changed pattern; those that survived are slowly repopulating vacant habitat (NMK).

It would be easy to characterise Rock Pipit as Meadow Pipit's ugly sister, a rejected prototype turned down on account of being bulky and, somehow, thrush-like. By midsummer, the cumulative effects of a hammering by salty wind, coupled with high levels of ultraviolet rays, are obvious. Atlantic coast populations and those inhabiting islands in the Irish Sea are the most dishevelled. Feather tracts that are constantly exposed to sunlight and spray, such as the tertials and central tail feathers, are dog-eared and bleached; in particular, wear can reduce the latter to a mere shaft by as early as May. Facially, a snuff-coloured whisker emerges through abrasion. Then, when plumage is moulted in late summer, patterns are reborn. At the same season, the new generation of juveniles undergo a partial moult, replacing body plumage and the smaller feathers of the wing. By autumn, all ages sport new garb, from House Mouse brown to Barbour jacket green. Nonetheless, compared to Meadow Pipit, detail looks blurry and 'smoked'. On home turf, dusky maiden colours are svelte and the bird treads lightly, like someone walking in the dark. The eye is alluring. Feathering between the bill and eye (topographically speaking, the loral area) is dark, exaggerating a white eye-ring. The throat is light and isolated like a baby's bib, entrapped by messy grey margins. A dribbled line of dark speckles denotes where a full-blown throat stripe should be, but is not. The line terminates in an anvil-shaped 'hotspot'. Drab tones are themed in legs and bill. In spring, adult bills turn shiny graphite-grey and the legs darken. On many, bill shape undergoes a minor modification. Presumably a reflection of growth modified by abrasion, the bill becomes attenuated, with the lower mandible angled slightly upwards, like a pencil over-sharpened on one side. Youngsters have a pale bill base bleeding across the lower mandible and, to begin with, dusty-pink legs.

In flight, or when the tail is spread at rest (see (3) below), pale plumage is revealed – restricted to a smoky sliver at the tail's corner. When closed, the pair of large central feathers cloaks the remainder. In so doing, they bear the brunt of tough conditions imposed by a life spent among salt spray and rock. Note their excessive wear in (3) below. By comparison, Meadow Pipits have bright white outer tails, which show a greater contrast with adjoining black feathers. Flight calls are similar to Meadow Pipit but sharper. Heard close, the note has a rasping 'sandpaper' quality; like hissing *fleece!* but removing the 'l'. Display and song flights are akin to Meadow Pipit. The aerial song flight is also similar to Meadow Pipit, but Rock Pipit display is performed exclusively along coastline, within a stone's throw of the sea. Compared to Meadow Pipit, Rock Pipit's fuller-voiced lisps are more vibrant, as though a treble setting has been overdone, and give the impression that their 'bounce' is enhanced by the acoustics of the gullies and rock faces that comprise the environment. This is fallacious: the notes have an inherent echo. A metallic stutter – *tseu, tseu, tseu* – serves as an opening salvo. The notes gain momentum and, like verbal stitches, align in a regular series to form a trill that is used in song flight. At other times, territorial individuals give just the introductory notes.

Rock Pipits are migrants. Juveniles move to unknown destinations and wintering birds are a combination of overseas visitors and adults defending breeding territories. On some, acquisition of breeding dress during March reveals hints of pink on the chest and bluish across the back. Such birds are Scandinavian Rock Pipits, mostly Norwegian. They arrive late in autumn but, at that season, are indistinguishable from local birds.

Underneath a gruff exterior lurks a gentle soul. Smoky markings and a drab countenance match habitat, not personality. 1) Winter plumage. 2) Adult in spring. 3) Tail pattern: low-key pale corner. 4) Juvenile in summer.

CHAFFINCH
Fringilla coelebs

Two tribes of Chaffinches grace gardens and woody retreats. Breeding birds are resident and sedentary; few stray more than 5km from where they were born. Locals are outnumbered in winter by a massive exodus of migrants from northern Europe. It is calculated that at least 10 million cross the North Sea.

FAMILIARITY CAN BREED CONTEMPT. Chaffinches are universal in all habitats that contain anything more than just a few bushes. The highest densities are reached in tall mixed woodland of uneven structure, where as many as 300 pairs per square kilometre may be found. Males are multicoloured and never look drab. Even in low-key winter livery they are decked out with an astro-turf green rump, fawn-pink chest and russet upperparts. In early spring, a stone-grey balaclava turns powder blue and the back becomes chestnut. The change in appearance is brought about, not through moulting plumage, but by a process of abrasion whereby a few millimetres of each feather tip wears down to expose a different underlying colour. In this way most finches and buntings attain a special breeding plumage without

recourse to moulting. Female plumage is muted doe brown. Her upperparts have a chameleon quality and can exude an olive lustre. The raiment is remarkably effective at blending in among vegetation, especially autumn leaves and winter stubbles. A sideways twist brings dark nape bands into view. Depending on posture, the head profile can be smooth or, in an instant, sprout a peculiar step or 'overhang' at the junction of crown and nape.

Chaffinches feed on seeds and grain in winter. Throughout the rest of the year they are insectivorous. Young are reared on animal matter, particularly caterpillars and foliage-defoliating insects, as well as beetles and various larvae, gleaned from the ground. From spring onwards, foraging adults dart and sally, chasing flies like a rookie flycatcher. Canopy feeding is regular

Both sexes have a tropical-green rump. Revealed in an obliging posture, it often comes as a surprise. For a small songbird, the Chaffinch is long-lived. Ringing recoveries indicate a life expectancy of up to twelve years, no mean feat for Scandinavian populations that clock up an annual round trip of 4,000km to Ireland and Britain. Where cause of death is known, the majority died at the claws of cats.

in autumn. Groups retire to sycamores and alders, working the underside of leaves and sunlit bark for basking bugs. In flight, no other common bird reveals so much white, comprising a shoulder patch, two wing-bars and outer tail feathers. Local populations are remarkably sedentary. Ringing recoveries indicate that almost 90 per cent move no further than 5km from their birthplace, and the rest less than 50km (Newton 1972). Mainly youngsters make the longer movements. Basically, once a Chaffinch has bred in an area it tends to remain for life. Commencing in October, overseas visitors arrive, originating chiefly from Scandinavia. Migrants stream south through Denmark, reaching the Low Countries and crossing the southern North Sea at its narrowest point before spreading across Britain. Some, an unknown

number, reach Ireland by following this route. Others arc west from Norway and pass over and around Scotland before reaching Ulster. From here, flocks push south. The sexes differ in migratory habits. In the Latin name, *coelebs* denotes bachelor, a reference to the fact that, of those that remain in winter in Scandinavia, almost all are males. Hence, visitors to our latitude are predominantly females and youngsters. Principally during hard weather, resident Chaffinches join the winter birds, although later they separate and form homogenous parties.

Old-hand males return to the same breeding territories year after year, having fed and roosted there if winter was mild. During the first calm days in March they proclaim their presence with a ringing *chink!* The bird's German name, Fink, is onomatopoeic, derived from the cheery signature note. Depending on mood, calling intensity varies. Agitated callers impart verve: *Pink! Pink!* Airborne singletons and small parties do not twitter but emit a 'soft-edged' *tup...tup.* Alternative transcriptions are *toop, teup* or *choop.* The quality is less jarring than Greenfinch's 'hard-edged', trilled *j'rrrup.* Perched loners announce presence by bleating *fink,* often prefaced with *tup* calls. Hence, *tup ... tup* (the bird lands and looks around) *fink, fink – Fink!* Singing males belt out an air-punching ditty. Lasting around three seconds, it consists of stereotyped notes that end in an upswinging flourish. The momentum and pace suggest that the bird changes gear more than once to reach the climax. As ever, to commit the sound to memory, it pays to invent our own analogy: possibly a fast bowler picking up speed and then unleashing the ball?

Minor variation enables neighbours to recognise each other. In fact, most males have a selection of song types. Rivalry tests the singing mettle of males; females listen intently and are drawn to males with the widest repertoire. For this reason, a challenged male attempts to copy the song of a duellist. Unmated males may sing for most of the day. That is, 6 times a minute, 360 times an hour and, even allowing for feeding and preening breaks, at least 3,300 times in a 12-hour day. Territorial males, as well as singing full stanzas, often resort to shorthand. Typical is a clipped couplet – *de-feet* – or a liquid *chillip,* the latter similar to House Sparrow. In rainy weather, tirelessly repeated desultory *de-feet* notes seem to serve as a marker, put down to confirm presence when the airwaves are quiet.

The nest, woven by the female, is exquisite. Materials include moss, feathers, hair and cobwebs. The sculpture is a dead ringer for a lichen-covered woody protuberance. Indeed, lichen that adorns its exterior is often stripped from surrounding bark. Most clutches are started in early May. During incubation the female feeds herself and leaves the nest briefly every hour to snack on insects; the male accompanies her on these nibbling trips. Just one brood is reared and both parents feed chicks with whole insects carried in the bill.

BRAMBLING
Fringilla montifringilla

Above: The Brambling is abundant throughout the forests of northern Europe, especially birchwoods across the northern taiga. Insects are its staple diet in summer but become unavailable in autumn. Millions take off and head south. Seeds are the winter mainstay. Flocks scatter continent-wide. Unfortunately, Ireland is optional. If autumn weather is dominated by easterly tailwinds, arrivals can be expected and may continue well into winter.

Inset: Bramblings forage on the ground but will patronise feeders. Females can be overlooked among Chaffinches. A glimpse of orange across the wing quickly gives the game away.

THE SWEET-SOUNDING sobriquet is meaningless. Bramblings are the acme of winter finch flocks, riches among a plainclothed horde. Weedy pasture, crop stubble or garden feeding stations – especially where sunflower seed is provided – may strike lucky. Highly migratory, this is the only finch that completely vacates breeding areas and travels mainly by night. Although wintering across a huge arc of Europe and Asia, movements are capricious until beechmast is located. Because mast is rarely plentiful in one area over consecutive winters, flocks embark on an annual treasure hunt. Where they find manna, prospectors halt. The most spectacular assemblage on record was seen in the winter of 1951–52 near the Swiss town of Hünibach (Muhlethaler 1952, Schifferli 1953). Birds feeding in the district converged in pre-roosting flocks, which poured non-stop through a small valley to spend the night in conifers. The stream was constant for almost an hour and the numbers could be estimated. Thirty-six million were counted from one watch point. A similar number were reckoned to approach from another direction!

Across Ireland variable numbers appear each October, usually on the coat tails of immigrant waves of Chaffinches from Scandinavia (see Chaffinch account, above). When easterly airflows coincide with autumn departures, more travel west. Unlike Chaffinches, Bramblings have orange, not white, wing-bars and shoulder patches. The bar across the greater coverts contrasts against a white 'handkerchief' at the base of the primaries, all the more prominent because it runs against the grain of the wing. On males, the chest is drenched in amber, aglow against a white belly; on females, the chest colour is cinnamon. Good views reveal tartan upperparts and a chunky,

black-tipped yellow bill. On both sexes, the flanks are splattered with black hailstones. Females have dove grey neck-sides, a stripe of which leaps from blackish tramlines on the nape. On males, the head is singed like burnt toast, chiefly around the eye and forehead. A white rump can be surprisingly difficult to see. The whiny voice is a boon in long-range detection. The most distinctive note is a braying *nay* (or *nyeeep*), reminiscent of uncorking wine (JW). In flight, lone birds utter *chuc … chuc … chuc*. The tooth-sucking snippet is subtle. Helpfully, it is often rounded off with a trademark whine (www.xeno-canto.org, catalogue number XC 41285, recorded by Matthias Feuersenger at Heligoland, Germany, on 12 October 2009).

During winter, Bramblings feed on the ground. Watched closely, perhaps from a kitchen window, the technique for removing husk can be observed. Powerful muscles operate tongue and mandibles. Two parallel grooves inside the palate accommodate the edges of the lower jaw. With the aid of the tongue, a seed is clamped in one groove. The edge of the lower mandible is then raised. To split the husk, force is applied. Next, the tongue rotates the kernel and the husk falls away, often disintegrating down one side of the lower mandible. Job done, the grain is pushed into the gullet and stored. Many seed-eating birds wait until later before digesting. Like cows, they chew the cud at a time of their own choosing. Often this is around midday. During feeding bouts, the mandibles are in constant motion, although the head is still and alert. Sometimes several seeds are gathered in the mouth and processed as a batch. Effectively, the bird is shelling nuts, although its actions are more suggestive of peeling spuds.

Left: Female plumage is variable and is less colourful and more sombre than a male's. The butch bill is not becoming; neither is a moustachioed look.

Right: Green plumage is complemented by yellow highlights on the wing and tail – but also by bubblegum-pink legs and morning-suit-grey tertial feathers. Although a common bird, the adult male Greenfinch is sublime.

Inset: Adults lead streaky offspring to feeders stocked with sunflower seed at an early age. Aggressive, they dominate proceedings until they have had their fill. Entire local populations may be attracted to bird tables, leaving them vulnerable to disease outbreaks from the very hand that feeds them.

GREENFINCH
Chloris chloris

GREENFINCH HAS A VARIED DIET; the large bill enables the bird to disembowel rose hips, a food source over which they have a virtual monopoly, as with seeds of Elm and Yew. Formerly, farmland provided rich pickings. Standing cereals were eaten while ripening in July. After harvest, spilled ripe grains were gleaned from stubble fields, followed by a glut of germinating annual weeds in spring. Modern cultivation methods have changed all that. In the past, Greenfinches assembled at stackyards and threshing places during hard weather. Nowadays, many birds rely on garden feeders to get them through the winter. Becoming a feeder junkie can have a high cost. The protozoan *Trichomonas gallinae* thrives in water and moist environments and causes a yellow canker, blocking the throat. The affliction, known as *Trichomoniasis*, means the victim starves to death. Listlessness and unnatural tameness are symptoms. Many Greenfinches (up to 35 per cent in some areas) have succumbed, infected from water in birdbaths and drinking troughs. The disease can be kept at bay by removing mouldy seed and cleaning feeders and drinking receptacles with a 10 per cent solution of bleach.

Males are unmistakable and *Chloris chloris* is a nod to Khloros, Greek goddess of green vegetation. Female garb is dull and includes a butch whisker. Juvenile body plumage is profusely 'ticked' with fine pencil streaks. Greenfinches inhabit tall bushy cover, including dense hedgerows. Mature gardens complete its universe. At the first sign of spring, males deliver a beautiful 'float like a butterfly' display flight. The heavyweight performer is surprisingly elegant. Floaters can be mistaken for the year's first Swallow. The ballet is accompanied by a wheezy, 'stretched'

jeeeeee, somewhat analogous to the sensation of a calf muscle tug when shifting slowly from flat feet to standing on tiptoe. While sometimes given in isolation, the wheeze is usually prefaced with a shuttled and mellow *choop choop choop*, which may develop into a throaty trill: *j'j'j'rrrup*. The sound has a reverberating quality, as though something is rattling inside the bird's throat – akin to the whirring bounce of a pea inside a whistle. This is a standard, year-round call. The notes are often repackaged to form a juddering trio: *jup-jup-jup*. To help forge a memory, visualise the burst fitting an image of tower blocks. Airborne individuals are often monosyllabic: *chup!* Confusingly, Chaffinch has a not dissimilar *yup* or *tupe*. Greenfinch is more emphatic. Lone birds perched incognito emit a forlorn, little-boy-lost sigh: *jew*. The note has a peculiar rising twang.

Greenfinches like to nest near their peers. By the mid-1970s, a quarter of a million had been ringed in Britain and Ireland. This established that birds begin to disperse within a few weeks after fledging; that they move longer distances in their first-year than later in life; and that, having bred in an area, they tend to remain there, although once a member of a winter flock, individuals roam over a wide radius (Boyd 1931). At a garden roost in England, over 1,000 were ringed during two months, although never more than twelve were seen at once. While a proportion of wintering birds return to adjacent parts of western Scotland and northwest England to breed, there is no evidence to suggest that British Greenfinches migrate between regular breeding and wintering grounds (Newton 1972). Apparently, very few cross to Ireland.

GOLDFINCH
Carduelis carduelis

Two actions accompany most Goldfinch behaviour: fluttering and twittering. In flight, the birds undulate like a colourful, high-powered butterfly.

GOLDFINCHES get to places that other finches only dream about – the recesses of seed heads on thistles, burdock and teasel. They have big, spreading toes and an anvil-shaped bill whose reach spans the distance between prickly spikes, some of which may be turned down to facilitate access. Embedded seeds are removed using a gaping movement that prises spines aside and facilitates access. Males, by just a millimetre, are longer-billed than females. The tiny difference in bill elongation has a bearing on diet. Both Darwin (1871) and Newton (1972) noticed that males were better suited to feeding on teasel. Indeed, captive females obtained only a quarter of the seed quantity extracted by males. Bill length may influence choice of food plant and possibly direct more females to migrate. Based on ringing data, most of the wintering birds in Britain are males. Unused land, where nature is left to run wild, is often a hotspot. The rougher the farm, the better the chances of seeing black and yellow flurries swirling like autumn leaves onto banks of thistles. Juveniles can be a puzzle. Adult insignia of a black, white and red head – bringing to mind a bloodied bandage – are missing. Youngsters are baldpates; offspring from second broods are still unpatterned in October. Many are black-tailed. The white tail spots on juveniles wear away quickly (NMK).

Goldfinches are seldom quiet. Even during winter, parties sit high among bare twigs and break into song. The boundary between song and calls is blurred. Twitters, trills and buzzes are stitched together and have a 'spitting' quality. Characteristic in flight is a tinkling, repeated *pickle-it*. At rest, a whiny upscale *bay-bee* is given, paralleled in the repertoire of Greenfinch and Lesser Redpoll. When 'feeder wars' break out, combatants hiss like sizzling sausages; the angst reinforced by vibrating wings and an open-billed glare.

The tiny deep-cupped nest is hidden in tree canopy. Spiders' webs, used to create a stable foundation, serve as a holdfast in high winds. In the heyday of the cage bird trade Goldfinches were heavily persecuted, both here and in Britain. In 1860, on the coast at Worthing in Sussex, 132,000 were caught. Despite presence in every month, most breeding birds migrate south in autumn: a harsh simplicity, especially when your place is filled by immigrant waves of winter visitors. Movements are complicated and recoveries chart simultaneous migration 'exchanges' across both sides of the Irish Sea. Thanks to a greater number of recoveries in Britain, that population shows two directional tendencies. In autumn, some travel southeast to the Low Countries and northern France before tracking southwest and, in some cases, wintering in Spain. Meanwhile, others travel west, some to Ireland. In short, Goldfinch migration is enigmatic and may conceal a difference in strategy with respect to age and sex.

SISKIN
Carduelis spinus

Siskins are a small, versatile finch. The bill is elongated and the tip is deceptively decurved. Like a car mechanic, feeding birds spend a lot of time at odd angles, frequently wrestling with dangling cones of alder and birch and extracting seeds upside down. Although some appear to be resident, migrants from an endless sea of fir, larch and pine stretching across northern Europe periodically irrupt west, especially when a prolific season is followed by poor seed production. Hungry birds tackle innovative food sources from Dandelion seedpods (left, male) to aphids on nettle stems (inset, female).

HARK THE WORDS OF THOMPSON (1849–52): 'To my ornithological friends and myself, the Siskin is known only as a winter bird of passage, resorting at uncertain intervals to Ireland. That they may occasionally breed in some parts of Wicklow, and certain suitable localities in the north, is not improbable.' The fashion for planting ornamental conifers in large demesne woodlands encouraged nesting attempts during the early part of the twentieth century. Then, to achieve self-reliance in timber in the wake of the Second World War, government policy enshrined commercial afforestation as an upland land use. As forests matured during the 1970s, Siskins exploited the habitat. In fact, the bird is not averse to nesting in mixed plantations or oakwoods. It is an abundant breeder in oakwoods in western Scotland and nests commonly in mature deciduous stands in north Antrim. Post-breeding influxes arrive from Scotland, Scandinavia and, in some cases, forested redoubts in the Carpathian Mountains of Eastern Europe. A ring from a Siskin trapped in Belfast was recovered in a Tengmalm's Owl nest in Finland.

Over the bird's European range, spruce seeds form the main food in early summer. Young of broods raised in April are fed seed from the opening cones. Later broods are fed seeds from pine cones, as well as insects. By the time the cones have emptied in July and August, conifer forests hold little food and Birch becomes important. In studies in Finland (Haapanen 1966) it was discovered that variation in the spruce crop affected overall breeding success and triggered irruptive movements during the following autumn. Legions move west, primarily seeking Alder seed. Invasions often involve thousands. Winter visitors attracted to garden feeders travel far. Birds ringed during winter in Britain subsequently reached France and Iberia. Others were retrapped on migration at points on a huge arc from Croatia to Finland. Titchy size, pendulous feeding habits and bright green and yellow colours can suggest titmice. Irrespective of sex or age Siskins have streaked, limey backs and bright yellow rumps. Adult males are black-crowned and canary-yellow below. Females and youngsters have finely streaked white bellies. Troupes shoulder and squirrel their way among clusters of catkins and cones, maintaining a patter of sputtery notes, not unlike rattling hail. Bouts of jumbled song can be overheard from garden birds in March. A Greenfinch-like wheeze functions as a full stop at the end of a song sentence. Then, like a busy typist, a new paragraph starts. In flight, singletons emit a high-pitched call, often the only clue to presence. Phonetically, this is a short 'slip of a pen' – *tsee-u* (or *pee-oo*) – that can be either rising or falling. A means of affixing the sound is to imagine the sigh of a firework streaking into the sky; the note attenuates and disappears.

LINNET
Carduelis cannabina

Left: First impressions conjure up an identification challenge. The sceptre of 'small and streaked' paralyses many would-be identifiers. Yes, there are several contenders, from Reed Bunting to Twite. Irrespective of age or sex, the head pattern is distinctive. The combination of a light blob on the cheek with an encircling 'doughnut' of pale plumage crimped around a dark, sequined eye is unique.

Right: Often unable to find seeding weeds on contemporary farmland, flocks of Linnets are forced to resort to such unlikely-seeming places as industrial estates and the periphery of out-of-town shopping malls. In the wake of building construction, the seed bank of disturbed ground flushes with annuals – plants that flower and set seed in one year. Debased by the term 'weeds', they sustain many small songbirds through the winter.

FROM LATIN, *linum* refers to plants in the flax family. Formerly, the cultivation of flax to produce linen led to a boom period for Linnets and other seed-eating passerines. Azure flowers presaged tiny tea-coloured seeds. Cultivation concentrated on stems, not seed. Stalks were cut and steeped ('retted') in dams, to prepare the fibres for threshing and weaving. Thompson (1849–52) witnessed an *embarrass de richesses*: 'The cultivator of flax in the north of Ireland, by placing no value on the home-grown seed, unwittingly presented a rich autumnal treat to the Linnet.'

Linnets feed on minuscule seeds throughout the year and raise young on a diet of green seed, fed to chicks as milky gruel. They have short, broad bills that cannot cope with seeds that are large or difficult to extract. Hence, pods are twisted free from plants whose seed capsules are attached to the stem and shed seed is picked from the ground. Acrobatic diners swing from heads of Knapweed, Fat-hen, Cat's ear and Dandelions, cavorting like mice when they squirm among prostrate clumps of Chickweed and Redshank. Autumn flocks nibble heather seed and bury themselves in bendy forests of Meadowsweet. Varied haunts include crop margins, quarry spoil, waste ground or the flush of weeds above the high-tide mark. Flocks rise and fall in unison and maintain a twittering cadence that reflects group excitement levels. In summer, juveniles utter a hard-sounding *d'jip … d'jip … d'jip*, especially in flight. The note is reminiscent of Greenfinch (*chup*) or even Crossbill (*plik*). Song is a fast discordant medley; a poor man's Canary. For this reason the species – known as a Whin-grey – was a popular cage bird.

Social by nature, pairs frequently nest in proximity, especially among gorse (whins). Courting males acquire a rosy crown and chest, not by moult but through plumage abrasion. Streaked plumage across the head and nape is reduced to plain grey and a brown-chequered back becomes smooth terracotta. Male finery

disappears in early autumn, this time lost by moult. Nonetheless, during winter, fresh-plumaged males show hints of raspberry among drab chest plumage. Females and young resemble each other. The chest is coarsely striated, yielding to stony white on the belly. Some, possibly first-winter males, are more sparsely streaked on a fawn background. All ages possess blackish wings and tail – combed with white along the outer webs of the central primaries and outer tail feathers. The pale edges stand out like a row of fish bones. Because Twite, Lesser Redpoll and Reed Bunting are not dissimilar, it is worth studying appearance in some detail. Linnets have cute, stripy faces that contain matching pale bands above and below the eye, which sits in a dark crease. At all times a pale 'porthole' centred on brown-grey cheeks is diagnostic. Bill colour is graphite grey, although some – perhaps youngsters – have a paler, olive tone.

The population, which is largely resident, has been hit hard. In Britain, 70 per cent of the population nests on farmland, where there was a 50 per cent drop in numbers between 1970 and 2001. Except in western Ireland, the bird is in similar straits on this side of the Irish Sea. More than any other finch, Linnets depend on the weeds of cultivation. The abundance and distribution of food is thus determined by farming practice; harvest operations reduce the seeds available, whereas the next cultivation brings a fresh flush to the surface. Many weeds are hardy, flowering and setting seed randomly throughout the year. In a quest to find them, Linnets roam widely and are one of the first finches to start nesting in spring, traditionally about the time that agricultural weeds became available. In the past, laying continued into August, so that a pair was capable of producing four broods. Nowadays, food shortages, caused by reduced availability of weed seeds in both arable and pastoral land due to pesticide use, force adults to subsist on dandelion seed in May and, where planted, oilseed rape between June and August. The reduction in quality and quantity of food has had an impact on breeding success. Instead of rearing two or more broods annually, one has become the norm. This is not enough to offset losses. Exacerbated by lower fecundity rates and an increasingly sanitised rural environment, flocks are becoming an anachronism. Ironically, waste ground on the margins of industrial estates often provides foraging habitat, thanks to nature running wild, free from chemical warfare. Some farmers are aware of the plight of Linnets, Yellowhammers and Skylarks. All rely on seeds to survive. The creation of small areas of wild bird cover incorporating kale, quinoa, mustard and oilseed rape can provide a lifeline.

TWITE
Carduelis flavirostris

Simply because the species superficially resembles a Linnet, Twites tend to be overlooked. In fact, even during winter, when both feed on the seeds of marsh plants in coastal locations, apartheid is typical. Rather than mingle, each species remains in a single-species flock. Hallmarks are a waxy yellow bill that goes with a curry powder 'face' and, a further distinction from Linnet, almost plain lores.

IN OLDER IRISH LITERATURE, the species went under the more explanatory moniker of Mountain Linnet. Formerly it was widespread across moorland and rugged coastal terrain where heather adorned cliff tops and extended inland. In feeding habits the bird resembles the Linnet: the weeds of pasture and of cultivated land provided much of the food in summer, albeit in upland districts. Times have changed and small-scale farm holdings in foothills and along wild coasts have gone. Hay meadows, weedy ground, corn stacks, poultry runs and patches of winter stubble scarcely exist. In Shetland, birds killed around corn stacks had been dining on weed seeds extracted from the butts of the sheaves (Saxby 1874). Much moorland breeding habitat has been lost or degraded through burning, reseeding, overgrazing or afforestation. Native Twites are close to extinction. A handful of breeding pairs hang on to a Noah's Ark remnant of mature heather interleaved with bouquets of seeding annuals near the Giant's Causeway. Best estimates of population size for the Republic of Ireland are hovering close to a paltry 100 pairs.

Thompson (1849–52) provides a flashback:

The Mountain Linnet breeds on the heathery top of Knockagh near Carrickfergus. Nests were generally placed in the heath, but in some instances were built near to the ground in dwarf whins. A venerable sporting friend has always observed these birds about their nests (in tufts of heather) when exercising his dogs on the Belfast Mountains preparatory to grouse shooting. It has been remarked as common and breeding on the mountainsides and occasionally on the wild seashore among furze or whins in many parts of Antrim and Down ... [It] breeds commonly and remains all the year on the low heathy tracts adjacent to, and little elevated above, Lough Neagh.

Nowadays most Twites are winter visitors, presumably from western Scotland. One colour-ringed on the Mull of Kintyre in October 2011 was seen at Whitehead, Antrim, in November. Post-breeding flocks move to low levels, primarily the seashore, where they have a penchant for feeding on low weeds close to the high-tide mark; a cordon sanitaire out of reach of agriculture. For the same reason, saltmarshes form an important refuge. Here, sea aster is one of several important food plants. Inland reports are usually misidentified Linnets whose bill colour in winter can, in good light, appear horn-coloured. Twites tend to maintain homogenous flocks and, even when Linnets are present in the vicinity, the two seldom mix. More so than Linnets, they creep and 'roll forwards' in short prancing flutters and are confiding.

Calls betray presence. A nasal *swee, swee, swee* is a barometer of agitation levels and often prefaces an aerial reconnoitre. A Lesser Redpoll-style *chet-chet* is used as a contact call. Other twittering notes are indistinguishable from Linnet.

Twites are equivalent in size to Linnet, yet their profile is closer to Lesser Redpoll. Examined in detail, echoes of both are manifest: the primaries match Linnet but the greater coverts fit Lesser Redpoll (NMK). The tail is longish and quite deeply forked; round shoulders and a bull neck create a blob-headed silhouette. A slash of white along the wing catches the eye. Unlike Linnet, a streaked tawny chest and flanks glow against an egg-shaped expanse of white across the belly. Concentrate on the face. In winter, the bill is yellow and the foreface is the colour of curry powder, fusing across the throat. A closer look reveals, not a short bill per se, but a feathered base with, unlike Linnet, a sheepskin noseband cloaking most of the cutting edges. The diagnostic pink rump is usually difficult to discern. Nonetheless, obliging views of winter flocks reveal some with candyfloss pink upper tail-coverts, outer tail feathers and primary edges. Later in spring the saturation deepens, on some becoming almost crimson. Subtle is, indeed, beautiful.

LESSER REDPOLL
Carduelis [flammea] cabaret

Small birds do the mightiest things. If spotted at a garden feeder alongside a House Sparrow, Lesser Redpoll looks not only half the size but also half the girth. Nonetheless, they are feisty customers and shoulder their way to feeder ports to extract seed, even though most of it is too big for their tiny bill and dribbles to the ground where larger, dislodged finches respectfully await showered titbits.

OUR LATITUDE lies at the southern edge of a circumpolar distribution across which redpolls occur in a vast swathe stretching from Scandinavia through Siberia to Alaska, Canada, Greenland and Iceland. Appropriately, the further north you travel, the frostier the plumage. Those in northern Greenland are amazing. To survive the harsh climate the bill, legs and feet are swaddled. Fluffed against the elements, the cherub resembles a snowball. Trying to marshal all the world's disparate tribes into order is a challenge. Large and white across Arctic tundra; grey and mealy in taiga forest; small, brown and swarthy in temperate woods: is each a species in its own right, or a manifestation of global adaptability? The debate rumbles on. Even DNA tests have failed to draw a line in the sand. In the overall scheme of things, our 'Lesser' Redpoll *Carduelis [flammea] cabaret* is a mighty midget, smaller even than a Blue Tit.

During spring, the main foods are the flowers and seeds of willows, supplemented by insects gleaned around opening tree buds, especially Larch. By early summer, seed from grasses and members of the Compositae plant family (such as dandelions) becomes the mainstay. Once Birch ripens in July, Redpolls respond by switching diet. The Birch crop exerts an influence throughout the coming winter as it determines the extent of migration. In autumn, flocks disperse from Scotland and Ireland and head southwest. Depending on abundance of food, numbers vary greatly from year to year. Consequently, individuals are not consistent in choice of winter quarters. Redpolls from Scotland, and probably Ireland, travel to southeast England, many reaching Belgium, some southern France. They are more likely to return to roughly the same natal area than to revisit wintering grounds in consecutive years. During late September and October, oscillating, jangly flocks arrive at Copeland Bird Observatory. Rather than being inbound, they are actually outbound, heading south and feeding as they go. Meadowsweet and willowherbs are popular and settled groups cling like titmice to the pendulous seed heads. As the season progresses, ripening alder seed becomes accessible. It has been suggested (Davis 1977) that, in autumn, those birds foraging on the ground may be first-years, which have been out of the nest for only a few weeks. It could be that they have to rely on the seeds dislodged by old hands feeding above.

'Poll' in the name refers to red on the forehead, separated from a tiny waxy yellow bill by a black 'soot-line' at the front of the face. Juveniles lack the poll. Siskins are frequent companions. Their plumage invariably contains green; Lesser Redpolls are brown and streaky. Lesser Redpolls produce a nasal and lilting triple salvo, *chi-chi-chi*. The tempo is fast, as though from a winged sewing machine. Displaying birds over nesting habitat – birch woodland across hillsides or bog, young conifer plantations or tall dense scrub – undulate deeply and intersperse a vibrating trill with the flight call. Another signature is a rising, upswinging *Joe-ee*, given at rest, mainly to advertise presence.

Food supplies in northern latitudes are locked away when winter bites. In consequence, populations wander. Thousands of kilometres may be travelled. Waves of refugees leapfrog home ranges, as though visiting a greater universe that, if called for at some future date, may be reoccupied. When such irruptions occur, birds from Greenland and Scandinavia reach us. Ringing demonstrates that pilgrims from China have reached the Low Countries. It is good to marvel at local birds and think that they are part of a global clan that has cracked survival techniques embracing wild places from Belfast to the Bering Sea.

COMMON CROSSBILL
Loxia curvirostra

A combination of habitat and voice readily draw attention to Crossbills. The increase in commercial 'softwood' forestry has added Ireland to the map of the bird's distribution – essentially an overlay of the world's coniferous forests.

TO UNDERSTAND the sporadic wanderings of Crossbills, it helps to also understand the fruiting of coniferous trees, to which the bird's life is geared. Much of the following account has been prepared after consulting Newton (1972). The seeds of all conifers form in late summer, and then remain on the tree until the cones open, up to two years later, depending on species. Importantly, the seeds of different species become accessible at different seasons. Crossbills can extract the seeds from cones at any stage of ripeness, but most easily from those that have begun to open naturally. In terms of food value, indispensable trees are spruce, pine, fir and larch. Ironically, once seeds have fallen, they are effectively lost, as Crossbills cannot easily pick them off the ground. Throughout European forests, cone crops are variable. In any year, hundreds of kilometres may separate productive areas. Each year, usually in summer, flocks move when the new crops are forming, settling where they find rich pickings. If the seeds hold out, they stay put until the next summer, moulting and breeding in the meantime. Occasionally, when high population levels coincide with an inadequate crop of seed, irruptions occur. Flocks spill west, leaving the core range in enormous numbers. In an invasion year, pilgrims may travel thousands of kilometres. Some, either driven by hunger or imbued with an explorer's death wish, reach Iceland and conifer-free Irish offshore islands. During a nineteenth-century invasion,

Colour distinguishes ages and sexes. Red signifies a male, although diet and age mean that some are the colour of a teddy bear. Bill size indicates preferred food. Photographed in the Netherlands, these birds are closely related Parrot Crossbills distinguishable by somewhat stouter bills designed to tackle pine cones, rather than spruce or fir.

flocks settled in orchards. Writing from Dublin on 3 February 1802, Mr Caldwell complained to his friend, Sir J. E. Smith, in Cork, echoing H. G. Wells' *The War of the Worlds*: 'The winter here has been severe. Vast flights of Crossbills made their appearance at the latter end of August and stayed until the beginning of October. They made great havoc in the orchards; they never ate the apple, but cut it to pieces, and picked out the pippins. They came first to the County of Cork, then proceeded to Waterford, Tipperary, Kilkenny, Wexford, Wicklow and Dublin, but no further north.'

Across Ireland in the latter part of the twentieth century, the invaders finally got what they wanted – conifers in seed. Many settled and became founder members of a breeding population. They clamber about like parrots, sidling along branches and pivoting to wrench at a cone, many of which are snapped off, carried to a perch and prised apart scale by scale; the seed is extracted with a purpose-made bill used like a trolley jack. Large feet help by gripping the cone. Groups fly high and break into a ringing chorus of *plik* calls. The fusillade can be 'deafening'. In general, groups are encountered. Only a tiny fraction attempt to breed. Ringing has provided evidence that, years later, some return to ancestral forests, even in the wake of transcontinental dispersal from Russia to Spain. Far from moving randomly, they irrupt in roughly the same direction each time. Admittedly, migrants only persist in a standard westerly vector until they

encounter seeding conifers. Given the homing ability of adults, this means that young raised in far-flung locations have to make their first 'homebound' migration against the grain. Being part of a flock of old hands probably facilitates navigation. Alternatively, the new generation's birthplace may become an adopted home. Perhaps this explains the year-round presence of Crossbills here? While the birds are prone to wander in search of coniferous seed, Ireland's new forests may have fostered a resident nomadic population, albeit topped up by periodic influxes from overseas.

Crossbills are wide-necked and short-tailed, and come in a hail of colours. Many males are understated red, the shade of aged cinema curtains. However, variation in male colour is considerable. Some are teddy bear orange-yellow; others are brassy. Yellow plumage is more common among first-years than among older males (Ticehurst 1915). Males that moult before the end of July grow yellow feathers; after this date, freshly moulted plumage is red. Those whose moult straddles July end up parti-coloured red and yellow (Weber 1963). The transition appears to accompany a change in feeding from old cones to new, so perhaps diet determines pigment. Female raiment is tropical lime green. Youngsters, whose mandibles lengthen but do not fully cross until they are about six weeks old, are mouse-coloured and streaky.

BULLFINCH
Pyrrhula pyrrhula

Females are brunettes. Pairs remain together throughout the year. In late summer, youngsters accompany parents and resemble mum, minus her black cap.

DESPITE A SHOT-PUTTER TORSO, Bullfinches are dextrous movers but messy eaters; detritus often dribbles down the side of calliper-shaped mandibles. Males with vivacious pink breasts are, for all the Crayola colour, not given to ostentation. If a Robin had the equivalent surface area in red breast, its cockiness would make it visible on Google Earth. Females are demure, with a grey-brown back and fawn underparts. Adults of both sexes have piggy eyes set in a black cape. Partners occasionally serenade each other with a quiet creaky warble. While pillow talk is seldom heard, calls are a different matter. A soft intoned pipe accompanies many activities. To imitate it, whistle the name 'Hugh'. Bullfinches love thickets and tall, straggly hedgerows. Flitting through cover, a useful spoor is revealed – the sight of a white rump on a loping black-tailed finch. Short legs discourage ground feeding.

'In nature's wild domain, the Bullfinch looks eminently beautiful and can be admired without the alloy associated with its appearance in the garden or the orchard, where it proves so destructive by eating the buds of the fruit trees' (Thompson 1849–52). Because the bird has been classified as a pest of commercial orchards, diet has been studied in detail. Damage affects apples, cherries, currants, gooseberries, pears and plums. They have distinct preferences as to variety, favouring dessert apples to cookers. Feeding is methodical and branch-by-branch. Given a choice in spring between ripening buds in orchards and those of Hawthorn (or the flowers of willow and oak), the bird can hardly be blamed in opting for commercially grown fruit trees. Newton (1972) undertook research and demonstrated a link between below-average years in the production of Ash seed, leading to severe bud damage in orchards. Basically, the failure of the Ash crop meant that, following a lean winter, ripening fruit buds were immediately attacked. This discovery meant that fruit growers were able to predict problem years, and plan their control accordingly. Trapping was the main method. By pre-emptively catching birds in those autumns when the Ash seed was poor, the remaining natural seed-crops were conserved, the date by which the birds turn to buds was delayed, and the total damage reduced.

Bullfinches are sedentary. Around 85 per cent move less than 5km. Control measures are effective because most travel short distances, so immigration is limited and local population surges are avoided. For the rest of the year, a great variety of seeds are eaten. Newton (1972) found that, in an English wood, at least four fifths of the tree species and half the herbaceous plants provide food at one time or another. The short bill is adapted to nibbling and for the most part they feed directly from the living plant, rather than off the ground. In the breeding season adults develop mouth pouches in which they store food for chicks. Feeding birds acquire a bulging throat. As capacity is reached, the chin's black feathers ruffle until nearly erect, over which globules of chewed green seed or pith spill like porridge. A pair visited a garden to feed on ripening Birch catkins each summer for at least seven years (AMG).

SNOW BUNTING

Plectrophenax nivalis

Snow Buntings are long-winged, an attribute that equips many to quit northern latitudes in autumn and make Atlantic crossings from Greenland and Iceland to Europe. Pressed against gravel, shingle or winter stubble, piebald plumage – similar to the shades of toasted white bread – is a perfect disguise and allows the wearer to slip away or be overlooked by remaining stock-still..

IF EVER A BIRD evokes a sense of Arctic wilderness, it is Snow Bunting. This is the most northerly breeding songbird and not just sporadically but regularly on all terrain, including scree and mountain tops above 1,000m. Food is mainly seeds with the addition of insects in the breeding season; young are reared exclusively on invertebrates. Nesting in rock crevices means that broods are safe until precocious offspring emerge with barely feathered, floppy wings. Weather rather than predators is the chief hazard for freshly fledged juveniles. Bitter cold or late snowfalls may cut off a vital supply of insect protein. If the season is not too inclement, snow patches are a boon to foraging adults who gather large numbers of hatching insects windblown from tundra vegetation and immobilised when they land on frozen snow. A silver lining of life in a vast stony landscape is the ease of camouflage. To boot, Snow Buntings creep like roly-poly mice and prostrate themselves, limpet-tight to the ground, at the first hint of danger – behaviour that emboldens them to opt for an ultra-rapid summertime moult of their flight feathers (of fewer than four weeks) and risk being virtually flightless. All other songbirds take twice as long to complete the process and none forsake powers of flight.

At the end of the breeding season flocks form and become nomadic. Flight jizz says 'lark' but the markings do not fit. Critically, although plumage variation is considerable, all show at least a narrow white bar on the central inner wing. On males, white predominates and occupies the core of the wing, embedded between a chequered back and a coal-black wing 'hand'. A musical rippling trill serves as a bead to presence, typically given at take-off. High overhead, loners attempt to summon comrades with a short whistle delivered with variable verve: from a soft clipped *teu* to a lazy disyllabic *peeyoo*. Summer haunts are vacated but males prefer to linger in the Arctic. Adult females and all members of the new generation are more migratory, explaining the low incidence of adult males among troupes that arrive to spend the winter in Ireland. Some try to winter on upland moors but most occur in coastal stubble, along stony beaches or among marram grass and strand-line vegetation behind sandy beaches. Feeding strategies can be feisty. The neck is stretched to reach pendulous seed heads and the bird may jump and shoulder-charge the base of bent stalks to dislodge seeds.

Snow Buntings breed abundantly in Greenland, Iceland and northern Scandinavia. Because the population in Iceland is subtly different in appearance, it has been possible, in Britain, to establish the origin of wintering birds. Ringing recoveries have helped. Data, mainly from Scotland, shows that the majority come from Iceland (Cramp *et al.* 1977–94). The source of the remainder is believed to be from Greenland. For those living in the highest latitudes, choice of migration route probably varies from year to year, depending on weather conditions. A wind of opportunity may steer migrants towards Ireland and Scotland, rather than Canada, where most Greenland birds overwinter. One ringed on Fair Isle, Scotland, in April 1959 and recovered in Newfoundland, Canada, in May 1960, provided proof of caprice.

Thompson (1849–52) remarked:

During the great snowstorm, early in March 1827, flocks [of Snow Buntings] appeared on the outskirts of the town of Belfast. Such numbers were killed on the seashore that they were purchased by Mr Sinclaire as the cheapest food he could procure for his trained Peregrines. In the winter of 1844–45 immense numbers came to the land opposite Rough Island, Strangford. Throughout a range of several miles they committed great devastation by picking up the sown wheat, which they got at along the edges of the ridges. The farmers were literally up in arms against them, and killed many, but the birds eventually became so wild as not to admit approach. They had never been there before, and were looked upon as some foreign species that came to destroy the wheat crop.

YELLOWHAMMER
Emberiza citrinella

'THIS HANDSOME BIRD, being a constant resident about the farm, is very well known. 'Yellow Yorlin' is the common name bestowed in the north of Ireland. Yellow-hammer is a term likewise used; but the word should be 'ammer', the German of bunting, and not 'hammer', which is meaningless' (Thompson 1849–52). That's one mystery solved! Yellowhammers are the Maasai tribe among buntings – lanky, slim and elegant. The tail is long, manifested in an undulating flight. The countenance is gentle and flocks are dignified with no bickering or squabbling. Among a range of fragmentary calls, one stands out. This is a pebbly 'tines of a steel comb being thrummed' series of clicks used when birds alight, take flight, or check the surroundings from a strategic perch. The sound is reminiscent of a speeded-up version of a Robin's *tick … tick … tick*.

Above: Male Yellowhammers are gloriously yellow-headed. In winter (when this photograph was taken) the bird's bust is actually less bright when greyish-green tips mute its luteous lustre. Full breeding plumage is produced through feather wear, not moult.

Inset: Female. The Yellowhammer's universe is small. Ringing reveals that 70 per cent of breeding pairs flock together and spend the winter within 5km of the nest site. Unless farmland contains the requisite foods, whole populations become extinct.

Yellow-headed males are unmistakeable. Some, possibly older individuals, are saffron with the faintest of head streaking. Some well-marked females look more like duller (perhaps younger) males. The plumage contains much to admire and is a tapestry of striated upperparts, delicately streaked underparts and distinctive 'tear-drop' ear-coverts. The bill is sky blue and the rump is unmarked bright rusty red. White tail corners are noticeable in flight or when the birds nervously twitch and half open the tail. Post-breeding flocks form in late summer and remain together until spring. Yellowhammers readily join forces with other seedeaters, such as Chaffinches and Tree Sparrows. Flocking not only means that a larger number of lookouts are likely to spot a predator but also, when attacking, the hunter may be confused by prey flying in different directions and may not be able to make up its mind which to go for. By March, males break into song, despite still being in peer groups. The verse is catchy and has traditionally been set to the metre of 'A-little-bit-of-bread-and-no – cheese.' The opening stanza is shuttling and has the buzz of a cicada, the final note is separate; a long, flat and monotone wheeze.

Tilled land, seed-laden winter stubbles, thick hedgerows, unsprayed and uncultivated margins alongside standing crops, scrub and small trees or telegraph poles for song-posts: these are a Yellowhammer's favourite things. From that list it is easy to deduce why it is in trouble. Yellowhammers nest along wide hedges, in patches of scrub or ditches, and are associated with boundaries that have wide grass margins. During summer, they forage close to the nest along hedges, on farm tracks, 'waste ground' and in open fields. Cereal fields become important feeding sites when crops come into ear and ripening grain can be accessed. The birds do best where cereals, mixed arable crops and a high density of hedgerows occur in combination. In winter, flocks seek out stubbles, newly sown fields, cereal-based game cover and grain in farmyards and at stock- and game-feeding sites. Often they become approachable where food is plentiful around livestock. All forage on the ground. As well as cereal grains and grass seeds, they eat the seed of nettles, Fat-hen, Chickweed, Dandelion, Knapweed and plantains. They seem to avoid oily seeds such as those of crucifers, including oilseed rape. Beetles, caterpillars, earthworms and other invertebrates are taken when available and chicks are reared on a combination of insects and unripe cereal grain. Because cereal grain was rare in the diet fed to chicks up until the 1960s, it is possible that a subsequent reduction in available insect food has been made up with less nutritious grain.

The bird is yet another casualty of a changed countryside. During the period 1970–2010, the bird disappeared from at least 65 per cent of Ireland. Nowadays, east Ulster, east Munster and Leinster hold those that remain – for now. Here are just some of the reasons that have fuelled decline. Since the Second World War, the rise of the internal combustion engine put paid to the workhorse and the cultivation of oats to feed draught animals (the crop helped sustain farmland seed-eating birds too). Low-intensity oat cultivation, once widespread across the land, ceased. In the autumn-sown, chemically boosted, weed-controlled monocultures that replaced spring-sown cereals, there is little succour for birds, insects or seed-producing wild flora – insulted by the term 'weeds'. Where crops have been replaced by grassland (for silage), populations have become extinct. Leaving a ryegrass meadow to seed after two silage cuts (with the third cut left ungrazed, thereby producing seed) has helped sustain some populations in England. Attempts to replicate this success in Northern Ireland have not, so far, borne fruit. What would Doctor Yellowhammer recommend? Traditionally, stubbles were the most important feeding habitat on the farm. In less pressured times, farm machinery was more forgiving. Reaper-binders cut the crop and spat it out in bundles of sheaves that were lifted and arranged manually into rows of stooks. The stooks were left to stand prior to being collected and threshed to remove cereal grain from the stalks. Harvesting took weeks and could be ruined by bad weather – the phrase 'all is safely gathered in' reflects the relief at a successful harvest. In the harvesting process, spilled seed was plentiful both on the ground, on the stooks and around farmyards. Thompson (1849–52) examined the winter stomach contents of Yellowhammers and his findings attest to the bird's close association with arable fields: 'The stomachs generally contained wheat, or some other grain.' In towns and villages transport was horse-drawn, providing spilled grain from feedbags and lodged in manure. In snowy weather flocks of Yellowhammers and Corn Buntings were recorded along roadsides: 'Buntings not only betake themselves to the roads for subsistence, but may be seen at such times in the less-frequented streets and stable-yards of the town of Belfast.'

Such practices have disappeared, as have many seed-producing weeds that grew in association with cultivation. The value of winter stubble largely depends on the abundance of broadleaved weeds producing seeds within it. Using herbicides, either pre-harvest or on stubbles, reduces the germination of these food plants. One of the key insects in the diet of farmland birds is the sawfly, which winters in the soil as a pupa. Cultivations drastically reduce numbers of pupae through harrowing. If stubble is retained into spring, the sawflies emerge, and the next generation of larvae provide food, especially for chicks. Alternatively, wild bird cover can be established in the spring to provide a winter seed source. High cereal proportion is beneficial. Triticale is the cereal with the best 'standing power' through winter. Rough grass margins adjacent to short, thick hedgerows are good news. Margins of at least 6m are best. The more variable the grass sward, the better the insect food for chicks. Varying the cutting regime enhances variety. Long rotations encourage tussocky margins; regular cutting allows the birds better foraging access. None of this is rocket science. Yellowhammers are not yet gone. They are remarkably fecund and, given a chance, can bounce back. A breeding pair at Ballycastle, Antrim, hatched four broods in both 1931 and 1932 (Deane 1954).

REED BUNTING
Emberiza schoeniclus

During summer, male headdress is predominantly black. Wear burnishes plumage and may even produce a glossy veneer on feathers whose tips are designed to flake off and reveal underlying colour. For other tracts, such as those across the back and wings, abrasion chafes. Compare the dog-eared look of this bird's tertials with those of the freshly moulted individual (see far left photo) photographed in October. By June, bright rufous along the outer webs has been reduced from a wide convex swathe to a narrow, almost concave, ragged rim.

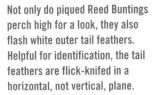

Not only do piqued Reed Buntings perch high for a look, they also flash white outer tail feathers. Helpful for identification, the tail feathers are flick-knifed in a horizontal, not vertical, plane.

In March, when this photograph was taken, unknown numbers head east. Ringing is yet to elucidate the true scale of Reed Bunting migration. Based on plumage features, one recent Irish winter visitor came from western Siberia.

Female Reed Bunting. The bill is peculiar. The upper mandible is thin and arched like a broken nail. Much bulkier, the 'digger bucket' lower mandible cradles seed and allows the tongue and jaw muscles to get to work and dehusk dinner.

EXCEPT WHEN IN COURTSHIP ROBES, cryptic plumage is preferred. Upperparts are drenched in black and tan etched with tramlines mimicking withered bracken and winter reeds. Males in breeding garb are black-shrouded; a wide white whisker divides head and chest and dangles like an ermine stole. Deep-pile white plumage encircles the neck. More so than other passerines, Reed Buntings reflect mood by alternately sleeking and puffing plumage. Displaying males inflate nape plumage, emphasising the white collar. The underparts are stony, while beige-white and bright grey gleams from the heart of a streaky, russet rump. Regard the tail. At rest its pattern is unremarkable, plain and brown-centred with white corners. Everything changes when seemingly bad nerves prompt tail twitching, revealing white on the two outermost feathers. If the alarm is false, tail flashing ceases and is replaced by a shallow dip. The bill is steel grey or horn-coloured, blackish on breeding males.

Following moult at the end of the breeding season, solid black disappears from the head and throat, replaced by sooty stripes and the ghost of a black bib, obscured by light feather tips. At the end of winter the tips abrade. Reed Buntings change feather patterns not by replacement, but abrasion. As early as February, male faces start to blacken. No two look the same and many are unsightly, as though they have mange. Female plumage is intricate. Russet, cinnamon and tawny tones achieve a demure feel. In particular, first-winter females are a 'perfect ten'. Their upperparts contain the fewest coppery hues, standard in other ages and males. Irrespective of age, females have a brown rump and an unmarked throat. At all ages, a helpful portfolio of field marks comprises a pale jaw line and, on a flying silhouette, a swollen look to the terminal portion of the tail.

While fond of overgrown damp habitats, Reed Buntings can also be found in dry situations where heavy cover is interspersed with scrub, especially tree saplings. Insects form the bulk of the diet in summer; seeds are a winter staple. Groups band together and seek out weedy fields, bushy woodland margins and crop stubble, especially where cabbage, cauliflower, broccoli and sprouts create screened, leafy runnels. Self-effacing by nature, flock members are peaceniks and silent when feeding. Calls are given in flight – jerky, but not undulating – or immediately after landing. A seamless, sweetly slurred *tseeeu* serves as a marker, often the first clue to an overhead migrant. Siskins have a similar (but higher-pitched) call. Playing second fiddle to the clear diction of the landmark *tseeeu*, a dry *chut* is also given. If close, the utterance 'expands' to become nasal and twangy. Song is mundane and formulaic. Tuneless introductory notes culminate in a jangle. The delivery is halting, the finale underwhelming: *chink, chink, chink, Chitty!*

Reed Buntings are struggling due to wetland drainage, zealous tidying of riverbanks and a reduction in insect food for chicks. Winter visitors from overseas create the impression that the species is widespread. Yet in the breeding season, distribution is local and increasingly fragmented.

CORN BUNTING
Emberiza calandra

WITH THE FASCINATION that accompanies being a witness to an upheaval that went down in history, it is possible that sometime in the future a young goggle-eyed questioner will ask me if I ever saw a living Irish Corn Bunting. Seeing an extinct bird – imagine that! Well, yes I did. I saw breeding birds singing their hearts out from telegraph poles at Malin Head, Donegal, and on The Mullet, Mayo. They were a bunting, not Beethoven, so the ditty was buzzing with a glass-splintering crescendo reminiscent of jangled car keys. That was 1983. By then the species was extinct as a breeding bird in Northern Ireland, although it was occasionally met with in winter. In 1984, I saw two on winter stubbles beside the sea at Groomsport, Down. They were among a blizzard of seedeaters that included Skylarks, Chaffinches, Bramblings, Linnets, Reed Buntings and, *mirabile dictu*, two Lapland Buntings. Then, in January 1989, I saw my last one. It was feeding in a stubble field with Skylarks and Linnets at Ardglass, Down. Views were good. As the feeding flocks rose and settled on a low hawthorn hedge, I spotted the big guy. A plump streaky character, big-eyed and looking a little lost. It tried to look inconspicuous but was bound to stick out as a gentle giant, a Great Auk of buntings. On the ground, invisibility was easier to achieve. General colour scheme and a low crouch nearly passed it off as half a Skylark. It was probably a migrant from dwindling populations that still existed at that time (and still do) in northwest England – Cheshire, maybe? So it was not born here. A *rara avis*, no less.

How sad that a species that in 1900 was known in every county except Leitrim has ceased to breed, although it is doubtful if the bird would have reached much of central and western Europe if it had not been for humans creating the agricultural landscape upon which it became dependent. In the halcyon days before pesticides, fertilisers, tractors and mechanisation, there was a close affinity between it and arable farms with cornfields and hedges. In coastal districts, populations thrived and nested in low gorse bushes (whins) and brambles, and fed among hay, corn and root crops. In Down, this rural idyll persisted up to the early 1970s on the Ards Peninsula (chiefly south of Cloughey) and in the hinterland of Cranfield Point (JSF). Then they were gone. Like ground-nesting Corncrakes, eggs and chicks were destroyed if, as seems to be the case, the species opted to nest among corn. Adults eat grain, but chicks are reared on insects. Until they fledge, youngsters are fed grasshoppers, ground beetles, harvestmen and spiders, and the caterpillars of butterflies, moths and sawflies. Foraging to feed hungry mouths is carried out within 200m of the nest.

Because Corn Buntings require grain and other large, starchy seeds, they have been susceptible to the loss of this food. They have been hit hard by the reduction of arable cropping in stock-rearing areas; early ploughing of stubbles and autumn sowing of arable crops; efficient harvest and bird-proof storage of cereal grain; wintering cattle indoors and feeding livestock with silage rather than seed-rich hay or cereals; and the unavailability of freshly drilled cereal grain at the end of the winter. Through nesting in crops now harvested at the height of the breeding season, nest-bound youngsters are born on death row. Post-breeding flocks roamed widely in search of cereal grain. It seems as though, right up to the present, winter survival is the hurdle crushing skeleton bands that remain in parts of eastern England, northeast Scotland and Lancashire. A precarious outpost of breeding birds and benign farming methods is hanging by a thread on the Outer Hebrides. This population has a lot in common with its vanished Irish counterpart. Cramp *et al.* (1977–94) tentatively recognised western Scottish and Irish birds as a subtly different subspecies, *Emberiza calandra clanceyi*. Distinguishing characteristics were darker and more heavily marked plumage, making them subtly different. Should there ever be an attempt to restore the bird to Ireland, possibly on a sympathetically farmed island, it is important to ensure the survival of the Hebridean population. The species' vital statistics are worrying. Numbers were estimated at 117 occupied territories in 2005, a decline of 17 per cent since 2002 and of at least 62 per cent since 1995 (Wilson *et al.* 2007). Ignorance is no longer an excuse for ignoring the bird's plight. The reasons for its decline are known. The problems lie with harvesting methods. Strips of cereal, mainly oats and rye, are grown on machair (coastal grassland) as winter stock feed. Traditionally, harvested cereals are stored in stacks made of ripe sheaths, from which the crop is removed to outdoor feed-stands for cattle over the course of the winter. Under this regime, grain is available throughout the winter, and the birds concentrate in flocks at feed-stands and stackyards. The continuance of cereal cultivation and the existence of secure nesting habitat in untouched dune grassland are crucial. During the 1980s cereals began to be harvested early, before grains ripened, and the crop was then stored as arable silage in black plastic bales. This removed a key winter food source, gathered with modern equipment that has ousted the labour-intensive, 'old-fashioned' reaper-binder. Harvesting and storage in outdoor corn stacks is in fast decline. It has been predicted (Hartley 1991) that this state of affairs will fritter away the population through lack of ripe grain, probably leading to extinction.

The French word 'Fin' should appear at this point. Let us leave a last refrain to Thompson (1849–52), to whom the 'Common Bunting' was ubiquitous. No doubt he felt that, by putting his observations on paper, he might, one day, do his birds – *our birds* – a favour by writing them into history. Little did he know that, for Corn Bunting, he did precisely that.

It is an inhabitant of the bare arable, and where some little portion of wildness still exists, as implied in the common

On drowsy high summer days when ripening corn stood golden in the fields until harvested in August, male Corn Buntings sang their jangling songs while females reared young on insects and seeds. Nests were safe in the nodding forest of cereals. Those days are gone. So too – tragically – are Ireland's Corn Buntings.

name of 'Briar Bunting'. The ditch bank run wild with brambles has more charms for this bird than the neat trim hedge. Within the shelter of such humble underwood its nest is made. It also builds frequently on the ground in meadows. In severe frost and snow, buntings not only betake themselves to the roads for subsistence, but may be seen at such times in the less frequented streets and stable-yards of the town of Belfast. Mr J R Garrett is inclined to believe in a migration,

from the circumstances that early every winter at Cromac, flocks consisting of from 100–200 birds appeared, and remained until spring. They were to be seen every evening in a plantation of elm trees, where they remained like Linnets for about an hour before retiring to roost in the adjoining shrubbery.

BACKYARD MOTELS

WATCHING BIRDS at close quarters is a special pleasure. How come they always look so smart, alert and triumphantly independent? They live among our back gardens but are self-sufficient and, maddeningly, they do not put on weight. Blackbirds stuff themselves with apple cores and berries, pig out on high-calorie cheese, suet and cold potatoes, yet they never develop flab. In truth, birds need all the grub they can get, especially in the winter months. Daylight feeding time is short, nights are long and cold and, as the season drags on, food resources become scarce.

Topping up your shopping trolley with a bag of peanuts to be festooned from the corner of the washing line is no guarantee that, next morning, you will have customers. A little more money buys a feeder. These come in a variety of sizes and may have individual feeding ports or consist of open wire mesh throughout. What should you fill them with? Some companies sell 'feeder seed', which is a mixture of different types. Black sunflower seeds are oily and nutritious and are best before Christmas, since the seed, which is inside the husk, starts to go soft in the New Year. However, smaller birds cannot crack open the husks, which are inedible and generate mess. Alternatively, use sunflower hearts – seed without the husk. These are eaten by a wider selection of birds. To save money and make stock last, you can grind them in a blender. For a real bargain, porridge oats (uncooked) are every bit as nutritious for birds as they are for us.

The range of foods eaten by birds is, of course, enormous. Do not be too disappointed if bossy Starlings monopolise fruit. Timid species prefer the pulverised remains that the Starling mob leaves behind. Birds go crackers for cheese. By propping a log clear of the ground and smearing it with cheese you can make an instant bird table. Use a lump of cheddar like a plane by rubbing it along the log's rough side, thereby allowing surface fissures and bumps to trap the food. Wedging peanuts into cavities adds more interest.

Birds need to drink every day and they also like to bathe. The aesthetics of a costly stone water feature are lost on them: an upturned bin lid is just as appealing. Put some rocks in the centre and a few convenient perches to enable easy access. With the exception of pigeons and doves, which sup and drink like us, all other birds have to dip their bills into water and tip the head back to swallow. Provision of water should not be embarked upon without a commitment to cleanliness. Be careful not to inadvertently offer a poisoned chalice containing microbes that cause diseases such as botulism or trichomoniasis. Try to deter predators. If you haven't got the location right, the customers will vote with their wings and will either not approach or fail to show up at all. Birds like to approach a bird table or feeding station by moving through protective cover until they are almost there. A feeder dangling on the lowest branch of a cluster of boughs, or bordered by a sheltering hedge, will provide safe passage and a sense of security.

How much food should you put out? The amount provided should allow for rapid turnover. Uneaten food rots and spreads disease. Should feeding stop in some seasons? Provided that food is eaten, you can continue throughout the year. In general, business slacks off in April when foliage insects emerge, marking

A tiny finch, Siskin tends to sneak in under the radar. Winter visitors and March migrants – many destined for Scandinavia – have learned to visit gardens for seed. Acrobatic skills and a bright, mainly greenish livery make them easy to overlook as titmice.

How birds adapt: in 1988, in T*he Complete Book of British Birds* (Automobile Association) Goldfinch was categorised as 'Not a bird table visitor'. In the intervening years, hordes of the small ebullient finch have taken to feeders. Goldfinches are fussy eaters and dislodge and discard seed, which falls away, creating a ground-level 'takeaway'. Too much spillage or, perversely, too many ground-feeding customers concentrated side by side, can lead to unsanitary conditions. Stations should be moved periodically and feeders cleaned scrupulously.

Left: Blue Tits' preparedness to accept food and nest-boxes cuts both ways – human and avian. Our Franciscan acts of giving have found a willing recipient. Yet, when we enter the realm of Blue Tits in our own backyard, the bird becomes irritated. Its sweet trill (see species account) is really a narky alarm call. Cockiness is an attribute of a bird that demonstrated a nationwide ability to transmit ideas when, during the 1970s, milk bottle tops were attacked every morning to remove cream. That was a step too far – the habit stopped when the cream was removed. Blue Tit is the only 'capped' tit to line the nest with feathers. This photograph was taken in a nest-box adapted for photography.

Right: In Britain alone, at least 5 million birds are killed annually by cats. Magpies are a scourge of eggs and nestlings. In many ways cats are worse because they take both breeding adults and full-grown fledglings before going home to eat cat food made from sand-eels, thus depriving seabird chicks of their dinner. In evolutionary terms, *Felis silvestris*, the Wildcat ancestor of all domestic strains, is a hunter. Hence bird-stalking pets are behaving naturally. Owners behave irresponsibly by allowing their mollycoddled moggies to wander neighbourhood gardens and slaughter wild birds that the rest of us try to nurture and enjoy.

a change in some bird diets. Of course, you too can switch menu. In the breeding season, Blackbirds, Robins and Dunnocks feed worms to nestlings. Mealworms are cheap to buy – even online – and can be scattered among lawn grass. Fear not, all will be found! In no time you can create a feeding hotspot. If cat-proof, you can provide a safe haven for juveniles, which will also be drawn to the cornucopia. Guard against disease. Outbreaks spread from contaminated droppings or by body fluids, especially saliva, of infected birds. The risk is greatest when many feed in the same area for prolonged periods. Obvious tips are to rotate feeding sites and clean and regularly disinfect feeders and bird tables, using a weak solution of domestic bleach. Trichomonas is not a word that trips off the tongue. It is a parasite that causes trichomoniasis in garden birds, infecting the back of the throat and gullet. Symptoms include laboured breathing, regurgitating food and having difficulty swallowing. The disease may progress over several days and the outbreak can last for weeks. It was first noticed in the UK in 2005 and outbreaks have recurred in every summer since. Greenfinches and Chaffinches are most affected. The Garden Bird Health Initiative maintains a dedicated website at www.ufaw.org.uk/gbhi that contains downloadable information.

Providing a nest-box is perhaps the greatest gift. Ensure that it is not a poisoned chalice. Can cats access it? Is it big enough inside? Is the entrance hole small enough to admit the desired tenant and nothing larger? Birds like plenty of room in which to construct a deep, comfortable nest. Many nest-boxes offered for sale are too shallow and are shoddy affairs that can split or are not weatherproof. Like us, birds need a proper home and space

for a growing family. An insane development in commercially produced boxes is a lid that cannot be lifted. *Used boxes must be opened and cleaned after the tenants have left.* Ticks and fleas attach themselves to birds and may lurk in a dormant state among old nest material. In particular, fleas develop in the nest during summer and cluster around the entrance the following spring, waiting for victims to enter. Large numbers cause discomfort and the box may be abandoned. Another reason to open the lid is to examine the floor. Some are left with large gaps – presumably for drainage. A weatherproof roof ought to negate this need. Plug all floor apertures: spaces in the floor will most likely put tenants off. Nest-boxes with floors that are damp or rotten have no chance of occupancy. If necessary, insert a dry plywood base over an existing mouldy base. Tits begin house-hunting in January – a cue for a New Year resolution? Avoid open-fronted boxes. The density of Magpies and cats in suburbia mean that birds are being invited to make a home in a death trap for eggs and chicks, never mind the likelihood of an incubating adult being taken. There is a paradox in erecting a nest-box nowhere near foraging habitat. The birds have been given a home but they must go elsewhere to find food. Why not plant trees that provide both? Native broadleaves, especially Willow, Birch, Oak, Hawthorn and Alder, are rich in insects and provide a cornucopia of chick food. The emerging foliage of deciduous trees supports the caterpillars that sustain many adult songbirds that, in turn, feed them to their young. If planting Alder, use native *Alnus canina* or *A. glutinosa*; Italian Alder *A. cordata* is commonly stocked by garden centres but is vastly inferior.

I GREW UP IN A HOUSING ESTATE where the only binoculars were owned by an aged bird-catcher. A prized pair of Bullfinches lit up his world. They lit up mine too, but a chance to hold a pair of binoculars rated higher. They had German writing and a distance scale superimposed on the view through large lenses that had a wonderful bloom of cobalt blue. Majestic peering brought to mind not birds but naval engagements and an imperious Teutonic voice yelling 'Feuer!' I felt blessed to be allowed to borrow them. Years later I got their little brother from, not Santa Claus, but a local schoolteacher, in time for my sixteenth birthday.

You become spiritually attached to binoculars. They become a portal to another world. The quality of the image is important but the touch of the magic instrument can matter just as much. Technology has created a selection of top models that share dizzy standards. Some are not only waterproof (the curse of my formative years was steamed-up lenses) but also bombproof, feather-light and image-stabilised. Amazing! However, old binoculars do not degrade or fail to resolve a perfect image. Unlike human eyes, they do not blur with age. If I could find my teenage pair I would still be able to see birds clearly, provided it was not a rainy day and they were turning the view into a sauna.

Second only to the tedious cliché, 'Is it the two-legged birds you're after?' comes the line, 'What binoculars should I buy?' In the past the question was easy to answer because few options were available. Choice has mushroomed and the enquiry is on a par with wondering which car to purchase. In addition, a technological change has occurred. Former 'conventional' binoculars had a stepped appearance that accommodated angled prisms reflecting light from large front-end objective lenses through internal gubbins (prone to being knocked out of alignment) to small viewing eyepieces. This generation – referred to as 'Porro prisms' after their inventor Ignazio Porro – has been superseded by 'roof prisms'. The novel configuration meant that models could be smaller and, with virtually no external moving parts, waterproof. Because they did not need to position prisms at vulnerable angles, a new robustness was born. Roof prisms are not susceptible to developing 'double vision' when dropped or accidentally whacked.

The next consideration is magnification. Exactly what do mathematical equations such as 7x42 mean? For binocular users, the answer is not 294. The first digit is the power of magnification, followed by the diameter in millimetres of the (objective) lens at the front of the optic. When Porro prisms were universal, it was useful to divide the smaller figure into the larger; the bigger the numerical result, the brighter the image. Hence, 7x50 binoculars, despite being lower-powered than 10x50 by a

factor of three, would resolve a brighter image. Because roof prism design delivers similar light-gathering abilities regardless of magnification, this quotient is largely obsolete. Nevertheless, there are factors to consider. At higher magnification, depth of field is somewhat reduced, as is overall brightness and field of view. Such trade-offs may count for nothing, depending on personal taste. Models boasting magnification above the power of ten tend to be fool's gold, except when exceedingly expensive, in which case they will also be large and, for best results, will require a tripod. As a general steer, avoid zoom magnifications and those with lenses made of synthetic glass. If possible, compare makes, making sure to try a top brand to get a yardstick for brightness, sharpness and field of view. Once those criteria have been experienced, the rest comes down to cost and intuition. Do you like the action of the focus wheel? Are they balanced and comfortable to hold? Once you have found Mr Right, many years of blissful monogamy should lie ahead.

Usually the most difficult challenge with new binoculars is working out how to assemble and then attach the strap and rain-guard. Setting the individual eyepiece adjustment can be fiddly too, although the principle is always the same: move the central focus until the image is sharp, and then slowly rotate (possibly by means of click-stops) the individual eyepiece adjustment to achieve fine focus. On some models, the setting can wander about. In the past, a frequent drastic remedy was to tape the eyepiece control ring into position. Cleaning lenses is best left until absolutely essential. Some birdwatchers acquire the habits of snooker players, constantly wiping lenses as though they were chalking a cue. This can result in lens coatings being removed, leading to a duller image. 'Lens pens' are an excellent cleaning aid and have a mushroom-shaped pad, containing dry chemical that absorbs greasy marks and light scum. However, a lens pen will not remove raindrops or spray. For this, a soft absorbent cloth is best. In heavy salt spray, continuous rubbing with coarse tissues is tantamount to cleaning lenses with sandpaper. Eyecups used to be permanent, immovable fixtures. Most of today's models allow the eyecup to be twisted down, narrowing the gap between eye-socket and eyepiece. Try a shallow position for the eyecups – it can produce the illusion of a wider field of view.

Within a generation telescopes have shaken off their drawtube design and are no longer the brass-and-glass monsters that they once were. Angled bodies have revolutionised viewing and, once you have made the mental leap of looking down to see ahead, the advantage of an angled body is considerable. No longer do you have to face into eye-watering wind or extend a tripod to a teetering maximum height. Furthermore, by peering down, your unused eye is already crooked at a favourable angle

Birds are among the most mobile creatures on Earth. Yet following them with optical equipment – especially a telescope or camera – can be difficult. How do wildlife film-makers produce such effortless moving images? The answer is to use a tripod head that has a panning action. How do you locate such a model? Many exist. To be sure that you have found the Real McCoy, once tensioning mechanisms are set, one lever should give full control and enable you – as with these sprinting Eider ducklings – to follow the subject 'in one smooth move'.

to check a field guide or make a sketch while the other eye is scrutinising a telescope image. A neat trick is a learned ability to look with both eyes open. Practise by holding something plain in front of your 'non-telescope eye' to fool it into not overlapping with the image. Once this technique is mastered, the benefit is a more relaxed view. If peering for long periods, it pays to switch from one eye to the other. This counteracts eyestrain and also the blanching of colour and contrast that occurs if just one eye is employed for prolonged periods.

Wide-angle eyepieces with set magnifications offer a panoramic field of view. Except for expensive makes, zoom eyepieces substantially reduce field of view, although the trade-off is an ability to crank up the power. Telescopes that incorporate special glass can be twice the price of the same model made in conventional glass. The difference can be surprisingly subtle and (good financial news) you might actually prefer the image filtered through standard glass. Do not neglect to acquire a solid tripod with a *smooth panning head*. A lot of telescopes are atop wobbly tripods. The difference in sharpness derived from a stable image is huge. Spending money on a superb telescope and clamping it to a cheap rickety tripod is heresy; it compromises the ability of the instrument to deliver. In today's digital age, compact cameras can be attached to telescopes (or binoculars) to resolve an image of sufficiently high quality to identify a mystery bird after the event. In an 'emergency' even a mobile phone can be grabbed and, literally, pressed into service if something unusual has been encountered.

HOOKED

I GREW UP in a slower, gentler time. Those were the days when bats counted as birds; and why not? They had wings, didn't they? Summers were long and winters were spent indoors reading *The Observer's Book of Birds*. In our house, apart from the rent book, there wasn't anything else to read. Half the book's plates were in black and white, which proved to be an identification pitfall until, on the cusp of my teens, I worked out what 'depicted in monochrome' actually meant. I realised that Siskins were not grey, black and white after all. Nevertheless, as a means of putting names to faces, the little brown book was brain food with the target-spotting potency of an al Qaeda training manual. An added incentive was the acquisition of flashcards depicting common birds that came with PG Tips tea. Armed with the set, my innate childhood desire to catalogue and understand was piqued. A latent interest in the variety of living things had netted birds. Pokémon cards were yet to be invented; otherwise I could have been misdirected towards man-made

artefacts. Nonetheless, the learning principle is important and conservationists should heed Pokémon (www.bioteach.ubc.ca/TeachingResources/GeneralScience/PokemonWildlife.pdf).

I yearned for a pair of wellies. Not knowing any other birdwatchers, I didn't miss binoculars. I remember my father taking me to a pawnshop to look at a pair with lenses scarcely larger than eyeballs. When the curmudgeon behind the counter said they cost 'two pounds, ten shillings and sixpence', my old man nearly had a coronary. I didn't like them anyway: actually they were opera glasses, and the tightwad shopkeeper was creepy; he had bad breath and bony fingers like my dentist. Instead, I desperately wanted a pair of 'water boots'. With my one pair of shoes, I was not allowed to thrash across wetlands questing for snipe, or go anywhere near the tickertape clouds of shorebirds on Belfast Lough. I felt trapped in a housing estate womb at Greenisland, Antrim. It was said that nasty things happened to people who ventured beyond the back fields. Tramping through

Even the sight of a flying archaeopteryx would not have been quite as memorable.

marshes or mudflats would have resulted in me being put up for adoption.

Without spyglasses – if you used words like 'binoculars' you ran the risk of being thumped for being a show-off – getting close to birds was a challenge. Forget seeing them close up in the garden. We did have a garden, but bird tables and strings of peanuts were unknown in Northern Ireland. The BBC patented them a few years later on *Blue Peter*. Sneaking up to a nest with a terrified Blackbird or Swallow incubating at arms' length was a good way to see details of adults – and then eggs. Singing birds required different tactics. Sedge Warblers tended to perch where you could see them, so I didn't have to throw rocks into vegetation to startle the songsters into view. On the other hand, unobtrusive Grasshopper Warblers were mortared.

One species remained steadfastly invisible for years. Corncrakes were a summer soundtrack playing in every pasture tall enough for the species to hide in. The phantom became an obsession. At nine, I ran after them in short trousers. By ten I was in jeans and could pursue them through nettles, but at eleven I still hadn't seen one. Short of flushing them out with napalm, I was bereft of ideas.

The darned bird even got me into trouble. I was playing outside right for the school soccer team and could hear one calling from meadows at the side of the pitch. It sounded close, much closer than the opposing team's outside left. In fact he was closer and streaked past me to score. My games teacher was furious when I told him that I had been distracted by a Corncrake, or Landrail (I got no reprieve for my erudition in supplying the species' alternative name). Perhaps he sensed that I was torn between soccer and birds. He need not have worried: I decided to combine the two. It happened like this. I persuaded

the rest of the forward line to help me nail a Corncrake. The nearest craking male to home was in the grounds of a local Presbyterian church. On a scale of fire and brimstone, trespassing there would risk punishment of fizzing white-hot intensity; but the draw was irresistible. The walls that bounded the site effectively isolated the quarry. If we all charged, surely the bird would reveal itself? I was so confident that I borrowed a pair of German Second World War spyglasses. Just the gear for the mission.

Climbing over a Protestant church gate felt like a mortal sin. The varnished wood, neatly trimmed lawns and weedless gravel pathways all seemed to be watching the act of trespass. Quickly and silently, we stepped into the jungle at the rear. As I now know, the Corncrake was using the church walls as an amplifier to throw its voice. The rasping echo made it a will-o'-the-wisp. We acted fast. Encircling what seemed to be the source, we rushed forward. We met at the epicentre, birdless. A second failure weakened resolve. It seemed better to scarper than wait for the police who, we imagined, were speeding towards us. Panic gripped big Joe Monaghan. I just knew he would be the first to chicken out. Florid-faced, he claimed that he heard movement in the church and legged it. That did the trick. He got an even bigger fright when a bird with bright ginger wings exploded at his feet. I could see it perfectly. It was wondrous. The pink bill shone like mother-of-pearl on a face of lapis lazuli blue. It was the embodiment of everything an iconic bird should be.

I was changed after that, and became umbilically connected with the wildlife of this planet. I do not know whether this was a road to Damascus or if the Corncrake was my forbidden fruit in the Garden of Eden. Either way, the operation's debrief established that life with birds in it certainly tasted sweeter.

HUGE

ACADEMIC LIFE might have suited me better if it had been more like school. Without a uniform I lost my sartorial compass. Inadvertently, I became a follower of fashion. The look was 'grunge refugee'. Long-haired and duffle-coated, it was easy to fit in. At times the thought crossed my mind that, at the end of all this, I was supposed to emerge as a svelte young man, educated and ready to make the world a better place. In the meantime I was able to exploit the New University of Ulster's laissez-faire timetables and fill my boots with birdwatching.

Home was a cold dungeon in Portstewart and early December 1976 witnessed a battle between threadbare hippie pretensions and frostbite. Hardy trendsetters stuck to cheesecloth tops and desert boots. The rest of us phoned home for woolly polo necks and gloves. Outdoors, in the bladder-shrinking cold, Redwings were everywhere. Groups of them hopped lethargically on frosted campus greens, for once not wings and tails rocketing away at human approach. Skylarks were also on the move and a severe

weather spectacular was playing out before my eyes at Portstewart Point. A new car park was sown with grass seed, despite the Siberian conditions. Among the local seedeaters a splendid male Snow Bunting arrived; its garb matched the season.

It was Wednesday, the best day of the week. The university film club screened inspired choices of movies on an enormous silver screen. No popcorn, just escapism and free heat. Reviews of today's offering contained tantalising snippets: 'It has been said that any story can be reduced to one of two basic plots: a person goes on a journey, or a stranger rolls into town.' The film was *High Plains Drifter*. It opens with a vaporous blur on a scorched plateau out of which emerges the silhouette of a galloping horseman. He is hardened and mysterious, unknown and probably dangerous. An antihero comes to life. Clint Eastwood played the lead. That did it. I sensed minimalist acting and gunslinger stereotyping. Not my cup of tea. I decided to go back to Portstewart Point. Besides, if I wanted to regard the antics of

People say that happiness springs only from the depths of our soul. On this occasion it sprang from behind a clump of grass.

an incorrigible hustler I needed to look no further than my flatmate Pat 'the Kid' Corry, a friend to every bookmaker in the seaside town (often with my money). Although a non-birder, Pat had fallen for my eulogising about the bunting's Snow White beauty and wanted to see it.

Pre-cast cobblestone blocks had been laid surrounding a raised plinth of soil. The designer had envisioned an elevated central doughnut of low grass around which vehicles could park and take in a panorama of sea and sky. Bare earth was raked level over both doughnut and cobbles; grass seed was everywhere. Linnets and Meadow Pipits hunkered squat to the ground on the summit. Alas, there was no sign of the star. Not to worry. The doughnut's ramparts offered a lee. Step by careful step we worked our way around the margins, following a clockwise route. 'Any moment now,' I predicted. And I was right. Firmly clamped to terra firma and dribbling flecks of seed was a small white blob sporting a waxy yellow bill and tawny breast-side patches suggesting that the wearer had just popped out of a toaster. Our tactics were spot-on. The quarry came closer. Pat was impressed, especially as he had my binoculars. He was not exactly excited, just savouring the view. Moments later he felt the full force of a rare bird discovery. I noticed a second bird shuffling around a bend. It was head-on and grovelling. Every once in a while I thought I saw a flash of yellow. Then, in an electrifying beat of time, it craned its neck and I beheld what looked like a black

and yellow liquorice allsort. Yikes! All the adrenaline drained from my body and squirted out of my ears. It was Northern Ireland's first Shore Lark. I wrenched the binoculars away from Pat, not realising that their strap was still around his neck. Our heads touched. However, it was obvious that my thoughts were elsewhere. In the ensuing tussle I grabbed the optics and babbled a blue streak. The Snow Bunting was eclipsed. I interpreted Pat's intake of breath as a sign that he too was gobsmacked. 'How rare is that one?' he whispered. 'Huge!' I replied.

I went back to the scene at first light: nuts to Statistics for Geographers: Module II. I was revved up like a submariner on shore leave but arrived in time only to see my erstwhile cornucopia run dry. The lark rose, said 'Donegal, here I come,' and sped off out to sea. It left me with a strange, flat feeling, as though living between two planets. In the distance the hills of Inishowen sparkled with snow. There was no shore to be seen, only a distant wall of white creeping in from the farthest limits of the sea. Maybe that sight made it think of a mountaintop home in Norway? Only a handful of House Sparrows remained. Cinderella had flown the coop and I was left with the Ugly Sisters. Rare birds can make us the gift of a larger life. They are shooting stars, flashes of brilliance and inspiration; noses thumbed at our definition of status quo. They are the strangers that roll into town.

SYSTEMATIC LIST OF SPECIES

This list provides a capsule summary of those species that have occurred in both Northern Ireland and the Republic of Ireland. Commencing in the nineteenth century with Thompson (1849–52), all published literature has been consulted to achieve utmost accuracy. Except for rare birds, additional information is contained in the main species accounts. Each entry includes a grading that reflects contemporary status. Judgements are somewhat subjective and use a narrow range of descriptive terms: Common (C), Fairly Common (FC), Uncommon (U), Rare (R), and Vagrant (V). These are defined below. Despite their imprecision, most birdwatchers understand what they mean. In all cases, knowledge of bird behaviour has to be borne in mind. Grasshopper Warbler is a common bird in suitable nesting habitat but is seldom seen due to a secretive lifestyle and, if not recognised by song, would be totally overlooked. Hence the number of individuals of a particular species that are present in a given habitat does not necessarily reflect the likelihood of discovery. Sadly, a few former resident species have become extinct, each as a result of human activity. Some, such as Great Auk, are gone for good. For others, there is little or no realistic prospect of natural recolonisation and they are classified as Extinct (EX).

C   **Common** Always or almost always present in preferred habitat at the appropriate season.

FC   **Fairly Common** Usually present, but sometimes only one or a few individuals.

U   **Uncommon** Occasional or localised, but not unexpected.

R   **Rare** Infrequent occurrence, not necessarily annual.

V   **Vagrant** Out of the blue; no more than a handful of appearances.

EX   **Extinct**

C FC U R V EX   ***Italicised letters*** in the list below indicate sightings in the Republic of Ireland.

Mute Swan *Cygnus olor* C *C*

Bewick's Swan *Cygnus columbianus* U *U*

Whooper Swan *Cygnus cygnus* C *C*

Bean Goose *Anser fabalis* R *R*

Pink-footed Goose *Anser brachyrhynchus* U *U*

White-fronted Goose *Anser albifrons* FC *C*

Lesser White-fronted Goose *Anser erythropus* V

Greylag Goose *Anser anser* C *C*

Snow Goose *Branta caerulescens* R *R*

Canada Goose *Branta canadensis* V *R*

Barnacle Goose *Branta leucopsisu* U *C*

Brent Goose *Branta bernicla* C *C*

Ruddy Shelduck *Tadorna ferruginea* R *R*

Shelduck *Tadorna tadorna* C *C*

Wigeon *Anas penelope* C *C*

American Wigeon *Anas americana* V *R*

Gadwall *Anas strepera* C *C*

Teal *Anas crecca* C *C*

Green-winged Teal *Anas carolinensis* R *R*

Mallard *Anas platyrhynchos* C *C*

American Black Duck *Anas rubripes* V

Pintail *Anas acuta* C *C*

Garganey *Anas querquedula* U *U*

Blue-winged Teal *Anas discors* V *R*

Baikal Teal *Anas formosa* V *V*

Shoveler *Anas clypeata* C *C*

Red-crested Pochard *Netta rufina* R *R*

Pochard *Aythya ferina* C *C*

Redhead *Aythya americana* V

Ring-necked Duck *Aythya collaris* R *R*

Ferruginous Duck *Aythya nyroca* R *R*

Tufted Duck *Aythya fuligula* C *C*

Scaup *Aythya marila* C *C*

Lesser Scaup *Aythya affinis* R *R*

Eider *Somateria mollissima* C *FC*

King Eider *Somateria spectabilis* V *V*

Long-tailed Duck *Clangula hyemalis* C *C*

Common Scoter *Melanitta nigra* C *C*

Surf Scoter *Melanitta perspicillata* V *R*

Velvet Scoter *Melanitta fusca* U *U*

Asian White-winged Scoter *Melanitta deglandi stejnegeri* V

Bufflehead *Bucephala albeola* V

Barrow's Goldeneye *Bucephala islanica* V

Goldeneye *Bucephala clangula* C *C*

Hooded Merganser *Lophodytes cucullattus* V

Smew *Mergellus albellus* U *U*

Red-breasted Merganser *Mergus serrator* C *C*

Goosander *Mergus merganser* U *U*

Red Grouse *Lagopus lagopus* FC *FC*

Capercaillie *Tetrao urogallus* EX *EX*

Grey Partridge *Perdix perdix* EX *R*

Quail *Coturnix coturnix* R *R*

Red-throated Diver *Gavia stellata* C *C*

Black-throated Diver *Gavia arctica* U *U*

Pacific Diver *Gavia pacificus* V

Great Northern Diver *Gavia immer* C *C*

White-billed Diver *Gavia adamsii* V *V*

Fulmar *Fulmarus glacialis* C *C*

Fea's Petrel *Pterodroma feae* V *R*

Bulwer's Petrel *Bulweria bulwerii* V

Cory's Shearwater *Calonectris diomedia* R *U*

Great Shearwater *Puffinus gravis* U *FC*

Sooty Shearwater *Puffinus griseus* FC *FC*

Manx Shearwater *Puffinus puffinus* C *C*

Balearic Shearwater *Puffinus mauretanicus* U *U*

Little Shearwater *Puffinus baroli* V *V*

Wilson's Petrel *Oceanites oceanicus* V *U*

Storm Petrel *Hydrobates pelagicus* FC *C*

Leach's Petrel *Oceanodroma leucorhoa* U *U*

Swinhoe's Petrel *Oceanodroma monorhis* V

Madeiran Petrel *Oceanodroma castro* V

Gannet *Morus bassanus* C *C*

Cormorant *Phalacrocorax carbo* C *C*

Double-crested Cormorant *Phalacrocorax auritus* V

Shag *Phalacrocorax aristotelis* C *C*

Magnificent Frigatebird *Fregata magnificens* V

Bittern *Botaurus stellaris* R *R*

American Bittern *Botaurus lentiginosus* V *V*

Little Bittern *Ixobrychus minutus* V *V*

Night Heron *Nycticorax nycticorax* V *R*

Green Heron *Butorides virescens* V

Squacco Heron *Ardeola ralloides* V *V*

Cattle Egret *Bubulcus ibis* V *R*

Little Blue Heron *Egretta caerulea* V

Little Egret *Egretta garzetta* FC *FC*

Great White Egret *Ardea alba* V *R*

Grey Heron *Ardea cinerea* C *C*

Purple Heron *Ardea purpurea* V *R*

Black Stork *Ciconia nigra* V

White Stork *Ciconia ciconia* R *R*

Glossy Ibis *Plegadis falcinellus* V *R*

Spoonbill *Platalea leucorodia* R *R*

Pied-billed Grebe *Podilymbus podiceps* V

Little Grebe *Tachybaptus ruficollis* C *C*

Great Crested Grebe *Podiceps cristatus* C *C*

Red-necked Grebe *Podiceps grisegena* R *R*

Slavonian Grebe *Podiceps auritus* FC *FC*

Black-necked Grebe *Podiceps nigricollis* R *R*

White-tailed Eagle *Haliaeetus albicilla* EX *EX*

Bald Eagle *Haliaeetus leucocephalus* V *V*

Griffon Vulture *Gyps fulvus* V

Osprey *Pandion haliaetus* U *U*

Golden Eagle *Aquila chrysaetos* R *V*

Red Kite *Milvus milvus* V *V*

Black Kite *Milvus migrans* V *V*

Marsh Harrier *Circus aeruginosus* U *U*

Hen Harrier *Circus cyaneus* FC *FC*

Montagu's Harrier *Circus pygargus* V *R*

Pallid Harrier *Circus macrourus* V *V*

Buzzard *Buteo buteo* C *FC*

Rough-legged Buzzard *Buteo lagopus* R *R*

Spotted Eagle *Aquila clanga* V

Honey Buzzard *Pernis apivorus* V *V*

Sparrowhawk *Accipiter nisus* C *C*

Goshawk *Accipiter gentilis* U *R*

Kestrel *Falco tinnunculus* C *C*

Lesser Kestrel *Falco naumanni* V

Red-footed Falcon *Falco vespertinus* V *R*

Merlin *Falco columbarius* FC *FC*

Hobby *Falco subbuteo* R *U*

Gyr Falcon *Falco rusticolus* R *R*

Peregrine *Falco peregrinus* C *C*

Water Rail *Rallus aquaticus* FC *FC*

Spotted Crake *Porzana porzana* R *R*

Sora *Porzana carolina* V

Little Crake *Porzana parva* V

Baillon's Crake *Porzana pusilla* V

Corncrake *Crex crex* R *FC*

Moorhen *Gallinula chloropus* C *C*

Coot *Fulica atra* C *C*

American Coot *Fulica americana* V

Crane *Grus grus* V *R*

Sandhill Crane *Grus canadensis* V

Little Bustard *Tetrax tetrax* V

Great Bustard *Otis tarda* V

Oystercatcher *Haematopus ostralegus* C *C*

Black-winged Stilt *Himantopus himantopus* V *V*

Avocet *Recurvirostra avosetta* R *R*

Stone Curlew *Burhinus oedicnemus* V *R*

Cream-coloured Courser *Cursorius cursor* V

Collared Pratincole *Glareola pratincola* V *V*

Black-winged Pratincole *Glareola nordmanni* V

Little Ringed Plover *Charadrius dubius* R *U*

Ringed Plover *Charadrius hiaticula* C *C*

Semipalmated Plover *Charadrius semipalmatus* V

Killdeer *Charadrius vociferus* V *V*

Kentish Plover *Charadrius alexandrinus* V *V*

Dotterel *Charadrius morinellus* R *R*

Golden Plover *Pluvialis apricaria* C *C*

Pacific Golden Plover *Pluvialis fulva* V *V*

American Golden Plover *Pluvialis dominica* V *R*

Grey Plover *Pluvialis squatarola* C *C*

Sociable Plover *Vanellus gregarius* V

Lapwing *Vanellus vanellus* C *C*

Great Knot *Calidris tenuirostris* V

Knot *Calidris canutus* C *C*

Sanderling *Calidris alba* C *C*

Semipalmated Sandpiper *Calidris pusilla* V *R*

Western Sandpiper *Calidris mauri* V

Red-necked Stint *Calidris ruficollis* V

Little Stint *Calidris minuta* U *U*

Temminck's Stint *Calidris temminckii* R *R*

Long-toed Stint *Calidris subminuta* V

Least Sandpiper *Calidris minutilla* V

White-rumped Sandpiper *Calidris fuscicollis* R *U*

Baird's Sandpiper *Calidris bairdii* V *U*

Pectoral Sandpiper *Calidris melanotos* U *U*

Sharp-tailed Sandpiper *Calidris acuminata* V

Curlew Sandpiper *Calidris ferruginea* FC *FC*

Stilt Sandpiper *Calidris himantopus* V *V*

Purple Sandpiper *Calidris maritima* C *C*

Dunlin *Calidris alpina* C *C*

Broad-billed Sandpiper *Limicola falcinellus* V *V*

Buff-breasted Sandpiper *Tryngites subruficollis* R *U*

Ruff *Philomachus pugnax* FC *FC*

Jack Snipe *Lymnocryptes minimus* FC *FC*

Common Snipe *Gallinago gallinago* C *C*

Wilson's Snipe *Gallinago delicata* V

Great Snipe *Gallinago media* V *V*

Short-billed Dowitcher *Limnodromus griseus* V

Long-billed Dowitcher *Limnodromus scolopaceus* R *R*

Woodcock *Scolopax rusticola* FC *FC*

Black-tailed Godwit *Limosa limosa* C *C*

Bar-tailed Godwit *Limosa lapponica* C *C*

Eskimo Curlew *Numenius borealis* EX

Whimbrel *Numenius phaeopus* FC *FC*

Curlew *Numenius arquata* C *C*

Upland Sandpiper *Bartramia longicauda* V

Terek Sandpiper *Xenus cinereus* V

Common Sandpiper *Actitis hypoleucos* C *C*

Spotted Sandpiper *Actitis macularius* V *R*

Green Sandpiper *Tringa ochropus* U *U*

Solitary Sandpiper *Tringa solitaria* V

Spotted Redshank *Tringa erythropus* U *U*

Greater Yellowlegs *Tringa melanoleuca* V *V*

Greenshank *Tringa nebularia* FC *FC*

Lesser Yellowlegs *Tringa flavipes* R *R*

Marsh Sandpiper *Tringa stagnatilis* V

Wood Sandpiper *Tringa glareola* U *U*

Redshank *Tringa totanus* C *C*

Turnstone *Arenaria interpres* C *C*

Wilson's Phalarope *Phalaropus tricolor* R *R*

Red-necked Phalarope *Phalaropus lobatus* R *R*

Grey Phalarope *Phalaropus fulicarius* U *U*

Pomarine Skua *Stercorarius pomarinus* U *U*

Arctic Skua *Stercorarius parasiticus* FC *FC*

Long-tailed Skua *Stercorarius longicaudus* U *U*

Great Skua *Stercorarius skua* FC *FC*

Ivory Gull *Pagophila eburnea* V *V*

Sabine's Gull *Xema sabini* U *FC*

Kittiwake *Rissa tridactyla* C *C*

Bonaparte's Gull *Chroicocephalus philadelphia* V *R*

Black-headed Gull *Chroicocephalus ridibundus* C *C*

Little Gull *Hydrocoloeus minutus* U *U*

Ross's Gull *Rhodostethia rosea* V *V*

Laughing Gull *Larus atricilla* V *V*

Franklin's Gull *Larus pipixcan* V *V*

Mediterranean Gull *Larus melanocephalus* U *FC*

Common Gull *Larus canus* C *C*

Ring-billed Gull *Larus delawarensis* U *U*

Lesser Black-backed Gull *Larus fuscus* C *C*

Herring Gull *Larus argentatus* C *C*

Yellow-legged Gull *Larus michahellis* R *U*

Caspian Gull *Larus cachinnans* V *V*

American Herring Gull *Larus smithsonianus* V *R*

Iceland Gull *Larus glaucoides* U *U*

Thayer's Gull *Larus thayeri* V *V*

Glaucous Gull *Larus hyperboreus* U *U*

Great Black-backed Gull *Larus marinus* C *C*

Sooty Tern *Onychoprion fuscatus* V *V*

Little Tern *Sternula albifrons* U *FC*

Gull-billed Tern *Gelochelidon nilotica* V *V*

Caspian Tern *Hydroprogne caspia* V

Royal Tern *Sterna maxima* V

Whiskered Tern *Chlidonias hybrida* V *V*

Black Tern *Chlidonias niger* U *U*

White-winged Black Tern *Chliodonias leucopterus* R *R*

Sandwich Tern *Sterna sandvicensis* C *C*

Elegant Tern *Sterna elegans* V *V*

Lesser Crested Tern *Sterna bengalensis* V

Forster's Tern *Sterna forsteri* R *R*

Common Tern *Sterna hirundo* C *C*

Roseate Tern *Sterna dougallii* U *FC*

Arctic Tern *Sterna paradisaea* C *C*

Guillemot *Uria aalge* C *C*

Brunnich's Guillemot *Uria lomvia* V

Razorbill *Alca torda* C *C*

Great Auk *Pinguinus impennis* EX *EX*

Black Guillemot *Cepphus grille* C *C*

Little Auk *Alle alle* U *U*

Puffin *Fratercula arctica* FC *FC*

Pallas's Sandgrouse *Syrrhaptes paradoxus* V *V*

Rock Dove *Columba livia* R *U*

Stock Dove *Columba oenas* FC *FC*

Woodpigeon *Columba palumbus* C *C*

Collared Dove *Streptopelia decaocto* C *C*

Turtle Dove *Streptopelia turtur* R *U*

Mourning Dove *Zenaida macroura* V

Passenger Pigeon *Ectopistes migratorius* EX

Great Spotted Cuckoo *Clamator glandarius* V *V*

Cuckoo *Cuculus canorus* FC *FC*

Black-billed Cuckoo *Coccyzus erythrophthalmus* V

Yellow-billed Cuckoo *Coccyzus americanus* V *V*

Barn Owl *Tyto alba* U *FC*

Scops Owl *Otus scops* V *V*

Snowy Owl *Bubo scandiacus* V *V*

Long-eared Owl *Asio otus* FC *FC*

Short-eared Owl *Asio flammeus* U *U*

Nightjar *Caprimulgus europaeus* R *U*

Common Nighthawk *Chordeiles minor* V

Chimney Swift *Chaetura pelagica* V

White-throated Needletail *Hirundapus caudacutus* V

Swift *Apus apus* C *C*

Pallid Swift *Apus pallidus* V *V*

Alpine Swift *Apus melba* V *V*

White-rumped Swift *Apus caffer* V

Little Swift *Apus affinis* V

Kingfisher *Alcedo atthis* FC *FC*

Belted Kingfisher *Megaceryle alcyon* V *V*

Bee-eater *Merops apiaster* V *R*

Roller *Coracias garrulus* V *V*

Hoopoe *Upupa epops* R *R*

Wryneck *Jynx torquilla* V *R*

Green Woodpecker *Picus viridis* V

Yellow-bellied Sapsucker *Sphyrapicus varius* V

Great Spotted Woodpecker *Dendrocopos major* U *U*

Philadelphia Vireo *Vireo philadelphicus* V

Red-eyed Vireo *Vireo olivaceus* R

Golden Oriole *Oriolus oriolus* V *R*

Brown Shrike *Lanius cristatus* V

Isabelline Shrike *Lanius isabellinus* V

Red-backed Shrike *Lanius collurio* V *R*

Lesser Grey Shrike *Lanius minor* V

Great Grey Shrike *Lanius excubitor* V *V*

Woodchat Shrike *Lanius senator* V *R*

Chough *Pyrrhocorax pyrrhocorax* U *FC*

Magpie *Pica pica* C *C*

Jay *Garrulus glandarius* C *C*

Jackdaw *Corvus monedula* C *C*

Rook *Corvus frugilegus* C *C*

Carrion Crow *Corvus corone* U *U*

Hooded Crow *Corvus cornix* C *C*

Raven *Corvus corax* C *C*

Goldcrest *Regulus regulus* C *C*

Firecrest *Regulus ignicapilla* R *R*

Blue Tit *Cyanistes caeruleus* C *C*

Great Tit *Parus major* C *C*

Coal Tit *Periparus ater* C *C*

Marsh Tit *Poecile palustris* V

Bearded Tit *Panurus biarmicus* R

Short-toed Lark *Calandrella brachydactyla* V *R*

Woodlark *Lullula arborea* EX *V*

Skylark *Alauda arvensis* C *C*

Shore Lark *Eremophila alpestris* V *V*

Sand Martin *Riparia riparia* C *C*

Swallow *Hirundo rustica* C *C*

House Martin *Delichon urbica* C *C*

Red-rumped Swallow *Cecropis daurica* V *V*

American Cliff Swallow *Petrochelidon pyrrhonota* V

Cetti's Warbler *Cettia cetti* V

Long-tailed Tit *Aegithalos caudatus* C *C*

Greenish Warbler *Phylloscopus trochiloides* R

Arctic Warbler *Phylloscopus borealis* V

Pallas's Warbler *Phylloscopus proregulus* V *V*

Yellow-browed Warbler *Phylloscopus inornatus* R *U*

Hume's Warbler *Phylloscopus humei* V

Radde's Warbler *Phylloscopus schwarzi* V *V*

Dusky Warbler *Phylloscopus fuscatus* V

Western Bonelli's Warbler *Phylloscopus bonelli* V

Wood Warbler *Phylloscopus sibilatrix* U *U*

Chiffchaff *Phylloscopus collybita* C *C*

Siberian Chiffchaff *Phylloscopus tristis* R *R*

Iberian Chiffchaff *Phylloscopus ibericus* V

Willow Warbler *Phylloscopus trochilus* C *C*

Blackcap *Sylvia atricapilla* C *C*

Garden Warbler *Sylvia borin* U *U*

Barred Warbler *Sylvia nisoria* V *R*

Lesser Whitethroat *Sylvia curruca* R *U*

Whitethroat *Sylvia communis* C *C*

Dartford Warbler *Sylvia undata* V

Subalpine Warbler *Sylvia cantillans* V *R*

Sardinian Warbler *Sylvia melanocephala* V

Pallas's Grasshopper Warbler *Locustella certhiola* V

Grasshopper Warbler *Locustella naevia* C *C*

Savi's Warbler *Locustella luscinoides* V

Eastern Olivaceous Warbler *Hippolais pallida* V

Booted Warbler *Hippolais caligata* V

Sykes's Warbler *Hippolais rama* V

Icterine Warbler *Hippolais icterina* V *R*

Melodious Warbler *Hippolais polyglotta* V *R*

Aquatic Warbler *Acrocephalus paludicola* V

Sedge Warbler *Acrocephalus schoenobaenus* C *C*

Paddyfield Warbler *Acrocephalus agricola* V

Blyth's Reed Warbler *Acrocephalus dumetorum* V

Marsh Warbler *Acrocephalus palustris* V

Reed Warbler *Acrocephalus scirpaceus* FC *FC*

Great Reed Warbler *Acrocephalus arundinaceus* V

Fan-tailed Warbler *Cisticola juncidis* V

Waxwing *Bombycilla garrulus* U *U*

Cedar Waxwing *Bombycilla cedrorum* V

Treecreeper *Certhia familiaris* C *C*

Wren *Troglodytes troglodytes* C *C*

Grey Catbird *Dumetella carolinensis* V

Starling *Sturnus vulgaris* C *C*

Rose-coloured Starling *Pastor roseus* R *R*

Dipper *Cinclus cinclus* C *C*

White's Thrush *Zoothera dauma* V *V*

Siberian Thrush *Zoothera sibirica* V

Hermit Thrush *Catharus guttatus* V

Swainson's Thrush *Catharus ustulatus* V

Grey-cheeked Thrush *Catharus minimus* V

Ring Ouzel *Turdus torquatus* R *U*

Blackbird *Turdus merula* C *C*

Black-throated Thrush *Turdus atrogularis* V

Fieldfare *Turdus pilaris* C *C*

Song Thrush *Turdus philomelos* C *C*

Redwing *Turdus iliacus* C *C*

Mistle Thrush *Turdus viscivorus* C *C*

American Robin *Turdus migratorius* V *V*

Spotted Flycatcher *Muscicapa striata* FC *FC*

Brown Flycatcher *Muscicapa daurica* V *V*

Rufous Bush Robin *Cercotrichas galactotes* V

Robin *Erithacus rubecula* C *C*

Thrush Nightingale *Luscinia luscinia* V

Nightingale *Luscinia megarhynchos* V *V*

Bluethroat *Luscinia svecica* V *R*

Red-flanked Bluetail *Tarsiger cyanurus* V

Black Redstart *Phoenicurus ochruros* U *U*

Redstart *Phoenicurus phoenicurus* U *U*

Whinchat *Saxicola rubetra* U *U*

Stonechat *Saxicola torquatus* C *C*

Isabelline Wheatear *Oenanthe isabellina* V

Wheatear *Oenanthe oenanthe* C *C*

Pied Wheatear *Oenanthe pleschanka* V

Black-eared Wheatear *Oenanthe hispanica* V

Desert Wheatear *Oenanthe deserti* V

White-crowned Black Wheatear *Oenanthe leucopyga* V

Rock Thrush *Monticola saxatilis* V

Red-breasted Flycatcher *Ficedula parva* V *R*

Pied Flycatcher *Ficedula hypoleuca* R *U*

Collared Flycatcher *Ficedula albicollis* V

Dunnock *Prunella modularis* C *C*

House Sparrow *Passer domesticus* C *C*

Tree Sparrow *Passer montanus* FC *FC*

Yellow Wagtail *Motacilla flava* R *U*

Citrine Wagtail *Motacilla citreola* V *V*

Grey Wagtail *Motacilla cinerea* C *C*

Pied Wagtail *Motacilla alba* C *C*

Richard's Pipit *Anthus richardi* V *R*

Tawny Pipit *Anthus campestris* V

Olive-backed Pipit *Anthus hodgsoni* V

Tree Pipit *Anthus triviali* R *U*

Pechora Pipit *Anthus gustavi* V

Meadow Pipit *Anthus pratensis* C *C*

Red-throated Pipit *Anthus cervinus* V *R*

Rock Pipit *Anthus petrosus* C *C*

Water Pipit *Anthus spinoletta* R *U*

Buff-bellied Pipit *Anthus rubescens* V *V*

Chaffinch *Fringilla coelebs* C *C*

Brambling *Fringilla montifringilla* FC *FC*

Serin *Serinus serinus* V

Greenfinch *Chloris chloris* C *C*

Goldfinch *Carduelis carduelis* C *C*

Siskin *Carduelis spinus* C *C*

Linnet *Carduelis cannabina* C *C*

Twite *Carduelis flavirostris* FC *FC*

Lesser Redpoll *Carduelis [flammea] cabaret* C *C*

Mealy Redpoll *Carduelis flammea* R *R*

Arctic Redpoll *Carduelis hornemanni* V

Two-barrred Crossbill *Loxia leucoptera* V *V*

Crossbill *Loxia curvirostra* FC *FC*

Common Rosefinch *Carpodacus erthyrinus* V *R*

Bullfinch *Pyrrhula pyrrhula* C *C*

Hawfinch *Coccothraustes coccothraustes* V *R*

Snow Bunting *Plectrophenax nivalis* FC *FC*

Lapland Bunting *Calcarius lapponicus* U *U*

Scarlet Tanager *Piranga olivacea* V *V*

Rose-breasted Grosbeak *Pheucticus ludovicianus* V

Indigo Bunting *Passerina cyanea* V

Fox Sparrow *Passerella iliaca* V

White-crowned Sparrow *Zonotrichia leucophrys* V

White-throated Sparrow *Zonotrichia albicollis* V *V*

Dark-eyed Junco *Junco hyemalis* V *V*

Pine Bunting *Emberiza leucocephalos* V

Yellowhammer *Emberiza citrinella* FC *FC*

Cirl Bunting *Emberiza cirlus* V

Ortolan Bunting *Emberiza hortulana* V *R*

Rustic Bunting *Emberiza rustica* V *V*

Little Bunting *Emberiza pusilla* V *V*

Yellow-breasted Bunting *Emberiza aureola* V *V*

Reed Bunting *Emberiza schoeniclus* C *C*

Black-headed Bunting *Emberiza melanocephala* V *V*

Corn Bunting *Emberiza calandra* EX *EX*

Bobolink *Dolichonyx oryzivorus* V

Baltimore Oriole *Icterus galbula* V *V*

Black-and-white Warbler *Mniotilta varia* V *V*

Blue-winged Warbler *Vermivora pinus* V

Northern Parula *Parula americana* V

Yellow Warbler *Dendroica petechia* V

Myrtle Warbler *Dendroica coronata* V

Blackpoll Warbler *Dendroica striata* V

American Redstart *Setophaga ruticilla* V

Ovenbird *Seiurus aurocapilla* V

Northern Waterthrush *Seiurus noveboracensis* V

Common Yellowthroat *Geothlypis trichas* V

Canada Warbler *Wilsonia canadensis* V

HONOURABLE MENTIONS

Potentially genuine vagrants whose credentials are undermined by the possibility that a captive origin might account for an apparently wild occurrence.

Red-breasted Goose *Branta ruficollis*

Wood Duck *Aix sponsa*

Greater Flamingo *Phoenicopterus roseus*

Booted Eagle *Aquila pennata*

Red-headed Bunting *Emberiza bruniceps*

DISHONOURABLE MENTIONS

Aliens established by human agency: 'Man's mixture of ignorance and sentimentality leads him to introduce animals and plants into finely balanced communities where, as often as not, they set off a long and tragic chain of unforeseen reactions' (Mountfort 1968).

Mandarin Duck *Aix galericulata*

Ruddy Duck *Oxyura jamaicensis*

Red-legged Partridge *Alectoris rufa*

Pheasant *Phasianus colchicus*

BIBLIOGRAPHY

Adderton, I. 2005. 'Ecology and Implications for Conservation of Increasing Corvid Numbers', PhD thesis, Queen's University, Belfast.

Allen, D. and Mellon, C. 'Northern Ireland Priority Species: Ring Ouzel' (updated 2010) www.habitas.org.uk.

Alerstam, T. 1996. 'The Geographical Scale Factor in Orientation of Migrating Birds'. *Journal of Experimental Biology* 199:9–19.

Anderson, B.W. 2010. *Evolution and Taxonomy of White-cheeked Geese*. Blythe CA: AVVAR Books.

Appleton, G.F., Adams, S.Y., Clark, J., Simmons, J.R. and Peach, W.J. 1997. 'Report on Bird Ringing in Britain and Ireland for 1995'. *Ringing and Migration* 18:113–58.

Armstrong, E.A. 1944. *The Birds of the Grey Wind*. London: Lindsay Drummond.

Armstrong, E.A. 1955. *The Wren*. London: Collins.

Ashoori, A. and Zolfinejad, K. 2008. 'The Ecology of the Corncrake in Stubble Paddyfields in the South Caspian Lowlands'. *Podoces* 3:92–6.

Attenborough, D. 2009. *Life Stories*: 'Collecting'. BBC audio.

Automobile Association. 1988. *The Complete Book of British Birds*. Hampshire, UK: Automobile Association.

Baha el Din, S.M., Salama, W., Grieve, A. and Green, R.E. 1996. 'Trapping and Shooting of Corncrakes on the Mediterranean Coast of Egypt'. *Bird Conservation International* 6:213–27.

Bairlein, F., Norris, D.R., Nagel, R., Bulte, M., Voigt, C.C., Fox, J.W., Hussell, D.J.T. and Schmaljohann, H. 2012. 'Cross-Hemisphere Migration of a 25g Songbird'. *Biology Letters* online, 15 February www.royalsocietypublishing.org, DOI: 10.1098/rsbl.2011.1223.

Balser, D.S., Dill H.H. and Nelson H.K. 1968. 'Effect of Predator Reduction on Waterfowl Nesting Success'. *Journal of Wildlife Management* 32:669–82.

Banks, R.C., Cicero, C., Dunn, J.L., Kratter, A.W., Rasmussen, P.C., Remsen, J.V., Rising, J.D. and Stotz, D.F. 2004. 'Forty-fifth Supplement to the American Ornithologists' Union Check-list of North American Birds'. *Auk* 121:985–95.

Bardarson, H.R. 1986. *Birds of Iceland*. Reykjavik: published by author.

Barn Owl Trust www.barnowltrust.org.uk.

Barrington, R.M. 1900. *The Migration of Birds as Observed at Irish Lighthouses and Lightships*. London and Dublin: R.H. Porter and Edward Ponsonby.

Barth, D., Heinze-Mutz, E.M., Roncalli, R.A., Schluter, I. and Gross, S.J. 1993. 'The Degradation of Dung Produced by Cattle Treated with an Ivermectin Slow-Release Bolus'. *Veterinary Parasitology* 48:215–27.

Batty, C. and Lowe, T. 2001. 'Vagrant Canada Geese in Britain and Ireland'. *Birding World* 14:57–61.

Beale, C.M., Burfield, I.J., Sim, I.M.W., Rebecca, G.W., Pearce-Higgins, J.W. and Grant, M.C. 2006. 'Climate Change may Account for the Decline in British Ring Ouzels'. *Journal of Animal Ecology* 75:826–35.

Benington, A. 2009. *Adventures of an Ulster Naturalist*. Brown's Fine Art Ltd.

Berg, A., Lindberg, T. and Kallebrink, K.G. 1992. 'Hatching Success of Lapwings on Farmland: Differences between Habitats and Colonies of Different Sizes. *Journal of Animal Ecology* 61:469–76.

Birding World 2007. 'Bird News', November 20:451.

Boere, G., Roselaar, K. and Engelmoer, M. 1984. 'The Breeding Origins of Purple Sandpipers Present in the Netherlands'. *Ardea* 72:101–9.

Booth, C.J. 1986. 'Raven Breeding for the First Time at Six Years Old'. *Scottish Birds* 14:51.

Bossema, I. 1979. 'Jays and Oaks: An Eco-ethological Study of a Symbiosis'. *Behaviour* 70:1–117.

Boyd, A.W. 1931. 'On some Results of Ringing Greenfinches'. *British Birds* 24:329–37.

Boyd, H. 2003. 'Spring Arrival of Passerine Migrants in Iceland'. *Ringing and Migration* 21:193–201.

Brodie, J. 1976. 'The Flight Behaviour of Starlings at a Winter Roost'. *British Birds* 69:51–60.

Brooke, M. de L. 1990. *Albatrosses and Petrels across the world*. Oxford University Press.

Bullock, I.D. 1980. 'Some Aspects of the Ecology of the Chough'. MSc thesis, University College of North Wales.

Bullock, I.D., Drewett, D.R. and Mickleburgh, S.P. 1983. 'The Chough in Britain and Ireland'. *British Birds* 76:377–401.

Burgess, J.P.C. 1982. 'Sexual Differences and Dispersal in the Blue Tit'. *Ringing and Migration* 4:25–32.

Burkitt, J.P. 1924. 'A Study of the Robin by Means of Marked Birds', *British Birds* 17, 294–303.

Busse, P. 1992. 'Migratory Behaviour of Blackcaps Wintering in Britain and Ireland: Contradictory Hypotheses'. *Ring* 14:1–2, 51–75.

Cabot, D. 2009. *Wildfowl*. Collins New Naturalist series. London: Collins.

Campbell, B. and Watson, D. 1964. *The Oxford Book of Birds*. Oxford University Press.

Campbell, L.H., Avery, M.I., Donald, P., Evans, A.D., Green, R.E. and Wilson, J.D. 1997. 'A Review of the Indirect Effects of Pesticides on Birds'. *JNCC Report* 227. Peterborough: Joint Nature Conservation Committee.

Casey, C. 1998. 'Distribution and Conservation of the Corncrake in Ireland, 1993–1998'. Irish Birds 6:159–76.

Cayford, J. 1981. 'The behaviour and dispersal of the Guillemot and Razorbill on the sea at Lundy'. Ms report in Edward Grey Library at Oxford University.

Chettleburgh, M.R. 1952. 'Observations on the Collection and Burial of Acorns by Jays in Hainault Forest'. *British Birds* 45:359–64.

Clark, J., Wernham, C.V., Balmer, D.E., Adams, S.Y., Blackburn, J.R., Griffin, B.M. and King, J. 2000. 'Bird Ringing in Britain'. *Ringing and Migration* 20:39–93.

Clowes, E. F. 1931. 'British Great Spotted Woodpecker in Co. Antrim: Observation on Drumming'. *Irish Naturalists' Journal* 3:208–9.

Coiffait, L., Clark, J.A., Robinson, R.A., Blackburn, J.R., Griffin, B.M., Risely, K.,

Grantham, M.J., Marchant, J.H., Girling, T. and Barber, L. 2006. 'Bird Ringing in Britain and Ireland in 2006'. *Ringing and Migration* 24:15–79.

Conder, P. 1989. *The Wheatear*. London: Christopher Helm.

Copeland Bird Observatory www.habitas.org.uk/cbo.

Corse, C.J. and Summers, R.W. 1999. 'The Seasonal Pattern of Numbers, Population Structure and Migration of Purple Sandpipers in Orkney'. *Ringing and Migration* 19:275–82.

Cowley, E. 1983. 'Multi-brooding and Mate Infidelity in the Sand Martin'. *Bird Study* 30:1–9.

Cox, R.B., Eddleston, C.R. and Newton, S.F. 2002. *Upland Bird Survey Report 2002: Donegal*. Birdwatch Ireland Conservation Report No. 02/04.

Cramp, S., Simmons, K.E.L. and Perrins C.M. (eds) 1977–94. *The Birds of the Western Palearctic* (nine volumes). Oxford University Press.

Cullen, C. and Williams, H. 2010. 'Sparrowhawk Mortality at a Wind Farm in Ireland'. *Irish Birds* 9:125–6.

D'Arcy, G. 1999. *Ireland's Lost Birds*. Dublin: Four Courts Press.

Darwin, C. 1871. *The Descent of Man*. London: Murray.

Davies, N. 1977. 'Prey Selection and the Search Strategy of the Spotted Flycatcher: A Field Study in Optimal Foraging'. *Animal Behaviour* 24:213–19.

Davies, N.B. 1983. 'Polyandry, Cloaca-Pecking and Sperm Competition in Dunnocks'. *Nature* 302:334–6.

Davies, N.B. 2011. 'Cuckoo Adaptations: Trickery and Tuning'. *Journal of Zoology* 284:1–44.

Davis, P.G. 1977. 'Changed Feeding Habits of Siskins and Lesser Redpolls'. *Bird Study* 24:127–9.

Davies, P. W. and Snow, D.W. 1965. 'Territory and Food of the Song Thrush'. *British Birds* 58:161–75.

Davis, T.A.W. 1960. 'Kestrel Pellets at a Winter Roost'. *British Birds* 53:281–4.

Deane, C.D. 1954. *Handbook of the Birds of Northern Ireland*. Bulletin of the Belfast Museum and Art Gallery 1:6.

Deane, C.D. 1979. 'The Capercaillie as an Irish Species'. *Irish Birds* 1:364–69.

Dempsey, E. and O'Clery, M. 2007. *Finding Birds in Ireland*. Dublin: Gill & Macmillan.

Dickinson, E.C. and Milne, P. 2008. 'The Authorship of *Parus ater hibernicus*'. *Bulletin of the British Ornithologists' Club*, 128(4).

Dimander, S.-O., Hoglund, J. and Waller, P.J. 2003. 'Disintegration of Dung Pats from Cattle Treated with the Ivermectin Anthelmintic Bolus, or the Biocontrol Agent *Duddingtonia flagrans*'. *Acta Veterinaria Scandinavica* 44(4):171–80.

Donaghy, A. 2011 'Catastrophic Curlew Declines Uncovered'. *Wings* 22, July.

Donald, P.F. and Morris, T.J. 2005. 'Saving the Skylark: New Solutions for a Farmland Bird'. *British Birds* 98:570–8.

Douglas, K. 2009. *The downfall of the Spanish Armada in Ireland*. Dublin: Gill & Macmillan.

Dubourdieu, J. 1812. *Survey of the County of Antrim*.

The Economist, 15 March 1879.

Edwards, C.A. and Bohlen, P.J. 1996. *Biology and Ecology of Earthworms*. London: Chapman & Hall.

Ellison, A. 1890. *The Zoologist*.

Eltringham, S.K. and Boyd, H. 1963. 'The Moult Migration of the Shelduck to Bridgewater Bay, Somerset'. *British Birds* 56: 433–44.

Environment and Heritage Service (Department of the Environment, Northern Ireland) 2006. 'DNA Analysis of Red Grouse: An Analysis of Taxonomy and Genetic Diversity. EHS reference: Con 2/1 190.

Eraud, C. and Boutin, J.-M. 2002. 'Density and Productivity of Breeding Skylarks in Relation to Crop Type on Agricultural Lands in Western France'. *Bird Study* 49: 287–96.

Evans, D. M. and Day, K. 2001. 'Migration Patterns and Sex Ratios of Diving Ducks Wintering in Northern Ireland with Specific Reference to Lough Neagh'. *Bird Study* 20:358–63.

Evans, E. E. 1951. *Mourne Country*. Dundalk: Dundalgan Press.

Fairley, J.S. 1975. *An Irish Beast Book*. Belfast: Blackstaff Press.

Fairley, J.S. and McLean, A. 1964. 'The Summer Food of Northern Ireland Kestrels'. *British Birds* 58:145–8.

Faulkner, J. and Thompson, R. 2011. *The Natural History of Ulster*. National Museums Northern Ireland Publication No.026. Nicholson & Bass.

Feare, C. J. 1966. 'The Winter Feeding of the Purple Sandpiper'. *British Birds* 59: 165–79.

Fisher, J. 1953. 'The Collared Turtle Dove in Europe'. *British Birds* 46:153–81.

Flegg, J.J.M. 1971. 'Birds in Ireland during 1966–69'. *British Birds* 64:4–19.

Fleming, F. 1998. *Barrow's Boys*. London: Granta.

Foster, J.W. 1998. *Nature in Ireland – A Scientific and Cultural History*. Dublin.

Fuller, R. J. and Glue, D. E. 1977. 'The Breeding Biology of the Stonechat and Whinchat'. *Bird Study* 24:215–28.

Fulton, D. 2010. 'The Breeding Population of Northern Wheatears at Clee Hill, Shropshire, 1998–2009'. *British Birds* 103:223–8.

Furphy, J.S., Hamilton, F.D. and Merne, O.J. 1971. 'Seabird Deaths in Ireland, Autumn 1969'. *Irish Naturalists' Journal* 17:2 (April), 34–40.

Garden Bird Health Initiative www.ufaw.org.uk/gbhi.

Garner, M. (2002). 'Identification and Vagrancy of American Merlins in Europe'. *Birding World* 15:468–80.

Gaston, A.J. 1973. 'The Ecology and Behaviour of the Long-tailed Tit'. *Ibis* 115: 330–51.

Gerard, J. 1597. *The Herball or General Historie of Plants*.

Gibbons, D.W., Reid. J.B. and Chapman, R.A. 1993. *The New Atlas of Breeding Birds in Britain and Ireland: 1988–1991*. London: T. & A.D. Poyser.

Giraldus Cambrensis (Gerald of Wales) [1187] 1982. *The History and Topography of Ireland*, trans. John J. O'Meara. London: Penguin.

Goldsmith, O. 1796. *History of the Earth and Animated Nature* (eight volumes).

Gompertz, T. 1961. 'The Vocabulary of the Great Tit and some other Related Species'. *British Birds* 54:369–94, 409–17.

Gooders, J. (ed.) 1970. *Birds of the World 1*, photograph, p. 323. IPC magazines.

Goodwin, D. 1952. 'Jays and Magpies Eating Wasps'. *British Birds* 45:364.

Gray, N. 2005. 'The Secret Life of Choughs on the Dingle Peninsula'. *Dingle Peninsula Bird Report 2002–2004*, 68–70.

Greenoak, F. 1979. *All the Birds of the Air*. London: Book Club Associates.

Guilford, T.C., Meade, J., Freeman, R., Biro, D., Evans, T., Bonadonna, A., Boyle, D., Roberts, S. and Perrins, C.M. 2008. 'GPS tracking of the foraging movements of Manx Shearwaters breeding on Skomer Island, Wales'. *Ibis* (2008), doi:10.1111/j.1474-919x.2008.00805.x

Gurney, J.H. 1868. 'An account of Great Auk in Co. Waterford.' *The Zoologist* 1449.

Gurney, J.H. 1921. *Early Annals of Ornithology*. London: H. F. & G. Witherby.

Gutierrez, R. 2003. 'The Balearic Shearwater: Apparently Heading for Extinction'. *Birding World* 16 (6):260–3.

Haapanen, A. 1966. 'Bird Fauna of the Finnish Forests in Relation to Forest Succession'. *Annales Zoologici Fennici* 2:153–196; 3:176–200.

Hall, J.J. 1981. 'The Cock of the Wood'. *Irish Birds* 2:38–47.

Hancock, M.H. and Wilson, J.D. 2003. Winter Habitat Associations of Seed-eating Passerines on Scottish Farmland'. *Bird Study* 50:116–30.

Harris, W. 1744. *The Antient and Present State of the County of Downe*.

Hartley, I.R. 1991. 'Polygyny, Parentage and Parental Investment in the Corn Bunting'. PhD thesis, University of Leicester.

Hauber, M.E., Russo, S.A. and Sherman, P.W. 2001. 'A Password for Species Recognition in a Brood-Parasitic Bird'. *Proceedings of the Royal Society of London B* 268:1041–8.

Henry, M., Béguin, M., Requier, F., Rollin, O., Odoux, J.F., Aupinel, J., Tchamitchian, S. and Decourtye, A. 2012 'A Common Pesticide Decreases Foraging Success and Survival in Honey Bees'. *Science* 1215039, published online 29 March.

Heppner, F. 1965. 'Sensory Mechanisms and Environmental Clues Used by the American Robin in Locating Earthworms'. *Condor* 67(3):247–56.

Hillis, J.P. 2009. 'Rare Irish Breeding Birds in 2008: The Annual Report of the Irish Rare Breeding Birds Panel'. *Irish Birds* 8:571–82.

Hoelzel, A.R. 1986. 'Song Characteristics and Response to Playback of Male and Female Robins'. *Ibis* 128:115–27.

Holling, M. 2011. 'Rare Breeding Birds in the United Kingdom in 2009'. *British Birds* 104:476–537.

Horgan, J. 2010. *The Song at Your Backdoor*. Cork: The Collins Press.

Hudson, R., Tucker, G.M. and Fuller, R.J. 1994. 'Lapwing Populations in Relation to Agricultural Changes: A Review' in G.M. Tucker, S.M. Davies and R.J. Fuller (eds) *The Ecology and Conservation of Lapwings*. Peterborough: Joint Nature Conservation Committee, pp. 1–33.

Hughes-Onslow G. 1949. 'Grey Geese in Ayrshire'. *Scot. Nat.* 61:123.

Hume, R.A.H. and Grant, P.J. 1974. 'The Upperwing Pattern of Adult Common and Arctic Terns'. *British Birds* 67:133–6.

Hutchinson, C.D. 1989. *Birds in Ireland*. T. & A.D. Poyser.

Jackson, J.B.C. 2007. 'Economic Incentives, Social Norms, and the Crisis of Fisheries'. *Ecological Research* 22:16–18.

Jackson, R.D. 1954. 'Territory and Pair-Formation in the Blackbird'. *British Birds* 47:123–31.

James, P.C. 1984. 'Sexual Dimorphism in the Voice of the European Storm Petrel'. *Ibis* 126:89–92.

Jenny, M. 1990. 'Territorialität und Brutbiologie der Feldlerche *Alauda arvensis* in einer Intensive Genutzten Agrarlandschaft'. *Journal für Ornithologie* 131:241–65.

Jonsson, L. 1976. *Birds of Wood, Park and Garden*. London: Penguin.

Jonsson, L. 1992. *Birds of Europe*. London: Christopher Helm.

Jonsson, L. and Grant, P.J. 1984. 'Identification of Stints and Peeps'. *British Birds* 77:293–315, July.

Kaiser, E. 1997. 'Sexual Recognition of Common Swifts'. *British Birds* 90:167–74.

Kee, R. 1972. *The Green Flag*. London.

Keillor, G. 1987. *Leaving Home*. London: Faber & Faber.

Keillor, G. 1991. *Radio Romance*. London: Faber & Faber.

Kennedy, Revd P.G., Ruttledge, R.F. and Scroope, C.F. 1954. *The Birds of Ireland*. London and Edinburgh: Oliver and Boyd.

Kiberd, D. 2000. *Irish Classics*. London.

Klinz, E. 1955. *Die Wildtauben Mitteleuropas*. Lutherstadt Wittenberg.

Krebs, J.R. 1982. 'Territorial Defence in the Great Tit: Do Residents Always Win? *Behavioural Ecology and Sociobiology* 11:185–94.

Lack, D. 1943. *The Life of the Robin*. London: Witherby.

Lack, D. and Owen, D.F. 1955. 'The Food of the Swift'. *Journal of Animal Ecology* 24:120–36.

Landsborough Thompson, A. 1975. 'Dispersal of First-year Gannets from the Bass Rock'. *Scottish Birds* 8:295–8.

Langslow, D.R. 1979. 'Movements of Blackcaps Ringed in Britain and Ireland'. *Bird Study* 26:239–52.

De Latocnaye, C. 1798. *A Frenchman's Walk Through Ireland*.

Lauga, B., Cagnon, C., D'Amico, F., Solange, K. and Mouches, C. 2005. 'Phylogeographyof the White-throated Dipper in Europe'. *Journal of Ornithology* 146:257–62.

de Leon, A., Minguez, E. and Belliure, B. 2003. 'Self-odour Recognition in European Storm-petrel Chicks'. *Behaviour* 140:925–33.

Levesque, A. and Yesou, P. 2005. 'Occurrence and Abundance of Tubenoses at Guadaloupe, Lesser Antilles 2001–2004'. North American Birds 59:672–7.

Lloyd, L. 1847. 'Woodcock and Snipe Shooting'. *Sporting Review*, October.

Lockley, R.M. 1983. *Flight of the Storm Petrel*. Vermont.

Long, R. 1975. 'Mortality of Reed Warblers in Jersey'. *Ringing and Migration* 1:28–32.

Lorenz, K. 1949. *King Solomon's Ring*.

Lynas, P., Newton, S.F. and Robinson, J.A. 2007. 'The Status of Birds in Ireland: An Analysis of Conservation Concern 2008–2013'. Irish Birds 8:149–66.

Lyngs, P. 2003. 'Migration and Winter Ranges of Birds in Greenland: An Analysis of Ringing Recoveries'. Danish Ornithological Society/BirdLife Denmark.

McCanch, N.V. 1997. 'Sparrowhawk Passage through the Calf of Man 1959–1993'. *Ringing and Migration* 18:1–13.

Macdonald, D. 1976. 'Predation on Nesting Collared Doves'. *Bird Study* 24:126.

Macdonald, M.A. 1977. 'An Analysis of the Recoveries of British-ringed Fulmars'. *Bird Study* 24:208–14.

Mayol, J. 2003. 'Estatus de *Puffinus mauretanicus* en Balears'. *Communicación en la I. Reunion del Grupo de Trabajo de la Pardela Balear de la Comision Nacional de Protección de la Naturaleza Comite Fauna i Flora*. Eivissa.

Merne, O. 1969. 'The Status of the Canada Goose in Ireland'. *Irish Bird Report, Seventeenth Annual Report*, 12–18.

Merne, O. 1986. 'Greylag Geese in Ireland'. *Irish Birds* 3:207–14.

Michl, G. 2003. *A Birders' Guide to the Behaviour of European and North American Birds*. Budapest.

Milton, K. 1990. *Our Countryside, Our Concern: Policy and Practice of Conservation in Northern Ireland*. Northern Ireland Environment Link.

Milwright, R.D.P. 2002. 'Redwing Migration and Wintering Areas as Shown by Recoveries of Birds Ringed in the Breeding Season in Fennoscandia, Poland, the Baltic Republics, Russia, Siberia and Iceland'. *Ringing and Migration* 21:5–15.

Milwright, R.D.P. 2003. 'Migration Routes, Breeding Areas and Between-Winter Recurrence of Nominate Redwings *Turdus iliacus iliacus* Revealed by Recoveries of Winter-Ringed Birds'. *Ringing and Migration* 21:183–92.

Mitchell, F. 1976. *The Irish Landscape*. Glasgow.

Mitchell, P.I., Newton, S., Ratcliffe, N. and Dunn, T.E. (eds). 2004. *Seabird Populations of Britain and Ireland*. T. & A.D. Poyser.

Mitschke, A., Rathje, H. and Baumung, S. 2000. 'House Sparrows in Hamburg: Population Habitat Choice and Threats'. *Hamburger Avifauna Beitr*. 30:129–204.

Moller, A. P. 1988. 'Infanticidal and Anti-infanticidal Strategies in the Swallow *Hirundo rustica*'. Behavioural Ecology and Sociobiology 19:365–71.

Moore, N. W. 1957. 'The Past and Present Status of the Buzzard in the British Isles'. *British Birds* 50:173–97.

Moryson, F. [1607] 1735. *An Itinerary*. Part published as *History of Ireland from the Years 1599–1603*. Dublin.

Mountfort, G. 1968. *Portrait of a Wilderness*. David & Charles.

Mühlethaler, F. 1952. 'Beobachtungen am Bergfinken-Schlafplatz bei Thun 1950–51'. *Ornithologische Beobachter* 49:173–82.

Neeson, E. 1997. 'Woodland in History and Culture' in J.W. Foster (ed.) *Nature in Ireland*. Dublin: Lilliput Press.

Nevitt, G.A. 2000. 'Olfactory Foraging by Antarctic Procellariiforms: Life at High Reynolds Numbers'. *Biological Bulletin* 198: 245–53.

Newton, I. 1972. *Finches*. Collins New Naturalist series. London: Collins.

Newton, I. 1986. *The Sparrowhawk*. T. & A.D. Poyser.

Newton, I. and Marquiss, M. 1982. 'Eye Colour, Age and Breeding Performance in Sparrowhawks'. *Bird Study* 29:195–200.

Norris, C.A. 1960. 'The Vanishing Corncrake'. *The Second BBC Naturalist*.

O'Connor, R.J. and Morgan, R.A. 1982. 'Some Effects of Weather Conditions on the Breeding of the Spotted Flycatcher in Britain'. *Bird Study* 29:41–8.

O'Donoghue, P.D., Cross, T.F. and O'Halloran, J. 1996. 'Carrion Crows in Ireland 1969–1993'. *Irish Birds* 5:399–407.

O'Flaherty, R. 1684. *A Chorographical Description of West or H-Iar Connaught*.

O'Huallachain, D.O. and Dunne, J. 2007. 'The Winter Diet of Pheasants: A Comparison of Estate-Reared and Wild Birds'. *Irish Birds* 8:189–94.

Okill, J.D. 1994. 'Ringing Recoveries of Red-throated Divers in Britain and Ireland'. *Ringing and Migration* 15:107–18.

Oliver, D. 1975. 'A Cause of Decline in Farmyard House Martin Colonies'. *Scottish Birds* 8:325–8.

Osborne, B.C. 1982. 'Foot-trembling and Feeding Behaviour in the Ringed Plover'. *Bird Study* 29:209–12.

Ottosson, U., Sandberg, R. and Pettersson, J. 1990. 'Orientation Cage and Release Experiments with Migratory Wheatears in Scandinavia and Greenland: The Importance of Visual Clues'. *Ethology* 86:57–70.

O'Tuama, S. and Kinsella, T. 1981. *An Duanaire 1600–1900: Poems of the Dispossessed*. Portlaoise.

Otway, C. 1827. *Sketches In Dublin*. Dublin.

Overskaug, K. and Kristiansen, E. 1994. 'Sex Ratio of Accidentally Killed Long-eared Owls in Norway'. *Ringing and Migration* 15:104–6.

Paradis E., Baillie, S.R., Sutherland, W.J., Dudley, C., Crick, H.Q.P. and Gregory, R.D. 2000. 'Large-Scale Spatial Variation in the Breeding Population of Song Thrush and Blackbird in Britain'. *Journal of Applied Ecology* 37:73–87.

Partridge, J.K. and Smith, K.W. 1992. 'Breeding Wader Populations in Northern Ireland, 1985–1987'. *Irish Birds* 4:497–518.

Patterson, R.L. 1880. *The Birds, Fishes and Cetacea of Belfast Lough*.

Payne-Gallwey, Sir R. [1882] 1985. *The Fowler In Ireland*. London: John van Voorst. (Reprinted Shedfield, Hampshire: Ashford.)

Perrins, C. 1979. *British Tits*. Collins New Naturalist series. London: Collins.

Perry, K.W. 1986. *The Irish Dipper*. Private publication.

Perry, K.W., Antoniazza, M. and Day, K.R. 1998. 'Abundance and Habitat Use by Breeding Great Crested Grebes at Lough Neagh (Northern Ireland) and Lake Neuchatel (Switzerland)'. *Irish Birds* 6:269–76.

Poxton, I.R. 1986. 'Breeding Ring Ouzels in the Pentland Hills'. *Scottish Birds* 14:44–8.

Preston, K. 1975. 'Census of Great Crested Grebes, Summer 1975'. *Irish Bird Report* 1975 38–44.

Price, R. and Robinson, J. A. 2008. 'The Persecution of Kites and Other Species in 18th-Century Co. Antrim'. *Irish Naturalists' Journal* 29(1):1–6.

Rackham, O. 1976. *Trees and Woodland in the British Landscape*. Phoenix Giant.

Risely, K., Renwick, A.R., Dadam, D., Eaton, M.A., Johnston, A., Baillie, S.R., Musgrove, A.J. and Noble, D.G. 2011. *The Breeding Bird Survey* 2010. BTO Research Report 597. Thetford: British Trust for Ornithology.

Robb, M. 2008. *Petrels Night and Day*. Dorset: The Sound Approach.

Robertson, H. 1991. 'Stock Doves Preyed on by Grey Squirrel and Brooding Young Squirrel'. *British Birds* 84:61.

Ronayne, S.T. 2011. 'Diet of the Little Egret in Southern Ireland'. *Irish Birds* 9:329–30.

RSPB (Royal Society for the Protection of Birds) 2007. *The Predation of Wild Birds in the United Kingdom: A Review of its Conservation Impact and Management*. RSPB Research Report No. 23. Sandy, Bedfordshire: RSPB.

Ruttledge, R.F. 1966. *Ireland's Birds*.

Rutty, J. 1772. *An Essay towards the Natural History of the County of Dublin*.

Ryall, C. and Briggs, K. 2006. 'Some Factors Affecting Foraging and Habitat of Ring Ouzels Wintering in the Atlas Mountains of Morocco'. *Bulletin of the African Bird Club* 13:17–31.

Salek, M. 2004. The Spatial Pattern of the Magpie: A Contribution to Predation Risk on Dummy Nests. *Folia Zoologica* 53(1):57–64.

Salomonsen, F. 1950. *Gronlands Fugle* [The Birds of Greenland]. Copenhagen: Munksgaard.

Salomonsen, F. 1967a. *Fuglene pa Gronland*. Copenhagen: Rhodos.

Salomonsen, F. 1967b. 'Migratory Movements of the Arctic Tern in the Southern Ocean'. *Biol. Medd. Dan. Vid. Selsk*. 24:1–42.

Sangster, G., Collinson, J.M., Helbig, A.J., Knox A.G. and Parkin, D.T. 2005. 'Taxonomic Recommendations for British Birds: Third Report'. *Ibis* 147:821–6.

Saxby, H.L. 1874. *The Birds of Shetland*. London: Simpkin, Marshall & Co.

Schifferli, A. 1953. 'Der Bergfinken-Masseneinfall 1950/51 in der Schweiz'. *Ornithologische Beobachter* 50:65–89.

Schlapfer, A. 1988. 'Populationsökologie der Feldlerche Alauda arvensis in der Intensiv Genutzten Agrarlandschaft'. *Ornithologische Beobachter* 85:309–71.

Schmaljohann, H. and Naef-Daenzer, B. 2011. 'Body Condition and Wind Support Initiate the Shift of Migratory Direction and Timing of Nocturnal Departure in a Songbird'. *Journal of Animal Ecology* 80:1115–22.

Schroeder, D., Heckroth, M. and Clemens, T. 2008. 'Against the Trend: Increasing Numbers of breeding Northern Lapwings and Black-tailed Godwits on a German Wadden Sea Island'. *Bird Study* 55:100–7.

Scott, D. 2008a. 'Hen Harrier Killed at Windfarm Site in Antrim'. *Irish Birds* 8:436–7.

Scott, D. 2008b. *Harriers: Journeys Around the World*. Tiercel.

Scott, D. 2010. *The Hen Harrier: In the Shadow of Slemish*. Whittles.

Scott, D., Clarke, R. and Shawyer, C.R. 1991. 'Hen Harriers Breeding at a Tree-nest'. *Irish Birds* 4: 413–22.

Sellersa, R.M. 1984. 'Movements of Coal, Marsh and Willow Tits in Britain'. *Ringing and Migration* 5:79–89.

Shaffer, S.A. et al. 2006. 'Migratory Shearwaters Integrate Oceanic Resources across the Pacific Ocean in an Endless Summer'. *Proceedings of the National Academy of Sciences* 103:12799–802.

Sharrock, J.T.R. (ed.) 1976. *The Atlas of Breeding Birds in Britain and Ireland*. T. & A.D. Poyser.

Sharrock, J.T.R. 1978. 'Did the Tree Pipit Formerly Nest in Ireland? *British Birds* 72: 41–2.

Shore, Malcolm H.M., Horne, J.A., Turner, S., and Weinburg, C.L. 2001. 'Rodenticide Residues in the Kestrel'. Unpublished report to English Nature by Centre for Ecology and Hydrology.

Shrubb, M. 1982. 'The Hunting Behaviour of Some Farmland Kestrels'. *Bird Study* 29:121–8.

Sim, I.J., Rebecca, G. and Ludwig, S. 2008. 'Understanding Ring Ouzel Declines'. Ring Ouzel Study Group www.ringouzel.info.

Slagsvold, T. and Lifjeld, J.T. 1985. 'Variation in Plumage Colour of the Great Tit in Relation to Habitat, Season and Food'. *Journal of Zoology* 206(3):321–8.

Smith, C. [1746] 1969. *The Ancient and Present State of the County and City of Waterford*. Cork: Mercier Press.

Smith, C. 1749. *History of Cork*. Dublin.

Smith, L. 2004. 'Upland Birds of the Long Mynd: Report of the Long Mynd Breeding Bird Project'. Shropshire Ornithological Society.

Sokolowski, J. 1969. *The Chaffinch*. Warsaw.

Spencer, K.G. 1953. *The Lapwing in Britain*. Hull: A. Brown & Sons.

Stanbury, A.and UK Crane Working Group 2011. 'The Changing Status of the Common Crane in the UK'. *British Birds* 104:432–47.

Stenhouse, I.J., Egevang, C. and Phillips, R.A. 2011. 'Trans-equatorial Migration, Staging Sites and Wintering Area of Sabine's Gull in the Atlantic Ocean'. *Ibis* 154:42–51; DOI:10.1111/j.1474-919X.2011.01180.x.

Stewart, J.Vandeleur. 1832. *Magazine of Natural History*.

Stoate, C. and Szczur, J. 2006a. 'Spotted Flycatchers at Loddington'. *Game Conservancy Trust Review of 2005*. Fordingbridge, Hampshire: Game Conservatory Trust.

Stoate, C. and Szczur, J. 2006b. 'Potential Influence of Habitat and Predation on Local Breeding Success and Population in Spotted Flycatchers'. *Ibis* 53:328–30.

Stokoe, R. 1958. 'The Spring Plumage of the Cormorant'. *British Birds* 51:165–79.

Summers-Smith, D. 1984a. 'Colonial Behaviour in the House Sparrow'. *British Birds* 47:249–65.

Summers-Smith, D. 1984b. 'Studies of Western Palaearctic Birds 197: Tree Sparrow'. *British Birds* 91:124–38.

Svensson, L., Mullarney, K. and Zetterstrom, D. 1999. *Collins Bird Guide*. London: HarperCollins.

Teunissen, W.A., Schekkerman, H. and Willems, F. 2005. 'Predators of meadow birds' [in Dutch]. *Sovon-onderzoeksrapport 2005/11*. Sovon Vogelonderzoek Nederland, Beek-Ubbergen. Alterra-Document 1292, Alterra, Wageningen.

Thompson, W. 1827. *The Birds of the Copeland Islands*.

Thompson, W. 1849–52. *The Natural History of Ireland* (four vols). London: Reeve, Benham and Reeve.

Thorup, K., Ortvad, T. E. and Rabol, J. 2006. 'Do Nearctic Northern Wheatears *Oenanthe oenanthe leucorhoa* Migrate Non-stop to Africa?' *Condor* 108:446–51.

Ticehurst, C.B. 1915. 'On the Plumages of the Male Crossbill'. *Ibis* 10(3):662–9.

Tompkins, D.M., Dickson, G. and Hudson, P.J. 1999. 'Parasite-Mediated Competition between Pheasant and Grey Partridge: A Preliminary Investigation'. *Oecologia* 119:378–82.

Trolliet, B. 2000. 'European Union Management Plan for the Lapwing'. European Commission, DG XI, Contract 97/162/3040/DEB/D2.

Tyler, S. 1972. 'Breeding Biology of the Grey Wagtail'. *Bird Study* 19(2):69–80.

UK BAP (United Kingdom. Biological Action Plans) 2010. www.ukbap-reporting.org.uk/plans/national_plan.asp.

Underhill, M.C., Gittings, T., Callaghan, D.A., Hughes, B., Kirby, J. S., and Delaney, S. 1995. 'Status and Distribution of Breeding Common Scoter in Britain and Ireland'. *Bird Study* 45:146–56.

Ussher, R.J. and Warren, R. 1900. *Birds of Ireland*. London: Gurney and Jackson. van Duivendijk, N. 2010. Advanced Bird Guide. New Holland.

Vera, F.W.M. 2000. *Grazing Ecology and Forest History*. Commonwealth Agricultural Bureau International.

Village, A. 1982. 'The Diet of the Kestrel in Relation to Vole Abundance'. *Bird Study* 29:129–38.

Viney, M. 2010. 'Crossing of Sheep Offers Hair Instead of Wool'. *The Irish Times*, 17 April.

Voous, K.H. 1960. *Atlas of European Birds*. Amsterdam and London: Nelson.

Walker, M.D. and Rotheram, I.D. 2011. '"Cool Dudes": Torpor in Common Swifts?' *British Birds* 104:219–20.

Wallace, D.I.M. 2004. *Beguiled by Birds*. Christopher Helm, London.

Watson, A.D. 1986. 'Bean Geese in South-West Scotland'. *Bird Study* 14:17–25.

Watson, D. 1972. *Birds of Moor and Mountain*. Edinburgh: Scottish Academic Press.

Watson, J. 1979. 'Food of Merlins Nesting in Young Conifer Forest'. *Bird Study* 26:253–8.

Weber, H. 1953. 'Bewirkung des Farbwechsels bei mannlichen Kreuzschabeln'. *Journal für Ornithologie* 94:342–6.

Weidinger, K. 2009. 'Nest Predators of Woodland Open-Nesting Songbirds in Central Europe'. *Ibis* 151:352–60.

White, G. 1789. *The Natural History and Antiquities of Selborne*.

Whitehead, S., Johnstone, I. and Wilson, J. 2005. 'Choughs Breeding in Wales Select Foraging Habitat at Different Spatial Scales'. *Bird Study* 52:193–203.

Whitehorn, P.R., O'Connor, S., Wackers, F.L. and Goulson, D. 2012. 'Neonicotinoid Pesticide Reduces Bumble Bee Colony Growth and Queen Production'. *Science* 1215025 online, 29 March.

Willughby, F. 1676. *Ornithologie libri tres* [in Latin, English edition published 1678]. London: John Martyn.

Wilson, H.J., Norriss, D.W., Walsh, A., Fox, A.D. and Stroud, D.A. 1991. 'Winter Site Fidelity in Greenland White-fronted Geese: Implications for Conservation and Management'. *Ardea* 79:287–94.

Wilson, J.D., Boyle, J., Jackson, D.B., Lowe, B. and Wilkinson, N.I. 2007. 'Effect of Cereal Harvesting Method on a Recent Population Decline of Corn Buntings on the Western Isles of Scotland'. *Bird Study* 54:362–70.

Witherby, H.F. 1928. 'A Trans-Atlantic flight of Lapwings'. *British Birds* 22:6–13.

Witherby, H.F., Jourdain, F.C.R., Ticehurst. N.F. and Tucker, B.W. 1938–41. *The Handbook of British Birds* (five vols). London: Witherby.

Wood, N.A. 1974. 'The Breeding Behaviour and Biology of the Moorhen'. *British Birds* 67:104–15, 137–58.

Wotton, S.R., Langston, R.H.W. and Gregory, R.D. 2002. 'The Breeding Status of the Ring Ouzel in the UK in 1999'. *Bird Study* 49:26–34.

Yalden, D.W. and Warburton, A.B. 1979. 'The Diet of the Kestrel in the Lake District'. *Bird Study* 26:163–70.

Yarrell, W. 1871–85. *A History of British Birds*, 4th edn (revised and enlarged by Alfred Newton and Howard Saunders) (four vols). London: John van Voorst.

Yeatman-Berthelot, D. and Jarry, G. 1994. *Nouvel Atlas des Oiseaux Nicheurs de France*. Societé d'Études Ornithologiques de Paris, France.

Zonfrillo, B. 1997. 'The Ecology of Seabirds on Ailsa Craig, Firth of Clyde'. PhD thesis, University of Glasgow.

PERSONAL OBSERVATIONS

Dominic Berridge (DB) – Kestrel

Oscar Campbell (OC) – Greylag Goose

James Cotter (JC) – Blackbird

Frank Craig (FC) – Chough

Campbell Douglas Deane (CDD) – Golden Eagle

Hill Dick (HD) – Wigeon

Tom Ennis (TE) – Stock Dove

Ian Forsyth (IF) – Oystercatcher

Joe S. Furphy (JSF) – Wigeon, Common Scoter, Red-breasted Merganser, Goshawk, Chough, Carrion Crow, Dipper, Corn Bunting

Trevor Goodbody (TG) – Corncrake

Tim J. Gordon (TJG) – Corncrake

George Henderson (GH) – Common Gull

Eleanor Keane (EK) – Meadow Pipit

Alexander Lees (AL) – Common Scoter, Peregrine, Curlew, Common Tern, Wheatear

Patrick P. Mackie (PPM) – Barnacle Goose, Teal

Bruce Mactavish (BM) – House Sparrow

Anthony McGeehan (AMG) – Pink-footed Goose, Greylag Goose, Wigeon, Long-tailed Duck, Grey Partridge, Black-throated Diver, Sparrowhawk, Kestrel, Corncrake, Lapwing, Turnstone, Sandwich Tern, Collared Dove, Dipper, Wheatear, Ring Ouzel, Sedge Warbler, Magpie, Jay, Jackdaw, Raven, House Sparrow, Bullfinch

Neville McKee (NMK) – Osprey, Black-headed Gull, Common Tern, Corncrake, Rock Pipit, Coal Tit, Robin, Willow Warbler, Carrion Crow, Starling, House Sparrow, Tree Sparrow, Twite, Goldfinch

Craig Nash (CN) – Woodcock

Steve Newton (SN) – Dipper

Michael O'Clery (MOC) – Kestrel

Aonghus O'Donnell (AOD) – Goshawk

Ken W. Perry (KWP) – Coal Tit

Julie Roe (JR) – Short-eared Owl

Hugh Thurgate (HT) – Common Gull

Shane Wolsey (SW) – Common Gull

Julian Wyllie (JW) –Stock Dove, Collared Dove, Sedge Warbler, Brambling

GAZETTEER

Annalong: County Down
Anne's Point [Strangford Lough]: County Down
Antrim Marina [Lough Neagh]: County Antrim
Antrim Plateau: County Antrim
Antrim Town: County Antrim
Ardee: County Louth
Ardglass: County Down
Ards Peninsula: County Down
Baldoyle: County Dublin
Ballycastle: County Antrim
Ballymacaw: County Waterford
Ballyshannon: County Donegal
Ballyworkan Moss [Portadown]: County Armagh
Bangor: County Down
Belfast: County Antrim
Belfast Harbour Estate: County Down
Belfast International Airport: County Antrim
Belfast Lough: Counties Antrim & Down
Belfast Mountains [Hills]: County Antrim
Blackrock [Island]: County Mayo
Blue Circle Island [Larne Lough]: County Antrim
Bog Meadows: County Antrim
Brown's Bay [Islandmagee]: County Antrim
Brownstown Head: County Waterford
Caledon: County Tyrone
Cape Clear Island: County Cork
Cardonagh: County Donegal
Carlingford Lough: Counties Down & Louth
Carnlough: County Antrim
Carrickfergus: County Antrim
Carrowdore: County Down
Carrowmore Lake: County Mayo
Cashel: County Tipperary
Castle Coole: County Fermanagh
Castlebar: County Mayo
Clandeboye Estate: County Down
Clare Island: County Mayo
Cleggan: County Galway
Cloghy: County Down
Clough: County Down
Coleraine: County Derry
Colin Glen: County Antrim
Copeland Islands: County Down
Corbally: County Antrim
Cork City: County Cork
Craigagh Wood: County Antrim
Crom Castle: County Fermanagh
Crom Estate: County Fermanagh
Crumlin: County Antrim
Cultra [Belfast Lough]: County Down
Dargan Bay [Belfast Lough]: County Antrim
Dargan's Island [Belfast Lough]: County Antrim
Deerpark: County Antrim
Derry City: County Derry
Downpatrick: County Down
Drogheda Bay: County Louth
Dublin: County Dublin
Dundalk Bay: County Louth
Dundrum: County Down
Dundrum Bay: County Down
Dunfanaghy: County Donegal

Eagle Island: County Mayo
Fair Head: County Antrim
Galbally Mountain [Carnlough]: County Antrim
Galway Bay: County Galway
Garron Point: County Antrim
Glenariff: County Antrim
Glenarm Park: County Antrim
Glencolmcille: County Donegal
Glenveagh National Park: County Donegal
Great Blasket: County Kerry
Great Saltee: County Wexford
Great Skellig/Skellig Michael: County Kerry
Groomsport: County Down
High Island: County Galway
Hook Head: County Wexford
Horetown: County Wexford
Horn Head: County Donegal
Inishbofin, Donegal: County Donegal
Inishbofin, Galway: County Galway
Ireland's Eye: County Dublin
Inishkea Islands: County Mayo
Inishshark: County Galway
Kenmare: County Kerry
Killard Point: County Down
Kirkiston: County Down
Knockagh: County Antrim
Lambay Island: County Dublin
Larne Lough: County Antrim
Lecale Peninsula: County Down
Lighthouse Island [Mew Island, outermost of
  Copeland Islands]: County Down
Lisburn: County Antrim
Little Skellig: County Kerry
Lough Beg: Counties Antrim & Derry
Lough Boora Parklands: County Offaly
Lough Conn: County Mayo
Lough Corrib: Counties Galway & Mayo
Lough Cullin: County Mayo
Lough Erne: County Fermanagh
Lough Foyle: Counties Derry & Donegal
Lough Gill: Counties Leitrim & Sligo
Lough Gur: County Limerick
Lough Mourne: County Antrim
Lough Neagh: Counties Antrim, Armagh, Derry,
  Down & Tyrone
Lough Ree: Counties Longford, Roscommon &
  Westmeath
Lough Swilly: County Donegal
Lurgan: County Armagh
Lurgan Green: County Louth
Magilligan: County Derry
Magilligan Point: County Derry
Mahee Island [Strangford Lough]: County Down
Maidens [the Maidens]: County Antrim
Malin Beg: County Donegal
Malin Head: County Donegal
Mallow: County Cork
The Maltings: County Down
Massereene: County Antrim
Mew Island [outermost of Copeland Islands]:
  County Down

Moira: County Down
The Montiaghs: County Armagh
Mount Sandel [Coleraine]: County Derry
Mountains of Mourne/The Mournes: County Down
Mounterlowney Mountains [Sperrin Mountains]:
  Counties Derry & Tyrone
The Mullet: County Mayo
Navan: County Meath
Newcastle: County Down
North Slob: County Wexford
Oxford Island [Lough Neagh]: County Armagh
Pettigo Plateau: County Donegal
Portmore Lough: County Antrim
Port Muck: County Antrim
Portrush: County Antrim
Puffin Island: County Kerry
Quoile Pondage: County Down
Ramore Head: County Antrim
Rathlin Island: County Antrim
Rathlin O'Byrne [Island]: County Donegal
Reagh Island [Strangford Lough]: County Down
River Bann: Counties Antrim, Armagh, Down & Derry
River Blackwater: Counties Cork, Kerry & Waterford
River Lagan: Counties Antrim & Down
River Maine: County Antrim
River Shannon: Counties Cavan, Clare, Fermanagh,
  Galway, Leitrim, Limerick, Longford, Offaly,
  Roscommon, Tipperary & Westmeath
Rockabill [Island]: County Dublin
Roscrea Castle: County Tipperary
Rosegarden: County Wexford
Rough Island [Strangford Lough]: County Down
St John's Point: County Down
Saltee Islands: County Wexford
Samphire Island: County Kerry
Shane's Castle: County Antrim
Shannon Callows: Counties Galway, Offaly,
Roscommon & Westmeath
Shannon Estuary: Counties Clare, Kerry & Limerick
Sheep Island: County Antrim
Sherkin Island: County Cork
The Skerries: County Antrim
Slieveanorra: County Antrim
Slieve Commedagh: County Down
Sperrin Mountains: Counties Derry & Tyrone
Stags of Broadhaven: County Mayo
Strangford Lough: County Down
The Tearaght: County Kerry
Templepatrick: County Antrim
Tollymore Park: County Down
Toome: County Antrim
Tory Island: County Donegal
Tuskar Rock: County Wexford
Upper Lough Erne: County Fermanagh
Wexford Harbour: County Wexford
Wexford Slobs: County Wexford
White Park Bay: County Antrim
Wolf Hill [Belfast]: County Antrim
Wood Quay Viking site: County Dublin
Youghal: County Cork

INDEX